# *Tru64™ UNIX® System Administrator's Guide*

Matthew Cheek, Scott Fafrak, Steven Hancock,
Martin Moore, and Gregory Yates

**Digital Press**
An imprint of Butterworth-Heinemann

Boston, Oxford, Auckland, Johannesburg, Melbourne, and New Delhi

A member of the Reed Elsevier group



Digital Press™ is an imprint of Butterworth–Heinemann.



Recognizing the importance of preserving what has been written, Butterworth–Heinemann prints its books on acid-free paper whenever possible. ∞

**Library of Congress Cataloging-in-Publication Data**

Tru64 UNIX system administrator's guide / Matthew Cheek … [et al.].

p. cm.

Includes bibliographical references and index.

ISBN 1-55558-255-9 (pbk. : alk. paper)

1. UNIX (Computer file) 2. Operating systems (Computers) 3. File organization (Computer science) I. Cheek, Matthew, 1965–

QA76.76.O63 T77 2002

005.4'4769—dc21

2001053698

**British Library Cataloguing-in-Publication Data**

A catalogue record for this book is available from the British Library.

The publisher offers special discounts on bulk orders of this book.

For information, please contact:

Manager of Special Sales

Butterworth–Heinemann

225 Wildwood Avenue

Woburn, MA 01801-2041

Tel: 781-904-2500

Fax: 781-904-2620

For information on all Digital Press publications available, contact our World Wide Web home page at: http://www.bh.com/digitalpress

10 9 8 7 6 5 4 3 2 1

Printed in the United States of America

*We dedicate this book to our wives—Sondra Cheek, Kris Fafrak, JoEllen Hancock, Beth Moore, and Beth Yates—without whose love and support this book would not have been possible.*

# *Contents*

# *Preface*

This book, *Tru64™ UNIX® System Administrator's Guide*, is the second edition of the popular book addressing Compaq Computer Corporation's powerful 64-bit UNIX operating system from the viewpoint of a system administrator. Originally released in 1992, Tru64 UNIX, which runs on high-performance Alpha microprocessor systems, has matured into the operating system of choice for a wide variety of applications, ranging from Internet search engines to popular e-commerce site systems used for mapping the human genome. Behind the scenes of these applications is the system administrator responsible for the care and feeding of these complex computer systems. With this book, it is our hope to meet the needs of the beginning Tru64 UNIX system administrator, while providing useful tips and resource information to the experienced administrator. If you are responsible for the management of Tru64 UNIX systems, either directly as a system administrator or indirectly as a manager or team leader, this book may be for you.

Matt Cheek was the sole author of the first edition. This revision is the work of five co-authors, and we shared the work of writing as follows: Matt had primary responsibility for Chapter 1 and Appendix B; Scott for Chapter 4; Steve for Chapters 3, 7, 10, and 11; Martin for Chapters 5, 6, and 9; and Greg for Chapters 2, 8, and 12 as well as Appendix A. We tried to give a consistent presentation of our information, but each of us comes from a different background and naturally brings a slightly different perspective to our writing. However, we hope that this has allowed us to take the best approach to each topic.

This volume is not intended as a replacement for the Tru64 UNIX product documentation; instead, it is offered as a complementary resource that addresses a broad range of system administration topics in what is hoped to be a more approachable style. In addition, we have tried to share useful, real-world system administration philosophies and techniques that the Compaq documentation cannot. As to our success, we respectfully leave that judgment to the reader.

In February of 1999, Compaq Computer Corporation, having acquired Digital Equipment Corporation in 1998, changed the name of Digital UNIX to Tru64 UNIX. The name change certainly reflected how Compaq was phasing out the Digital brand name, but also emphasizes that this version of UNIX is a "true" 64-bit operating system, one that fully leverages the capabilities of Compaq's 64-bit Alpha microprocessor.

The first edition of this book was based upon version 4.0 of what was at that time known as Digital UNIX. Later, the name officially became "Tru64 UNIX V. 4.0." Digital UNIX V. 4.0 and Tru64 UNIX V. 4.0 are, indeed, the same product.

This book is based upon Tru64 UNIX version 5.1, which as of this writing is the currently released version of Compaq's UNIX product. The 5.1A version was only a month or two from shipping at press time, and all effort has been made to make the content applicable to that version as well.

# *Acknowledgments*

Without the contributions of some special folks over the last 12 months, this book would never have seen the light of day. This support, both technical and moral, kept us going, especially in the final months of the project.

We offer our sincere thanks to Ernie Heinrich, Robert Katz, Sandy Levitt, Tim Mark, and Dan McGraw of Compaq Computer Corporation and Dennis O'Brien of Bruden Corporation for their assistance with the technical review of this book.

We cannot begin to express our gratitude to Theron Shreve and Pam Chester, our editors at Digital Press, for taking a chance on us and supporting this project. Thanks for offering encouragement when we needed it and kicking us in the behind when that was warranted, too.

Finally, we want to express our appreciation to our wives, Sondra, Kris, JoEllen, and the two Beths. Without their love and support this project would never have gotten off the ground.

*Matt*
*Scott*
*Steve*
*Martin*
*Greg*

1

# *Introduction to Tru64 UNIX System Administration*

For all the advances in computing architectures and operating systems, complex computers still require a great deal of care and feeding. No operating system typifies this statement more than UNIX. UNIX is a mature operating system that runs on a wide range of systems—from small single-user desktops to the world's fastest supercomputers. The broad spectrum of applications that run on UNIX ranges from banking and financial applications to telecommunications, manufacturing, and health care processes. Simply put, UNIX is everywhere. However, for all its success in the marketplace and all the development work that various UNIX vendors lavish on fancy graphical user interfaces and dynamic this and automatic that, a UNIX system still, more than 30 years after its creation, cannot manage itself. Enter the UNIX system administrator.

## 1.1 What Is UNIX System Administration?

A UNIX system administrator is the individual responsible for managing the complex collection of hardware and software that is a UNIX system. The UNIX operating system comprises a wide variety of services and processes that must be kept running and available and distributed among the system's users. A typical day for a UNIX system administrator may include installing systems, creating user accounts, stringing cables, troubleshooting and replacing failed hardware, performing system and user backups, and any of a hundred other tasks. UNIX system administration is frequently a thankless task. If everything is running smoothly, users and management often forget about the hard work that goes on behind the scenes. However, when a problem occurs and the system is down, it is frequently the system administrator who bears the brunt of user and management unhappiness.

Having said that, UNIX system administration is a booming career field frequently seen in lists of the most desirable or most needed occupations. UNIX system administrators seem to fall into one of three categories. The first is the individual who was "volunteered" for the job. These folks typically already have a "real" job, but for one reason or another, the system administration role was added to their job description. The second type is the professional system administrator who has chosen UNIX system administration as a primary career and has worked and studied to be the very best. This type of system administrator is becoming more common as colleges and universities continue to develop UNIX system administration curriculums and the career field gains respectability. Finally, perhaps the most common type of UNIX system administrator is the person who just accidentally became one. These folks stumbled into it after being programmers or engineers or something completely unrelated to computers, such as musicians. After discovering the ever-changing variety, constant challenges, and deep satisfaction that comes from managing the complex entity that is a UNIX system, they were hooked.

Tru64 UNIX is one of many implementations of the UNIX operating system, and while many aspects of using a UNIX system are similar from one flavor to another, the details of UNIX system administration are all too frequently highly vendor-specific. Because of this, vendor-specific UNIX system administration books will continue to be necessary.

Before outlining the topics covered by this text, it might be helpful to understand the history of Tru64 UNIX and what versions of the operating system will be addressed in these pages. Following this will be a brief discussion of the Alpha family of computer systems.

Tru64 UNIX was originally a product of Digital Equipment Corporation called "DEC OSF/1" because it was based on the Open Software Foundation's OSF/1 UNIX standard. Version 1.0, the first fully supported OSF/1 version, was released in March 1992. This version was primarily an internal release and was not shipped to customers. A year later, Digital shipped OSF/1 version 1.2 to customers. This version, the first fully functional release, was also the first that supported the new Alpha-based systems. From that point forward, OSF/1, then Digital UNIX, and finally Tru64 UNIX, would only run on systems with Alpha processors. In June of 2001, however, Compaq and Intel Corporation announced that Tru64 UNIX was to be ported to Intel's 64-bit IA-64 processor; the first IA-64-based Tru64 UNIX systems will be available by 2003 or 2004. Throughout the rest of 1993, Digital continued to release minor updates to OSF/1, each adding new functionality or support for new hardware. In March 1994, Digital released OSF/1 version 2.0. This was a major release that introduced many of the modern operating system features, such as the Advanced File System (AdvFS) and CD-ROM, RAID, and Token Ring support. The next major release of OSF/1 was version 3.0 in August 1994. This release continued the tradition of enhancement by adding support for Symmetric Multiprocessing (SMP) and loadable drivers. Following in February 1995 was version 3.2 of OSF/1, which added support for Asynchronous Transfer Mode (ATM) and the Common Desktop Environment (CDE). With the release of version 3.2C in August 1995, the name of the operating system was changed from DEC OSF/1 to Digital UNIX. This was primarily a marketing decision made to better differentiate the product in an increasingly crowded market.

The next major release (version 4.0) of Digital UNIX was released in March 1996. This version added a host of new features to improve system management, portability, and performance. A string of minor releases followed, each one adding new features and enhancements to the operating system.

In 1998, Compaq Computer Corporation acquired Digital Equipment Corporation and began phasing out the Digital brand name. With the release of version 4.0E in December 1998, Compaq renamed "Digital UNIX" to "Tru64 UNIX" in order to capitalize on its 64-bit nature.

Version 5.0 of Tru64 UNIX was released in August 1999. This major release again introduced a host of new features and enhancements. The most significant of these was the close integration of Compaq's TruCluster product. Although TruClusters were supported as early as Digital UNIX version 3.2E, they were now much more tightly coupled with the operating system. This allowed a cluster of up to eight Alpha systems to present a "single system image," greatly increasing the power and flexibility available to end users, while simplifying the management of multiple systems.

At the time of this writing, the most current release of Tru64 UNIX is version 5.1. This book will primarily discuss system administration on Tru64 UNIX version 4.0D and later. Where there are differences between version 4.0 and 5.X, they will be noted.

The future of Tru64 UNIX looks very bright. The 64-bit operating system combined with the 64-bit architecture of the Alpha and IA64 processors, positions Tru64 UNIX in the lead for high-performance UNIX platforms.

## 1.2 The Alpha Architecture

Digital Equipment Corporation was a trailblazer in the area of 64-bit microprocessors with its family of Alpha processors. Tru64 UNIX has historically been married to the Alpha processor, but this will change in the near future with the port to the IA-64 processor.

The Alpha RISC processor was announced by Digital in February of 1992 and its top speed was 200MHz. This was an astonishing feat, since the Alpha's contemporaries were running at speeds in the double digits. Digital followed up by announcing the first generation of Alpha-based systems in November of that year. The first lineup ranged from the DEC 3000 workstation and the DEC 4000 departmental server all the way to the mainframe class DEC 7000 and 10000 systems. In October 1993, the second-generation Alpha systems were delivered, strengthening Digital's lead in high-per- formance systems. Six months later, Digital announced the AlphaServer™ 2100, which was one of the first of a new breed of Alpha-based multiprocessing midrange servers. The 2100 quickly became a best seller for Digital. In August 1995, Digital announced the 300MHz Alpha, and eight months later it delivered the AlphaServer 8400 supporting up to 12 of the new 300MHz processors. The 8400 was truly a mainframe replacement system and broke every performance record in existence. Digital continued pushing the Alpha technology and announced 500MHz parts in July 1996.

Digital—and Compaq, after it acquired Digital—continued to press the development of the Alpha, releasing new generations of the chip with more features, smaller footprints, and faster clock speeds. At the time of this writing, 1 GHz processors are available in the GS-series of AlphaServers. This series (the GS80, GS160, and GS320), was a major leap forward when it was announced in June of 2000. These new systems are the most powerful yet, and were the first Alpha systems to support a Non-Uniform Memory Architecture (NUMA). The GS series has a modular, "building block" design that allows the systems to be partitioned into several independent "virtual systems," each running its own copy of Tru64 UNIX—or even another operating system, such as Compaq's OpenVMS.

From the very first Alpha to today's fastest systems, compatibility has been maintained. Tru64 UNIX runs on the entire range of Alpha-based systems. Compaq has ceased supporting the Tru64 UNIX product on the very earliest Alpha systems, but there is a good possibility that the operating system will still run on them.

# 1.3 The Organization of This Book

This text is divided into 12 chapters, each covering a different topic or discipline. The book is not intended to replace the Tru64 UNIX documentation; rather, it is presented as a supplement. The authors hope that this volume meets the needs of the target audience, the Tru64 UNIX system administrator, and contributes to successful system management.

## 1.3.1 Installation

Before a Tru64 UNIX system can be administered, it must be installed. The steps necessary to prepare a system for installation and to successfully install Tru64 UNIX are covered in Chapter 2. In addition, the steps to update a Tru64 UNIX system to a later version of the operating system are covered.

## 1.3.2 Storage

Chapter 3 reviews both physical disk configuration and operations, and the selection and management of the various file systems and volume management options available on the Tru64 UNIX system.

## 1.3.3 System Configuration

Once a Tru64 UNIX system is successfully installed, there are many configuration activities that must take place before the system is ready for use. These activities include managing software subsets, licenses, and other system definition and configuration data, all of which are discussed in Chapter 4.

## 1.3.4 User Accounts and Security

The most visible of system administration responsibilities is managing users. Chapter 5 covers user account management, and Chapter 6 covers the maintenance of system integrity and security.

## 1.3.5 Networking

Chapter 7 covers the configuration of the TCP/IP networking subsystem and associated services on a Tru64 UNIX system. This is an important responsibility as most systems are networked to share resources and distribute loads.

### 1.3.6 Printing

Being able to print is an important facility for most users, and configuring printers and the spooling system is frequently a frustrating task for system administrators. Chapter 8 reviews the steps necessary to tame the printing beast.

### 1.3.7 Processes and Resources

A great deal of a system administrator's time and energy is spent managing the myriad UNIX processes and resources. Users learn to depend on the availability of their favorite subsystem, and the administrator's job is to make sure that these many services are available and managed correctly. These topics are discussed in Chapter 9.

### 1.3.8 Performance Monitoring and Tuning

Chapter 10 looks at some of the tools and techniques that can be used to identify and resolve performance problems on a Tru64 UNIX system. UNIX performance tuning is not an exact science, but after reviewing this chapter, a system administrator should be able to understand many of the variables that affect system performance.

### 1.3.9 Backups

Safeguarding the user community's data is a sacred trust for a system administrator. Chapter 11 explains the development of a backup strategy and covers the various backup and recovery tools provided on Tru64 UNIX.

### 1.3.10 System Logging and Troubleshooting

Finally, what happens when something breaks? Chapter 12 covers system monitoring and error recovery techniques, and introduces several Tru64 UNIX tools for troubleshooting hardware and software problems.

# 2

# *Installation*

## 2.1 Introduction

The initial installation of a Tru64 UNIX system can be an exciting process. Whether you are installing it on a brand-new system or a doing complete reinstallation of an existing system, the opportunity exists to define many aspects of the final configuration. The key to achieving the desired results is thorough planning. Some of the configuration decisions to be made prior to starting a Tru64 UNIX installation are disk and file system layouts, the method of installation, and which optional Tru64 UNIX software subsets to install. The first part of this chapter will consider these issues.

Once you have decided how the system will be configured, it is necessary to ensure that the system is properly prepared for the installation. This means that all components of the system are at the proper firmware revision for the version of Tru64 UNIX you will be installing. In addition, depending on the method of installation selected, either a local CD-ROM drive must be installed or, if installing from a Remote Installation Server (RIS), the system must be connected to a network. Next, you must have console access to the system. This console can be a serial terminal or a graphics display; Tru64 UNIX supports installations from either console type. Next, your system needs a suitable boot disk. This requirement may seem obvious, but this is worth mentioning because Compaq hardware makes it very easy to have multiple versions of Tru64 UNIX installed on a system. This capability can allow you to evaluate a new version of Tru64 UNIX by installing the later version on a spare disk rather than upgrading your current version. Simply boot from that new installation and you can determine if the upgrade is right for you. Finally, the procedure for checking and updating system firmware is outlined.

This chapter describes the installation process and provides examples of the graphical installation utility available on Tru64 UNIX V5.1 and above. Regardless of the installation interface used (graphical or character-cell), you will have the ability to select the boot disk; the root, swap, /usr and /var partitions and file system types; and the Tru64 UNIX software subsets to install. After loading the selected subsets, the installation program prompts you to rebuild the kernel (depending on how you answered the kernel options question, it may build it for you). Later in the chapter recommendations will be made regarding which optional subsets to install and which kernel options to select.

Once the installation is complete and the system reboots, the remaining system configuration must be done before the system is ready for use. The bulk of the post-installation configuration will be covered in Chapter 4, "System Configuration," but some minor configuration details will be mentioned in this chapter. Other areas of system configuration, such as user accounts and network management, are dealt with in Chapters 5 and 7, respectively.

An alternative to doing a full installation is an update installation. An update installation updates an existing Tru64 UNIX system to a later version. For instance, you can do an update installation to update a Tru64 UNIX V4.0G system to Tru64 UNIX V5.1. An update installation preserves existing disk partitioning, LSM configuration, file systems, user accounts and files, and the network and printer configuration. The advantage of an update installation over a full installation is that all local customizations remain intact. The disadvantage is that you carry any bad habits and old baggage forward, and if the existing version is quite old, it could require more work do update than to perform a fresh install. Sometimes a fresh installation is worth the extra effort. In fact, Compaq recommends that you perform a fresh installation once you decide to move to a new major release. The details of an update installation are covered; some of the limitations of an update installation are also mentioned.

Finally, Compaq's Remote Installation Services (RIS) will be explained. RIS is a facility for installing a Tru64 UNIX system from a remote server that contains the Tru64 UNIX distribution. The main advantage of RIS is that multiple systems can be installed without having to have the Tru64 UNIX distribution CD-ROM in each system. All that is required is copying the Tru64 UNIX distribution into a remote installation environment on an already installed system that will function as the RIS server. Once this RIS environment is configured and remote clients are registered with the RIS server, remote installations on those remote clients can begin. The special requirements of using RIS will be detailed.

## 2.2 Tru64 UNIX Preinstallation Planning

To guarantee a successful Tru64 UNIX installation, several areas require some consideration and planning:

- Installation media (local CD-ROM or RIS server)
- Installation method (default, custom, or cloned)
- Selection of optional subsets
- Boot disk partitioning (size and location)
- File system type
- Swap areas (size and quantity)

### 2.2.1 Review Tru64 UNIX Installation Documentation

The very first step is to read the Tru64 UNIX Installation Guide and the Tru64 UNIX Release Notes for the version of Tru64 UNIX you are planning to install. Both of these documents contain information that will assist you while planning the installation. Some of these issues can wait to be resolved until after the system installation is complete, but most must be decided before the installation can begin.

The Tru64 UNIX Installation Guide is the authority for the installation process. This manual contains specific information for each computer system supported by the version of Tru64 UNIX covered by the document. This information includes the required console flag settings and instructions on initially booting the system to begin the installation, either from CD-ROM or over a network connection to an RIS server. In addition, the processor-specific section indicates any unique settings or requirements necessary to install Tru64 UNIX. Finally, the Installation Guide contains detailed listings of the mandatory and optional software subsets contained in the particular version of Tru64 UNIX. This information includes subset descriptions. You will find the disk space requirements for each software subset in the Release Notes. A separate section in the Installation Guide contains the default disk partitions for the supported Compaq-manufactured disks.

The Tru64 UNIX Release Notes should also be read before beginning an installation. The Release Notes document any last-minute changes to either the particular version of the Tru64 UNIX software or to the installation process itself. Pay close attention to any section in the Release Notes that refer either to the type of Compaq system being installed or to optional software subsets you have selected. In addition, the Release Notes describe features of the operating system that are new or have changed significantly from previous releases of Tru64 UNIX.

Both the Tru64 UNIX Installation Guide and the Tru64 UNIX Release Notes are included in the Tru64 UNIX Software Distribution Kit, along with the Tru64 UNIX CD-ROM media. In addition, the most recent versions of these two documents are available online via the World Wide Web (WWW) at Compaq's Publications homepage:

```
http://www.tru64unix.compaq.com/faqs/publications/pub_page/
  doc_list.html
```

### 2.2.2 Selecting Installation Media

The first choice you should make when planning a Tru64 UNIX installation is whether to install a system from a locally mounted Tru64 UNIX CD-ROM or from a Remote Installation Services (RIS) server. Which method you choose depends mostly on whether an RIS server is available. The special requirements of an RIS server may rule out an RIS installation. If an RIS server is available, reachable via the network, and has the correct version of Tru64 UNIX installed in its repository, RIS can simplify a client system installation.

Regardless of whether an RIS server is available, installing a system via a local CD-ROM is always an available option. The only requirements to do so are the correct version of the Tru64 UNIX installation CD-ROM and a CD-ROM drive connected to the target system. At a minimum, you need two CD-ROMs: The Tru64 UNIX base operating system software CD-ROM that is labeled Tru64 UNIX Vx.yz Operating System Volume 1 (here, the x.yz stand-in for the major, minor, and maintenance release number and letter, such as V5.1A), and the firmware CD-ROM that is labeled Alpha Systems Firmware Vx.y.

### 2.2.3 Selecting the Installation Method

The next decision that should be made concerns the installation type. This choice assumes that you are conducting a new or overwrite installation; update installations are discussed later in this chapter. The choices are Full and (new in Tru64 UNIX version V4.0 and above) Cloned installations. The following sections describe these two types of installations.

### 2.2.3.1 Full Installation

The Tru64 UNIX full installation is a straightforward installation where you answer a few questions up front and then the installation process proceeds unattended until the operating system is ready for the post-installation activities.

The questions that you have to answer in the full installation are categorized into four basic areas:

- General (and mandatory) information
- Software subsets
- Kernel options
- File system layout

After a full installation has been completed, you can make further configuration changes; for example, you can add or remove software subsets using setld(8).

Selecting a full installation provides the freedom to customize almost every aspect of the installation. This includes selecting the boot disk; specifying the location of the root, /usr, and, if desired, the /var file system; and specifying the location of the primary and secondary swap areas. When creating the file systems, the option of selecting either the Advanced File System (AdvFS) or the UNIX File System (UFS) is presented. In addition, the full installation allows placing all file systems on different physical disks. Compaq recommends using the AdvFS file system.

Equally important, the opportunity is provided to select any or all optional Tru64 UNIX software subsets to be installed. The full installation option evaluates and resolves any subset dependencies, possibly selecting dependent subsets automatically. The ability to choose which kernel options will be built into the resulting Tru64 UNIX kernel is also provided.

A full installation provides the system administrator with nearly absolute control over the configuration of the resulting Tru64 UNIX system. Given adequate planning, the full installation is the recommended method of manually installing a Tru64 UNIX system. Of course, without the proper knowledge, selecting a full installation could result in a system either poorly configured or completely inoperable. The most important prerequisite to a full installation is disk planning. This includes determining the software subsets you wish to install; calculating the space required for the root, /usr, and /var file systems in addition to swap space requirements; being prepared to partition the disk(s) based on these calculations; and choosing the file system types.

#### 2.2.3.2 Cloned Installation

New as of Tru64 UNIX version V4.0 is the cloned installation type. A cloned installation is one in which a system is installed based on the contents of a predefined configuration file. This facility provides the ability to install a system with minimal user interaction. For sites with many similarly configured systems, this can result in quick, consistent, and accurate installations. The key to the cloned installation is the Configuration Description File, or CDF. The CDF contains the following information describing how to install a system:

- Details about the file systems to be created, including name, disk, and partition in which they will reside, and file system type
- Swap area(s) to be created and disk and partitions where they will reside
- Installation Media (CD-ROM or RIS)
- Various system-specific details, such as host name, root password, geographic locations and time zone, and options to use when initially building the kernel
- Software subsets to be installed

See Figure 2.1 for an example of a CDF.

When preparing for a cloned installation, the CDF for a given system may be created from scratch as long as the documented layout and format are

**Figure 2.1**
*Example CDF file.*

```
install:
        _item=Inst_islinfo
        _action=create
        media_type=CDROM
        srcloc=/ALPHA/BASE

install:
        _item=Inst_disklabel
        g_size=3362513
        c_offset=0
        e_offset=6274033
        b_size=2052443
        g_offset=2467299
        d_size=5749745
        b_offset=414856
        f_size=5749746
        name=dsk1
        h_size=11943712
        d_offset=524288
```

**Figure 2.1**
*Example CDF file (continued).*

```
        a_size=414856
        f_offset=12023778
        c_size=17773524
        _action=create
        h_offset=5829812
        e_size=5749745
        a_offset=0

install:
        _item=Inst_filesystem
        disk_number=0
        disk_name=dsk1
        controller_type=SCSI
        name=root
        partition=a
        controller_number=0
        disk_type=BD009222C7
        file_system_type=AdvFS
        _action=create

install:
        _item=Inst_filesystem
        disk_number=0
        disk_name=dsk1
        controller_type=SCSI
        name=usr
        partition=g
        controller_number=0
        disk_type=BD009222C7
        file_system_type=AdvFS
        _action=create

install:
        _item=Inst_filesystem
        disk_number=0
        disk_name=in_usr_domain
        controller_type=SCSI
        name=var
        partition=g
        controller_number=0
        disk_type=BD009222C7
        file_system_type=AdvFS
        _action=create

install:
        _item=Inst_filesystem
        disk_number=0
        disk_name=dsk1
        controller_type=SCSI
        name=swap1
        partition=b
        controller_number=0
        disk_type=BD009222C7
```

**Figure 2.1**
*Example CDF file (continued).*

```
        file_system_type=swap
        _action=create

install:
        _item=Inst_filesystem
        disk_number=0
        disk_name=in_usr_domain
        controller_type=SCSI
        name=i18n
        partition=g
        controller_number=0
        disk_type=BD009222C7
        file_system_type=AdvFS
        _action=create

install:
        _item=Inst_subsets
        volume_name=DISC1
        name=BASE

ss_names=OSFACCT510,OSFADVFS510,OSFADVFSBIN510,OSFADVFSDAEMON51
0,OSFAFM510,OSFATMBASE510,OSFATMBIN510,OSFATMBINCOM510,OSFBASE5
10,OSFBIN510,OSFBINCOM510,OSFC2SEC510,OSFCDEAPPS510,OSFCDEDEV51
0,OSFCDEDT510,OSFCDEMAIL510,OSFCDEMANOP510,OSFCDEMANOS510,OSFCD
EMIN510,OSFCLINET510,OSFCMPLRS510,OSFDCMT510,OSFDCMTEXT510,OSFD
ECW510,OSFDMS510,OSFDOSTOOLS510,OSFEMACS510,OSFENVMON510,OSFEUR
LOC510,OSFEXAMPLES510,OSFEXER510,OSFFONT15510,OSFFONT510,OSFHWB
ASE510,OSFHWBIN510,OSFHWBINCOM510,OSFIMXE510,OSFINCLUDE510,OSFI
NET510,OSFJAVA122510,OSFJAVA510,OSFKBDLK201510,OSFKBDLK401510,O
SFKBDLK411510,OSFKBDLK421510,OSFKBDLK444510,OSFKBDPCXAL510,OSFK
TOOLS510,OSFLAT510,OSFLDBBASE510,OSFLDBDOC510,OSFLEARN510,OSFLI
BA510,OSFLSMBASE510,OSFLSMBIN510,OSFLSMX11510,OSFMANOP510,OSFMA
NOS510,OSFMANWOP510,OSFMANWOS510,OSFMH510,OSFMITFONT510,OSFNETC
ONF510,OSFNETSCAPE510,OSFNFS510,OSFNFSCONF510,OSFOBSOLETE510,OS
FOLDDECW510,OSFPERL510,OSFPGMR510,OSFPRINT510,OSFRCS510,OSFRIS5
10,OSFSCCS510,OSFSDE510,OSFSDECDE510,OSFSER510,OSFSERPC510,OSFS
ERTC510,OSFSERVICETOOLS510,OSFSVID2510,OSFSYSMAN510,OSFTCLBASE5
10,OSFTERM510,OSFTKBASE510,OSFTRUETYPE510,OSFUUCP510,OSFX11510,
OSFXADMIN510,OSFXADVFS510,OSFXC2SEC510,OSFXDEMOS510,OSFXDEV510,
OSFXEXAMPLES510,OSFXIEDOC510,OSFXINCLUDE510,OSFXLIBA510,OSFXMIT
510,OSFXNEST510,OSFXOEM510,OSFXPRINT510,OSFXPRT510,OSFXSYSMAN51
0,OSFXVFB510


  advflag=1
        _action=create

install:
        _item=Inst_cinstall
        kernel_option=all
        lang_env=C
        timeset=yes
        password=CyrPiMbOqwlLU
```

**Figure 2.1**
*Example CDF file (continued).*

```
timezone=New_York
locality=America
_action=create
hostname=justice
```

followed. Typically, however, a CDF for a new cloned installation is based on an existing system that has a similar or identical hardware configuration. When Tru64 UNIX is installed on a system using the full installation method, a CDF is generated and placed in the /var/adm/smlogs directory and named install.cdf. This generated CDF can then be used as the source for further cloned installations. For example, given a set of systems with the same or similar hardware configuration, the first system could be installed manually, then the resulting CDF could be used to replicate the remaining systems simply by changing the host name field. As this example shows, a cloned installation is well suited for the mass-installation of similar systems—they must be similar or this technique will not work. However, with careful modifications to the CDF to describe a system's desired configuration, the cloned installation can also be used to install individual systems. An example of this could be a site with a large quantity of differently configured systems that must be installed quickly and accurately. By preparing a set of CDFs ahead of time, one for each system, all the systems could be quickly and reliably installed with minimal system administrator involvement.

The CDF of the cloned installation process only addresses the initial system installation and configuration and cannot, for example, change the default partitioning of the boot disk prior to or add user accounts after the installation. Compaq has extended the cloned installation, starting at V4.0B, to allow for this type of optional pre- and post-installation activity. See the current Tru64 UNIX Installation Guides for details on how to execute user-supplied scripts before or after the installation process.

You can also clone a configuration, which is a little different than performing installation cloning. See Chapter 4, "System Configuration", for more information.

### 2.2.4 Selection of Optional Subsets

During a full installation, the opportunity to select from a set of optional software subsets is presented. Regardless of the installation type, however, optional software subsets may be installed after the system has been installed.

When installing Tru64 UNIX on a system, a mandatory set of subsets is selected for installation. This mandatory set includes a minimal set of software necessary for installation and basic functionality that is always selected. In addition, other mandatory software subsets are selected based on the hardware configuration of the system. For example, if the system has graphic capability, the minimal X Window System environment subsets are also mandatory. Beyond these mandatory subsets, there are roughly 100 optional subsets that can be selected for installation during the initial system installation. These optional subsets fall into a dozen different categories:

- General applications
- Mail applications
- System administration tools
- Network utilities
- Printing environment
- X Window System applications
- X Window System environment support
- Kernel build environment
- Kernel development environment
- General software development environment
- Reference pages
- Text processing utilities

The Tru64 UNIX Installation Guide contains descriptions of each of the various optional software subsets. Additionally, the Release Notes contain an appendix detailing the disk space requirements for each of the mandatory and optional subsets. Before beginning a system installation, determining which optional subsets will be installed will assist you in disk planning (layout and sizing), which is the next step in installation planning.

Determining which optional subsets to select is best accomplished by first deciding how the system will be used. If, for instance, the system is a graphics workstation that will be used for software development, it is likely that many of the X Window System and software development environment optional subsets will be installed. Conversely, if a system will be a production server supporting remote clients, the installation of software development utilities or X Window System applications and fonts might not be appropriate. Finally, if the system will run third-party applications, examine the installation documentation for these products to determine if they require Tru64 UNIX software subsets to operate, and see what their disk requirements are.

One helpful strategy for selecting which optional subsets to install is to determine which subsets should not be installed. Once you have decided what not to install, select the remaining subsets for installation. Keep in mind that the selection or rejection of any particular subset is not permanent. If you determine after the system has been installed that some subsets that were not installed are required, simply install them from the installation media using the setld command. If it becomes apparent that some subsets that were initially installed are not necessary, removing them is equally simple. Compaq's recommendation, if you are unsure about whether to install a particular subset, is to select it for installation. Most Tru64 UNIX optional subsets function satisfactorily well together, and selecting all optional subsets will result in a functioning, though perhaps not optimally configured, system.

Some optional subsets are fairly easy to rule out based on the hardware configuration of your system. For example, there are separate X Window System server subsets for specific supported graphics cards. It is necessary to load only the subset for the graphics card installed in your system. If a particular system has a PCI bus graphics card, the X Servers for PCbus subset is the only necessary subset of these three:

- X Servers for PCbus (windowing environment)
- X Servers for Open3D (windowing environment)
- X Servers for TurboChannel (windowing environment)

There is no point in installing the X Servers for Open3D or TurboChannel when there is not an Open3D or TurboChannel graphics card present. Likewise, if your system does not have ATM hardware, it is unnecessary to load the following subsets:

- ATM commands (network-server/communications)
- ATM kernel modules (kernel build environment)
- ATM kernel header and common files (kernel build environment)
- ATM kernel objects (kernel software development)

### 2.2.5 Boot Disk Partitioning

For full installations the default layout of the boot disk is sometimes inadequate, depending on the selection of optional software subsets. Once you have decided which optional software subsets will be installed, the next step is to calculate the amount of disk space required given that set of software. The Tru64 UNIX Release Notes list the disk space requirements for each mandatory and optional software subset. The sizes are listed as the number of

512-byte blocks required in the root, /usr, and /var file systems. Simply consult the table in the Release Notes and sum the values of each selected subset for each file system. This will result in the minimum size of the root, /usr, and /var file system. If /var will reside in the /usr file system, which is an option of the Tru64 UNIX installation, add the /var size to the /usr file system size. Since the Release Notes list subset sizes in 512-byte blocks, divide this value by 2048 to convert the size to megabytes and round up. These resulting minimum values for the root, /usr, and /var file systems, however, are just the base for calculating the layout of the system disk. Other variables that influence disk layout are:

- The size and number of swap areas
- Crash dump space requirements
- The location of user home directories
- The file system type (UFS or AdvFS)
- Future growth
- Performance (spreading the I/Os to multiple disks)

#### 2.2.5.1 Swap Space Requirements

The Tru64 UNIX installation procedure requires that a primary swap space be allocated; it also provides the option to create a secondary swap space during the installation. By default, the primary swap space is placed on partition b of the system boot disk. This default location is by convention only, and the primary swap area can be located in any boot disk partition except partition a, which is required to be the root file system. Alternately, the primary swap area can be located on a disk other than the boot disk.

Unless special configuration requirements dictate otherwise, the recommended boot disk layout is to place the primary swap area on the boot disk in partition b. This will keep the boot partition and the primary swap partition together on the same disk and ensure that the system has, on a single disk, the necessary partitions to start up. Given this configuration, the optimal size of the primary swap partition depends on whether the system will have additional secondary swap partition(s). This decision is based primarily on the physical memory size of the system, as well as the size and number of disks in the system. If, for example, the system is a desktop AlphaStation with 64 MB of memory and two 9 GB disks, a single 128-MB swap area on partition b of the boot disk is likely to be sufficient. A larger system, such as an AlphaServer with 512-MB or more of memory and many disks, may benefit from a primary 256-MB swap area on partition b of the boot disk plus two additional

512-MB secondary swap areas on other disks. These two examples illustrate the strategy of placing a relatively small primary swap area on the boot disk and, if necessary, placing secondary swap area(s) on other disks.

#### 2.2.5.2 *Crash Dump Space Requirements*

When a Tru64 UNIX system crashes, by default the resulting crash dump is copied into one of the swap partitions and upon subsequent reboot it is moved into /var/adm/crash by the savecore(8) utility. The default location can be changed; see the man page for savecore for details. The crash files are composed of a partial or full memory image at the time of the crash and a copy of the current kernel, usually /vmunix. The file system that contains the directory /var/adm/crash must be large enough or, more accurately, have sufficient free space to contain at least one crash dump. The size of a system's crash dump is determined by several factors—the amount of physical memory and whether partial or full dumps, compressed or not compressed, are selected just to name a few. On systems configured for full crash dumps, the /var/adm/crash area should be at least as large as the size of the system's physical memory, and on systems configured for partial dumps, it can be somewhat smaller. The vast majority of the time you will configure your system to produce partial crash dumps. The purpose of mentioning this now is to make you aware that initially this destination is contained in the /var file system, or in the /usr file system if a separate /var file system is not selected. Ensure that enough space is allocated for at least one crash dump in the file system where the /var/adm/crash directory will be.

One recommendation is to create a separate file system solely to contain crash dumps. Mount this file system either at /var/adm/crash, or select a different mount point and configure the system to save crash dumps to this new location. Following this strategy means that no space need be allocated in either the root, /usr, or /var file systems for crash dumps. See Chapter 12, "System Logging and Troubleshooting," for guidelines on configuring and managing crash dumps.

#### 2.2.5.3 *User Home Directory Location*

The Tru64 UNIX user creation utilities, adduser, useradd, SYSMAN, and the CDE Account Manager, all default to creating user account home directories in the /usr/users directory. Depending on the number of user accounts a system will support, this may be an unwise choice. A better alternative is to create a separate file system after the installation is complete to contain user account home directories. Placing user account home directories in a file system other than /usr, or for that matter the root or /var file system, prevents users from impacting system operation by filling any of these three important system file systems. If, however, the decision is made to place user account home directories in the root, /usr, or /var file system, a rule of thumb to follow is to allocate approximately 100 MB for each user account. This will provide some amount of buffer space to reduce the possibility of a particular user filling the file system containing the home directories. Of course, decrease or increase this per-user disk space preallocation if you have an accurate understanding of the amount of disk space any particular user may need.

For backup purposes, if you have users with large directories, it is a good idea to break up the user directory structure into manageable file system sizes. How large is large depends on your backup strategy and tape drive capacity. For example, you might create a structure with two file systems, /usr/staff/1 and /usr/staff/2, and equally distribute the users between the two. A couple of benefits of this strategy are that you can more easily and quickly back up and restore smaller file systems, and if you have a file system or storage problem it does not have to affect all of your users.

#### 2.2.5.4 File System Overhead

After calculating the minimum size of the boot disk file systems based on the mandatory Tru64 UNIX subsets, plus any optional subsets, and taking into consideration the issues described above, the final variable in the boot disk partitioning equation is related to the file system overhead. A certain percentage of the total space allocated is unavailable for use. As a rule of thumb consider this to be 5%. This means that when you are planning the size for a particular file system, this percentage should be added to the calculated value to arrive at a final partition size. This percentage is used by the operating system for file system housekeeping. In addition, UFS file systems are created with an additional percentage of space marked as unavailable to non-root users. The root user or root-owned processes can make use of this reserved space. The percentage held back, by default 10%, can be changed by specifying a different value for the minfree parameter of the newfs(8) and tunefs(8) commands. See Chapter 3, "Storage," for details on adjusting this minfree value.

#### 2.2.5.5 Performance

In deciding file system layout and how many disks to use for root, /usr, /var, swap, and data, do not forget the performance considerations. Spreading the disk I/Os across multiple disks or even buses can improve performance by eliminating I/O bottlenecks. Some of the I/O behavior will be known at installation time, but much of this will be learned once the system is in production. Monitor the I/O performance and be prepared to change the configuration as needed based on hot file systems.

## 2.3 System Preparation

Once the preinstallation planning has been completed, the next step prior to actually beginning the installation is ensuring that the system itself is suitably prepared. This means surveying the system to see that its configuration is compatible with a Tru64 UNIX installation. This is especially important for older systems, which may need to be updated to support the version of Tru64 UNIX being installed. The following are the system prerequisites of a Tru64 UNIX system installation:

- Any existing data is backed up
- Installation media is available
- A system console is in place
- A suitable boot disk is available
- The system's firmware is at the required version

### 2.3.1 Back Up Existing Data

If the installation is to be onto a Compaq system currently running an instance of either Tru64 UNIX or another operating system such as OpenVMS, take the time to back up and verify any important data before proceeding to install Tru64 UNIX. This is not so much a requirement as a recommendation. Even if the system was being backed up regularly, make two copies of the data deemed important and ideally make two full backups. This step is inexpensive insurance and could save you or your organization a great deal of pain.

### 2.3.2 Available Installation Media

This requirement simply means that the Compaq system must have access to the installation media. If you will be installing Tru64 UNIX from the distribution CD-ROM, a CD-ROM drive must be installed on the target system and the selected version of the Tru64 UNIX distribution installation CD-ROM must be available.

If, however, you plan on installing the system from an RIS (Remote Installation Services) server, the target system must be connected to a network via Ethernet, Token Ring, or FDDI. The RIS server must be reachable by the target system across the network, and unless special requirements are met, both the target system and the RIS server must be on the same network segment or subnet in order to allow remote booting. In addition, the target system must be registered as a client with an RIS server that is serving the desired version of Tru64 UNIX.

### 2.3.3 System Console

In order to install Tru64 UNIX, the target system must have a system console. The system console is the display/keyboard from which many important system administration activities, including installation, must occur. There are two types of supported system consoles for Compaq systems:

- A graphical display, keyboard, and mouse, such as those commonly found on a desktop workstation
- A character-based display and keyboard, such as a serial terminal connected to the system's console or serial port

An additional supported console interface is a modem connected to the console port, but this feature is only available on Compaq AlphaServers that support Remote System Management. This allows a remote system to be installed over a dial-up connection. Consult the system documentation to determine if this remote console is an option for your system.

If you are installing Tru64 UNIX on a system with graphical display capabilities, a graphical point-and-click Installation Setup application is displayed. The two installation procedures, text-based and graphical, provide equivalent flexibility when installing a Tru64 UNIX system.

### 2.3.4 System Disk

Before beginning a Tru64 UNIX installation, the disk that will be the system disk must be selected. The system disk, or more accurately the disk that will contain the root file system, will be the disk from which the installed operating system will boot. There are two requirements for this disk:

- The selected disk must be a supported disk for your platform. These specifications can be found at:

  ```
  http://www.compaq.com/alphaserver/platforms.html
  ```

  Select your platform and select the supported options link.

It may be possible to successfully install Tru64 UNIX on a disk not listed, but Compaq may or may not provide support in the event of problems. Since most Compaq systems are delivered with at least a single disk, it is strongly recommended that the system disk be one of the supported types.

- The selected disk must have partition a available. The Tru64 UNIX root file system must be located on partition a, and this partition must start at block 0 and be, at a minimum, 128 MB in size.

A complete Tru64 UNIX operating system installation can reside on a single, sufficiently large disk. Such an installation would mean the root and /usr file system plus a swap partition are contained on one disk. This is an acceptable configuration, especially for a small desktop or server system. However, only the root file system must reside on the system disk. Other file systems and swap partitions can be placed on additional disks. For instance, the custom installation allows the selection and creation of a root file system, a /usr file system, a /var file system, and two swap partitions. By placing each of these on distinct disks, a custom Tru64 UNIX installation could be placed on five disks.

### 2.3.5 System Firmware

Before beginning a Tru64 UNIX installation, you must check that the version(s) of firmware on the target system are at a minimum level for the version of Tru64 UNIX to be installed. Firmware is software that is stored in programmable read-only memory (PROM) on a Compaq Alpha system that is responsible for certain hardware behavior. The most important firmware on an Alpha system running Tru64 UNIX is the Alpha System Reference Manual (or SRM) Console firmware. This firmware is commonly referred to as simply the Console Firmware, and its main role is to load the Tru64 UNIX operating system from disk or from a network and then pass control to it. The SRM is also where a Tru64 UNIX installation is begun.

Other firmware to be aware of includes:

- Advanced RISC computing (ARC) firmware
- EISA configuration utility (ECU)
- I/O adapter firmware

The ECU is used on Compaq Alpha systems with an Extended Integrated System Architecture (EISA) bus. While most newer Compaq Alpha systems use the PCI bus for expansion cards, many Compaq Alpha systems also support the EISA bus. Before installing Tru64 UNIX on a system with an EISA bus, you must run the EISA Configuration Utility to identify any installed EISA boards. The ECU is included on a separate floppy disk. Refer to the system owner's guide for information on running the ECU. Always update the firmware before running the ECU.

Many Compaq I/O boards also have their own firmware that defines their functionality. Some examples of these boards include SCSI adapters, RAID controllers, and I/O modules. The firmware level on any such components in a system must be verified to be at a minimum level for the version of Tru64 UNIX being installed.

### 2.3.6 Determining Firmware Requirements and Current Version

Before installing Tru64 UNIX, make sure that your system has the correct Console firmware version[1]. To determine the minimum firmware revision for your system, consult either the Firmware Release Notes for the version of Tru64 UNIX being installed or the Release Notes for the Alpha Systems Firmware Update. The Alpha Systems Firmware Update Release Notes contains a table that identifies the minimum acceptable firmware version based on the operating system and version. Table 2.1 contains the Tru64 UNIX–specific portion of this table from the V6.0 Firmware CD. Notice that it lists the version of the CD, not necessarily the version you see at the console. Further down in the document is another table that shows the specific version of the firmware based on the hardware and software platforms. For example, the V6.0 Firmware Release Notes indicate that updating an AlphaServer ES40 with the V6.0 CD will result in V6.0 of the SRM console. Note however, that

**Table 2.1** *Firmware OS Minimum Version for an ES40*

| OS | OS Version | Minimum Acceptable FW CD Versions |
|---|---|---|
| Tru64 UNIX | V4.0F | FW CD V5.4 |
| | V5.0 | FW CD V5.5 |
| | V5.0A | FW CD V5.6 |
| | V5.1 | FW CD V5.8 |

1. In most cases, the correct Console Firmware is delivered in the same package as the Tru64 UNIX CDROM media.

the CD version and the firmware version do not always match. As an example of this, updating an XP1000 Workstation from the same V6.0 CD will result in V5.9 of the SRM console.

Once the minimum Console firmware level has been determined, display the target system's current Console firmware level by getting to the system's SRM Console prompt (>>>) and issuing the following command:

```
>>>show version
   version          V5.9-4 Jan  9 2001 16:38:48
```

In this example, the Console firmware version is 5.9-4. Again, referring to Table 2.1, the minimum required Console firmware level for Tru64 UNIX version V5.1 must be at least from the V5.8 CD and from the Release Notes of the Alpha Systems Firmware Update CD V5.8; that means that the ES40 firmware version should be of the V5.8 family (possibly V5.8-nn). Now since a new release of the firmware is available, that being the V6.0 CD, it makes sense to consult the V6.0 CD's documentation to see if it is appropriate to update to that newer version.

If the system is already up and running Tru64 UNIX, you can quickly determine the current Console firmware version by running the following commands:

```
# consvar -g version
version = V5.8-43 Aug 21 2000 16:22:48
# consvar -g pal
pal = OpenVMS PALcode V1.84-101, Tru64 UNIX PALcode V1.79-101
```

Note that new Compaq Alpha systems may have a higher firmware revision than the firmware level specified in the latest version of Tru64 UNIX. A higher firmware revision usually indicates changes to support the operating system version that shipped with the system. Compaq recommends that Alpha systems should not be loaded with earlier (lower) versions of firmware than is currently installed. The later firmware is almost always backward compatible with earlier versions of the Operating System. An exception to this recommendation might be if a firmware upgrade caused system problems and it became necessary to back-out the firmware upgrade to the previous version.

### 2.3.7 Upgrading Firmware

If it is determined that the Console firmware needs to be upgraded before a Tru64 UNIX installation can begin, the procedure for updating a system's firmware follows. Updating the Console firmware is a fairly quick procedure, and there are three main update methods supported by Compaq:

- A Compaq Alpha Systems Firmware Update CD-ROM
- A bootable floppy disk
- Over a network using the BOOTP protocol

These three methods are basically different ways to load and run the firmware update utility on the target system. Once this update utility is running, the procedure to actually update the firmware is identical regardless of the delivery method (CD-ROM, floppy, or BOOTP).

Below are details for using each of these delivery methods followed by the generic instructions for the actual firmware update utility. In each of the following sections, the particular boot device (CD-ROM, floppy, or the network for BOOTP) is referenced. Enter the following command from the SRM Console prompt (>>>) to determine this boot device on your system:

```
>>> show device
```

A device information table similar to the following is displayed:

```
dka0.0.0.15.0        DKA0        COMPAQ BD009222C7  B016
dka100.1.0.15.0      DKA100      COMPAQ BD009222C7  B016
dqa0.0.0.13.0        DQA0          COMPAQ CDR-8435  0013
dva0.0.0.0.0         DVA0
ewa0.0.0.9.0         EWA0          08-00-2B-86-8B-0E
ewb0.0.0.11.0        EWB0          08-00-2B-86-8C-0E
ewc0.0.0.17.0        EWC0          08-00-2B-C4-15-DA
pka0.7.0.15.0        PKA0          SCSI Bus ID 7
```

The second column displays the boot device name for each device in the table. For network interfaces, the hardware or Media Access Control (MAC) address is shown in the third column. For instance, using the above table:

- DKA0 and DKA100 are the SCSI disks.
- DQA0 is the CD-ROM drive.
- DVA0 is the floppy disk.
- EWA0 – EWC0 are the Ethernet network interface cards (See documentation for a current list of supported network interfaces types).
- 08-00-2B* are the network interface hardware address.
- PKA0 is the SCSI controller.

#### 2.3.7.1 Firmware Update CD-ROM

The simplest method of loading the firmware update utility is via a Compaq Alpha Systems Firmware Update CD-ROM. This CD-ROM is usually included with the Tru64 UNIX Software Distribution Kit but is occasionally shipped separately from Compaq as the CD-ROM is updated on a quarterly basis. This CD-ROM is versioned and contains the latest version of the Console firmware for each Compaq Alpha system. The Firmware Update CD-ROM also contains one previous version of each system's Console firmware so that the firmware can be downgraded in the event a problem arises after updating a system to the latest version. In addition, system-specific Release Notes on the CD-ROM provide information about the Console firmware version.

#### 2.3.7.2 Booting from the Firmware Update CD-ROM

To boot from the Firmware Update CD-ROM, simply insert the CD into the CD-ROM drive and from the SRM Console prompt (>>>), issue the following command:

```
>>> boot <CD-ROM drive Device Name>
```

Substitute the previously determined CD-ROM device name in the boot command. Using the previous example, the command would be:

```
>>> boot DQA0
```

The system will then proceed to boot from the Firmware Update CD-ROM, and after several minutes of boot activity, the first screen of system-specific README-First information announcements will be displayed. This README information may include details of firmware changes or enhancements, known problems, and the directory location on the CD of the firmware Release Notes. Simply press the <Return> key to scroll through the information or press <CTRL/C> to skip the remainder of the screens. It is a good idea to scan this information for issues that may impact your system at this time.

After the final screen of README information, the default firmware update utility bootfilename will be displayed, followed by the prompt Bootfile:. At this point, simply press <Return> to load the default (latest) version of the update utility, or type a specific firmware update utility bootfilename to load an alternate, usually older version. For example:

The default bootfile for this platform is

```
[DS10]DS10_V5_9.EXE
```

Hit <RETURN> at the prompt to use the default bootfile.

```
Bootfile:
```

After either selecting the default or an alternate firmware update utility bootfilename, the system will proceed to load that version and present the main menu of the firmware update utility. Continue to Section 2.3.10, "Firmware Update Utility," later in this chapter to proceed with the firmware update.

### 2.3.8 Bootable Firmware Update Floppy Disk

While the Alpha Systems Firmware Update CD-ROM is the most convenient method of updating a system's firmware, there may be times when using the CD-ROM is not possible. Perhaps the correct CD-ROM is simply unavailable, or Compaq has released an interim firmware release between the regularly scheduled releases of the Firmware Update CD-ROM, which is upgraded quarterly. For these situations, Compaq has provided a second method of updating many AlphaSystem's firmware: a bootable floppy disk. Updating a system via a bootable floppy is not as convenient as a CD-ROM since you must download the necessary firmware image from Compaq and copy this image to a floppy disk. The advantage, of course, is that if you need the very latest firmware update, you do not have to wait for the next release of the Firmware Update CD-ROM.

Compaq provides a Web site specifically for the distribution of firmware updates. This page provides the contents of the most recent Firmware Update CD-ROM for those without access to a local copy. In addition, any interim firmware updates that have not yet been released on a Firmware Update CD-ROM are also available for download. The firmware updates are listed by supported Alpha systems. The URL for this Firmware Update page is:

```
http://gatekeeper.research.compaq.com/pub/DEC/Alpha/firmware/
```

Additionally, the firmware updates are also available via anonymous FTP from:

```
ftp://gatekeeper.research.compaq.com/pub/DEC/Alpha/firmware/
```

Each system has its own directory containing the appropriate firmware updates. The /pub/DEC/Alpha/firmware/vX.Y/doc/ directory (where X.Y is the version of the Firmware Update CD-ROM) contains the Release Notes for each system, as well as the necessary information for updating the firmware from the images. The /pub/DEC/Alpha/firmware/readmes/ directory contains HTML and text files for each system, which describe the methods for updating the firmware from files downloaded from this FTP area. This readmes directory, in conjunction with the Release Notes for a given Alpha system, should provide the necessary information for updating a particular system's firmware. Any individual Alpha system firmware releases that occur between Firmware CD-ROM releases will be located in the /pub/Digital/Alpha/firmware/interim directory.

#### 2.3.8.1 Creating a Bootable Firmware Update Diskette

The process for updating the firmware by floppy disk can vary between different systems. This example is for the AlphaServer ES40 and will be similar but not exactly the same as for other platforms.

The first step in updating an Alpha system's firmware via floppy disk is to create a bootable firmware floppy disk. Several prerequisites are necessary in order to create such a bootable diskette:

- The appropriate firmware update image for the system to be updated
- A 3.5-inch floppy diskette
- An Alpha system running Tru64 UNIX with a 3.5-inch floppy diskette drive

The third item is a requirement both for the system that will be used to actually create the bootable floppy disk and for the system whose firmware is to be updated via the resulting bootable floppy disk. Obviously, the system that creates the bootable floppy disk can be the same system being updated. Certain Compaq Alpha systems (e.g., the AlphaServer GS60 and GS140) do not have floppy drives and, as such, cannot be updated via the bootable floppy disk. For the same reason, such Alpha systems cannot be used to create bootable floppy disks either.

#### 2.3.8.2 Download the Firmware Image

Compaq provides bootable firmware update images that fit on a single 3.5-inch floppy disk. Due to the limited capacity of a floppy disk, however, Compaq prepares an individual image for each type of Alpha system, and the appropriate image must be downloaded for transfer to a floppy disk. Using either the Compaq Alpha Systems Firmware Update Web page or Compaq anonymous FTP server, download the appropriate image to a Tru64 UNIX system. The Firmware Update Web page makes it simple to download the correct file for a particular system; simply click on the link for the desired system, then scroll down to the Boot Floppy (Tru64 UNIX systems) section and select the link for the correct firmware update image.

In the event the Web site is unavailable or inaccessible, firmware update images may also be downloaded from Compaq's anonymous FTP server. Unfortunately, you will have to know which file to download as opposed to selecting it from a Web page. Each individual system type's firmware update image is located in a directory named for the type of system. The naming convention of the firmware update image itself varies from system type to system type, but typically the file name contains the system type, optional architecture, version, and ends with a ".exe". For example, consider this example:

```
Compaq Alpha System Model Firmware Update
  Image File

Compaq AlphaServer ES40, ES40cv, & ES40lp Systems Model 6/xxx
  es40_v6_0.exe
```

The following is an example session of downloading a firmware update image for an AlphaServer ES40:

```
# ftp gatekeeper.research.compaq.com
Connected to gatekeeper.research.compaq.com.
.
.
.
Name (gatekeeper.research.compaq.com:yates): anonymous
331 Guest login ok, send ident as password.
Password:
230 Guest login ok, access restrictions apply.
Remote system type is UNIX.
Using binary mode to transfer files.
ftp> cd /pub/DEC/Alpha/firmware/v6.0/es40
250 CWD command successful.
ftp> bin
200 Type set to I.
ftp> get es40_v6_0.exe
200 PORT command successful.
150 Opening BINARY mode data connection for es40_v6_0.exe
(2686464 bytes).
226 Transfer complete.
2686464 bytes received in 14.39 secs (14.39 secs, 182.31
Kbytes/s)
```

```
ftp> bye
221 Goodbye.
```

This example copies the ES40 image that will work with all ES40s. In the next section, the platform-specific image will be copied since only it will fit on a floppy disk.

#### 2.3.8.3 Download the Bootable Floppy Creation Utility

Compaq provides a utility, mkbootfirm, which is used to convert the downloaded firmware update image to the appropriate format for copying to a low-level formatted floppy disk. This utility is available from the same Web page or FTP site as the firmware update images. The URL for this utility is:

```
http://gatekeeper.research.compaq.com/pub/DEC/Alpha/firmware/
  utilities/mkbootfirm.tar
```

Download this file to a convenient place on your Alpha system and unpack it with the following command:

```
# tar -xvf mkbootfirm.tar
```

This will result in a directory named mkbootfirm in the current directory that contains the mkbootfirm utility itself and a README file.

#### 2.3.8.4 Create the Bootable Floppy

The files required to update the console firmware by floppy disk are:

- mkbootfirm.tar (contains the mkbootfirm utility)
- clu.exe (Loadable Firmware Utility)
- clsrmrom.exe (EV6 SRM console image) or cl67srmrom.exe (EV67 SRM console image)
- clarcrom.exe (AlphaBIOS console image)

As mentioned above, the mkbootfirm.tar file is located on the ftp server at:

```
http://gatekeeper.research.compaq.com/pub/DEC/Alpha/firmware/
  utilities/
```

The other files are located in:

```
http://gatekeeper.research.compaq.com/pub/DEC/Alpha/firmware/
  vX.Y/platform-name/
```

Once you have downloaded the firmware update images and the mkbootfirm utility, the next step is to create a bootable firmware update floppy. Insert a blank or scratch 3.5-inch floppy disk into the floppy drive and low-level format the diskette with the following command. Note that this command is for a floppy in the first (zeroth) floppy drive.

```
# /sbin/fddisk -f -fmt /dev/rdisk/floppy0c
```

After low-level formatting the floppy, transfer the firmware update image to the diskette with the following command:

```
# mkbootfirm/mkbootfirm clu.exe |
  dd of=/dev/rdisk/floppy0c bs=64k
```

Eject the floppy and insert a second one in the drive and format it:

```
# /sbin/fddisk -f -fmt /dev/rdisk/floppy0c
```

Create a link to your floppy drive called /dev/fddrive. This is required for the use of the mtools(1) utilities below:

```
# ln -s /dev/rdisk/floppy0c /dev/fddrive
```

Now add DOS format to the floppy that you just formatted and copy the console images to the floppy. Also, in this case since this is for an EV67, rename the longer cl67srmrom.exe to clsrmrom.exe so mtools does not have a problem with the filename length.

```
# /usr/bin/mtools/mformat -s 18 a:
# mv cl67srmrom.exe clsrmrom.exe
# /usr/bin/mtools/mwrite clsrmrom.exe a:\clsrmrom.exe
# /usr/bin/mtools/mwrite clarcrom.exe a:\clarcrom.exe
```

#### *2.3.8.5 The I/O Options Firmware Update Floppy Disk*

The limited capacity of a 3.5-inch floppy disk prevents Compaq from including any firmware images other than for the SRM and ARC consoles. Since some I/O options, such as SCSI adapters, network interface controllers, and I/O modules also have upgradable firmware, Compaq distributes firmware updates for these options also. If you wish to update the firmware on these I/O options when using the bootable floppy method, you must create a second floppy that contains these firmware updates. Creating an I/O options firmware update floppy disk is entirely optional—you will be prompted for it during the process of booting the console firmware update floppy disk. If you have elected not to create the I/O options firmware update diskette, simply press <Return> at that prompt.

These I/O option firmware updates are available as a single image from the same Web page or FTP site as the system firmware update images. The URL for this image is:

```
http://gatekeeper.research.compaq.com/pub/DEC/Alpha/firmware/
   v6.0/options/option s.dd
```

where X.Y is the version of the Firmware Update CD-ROM.

Once you have downloaded the I/O options firmware update image, the next step is to copy this image to a floppy disk. Insert a blank or scratch 3.5-inch floppy disk into the floppy drive and low-level format the diskette with the following command:

```
# fddisk -f -fmt /dev/rdisk/floppy0c
```

After low-level formatting the floppy, transfer the I/O options firmware update image to the diskette with the following command:

```
# dd if=options.dd of=/dev/rdisk/floppy0c bs=64k
```

This command assumes that the I/O options firmware update image is named options.dd and that the floppy disk is in the first floppy drive.

Always consult the directions on the Alpha Firmware pages to get the most up-to-date directions for applying the I/O options.

#### 2.3.8.6 Booting from the Firmware Update Floppy Disk

To boot from a Firmware Update floppy disk, insert the floppy into the floppy drive and from the SRM Console prompt (>>>), issue the following command:

```
>>> boot <floppy drive Device Name>
```

Substitute the previously determined floppy drive device name in the boot command. Using the previous example, the command would be:

```
>>> boot DVA0
```

The system will then proceed to boot from the Firmware Update floppy disk, and after several minutes of boot activity, you will be prompted to insert a floppy containing option firmware. If an I/O Options Firmware Update diskette was previously created, remove the Firmware Update floppy and insert the I/O Options Firmware diskette and hit the <Return> key; otherwise, simply hit the <Return> to continue. After this prompt, the load will proceed and finally present the main menu of the firmware update utility. Continue to Section 2.3.10, "Firmware Update Utility," later in this chapter to proceed with the firmware update.

### 2.3.9 Updating Firmware Across the Network via BOOTP

Compaq provides the ability to update an Alpha system's console firmware by booting a firmware update image located on another system across the network using BOOTP (Boot Protocol). This can be a useful alternative to either the Firmware Update CD-ROM or a bootable Firmware Update floppy disk, especially when there are many systems to be updated. Simply copy the appropriate firmware update image(s) to a suitable system and configure the BOOTP server on that system for each client system to be updated. Once these steps are completed, each target system can be booted from the BOOTP server and the firmware update can proceed. Note that as of V5.0 of the Alpha Systems Firmware Update, there is no BOOTP support for updating the I/O options firmware—only the SRM and ARC firmware can be updated via BOOTP.

When selecting a system to be a BOOTP server for firmware updates, there are several requirements to consider. To be a BOOTP server, a system must be on the same network segment as the systems to be updated, and the systems must be able to communicate with each other. Check connectivity with the ping(8) command. See Chapter 7, "Networking," for details on Tru64 UNIX network configuration. In addition, the optional Additional Networking Services subset containing the BOOTP daemon must be loaded. This subset is named OSFINETxxx, where the xxx specifies the version of the subset. To determine if this subset is loaded, execute the following command, searching for the correct subset:

```
# /usr/sbin/setld -i | grep -i osfinet

OSFINET510    installed    Additional Networking Services
(Network-Server/Communications)
```

Based on this output, the subset is installed. If you do not receive any output, or if the installed keyword in the second column is absent, you must install the subset from the master Tru64 UNIX operating system installation media using the setld command. For assistance in installing optional Tru64 UNIX subsets, see Chapter 4, "System Configuration."

#### 2.3.9.1 Copy the Firmware Update Images to the Server

After determining that the chosen system meets the requirements of a BOOTP server, the next step is to copy the firmware update image(s) to a directory on the BOOTP server. The images can be copied from the Firmware Update CD-ROM or downloaded from Compaq's Alpha Systems Firmware Update Web site or FTP server. See earlier Section 2.3.8.1, "Creating a Bootable Firmware Update Diskette," for details on downloading the appropriate firmware update image from Compaq's Web site or FTP server.

Place the resulting firmware update image(s) in a directory on the BOOTP server. A suggested directory is /usr/firmware, but the location is completely arbitrary. The following is an example session of mounting the Firmware Update CD-ROM and copying the firmware update image for an AlphaServer ES40 into a directory on the BOOTP server:

```
# mkdir /usr/firmware
# mount -rt cdfs -o noversion /dev/cdrom0c /mnt
# cp /mnt/es40/es40_v6_0.exe /usr/firmware
```

#### 2.3.9.2 Modify or Create the Client Entry in the /etc/bootptab File

The BOOTP daemon's configuration file is /etc/bootptab, and this configuration file is read when the daemon receives a boot request packet. This configuration file defines information for remote clients. Edit the /etc/bootptab file and add or modify an entry for each system whose firmware will be updated. The format of an /etc/bootptab client entry is:

```
<host_name>:ht=<hw_type>:ha=<hw_address>:bf=<filename>:
  ip=<ip_address>
```

where:

- host_name is the client's system name as specified in /etc/hosts.
- hw_type is the network interface type. Ethernet and FDDI are ht=1, and Regular token-ring (IEEE 802) is ht=6.

- hw_address is the network interface hardware address (MAC address): use the console command show device.
- filename is the full pathname of the bootable firmware update image.
- ip_address is the corresponding Internet protocol address of the system name in /etc/hosts.

The following is an example of a bootptab file:

```
saturn:ht=1:ha=00-00-F8-01-42-5F:bf=/usr/firmware/
  es40_v6_0.exe:ip=10.0.0.5
```

#### 2.3.9.3 Invoke BOOTP and tftpd Daemons

To activate the BOOTP process, two system daemons must be enabled, the BOOTP Daemon (joind) and the Trivial File Transfer Protocol Daemon (tftpd). The tftpd daemon actually does the work of transferring the bootable firmware update image across the network to the client

Both of these daemons are controlled by entries in the /etc/inetd.conf configuration file. Simply edit this file and modify or create the entries for the BOOTP and tftpd daemons. Ensure that the entries in /etc/inetd.conf for these daemons do not have a # character at the beginning of the line. For the BOOTP daemon, modify or create the joind entry. In addition, modify the tftpd entry to reflect the directory where the bootable firmware update image is by appending the directory name to the end of the line. The entries should be similar to the following examples:

```
tftp  dgram udp wait root /usr/sbin/tftpd tftpd /tmp
  /usr/firmware
bootps dgram udp wait root /usr/sbin/joind  joind
```

After modifying the /etc/inetd.conf file, you must force the inetd process to reread its configuration file by sending the process a hang-up signal. This enables the BOOTP process and causes future boot requests received by inetd to be forwarded to the BOOTP daemon. To force inetd to reread /etc/inetd.conf, issue the following command:

```
# kill -HUP 'cat /var/run/inetd.pid'
```

#### 2.3.9.4 Boot the Client

Once the appropriate bootable firmware update image is copied to the BOOTP server and the BOOTP and tftpd daemons are configured and enabled, the next step is to begin the firmware update from the client's console. From the client's SRM Console prompt (>>>), issue the following command:

```
>>> boot -protocol bootp <network interface Device Name>
```

Substitute the previously determined network interface device name in the boot command. Note that the -protocol option is used to specify the boot protocol—in this case BOOTP. Using the previous example, the command would be:

```
>>> boot -protocol bootp EWA0
```

The client system will then broadcast a BOOTP request packet and, if the BOOTP server is available and configured correctly, proceed to boot the firmware update image served by the BOOTP server. The following is an example session of booting a client with BOOTP:

```
>>>boot -protocol bootp EWA0
(boot ewa0.0.0.11.0 -flags A)
FRU table creation disabled
Trying BOOTP boot.
Broadcasting BOOTP Request...
Received BOOTP Packet File Name is:/usr/firmware/
  es40_v6_0.exe
local inet address: 10.0.0.5
remote inet address: 10.0.0.3
TFTP Read File Name: /usr/firmware/es40_v6_0.exe
netmask = 255.255.255.0
Server is on same subnet as client.
(The boot proceeds…)
```

After several minutes of boot activity, you will be prompted to hit the <Return> key. After this prompt, the load will proceed and finally present the main menu of the firmware update utility. Continue to Section 2.3.10, "Firmware Update Utility," below to proceed with the firmware update.

### 2.3.10 The Firmware Update Utility

Regardless of the method used to load the firmware update utility (CD-ROM, bootable floppy disk, or across the network via BOOTP), the process of actually updating a system's firmware is essentially the same. Once the load process is complete, the main menu of the Firmware Update Utility is displayed:

```
***** Loadable Firmware Update Utility *****
-------------------------------------------------------------
Function    Description
-------------------------------------------------------------
Display     Displays the system's configuration table.
Exit        Done exit LFU (reset).
List        Lists the device, revision, firmware name, and
            update revision.
Readme      Lists important release information.
Update      Replaces current firmware with loadable data image.

Verify      Compares loadable and hardware images.
? or Help   Scrolls this function table.
-------------------------------------------------------------

UPD>
The Firmware Update Utility's prompt is UPD> and the various
functions are selected by entering the function name followed
by <Return>. From this prompt, it is actually only necessary to
enter the first letter of each of the functions. The first step
is to issue the List command, which displays all firmware
options available for update, their current revision, and the
revision they would be updated to. For example:

UPD> list

Device          Current Revision      Filename      Update Revision

nt              5.69                  nt_fw         5.70

srm             5.8-10                srm_fw        5.9-4

                                      cipca_fw      A420
                                      dfxaa_fw      3.20
                                      kzpsa_fw      A12
```

After listing the components available for firmware update, the next step is to actually do the firmware update. Simply issue the Update command to update all the devices to the firmware version displayed in the fourth column of the list output. If only a single device is to be updated, specify that device's name after the Update function. For instance, to update just the SRM, issue the following command:

```
UPD> update SRM
```

After entering the Update command, you will be prompted to confirm the update and, after entering a Y, the update will begin. Once the firmware update has begun, it is important not to interrupt the update as one or more devices could be left in an inoperative state. Do not reset or remove power from the Alpha system being updated. An example update sequence:

```
UPD> update
Confirm update on:
ARC
SRM
kzpsa0
kzpsa1
[Y/(N)]y
WARNING: updates may take several minutes to complete for each
 device.

    DO NOT ABORT!
ARC  Updating to v5.70... Verifying v5.70... PASSED.
SRM  Updating to v5.9-4... Verifying v5.9-4... PASSED.
kzpsa0  Updating to vA12... Verifying vA12... PASSED.
kzpsa1  Updating to vA12... Verifying vA12... PASSED.
UPD>
```

Once the update is complete, the Verify function can be used as confirmation that the update was successful:

```
UPD> verify
ARC   Verifying v5.70... PASSED.
SRM   Verifying v5.9-4... PASSED.
kzpsa0   Verifying vA12... PASSED.
kzpsa1   Verifying vA12... PASSED.
```

Note that if the update is booted from a floppy, you may have to specify the path to the firmware:

```
UPD> update srm -path fat:clsrmrom.exe/dva0
```

Finally, issue the Exit command to exit from the Firmware Update Utility. This will reinitialize the system, and the value of the auto_action console environmental variable will determine the system's next action. If auto_action is set to BOOT or RESTART, the system will attempt to boot; if auto_action is set to HALT, the system will return to the console prompt (>>>).

Note that the Firmware Update Utility may appear slightly different on different Alpha platforms. These differences are typically minor menu formatting changes or command output alterations. Read the firmware update Release Notes and README files for the particular model and version being updated so as not to miss any new or changed features of both the Firmware Update Utility and the firmware upgrade itself.

## 2.4 Tru64 UNIX Installation

After completing the necessary preinstallation planning and ensuring that the system itself is suitably prepared, you are ready to begin the actual installation of Tru64 UNIX on your system. This section will detail the actual installation process including a comparison of both the character and graphical installation utility interfaces. Note that the installation to be detailed here is a Full installation, where the Alpha system is booted from the installation media—either a local CD-ROM or across the network from an RIS server. An Update installation, which is outlined later in this chapter (see Section 2.5.1, "Update Installation Steps"), is performed with the Alpha system running the version of Tru64 UNIX to be updated from single-user mode.

### 2.4.1 Full Installation Steps

1. Complete preinstallation planning and preparation.
2. Take the System to the Console Prompt (>>>). Power up the system. After the Power On Self-Test (POST) and other startup and diagnostic messages, the console prompt should be displayed. If the system begins to boot, halt the system by pressing the Halt button. If the system is already running a version of Tru64 UNIX or another operating system, shutdown and halt the system with a command similar to the following:

```
# shutdown -h +1 "Shutting down for full installation"
```

3. Set the Necessary Console Flags. Refer to the "Processor-Specific Boot Instructions for Full Installations" chapter in the Tru64 UNIX Installation Guide for system-specific console variable settings. The following flags are typically specified on all Alpha systems prior to beginning a full installation:
   - This command clears the boot_osflags variable to ensure the kernel takes the correct action upon bootup:

```
>>> set boot_osflags ""
```

   - This command sets the auto_action variable to halt, which causes the system to return to the console prompt after the system is powered up or initialized:

```
>>> set auto_action halt
```

- Typically, after the installation is complete, the auto_action variable is reset to boot or restart so the system will automatically boot upon power-up.

This command sets the os_type variable to UNIX, which specifies that the SRM Console firmware will be booted when the system is powered on:

```
>>> set os_type unix
```

4. Beginning in V5, if the bootdef_dev variable is set and points to an existing V5 system disk, the installation will use the device database from that existing installation. In other words, if you had customized the device database by renaming dsk0 to dsk30 and dsk1 to dsk50, the new installation would know your disks by their new names, dsk30 and dsk50, if the bootdef_dev pointed to the old system disk at the time of the new installation. If you want a fresh device database, set the bootdef_dev variable to null:

```
>>> set bootdef_dev ""
```

5. Initialize the System. Whenever certain SRM environment variables are changed, it is necessary to reinitialize the system in order to activate the new variable values. Issue the following command from the SRM Console prompt (>>>) to reinitialize the system:

```
>>> init
```

6. Identify Boot Device. Once the system has been reinitialized and the SRM Console prompt (>>>) is presented, enter the following command from the prompt to determine the boot device of either the CD-ROM or the network interface on your system:

```
>>> show device
```

A device information table similar to the following is displayed:

```
dka0.0.0.15.0       DKA0        COMPAQ BD009222C7   B016
dka100.1.0.15.0     DKA100      COMPAQ BD009222C7   B016
dqa0.0.0.13.0       DQA0          COMPAQ CDR-8435   0013
dva0.0.0.0.0        DVA0
ewa0.0.0.9.0        EWA0        08-00-2B-86-8B-0E
ewb0.0.0.11.0       EWB0        08-00-2B-86-8C-0E
```

```
ewc0.0.0.17.0        EWC0             08-00-2B-C4-15-DA
pka0.7.0.15.0        PKA0                 SCSI Bus ID 7
```

The second column displays the boot device name for each device in the table. For instance, using the above table:

- DQA0 is the CD-ROM drive—Use this boot device when installing from CD-ROM media.
- EWA0-EWC0 is the Ethernet network interface—Use this boot device when installing from an RIS server.

Boot from Installation Media. Boot the system and begin the installation by issuing the following boot command:

```
>>> boot <Device Name>
```

If you are installing from CD-ROM, substitute the previously determined CD-ROM device name in the boot command. Using the previous example, the command would be:

```
>>> boot DQA0
```

Output similar to the following will be displayed as the system boots from the CD-ROM:

```
(boot dqa0.0.0.13.0 -flags a)
block 0 of dqa0.0.0.13.0 is a valid boot block
reading 16 blocks from dqa0.0.0.13.0
bootstrap code read in
Building FRU table
base = 1be000, image_start = 0, image_bytes = 2000
initializing HWRPB at 2000
initializing page table at 3ff0000
initializing machine state
setting affinity to the primary CPU
jumping to bootstrap code
Tru64 UNIX boot - Fri Nov 16 21:24:46 EST 2001
```

If the installation will be from an RIS server, boot from the network interface and specify the protocol as BOOTP. For example:

```
>>> boot -protocol bootp EWA0
```

Output similar to the following will be displayed as the system boots from the RIS server:

```
(boot fwa0.0.0.12.0 -flags a)
FRU table creation disabled
Trying BOOTP boot.
Broadcasting BOOTP Request...
Received BOOTP Packet File Name is:
  /var/adm/ris/ris0.alpha/hvmunix
local inet address: 10.0.0.5
remote inet address: 10.0.0.3
TFTP Read File Name: /var/adm/ris/ris0.alpha/hvmunix
netmask = 255.255.255.0
Server is on same subnet as client.
......................................
......................................
..................
bootstrap code read in
base = 1cc000, image_start = 0, image_bytes = 9d67a0
initializing HWRPB at 2000
initializing page table at 3ff0000
initializing machine state
setting affinity to the primary CPU
jumping to bootstrap code
Secondary boot program - Wed Jul 18 17:50:38 EDT 2001
```

7. Begin the Actual Installation. Once the system completes the boot process, what you see next depends on the version of Tru64 UNIX being installed and the system's hardware configuration. If you are installing Tru64 UNIX V4.0 or greater and the system has graphical display capabilities, refer to Section 2.4.2. If the system being installed does not have graphical display capabilities, refer to Section 2.4.3.

8. Reboot the System. After the installation of the system is complete, the system is halted and a message is displayed on the screen instructing the installer to set several console variables and boot. For instance:

   Issue the following console commands to set your default bootpath variable and to boot your system disk to multiuser:

```
>>> set boot_osflags A
>>> set bootdef_dev DKA0
>>> boot
```

Issuing these commands will boot the newly installed system to multiuser mode and continue the installation. In most cases these changes are made for you and the system boots automatically.

9. Initial System Configuration. After the newly installed system boots, the process of configuring the system begins. First, the mandatory and any optional software subsets are configured for the newly installed system. This software configuration occurs automatically with no user input necessary. The name of each software subset is displayed as it is configured. This process is fairly quick; depending on the number of installed subsets, the configuration should take no more than five minutes to complete. The output is similar to the following:

```
*** SYSTEM CONFIGURATION ***
Configuring "Base System " (OSFBASE510)
Configuring "Base System - Hardware Support " (OSFHWBASE510)
Configuring "Compiler Back End " (OSFCMPLRS510)
Configuring "Ref Pages: CDE Development " (OSFCDEMANOP510)
Configuring "Ref Pages: CDE Admin/User " (OSFCDEMANOS510)
```

   In addition, this initial system configuration is when the system's personality (host name, date and time, root password) is actually configured. If any of these parameters were not specified at the time of installation, you will be prompted to enter them at this point.

10. Kernel Build. Immediately after the initial system configuration, the custom system kernel is built for the first time. The kernel is built based on whether you chose Mandatory Only, All Options, or Customize earlier in the installation process. If you choose Customize, you will pick the appropriate kernel options from the list; otherwise the choice list is skipped.

   At this point, the system builds this initial kernel and then reboots. This completes the actual installation of Tru64 UNIX.

11. Login as Root to Continue System Configuration. After the system reboots, login as root using the previously specified root password to continue the system configuration. Refer to Chapter 4, "System Configuration," for details on post-installation tasks.

### 2.4.2 The Tru64 UNIX Full Installation

When installing Tru64 UNIX on a system with graphics capabilities, an X Window System server is started after booting from the install media and the first of several Tru64 UNIX Installation Setup windows is displayed (Figure 2.2). The installation utility walks the installer through several configuration windows and then presents a summary window so that the selections can be verified.

The Installation utility is an X Window System application with a series of windows, fields, buttons, and drop-down menus for entering system characteristic parameters. Provided that the installer has completed the system configuration planning, performing a Full Installation is a straightforward exercise in answering a few basic questions.

#### 2.4.2.1 Host Information

The first window that you will see after the Installation Welcome window is the Host Information dialogue. The modifiable fields include the host name, area, location, date, and time (Figure 2.3). The host name is the name that you and others will use to refer to this system on the network. What you choose for the Area and Location establishes the time zone information. The date field order is Month/Day/Year and the time is in 24-hour format so 4PM is 16:00. If you do not specify a date and time, the installation will proceed but will ask for the current date and time before building the custom kernel.

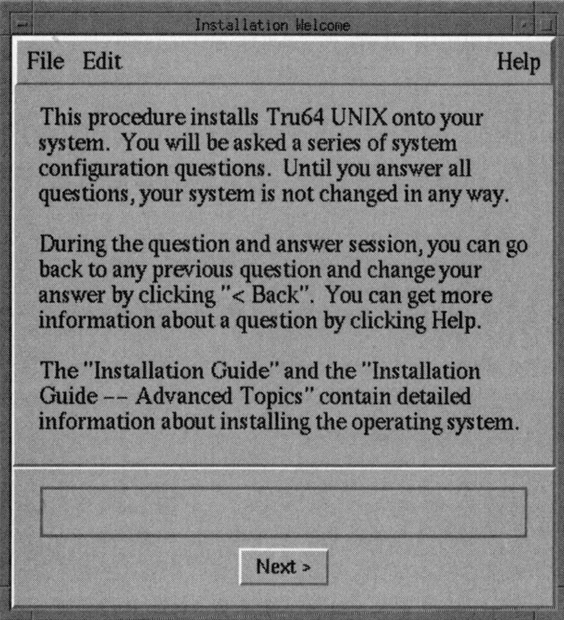


**Figure 2.2** *Installation welcome.*

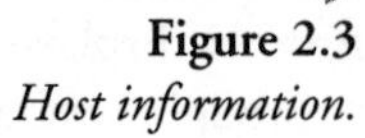


**Figure 2.3**
*Host information.*

#### 2.4.2.2 Root Password

The next data required is the root password (Figure 2.4). The root user, also known as the superuser, has privileges above that of regular users. For example, the superuser (or root user) can shut down the system, add users, mount file systems, etc. For this reason it is important that the root password be secure. The installer must select a password that has at least six characters and contains upper and lower case characters. One of the first six characters must be a number, special character, or upper case letter. When you type the password it will not be displayed for security reasons, but it is being recorded by

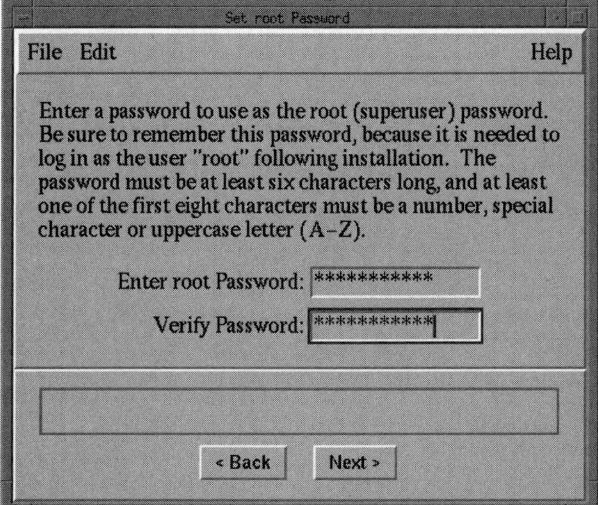


**Figure 2.4**
*Set root password.*

the system. You also have to type it a second time for verification. After the system has booted you can change the password using the passwd(1) command.

#### 2.4.2.3 *Software Selection*

The important next step is selecting the software subsets to install. You can choose which software subsets will be installed (Figure 2.5) first by selecting Mandatory Only, All Software, or Customize. If you choose Mandatory Only or All Software, no further choice is required at this time. Choosing Customize and clicking on the Edit List... button will display a detailed choice window (Figure 2.6). Which option you choose depends on what kind of system this will be and this should be determined in the planning phase. If you do not want all subsets, select Customize and pick and choose. Otherwise select all subsets or just the mandatory ones. Installing all subsets will use more disk space but will not adversely affect the operation of the system. Selecting only the mandatory subsets will probably not be sufficient in most cases. You can add and remove subsets at any time using the setld command.

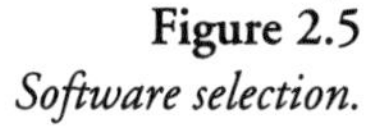

**Figure 2.5**
*Software selection.*

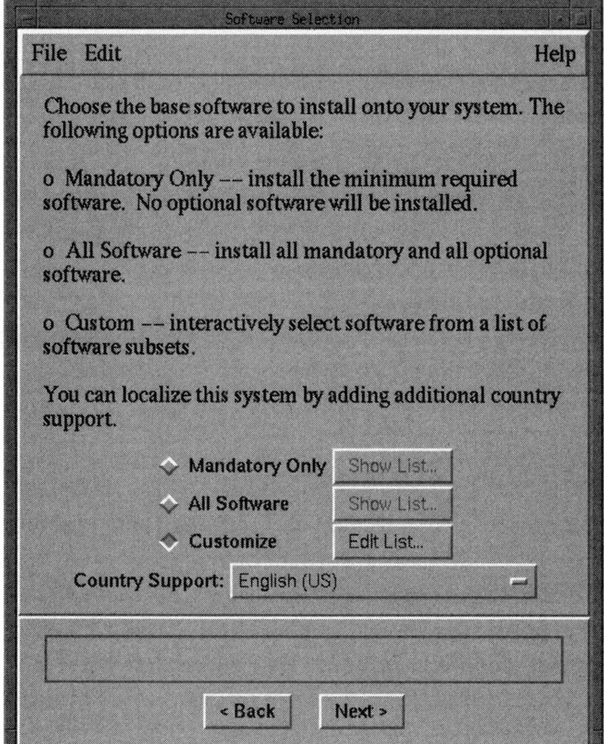

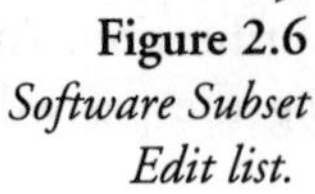

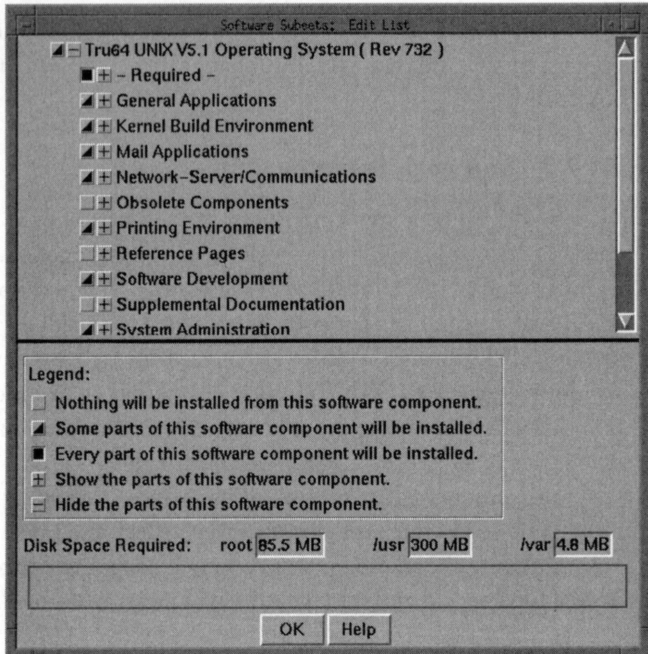


**Figure 2.6** *Software Subset Edit list.*

Also chosen in this window is Country Support. You can select support for one or more additional languages for the graphical user interface.

After selecting Customize and clicking on Edit List… you can make subset selections by category, for example Reference Pages, or by expanding the category by clicking the + and selecting individual subsets from that category. If you choose a subset that has a dependency on another subset, the required subset will automatically be selected. Note the key at the bottom of the window that shows if any or all of a particular software category is installed. Also at the very bottom is a running total of the file system space required based on current selections.

### 2.4.2.4 Kernel Options

The next step is to select which kernel options (Figure 2.7) will be built into the custom kernel after the installation procedure has completed. The options are Mandatory Only, All Options, and Customize. As you might guess, if you don't choose Customize there will be no choose list before the kernel is built. If you do choose Customize, you must select the specific kernel options for your system when prompted just prior to kernel build.

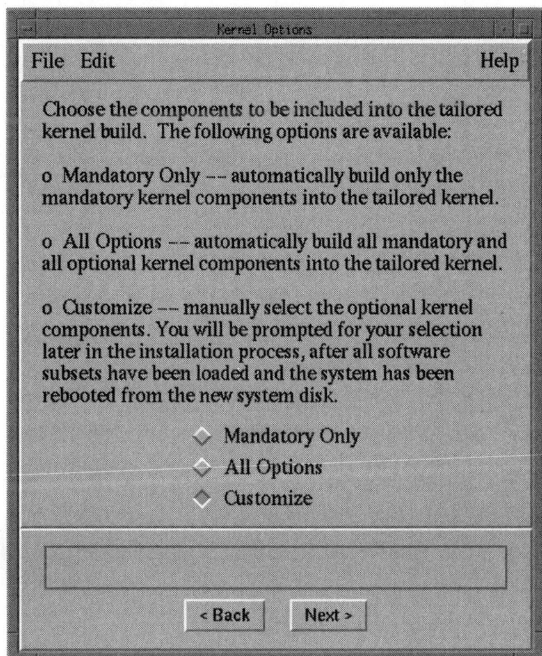


**Figure 2.7**
*Kernel options.*

### 2.4.2.5 File System Layout

Now that you know what you are installing you have to decide where to install it and what type of file system to use. The File System Layout dialogue (Figure 2.8) offers two main options, Default File System Layout and Custom File System Layout. Since the default layout does not give much room for customization this chapter will only consider the customized layout (Figure 2.9).

The custom file system layout allows many selections. For example you can place each file system on a separate disk, choose multiple file system types, include the Logical Storage Manager, and repartition your disks. Also if you are not sure which disk is which, for example you do not know which physical disk is dsk1, you can select the Identify Disk... button and it will turn the disk activity light on for that disk.

Assuming that the preinstallation planning has been completed, it is a simple matter of selecting the disk and partition and possibly resizing the partition to the required size. Note that /var can be specified to be in /usr or it can have its own file system. This is entirely up to the installer.

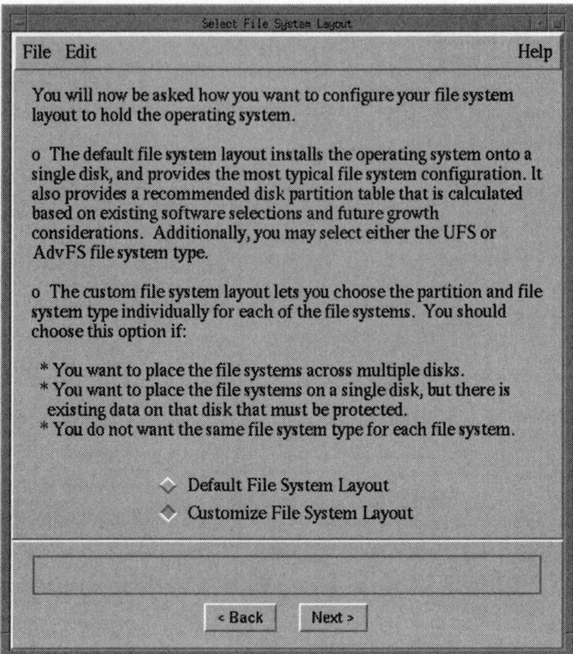


**Figure 2.8**
*File System layout selection.*

While you can install into LSM volumes by selecting the LSM pop-up menu it is not required to select LSM during this phase to use LSM on the system. You can easily add this option after the system has been completely built.

If you need to resize the partition of a disk at this point select the Edit Partitions... button and you will see a graphical utility (Figure 2.10) that you can use to easily resize the partitions. Simply use the sliders to grow or shrink the partitions to the size you need. When you are finished, select OK and you will return to the Custom File System Layout. The customized sizes will be reflected in the layout window.

### 2.4.2.6 Installation Summary

Finally, the Installation Summary window (Figure 2.11) is displayed with all of your choices to this point. You should verify that your selections are correctly reflected in the summary. If not, or if you have decided to change something you can still make modifications now. If you had to exit the installation procedure at this time, at most, all you would have to do is repartition any disks that were modified during the File System Layout phase and possibly modify the date to have the system in its original state.

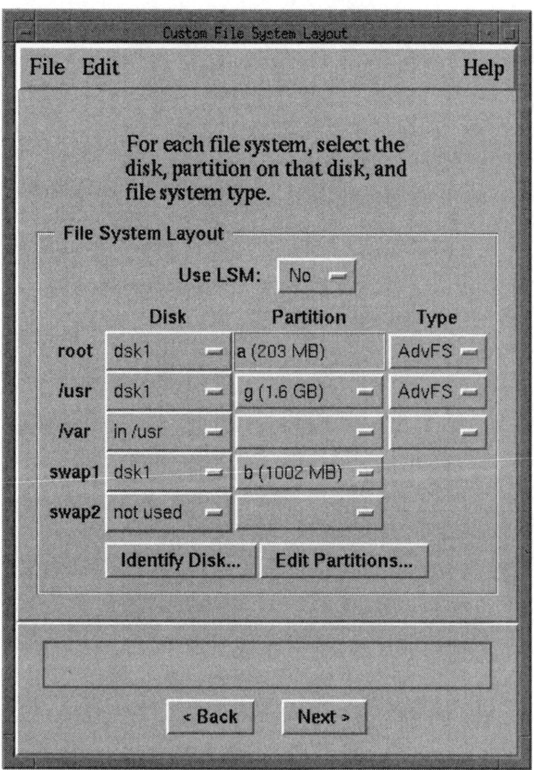


**Figure 2.9** *Custom file system layout.*

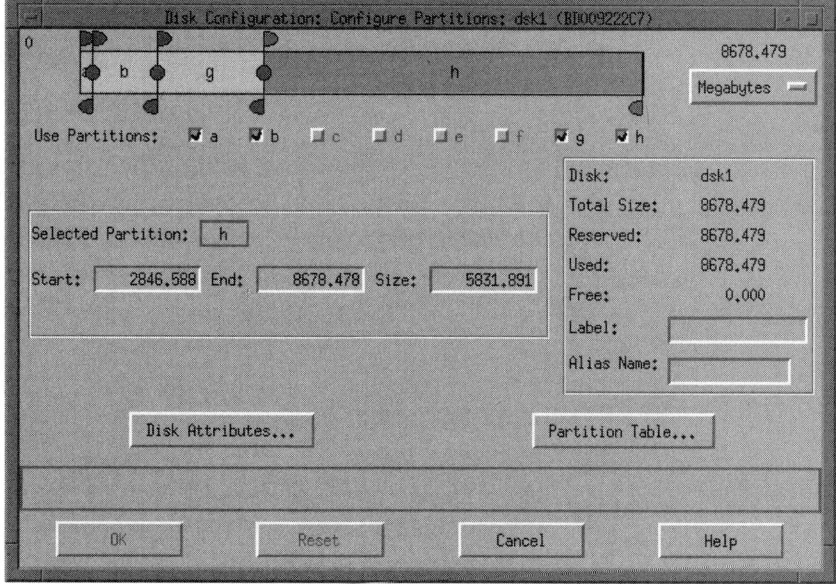


**Figure 2.10** *Disk configuration utility.*

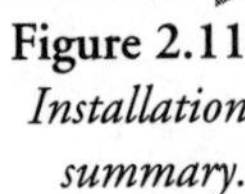


**Figure 2.11**
*Installation summary.*

Once satisfied with the selections, select the Finish button and the installation procedure will proceed to install the operating system and will not require any additional input until the subsets are installed and the system has rebooted.

### 2.4.2.7 System Load

After you confirm that you want to proceed with the installation, the installation will proceed and the file systems will be created, swap will be added, and the subsets will be installed. You will see a status display (Figure 2.12) that will show you how the installation is progressing. After the software is loaded the system will automatically reboot and perform the Software Configuration. This is a rather quick operation. Then a new kernel will be built.

### 2.4.2.8 Custom Kernel Build

If you chose either Mandatory Only or All Options in the Kernel Options section, the custom kernel will automatically be built and moved into the root

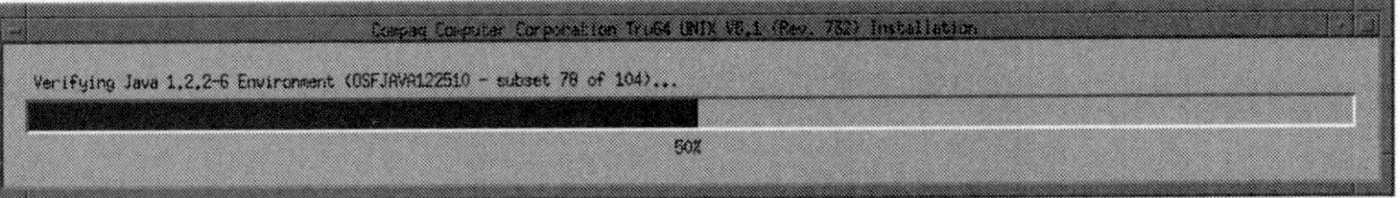


**Figure 2.12**
*Installation status window.*

directory. If you selected Customize, you will be presented with the Kernel Option Selection menu. Select the options you need and the custom kernel will be built. You can always return to this point by using the doconfig(8) utility. The menu that you see will differ from system to system but will look similar to this:

```
*** KERNEL OPTION SELECTION ***

    Selection   Kernel Option
--------------------------------
        1       System V Devices
        2       NTP V3 Kernel Phase Lock Loop (NTP_TIME)
        3       Kernel Breakpoint Debugger (KDEBUG)
        4       Packetfilter driver (PACKETFILTER)
        5       IP-in-IP Tunneling (IPTUNNEL)
        6       IP Version 6 (IPV6)
        7       Point-to-Point Protocol (PPP)
        8       STREAMS pckt module (PCKT)
        9       X/Open Transport Interface (XTISO, TIMOD,
                  TIRDWR)
       10       Digital Versatile Disk File System (DVDFS)
       11       ISO 9660 Compact Disc File System (CDFS) Audit
                  Subsystem
       13       ATM UNI 3.0/3.1 ILMI (ATMILMI3X)
       14       IP Switching over ATM (ATMIFMP)
       15       LAN Emulation over ATM (LANE)
       16       Classical IP over ATM (ATMIP)
       17       ATM UNI 3.0/3.1 Signalling for SVCs (UNI3X)
       18       Asynchronous Transfer Mode (ATM)
       19       All of the above
       20       None of the above
       21       Help
       22       Display all options again
--------------------------------

Enter your choices.

Choices (for example, 1 2 4-6) [20]:
```

Keep in mind that building a kernel with options that are not required makes the kernel larger, which means it will take a bit more memory. Not building something into the kernel that you will need means that you have to schedule downtime so that a new kernel can be moved into production.

For instance, to use the IP Version 6 (IPV6) on the system, the IPV6 kernel option must be selected. Note that an exception to this is the ISO 9660 Compact Disc File System (CDFS) option. Starting at Tru64 UNIX V4.0D, this option is dynamically loaded by the kernel when a CDFS file system is mounted. This option may still be statically loaded into the kernel, but it is unnecessary and the resulting kernel will be larger, thereby consuming a small amount of memory at all times.

Once the custom kernel is built and copied into the root directory, it takes one more reboot and the installation is complete. The next steps are called the post-installation steps. This involves logging in as root and configuring the system for use. These tasks are covered in Chapter 4, "System Configuration."

### 2.4.3 The Tru64 UNIX Character Installation Utility

When installing Tru64 UNIX on a system without graphical capabilities, the installation interface is a character-cell menu-driven application. This application provides essentially the same functionality as the Graphical Installation Utility. The only exception is access to an easy disk-partitioning utility such as the Disk Configuration window available when doing a Graphical installation. If it becomes necessary to customize the partitions of disks, the disklabel(8) command must be used manually from the UNIX Shell mode. See Chapter 3, "Storage," for details on use of the disklabel command.

After the initial boot from the installation media, the following information is displayed, followed by the three-option installation menu:

```
          Welcome to the Tru64 UNIX Installation Procedure

This procedure installs Tru64 UNIX onto your system.  You will
   be asked a series of system configuration questions.  Until
   you answer all questions, your system is not changed in any
   way.

During the question and answer session, you can go back to any
previous question and change your answer by entering:
  "history"
You can get more information about a question by entering:
  "help"

Refer to the "Installation Guide" and "Installation Guide -
  Advanced Topics" for more detailed information about
  installing Tru64 UNIX.

** This system is currently running firmware revision: 5.0A
   See the "Tru64 UNIX Release Notes" for information regarding
     the required firmware revision.
   The following options are available:

   o  The "U.S. English Installation" installs only the Tru64
      UNIX base software onto your system.
```

```
    o  The "Installation with Worldwide Language Support" (WLS)
       allows you to internationalize your system. This option
       will allow you to install the Tru64 UNIX base software as
       well as WLS software. The additional software subsets
       provide support for various countries and their native
       languages.

    o  The "Exit Installation" option stops the installation,
       and puts your system in single-user mode with superuser
       privileges. This option is intended for experienced UNIX
       system administrators who want to perform file system or
       disk maintenance tasks prior to the installation. This
       option may also be used for disaster recovery on a
       previously installed system.


Remember, you can always get extra information by typing help.

1) U.S. English Installation
2) Installation with Worldwide Language Support
3) Exit Installation

Enter your choice:
```

The installer will be asked the same questions as in the Graphical installation.

## 2.5 Upgrading Tru64 UNIX

The process of upgrading an existing installed version of Tru64 UNIX to a later version of Tru64 UNIX is called an Update installation. An Update installation is performed on an existing system and results in an upgraded system while preserving disk and file system configuration, user accounts, printer and network configurations, and any other custom configurations that existed prior to the upgrade. An Update installation is similar to a Full installation in two important ways:

- Many of the preinstallation tasks are the same. These include backing up the system prior to beginning, updating the system firmware if necessary, and planning disk space.

- Updates can be done from CD-ROM or across the network from a Remote Installation Services (RIS) server

The Update installation process is different from a Full installation primarily in the way the update is begun. While a Full installation is started from the console prompt (>>>), an Update installation is begun while the system is running and in single-user mode.

In addition, Compaq has provided only certain update paths. For instance, to upgrade to V5.1 of Tru64 UNIX, the system must already be at V4.0G, or V5.0A. Unfortunately some system upgrades may take two or more updates to get the system to the desired target version. As an example, consider a Tru64 UNIX V4.0F system. In order to upgrade this system to V5.1, the supported path is:

1. Update from V4.0F to V5.0A, followed by an:
2. Update from V5.0A to version V5.1.

See the Performing an Update Installation chapter in the appropriate Tru64 UNIX Installation Guide for details on the supported update paths.

## 2.5.1 Update Installation Steps

A Tru64 UNIX Update installation requires as much, if not more, preinstallation planning as a Full installation. This is so because the system being upgraded is likely an existing system that is depended upon by users. A successful Update installation is very nearly transparent to the users, and adequate planning is the first step in achieving this goal. The following steps describe an Update Installation.

### *2.5.1.1 Prepare for the Update Installation*

Complete all preinstallation planning and preparation. Planning for an Update is similar to a normal Full installation and includes:

- Back up the system prior to beginning the update.

  Anything can happen during an upgrade, and you want to prepare for success no matter what that may mean. Take a vdump(8) of the root, /usr, and (if it is separate) /var before beginning an update. If there is any failure you will be able to quickly and easily return to your preinstallation environment.

- Ensure there is sufficient disk space for the upgraded and new software subsets.

Check existing disk space and look at the Release Notes to see if you have enough space before beginning. Some housekeeping may be in order.

- Upgrade the system's firmware if necessary.

  You are already scheduling down time, so even if the firmware currently on the system is at least at the minimal, update to the latest that you have on hand.

- Check the Release Notes for any Update Installation information.

  Release Notes contain important information and should always be reviewed before any upgrade or install. At least review the new features or platform-specific notes.

- Determine the CD-ROM device name.
- Run verify on any AdvFS file systems.

  Prior to beginning the update, umount all AdvFS file systems (besides root) and run verify on them. For root, use 'verify –a'. If verify uncovers a problem correct the problem (this could range from letting verify fix it (-f) or re-creating the domain and restoring the data. You do not want to proceed to a later version with domain corruption so fix it now.

- Verify that all layered products are supported at the new operating system version.

#### 2.5.1.2 Shut Down to Single User

If in multiuser mode, either log in as root or 'su' to root and shut down the system:

```
# su -
password:
# shutdown +10 "Shutting down for planned operating system
update"
```

#### 2.5.1.3 Start the Update Installation

Depending on how many subsets you will be installing, the class of system and speed of CD-ROM, it will take between 45 minutes to a couple of hours to update the system.

1. If you want update(8) to run without any intervention necessary, start it with the '-u' option:

```
# /sbin/update -u
```

2. Mount local file systems and start LSM if it is installed:

```
# /sbin/bcheckrc
```

3. Place the operating system in the CD-ROM.
4. Mount the CD-ROM:

```
# /sbin/mount /dev/rz4c /mnt              # V4
# /sbin/mount /dev/disk/cdrom0c /mnt      # V5
```

5. Begin the installupdate procedure:

```
# /sbin/installupdate [-nogui] <location>
```

Where <location> can be:
• local device (/dev/rz4c, /dev/disk/cdrom0c, etc.)
• mount point to which the CD-ROM has been mounted (/mnt)
• RIS server (loader1:)

#### 2.5.1.4 Choose Options

The set of choices you see are the Update Installation Options.

- Select Optional Kernel Components

  Select this option if you are already running a customized kernel or if you want to customize the kernel. If you do not select this option, only the mandatory kernel options will be built into the new kernel.

- Archive Obsolete Files

  Select this option if you want the obsolete files that are no longer required by the new version to be archived before they are deleted.

#### 2.5.1.5 Monitor Analysis

After the options are selected, the next thing you see is the PreLoad Analysis. The update process is:

- Checking for conflicting software
- Determining Installed base operating system software
- Determining kernel components

- Checking for file type conflicts
- Checking for obsolete files
- Checking file system space

See the Installation Guide for details about each check.

#### 2.5.1.6 *Begin Software Load*

After the Analysis Phase has completed, you are asked to confirm the start of the Update. If you are satisfied and confirm, the Update will proceed.

#### 2.5.1.7 *Post Update Tasks*

Once the Update is complete, login as root and perform the post-update tasks. The next two sections describe the post-update tasks.

#### 2.5.1.8 *Manually Merge Customizations if Necessary*

Review the log files produced by the Update installation. These files are:

- Update installation log:

  `/var/adm/smlogs/update.log`

- Configuration log:

  `/var/adm/smlogs/it.log`

- Customized files (if there were any):

  `/var/adm/smlogs/upd_custom_files`

- Failed merges (if there were any):

  `/var/adm/smlogs/upd_mergefail_files`

#### 2.5.1.9 *Manually Merge Customizations if Necessary*

The Update may not have been able to merge all of the customizations for one reason or another. If this is the case, you will have to do this manually. Manually merging is simply editing new versions of system files to include your customizations. Review the upd_custom_files and upd_mergefail_files as well as the kernel configuration file, /sys/conf/HOSTNAME to see if you need to take any action. More details are found in the Installation Guide.

Once any required manual merges are complete the system is ready for use and you can put the system back into production or install additional software. Additionally you may wish to perform some update installation cleanup.

#### 2.5.1.10 Update Installation Cleanup (Optional)

You should clean up (remove and archive) files created by the Update procedure. This should be done last (after fixing any merge issues) and can be done through Sysman:

```
# sysman updadmin
```

This menu leads you through removing the .PreUPD and .PreMRG files.

## 2.6 Patches

No installation can be considered complete until the aggregate current patch kit (if one exists) has been applied. The purpose of this section is to give an overview of applying an aggregate patch kit. Compaq customers who have chosen to get the patches quarterly by CD-ROM can install directly from the CD-ROM, but most customers will download the patches from the public patch web site:

```
http://ftp.support.compaq.com/public/unix/
```

From this directory locate the version of Tru64 UNIX that you will be patching and select the patch kit from that location.

The file that you will download has the form t64vXYasNNNN-<datetimestamp>.tar, where XY is the version and NNNN is the patch kit number. For example, t64v51as0003-20010521.tar is referred to as Patch Kit 3 for V5.1.

Once the patch kit tar file is downloaded, untar it:

```
# tar xvf T64V51AS0003-20010521.tar
blocksize = 256
x patch_kit
x patch_kit/patch_tools
x patch_kit/patch_tools/product_map, 656 bytes, 2 tape blocks
x patch_kit/patch_tools/instctrl
x patch_kit/patch_tools/instctrl/OSFPAT00000030510.inv, 1893
   bytes, 4 tape blocks
```

.
.
.

Now cd to the directory where the dupatch command is (it will be the relative path patch_kit) and run the version of dupatch that is contained in the kit:

```
# cd patch_kit
# ./dupatch

          * Previous session logs saved in session.log.[1-25]

Tru64 UNIX Patch Utility (Rev. 29-02)
==========================
          - This dupatch session is logged in
            /var/adm/patch/log/session.log

    Main Menu:
    -----

    1)   Patch Installation
    2)   Patch Deletion
    3)   Patch Documentation
    4)   Patch Tracking
    5)   Patch Baseline Analysis/Adjustment
    h)   Help on Command Line Interface
    q)   Quit

Enter your choice:
```

From this menu you can install and delete the patches as well as some more advanced patching operations. The installation steps will be familiar to you since the installation engine behind dupatch is setld. You can install the patches while in multi-user mode but the preferred method is from single-user mode. In either case the kernel will have to be rebuilt and the system rebooted for the patches to take effect.

The dupatch installation guide is included in the tar file that was extracted. Reference this guide for more detailed and up-to-date directions for using dupatch. Also refer to the Best Practices Web page for Compaq's recommendations regarding patches and other important system administration matters:

```
http://www.tru64unix.compaq.com/faqs/publications/best_practice
s/index.html
```

# 3

# Storage

In this chapter, we explore Tru64 UNIX storage. The goal of this chapter will be to provide information to the reader in order to understand enough about devices to handle most system administration tasks. Naturally, a complete discussion of this topic could take many more pages than are available here. In this chapter, we will start with some theory and then move on to very practical concepts.

## 3.1 Storage Systems Concepts

To better understand how UNIX file systems are implemented in later discussions, it is important to know some of the terminology and concepts of storage. This section is an examination of generic concepts of storage and disk drive terminology so these ideas will make sense in the discussion of file systems.

### 3.1.1 Disk Drive Terminology

A single disk is based on a single individual spindle that comprises a storage subsystem. Sometimes a RAID device, which can comprise many individual disks, is referred to as a single disk since it presents itself to UNIX that way. For our purposes in this section, we are referring to concepts related to a single disk device; later sections will cover the RAID device concepts and terminology.

A *disk drive* is a mechanical device. It consists of moving parts such as servos and drive motors that can wear out after a certain period of time. Despite this, these devices have become very reliable over time with very high mean time between failures (MTBF) associated with them. A MTBF of over

500,000 hours is common these days, which means that in the absence of a manufacturing defect, the drive will likely outlive the useful life of the computer system to which it is attached. Historically, it has been important to understand the mechanics of disks since these were used in calculations for optimal UNIX file system structure. We will see later that these calculations still exist, but are far less relevant than they used to be, due to the advent of hardware and software RAID products that mask the underlying details. It is also important to understand that these devices still do fail. A single block or an entire drive can go bad, but in either case it is possible, using RAID techniques, to mask the failures from the operating system's point of view.

A *spindle* is a single rotating axle to which the platters that contain the data on the disk are attached. A single circumference of a disk platter under a single head located a fixed distance from the disk spindle is known as a *track*. This is the amount of data that can be read by a single drive head in one rotation of the platter. A disk *sector* is a fixed-sized piece of a track located on disk. A disk *block* is a fixed-sized, contiguous area on disk. This is the minimum amount of information transferred between the operating system and a disk, thus it is the smallest addressable entity on a disk device. For all Compaq-supported disk drives, disk sectors and blocks are both equal to 512 bytes of data.

A *head* is a physical device that reads the data on a single side of a platter. All heads for a single drive are connected to a device known as an *actuator arm* that moves all the heads together. Since all the heads must move at the same time and all the heads can read data in parallel, a logical construct known as a *cylinder* has been developed to describe all the tracks located on all the platter sides located the same fixed distance from the disk spindle. Since a *seek* is the most time-consuming event needed to read and write data to or from a disk drive, it is important to reduce the number of seeks. One way this is accomplished is to place related data in the same or adjacent cylinders; thus the concept of a cylinder group was developed. A *cylinder group* simply refers to a contiguous set of cylinders used to store file system data. Cylinder groups have historically been used to improve the performance of UFS file systems.

### 3.1.2 Controller Technology

A *controller* is a term that can have many meanings depending on the context in which it is used. In the context of this chapter, we simply use the term as another name for an adapter. Thus, a SCSI controller is simply a device that converts signals from a computer system's main I/O bus to the SCSI standard protocol. A RAID controller is a device that connects to a standard bus interface (e.g., SCSI) and translates the I/Os to a set of devices connected to the back end of the device. Thus, a RAID controller is much more sophisticated and complex than a simple SCSI adapter. A RAID controller has a CPU and memory associated with it and runs a specialized program, called the firmware, that determines how the device can be configured and how it will react to various events.

Today, a vast majority of storage attached to UNIX systems is connected using the Small Computer System Interface (SCSI) bus standard. Later we will be covering SCSI in greater depth, since the standard has evolved over time and there are many options to support the different speeds and signal types that the standards allow. Even with these changes, the SCSI standard has simplified disk interconnects considerably from the old days of proprietary disk protocols.

One other rapidly evolving and popular storage mechanism today is Fibrechannel or Storage Area Network (SAN) technology. Fibrechannel uses optical fiber interconnects between the systems and devices, rather than copper-based cables, in much the same way that hosts are interconnected in a local area network. These fiber interconnects are simply a different transport used to ship the SCSI commands and data between the systems and storage. Thus, Fibrechannel does not really represent a new protocol distinct from SCSI, but rather is a new way to transport the bits back and forth. There are several good books devoted to Fiberchannel and we cannot hope to cover it fully here, so we refer the reader to one of those for further reading on this subject. As a systems administrator for a large Tru64 UNIX system, you will undoubtedly want to understand how this important new technology works before implementing it at your site. At the time of this writing, the technology is still evolving; therefore great skill is still required to install and manage these SANs properly.

### 3.1.3 SCSI Concepts

SCSI (pronounced "scuzzy") is not just a single standard but is actually a suite of standards. In this section, we explain the different SCSI terminology and develop concepts needed to discuss the interaction between SCSI devices and the host.

SCSI (or what is now often referred to as SCSI-1) was the original SCSI specification proposed by the American National Standards Institute (ANSI). The work on the specification began in 1982 and was originally designed for attaching storage devices to workstations (ANSI X3.131-1986). It supported a single-ended, narrow bus structure with maximum support for only eight devices. The maximum speed that could be achieved was only 5MB/sec with a maximum bus length of 6 meters. In addition, the roughly 200-page document initially defined only six devices. Although this standard was quite useful and was used in many small computer systems, there were significant weaknesses, particularly for larger systems. Technology and system sizes began to change significantly; thus, the need for improvements became evident. The committee began working in 1992 on the second revision of the standard.

The SCSI-2 specification (ANSI X3.131-1994) was the result of the second committee's work and is still in widespread use today. This standard was a great improvement because it defined much faster device speeds, four new devices, "fast" and "wide" concepts, differential device specifications, and new cabling standards. In addition, it allowed for multiple initiators on a single bus at one time, paving the way for clustering technologies like Compaq's TruCluster product. The new standard allows up to 16 devices per SCSI-2 bus and up to 8 logical unit numbers (LUNs) per device. The SCSI-2 specification was vastly better than SCSI-1, and truly brought SCSI into the mainstream of computing for both low-end and high-end systems.

As of this writing, the SCSI-3 specification is emerging as the new SCSI standard. SCSI-3 is different from its predecessors in that it is really an architecture for adding new interfaces and devices into the standard. It has been intelligently crafted with the thought that any useful standard must continue to evolve and will never remain static. As of this writing, many devices have implemented various pieces of the specification to one degree or another. For example, the very popular Ultra and Ultra Wide SCSI (also known as Fast 20 and Fast 20 Wide) devices are an implementation of part of the SCSI 3 standard. These two fall into the SPI (SCSI Parallel interface), which is a synchronous extension to the SCSI standard with a negotiated period of between 50 and 96 nanoseconds. As a result, the Ultra standard is roughly twice the speed of regular Fast SCSI, allowing a 20MB/second transfer rate for narrow devices and 40MB/second for wide. The SCSI-3 standard increases the number of supported LUNs per device to 64 from 8.

## 3.2 Redundant Array of Independent Disks

In the 1980's, when disk drives began to come down in price and improve in reliability, a group of three University of California at Berkeley professors realized that if you took a bunch of off-the-shelf disks, you could make them perform as well as or better than a Single Large Expensive Disk (SLED). At that time, for performance and reliability, you still needed to spend lots of money for proprietary drives to attach to your mainframes and minicomputers. The introduction of smaller, standard drives, combined on a large scale, began to emulate the bigger drives in what became known as a Redundant Array of Independent Disks (RAID). These devices have all but replaced the big, proprietary drives for high-end systems. An entire industry has been built around RAID technology, accounting for billions of dollars in sales each year. All indications are that requirements for storage will continue to grow at a rapid rate and this industry will continue to prosper.

### 3.2.1 RAID Terminology

Before we move any further into our discussion of RAID terminology, let's define a few terms that we will need later on. A RAID device is any highly intelligent controller that implements some or all parts of the RAID specifications. One example of such a device connected to a Tru64 UNIX system is Compaq's StorageWorks HSZ family of storage controllers. These controllers connect to your Alpha system via a SCSI interface and offer features such as dual-redundancy, spare device management, multi-pathing, write-back cache with battery backup, and intelligent manageability. There are other popular non-Compaq brands available that have been used successfully with Tru64 UNIX.

Fundamental to our discussion of RAID is striping, which is a method of concatenating multiple drives into one logical storage unit. Striping involves partitioning each drive's storage space into "stripes" that may be as small as one disk sector (512 bytes) or as large as several megabytes. These stripes are then interleaved in a round-robin fashion, so that the combined space is composed of alternating stripes from each drive. In effect, the storage space of the drives is shuffled like a deck of cards. The type of application environment you have will determine whether large or small stripes should be used. A typical stripe size is 128 or 256 blocks (64 or 128 kilobytes). In HSZ terminology, a stripe is also known as a "chunk"; for example, the "CHUNKSIZE" keyword is used to alter the default stripe size.

Parity is a mechanism by which data can be verified when written to a device. When the number of all of the "on" bits is counted, an additional bit is added to the existing bits to make the resulting sum of all bits even or odd. Thus, there are two types of parity: even and odd. Odd parity means the sum of the bits, including the parity bit, is an odd number, while even parity means the sum is an even number.

### 3.2.2 RAID Levels

There were five theoretical levels of RAID defined by the original work done at the University of California at Berkeley, and they are known as RAID 1 through RAID 5. Some of these are never seen in practice because they offer little differentiation from the more common levels. Each level offers different performance or redundancy features, and each has different trade-offs in its implementation. Later on, RAID 0 and RAID 0+1 levels were added to provide some features that were missing from the original theory. RAID levels 2, 3, and 4 are rarely, if ever, seen in practice, but we include them here for completeness. The following is a list of each RAID level and its definition:

- RAID 0—This RAID level is also known as striping. RAID Level 0 is not redundant, and hence does not truly fit the "RAID" acronym. In level 0, data is distributed across drives, resulting in higher data throughput. Since no redundant information is stored, performance is very good, but the failure of any disk in the array results in data loss.
- RAID 1—RAID Level 1, also known as mirroring, provides redundancy by writing all data to two or more drives. The performance of a level 1 array tends to be faster on reads and slower on writes than a single drive, but if either drive fails, no data is lost. This is a good entry-level redundant system, since only two drives are required. On the other hand, since the data is completely duplicated, the cost per megabyte is relatively high.
- RAID 0+1—This level was never referred to in the original Berkeley paper, but it is a logical extension of it. This is the combination of mirroring with striping, and it provides complete redundancy along with the performance improvement of using striping for each copy of the data. The cost per megabyte for this RAID level is the same as for RAID 1, but the performance tends to be better.
- RAID 2—RAID Level 2, which uses Hamming error correction codes, is intended for use with drives that do not have built-in error detection. All SCSI drives support built-in error detection, so this level is of little use when using SCSI drives. Thus, you will never see this RAID level implementation in the real world.
- RAID 3—RAID Level 3 stripes data at a byte-level across several drives, with parity stored on one drive. It is otherwise similar to level 4. Byte-level striping requires hardware support for efficient use.
- RAID 4—RAID Level 4 stripes data at a block level across several drives, with parity stored on one drive. The parity information allows

recovery from the failure of any single drive. The performance of a level 4 array is very good for reads (the same as level 0). Writes, however, require that parity data be updated each time. This slows small random writes, in particular, though large writes or sequential writes are fairly fast. Because only one drive in the array stores redundant data, the cost per megabyte of a level 4 array can be fairly low.

- RAID 5—RAID Level 5 is similar to level 4 but distributes parity among the drives. This can speed small writes in multiprocessing systems, since the parity disk does not become a bottleneck. Because parity data must be skipped on each drive during reads, however, the performance for reads tends to be considerably lower than a level 4 array. The cost per megabyte is the same as for level 4.

### 3.2.3 Hardware vs. Software RAID

With the changes in LSM implemented in Tru64 UNIX 5.0, you'll find there is a considerable blurring of the lines in terms of what can (and should) be done with respect to RAID in hardware and/or software. As usual, there are trade-offs to consider when deciding whether to implement RAID in software or hardware. When deciding whether to implement RAID in hardware or software, you must usually choose between the three main factors of performance, complexity, and flexibility. Any change in one of these factors could cause a detrimental impact in the others. Below are some tips (gained through extensive experience) designed to help guide you when deciding on a hardware or software RAID solution.

First, as a general rule, the highest performing RAID should be implemented in hardware (smart controller firmware), but greater flexibility is gained by implementing RAID using a volume manager like LSM. Therefore, when performance is the primary factor, try to implement RAID in hardware as much as possible. Not only will this provide the best performance, but it will reduce complexity of the solution. Any reduction of complexity in the system is a real plus when considering the effort by the system administration staff to deal with device failures. Complex systems can and do fail in unpredictable ways, so simpler tends to be better. On the other hand, if flexibility is the primary objective, then software RAID is the clear choice.

Second, don't over-implement RAID. We have many options to choose from, including LSM, hardware RAID controllers, and AdvFS file striping. Therefore, it would be easy to implement RAID at the wrong level and unintentionally reduce performance, increase complexity, or reduce availability.

For example, if mirroring were implemented at the hardware level and also between devices in LSM, then there would be almost no improvement in availability gained at the expense of disk space. Another foolish example is a stripe set on a hardware RAID controller that can be carved into pieces that can then be striped again using LSM. This additional striping would actually slow write performance, rather than improving it as was intended. This is like compressing a file twice because we hope to get a smaller file the second time around. The actual result is usually a larger file. The same thing can happen with RAID implementations. Too much of a good thing can actually have the opposite effect.

Third, be careful to implement RAID at the appropriate level. For example, prior to version 5.0, LSM would not support RAID 5 but only RAID levels 0, 1, and 0+1. However, it is important to distinguish the difference between what can be done and what should be implemented. We believe the cases in which software RAID 5 should be implemented are very limited. The LSM implementation of RAID level 5 has low overhead and provides redundancy, but we don't recommend using software-based RAID 5 when I/O performance is an important factor. In those cases, hardware RAID 5 should be used to maximize performance and reduce complexity.

Fourth, combining software and hardware RAID may be the best option in some cases. For example, some amount of redundancy is not available with hardware RAID (e.g., mirroring across buses), so a software solution may be the only option.

## 3.3 Tru64 UNIX Device Management

This section introduces the concepts required to understand devices in Tru64 UNIX. For the most part, Tru64 UNIX is similar to other UNIX flavors in some ways and very different in others. It is important to understand these similarities and differences so that a thorough coverage of the file systems is possible. We will begin rather generically with an overview of device management, but our end goal is to get into an in-depth discussion of the management of disk devices, since those are the devices used in the management of the file systems.

We will be discussing only the Version 5.0 device naming and structure here. Beginning with 5.0, Tru64 UNIX device management was changed dramatically not only from the user's perspective (since the naming scheme changed), but also in the kernel. There were two main reasons why changes needed to be made. First, they are required to enable TruCluster 5.x Single System Image (SSI), which means that disk and tape devices are seen consistently across the entire cluster. Second, the changes were needed to allow SCSI Wide Device and Fibrechannel support. In order to support these new requirements, the old device-naming scheme had to be changed.

### 3.3.1 Device Special Files in Tru64 UNIX

As with any UNIX operating system, the Tru64 UNIX system device files are located in the /dev or the /devices directory in the root file system. Device files represent the user-level process "handle" into the device drivers that control various hardware devices on the system. Each device driver is assigned a major number, which uniquely defines it to the kernel. The major number is an offset into one of two tables, known as the *switch* tables, which define the operations that are permissible on the devices. The reason we have two switch tables is that we have one for character devices and one for block devices. It is possible to have a single device with both a character device file and block device file associated with it, but the operations that are supported will be different and thus the code to perform those operations will also be different.

SCSI disk device naming on Tru64 UNIX has traditionally followed the BSD standard conventions. The older device-naming scheme was severely limited in some important ways. Primarily, the old scheme could not be adapted for use in a Single System Image (SSI) cluster environment. What this means is that for a cluster to behave as a single system, the devices must be cluster-wide, rather than local. The BSD-style SCSI disk devices were named based on a formula that includes the local bus and target numbers. There is simply no way to make this number unique for all nodes in the cluster. The second main reason for the device nomenclature change in Tru64 UNIX 5.0 was to accommodate the SCSI-3 standard, which supports up to 64 LUNs per device. The BSD method of using letters to delineate the LUNs could not be easily adapted for SCSI-3. Therefore, device naming in Tru64 UNIX 5.0 has changed significantly from the BSD-derived naming of prior versions. Table 3.1 lists the most commonly used device type naming conventions.

In addition to device naming, the major numbering scheme changed dramatically in Tru64 UNIX 5.0. The older scheme used a different major number for all device types. In the new method, only the major number 19 is used for all cluster devices. This greatly simplifies some of the kernel device management.

**Table 3.1** *Device special files for Tru64 UNIX*

| Device | Description |
|---|---|
| /dev/disk/dsk[x] | SCSI disk block special device |
| /dev/rdisk/dsk[x] | SCSI disk character special device |
| /dev/tape/tape[x]_d[y] | SCSI tape character (rewind) device |
| /dev/ntape/tape[x]_d[y] | SCSI tape character no-rewind device |
| /dev/disk/floppy[x] | Floppy block special device |
| /dev/rdisk/floppy[x] | Floppy character special device |
| /dev/disk/cdrom[x] | CD-ROM block special device |
| /dev/rdisk/cdrom[x] | CD-ROM character special device |

As most UNIX system administrators know, devices come in two flavors: character and block special. Character device special files are used for reading from and writing to those devices that must be accessed one character at a time. Some examples of this type of device are a terminal (tty) or a SCSI tape (tz) device. On the other hand, block devices must be accessed one disk block (512 bytes) at a time. The block devices seen every day on a typical Tru64 UNIX system are disk devices such as SCSI hard, CD-ROM disks and floppy. In this section, we will discuss some of these different devices (disks and tapes).

### 3.3.2 SCSI Disks

SCSI disks are the most common device for storing and retrieving files on a computer system. On a Tru64 UNIX system, the SCSI disks are normally contained in a shelf or are internally mounted in a system cabinet. Disks can be used in either a raw or block-oriented fashion, depending upon what the application requires. If raw disks are used, then the application, such as a commercial database product, must keep track of the disk organization and manage the available space. Normally, disks will be used in a block-oriented fashion and will therefore have file systems on them. In that case, the operating system will keep track of the on-disk organization for you and provide tools for backing up and otherwise manipulating the files. See the discussion in Chapter 11 for more information on making system backups for both character and block devices.

The disk device name format used in Tru64 UNIX is as follows:

```
Device name format:

/dev/disk/dskXP
/dev/rdisk/dskXP
```

where the mnemonics above refer to the following:

```
P = Partition. This is a lower case letter from a to h
representing the first through eighth partition.
X = The cluster-wide unique device number.
```

**Example:**

Here we show an example of looking at the device files on a Tru64 UNIX 5.x system. This device is located on bus #2, target #6, LUN 0, and is an RZ28D device type.

```
# cd /dev
# ls -l *disk/dsk46*
brw——-   1 root     system    19,593 Mar 15 11:04 disk/dsk46a
brw——-   1 root     system    19,595 Mar 15 11:04 disk/dsk46b
brw——-   1 root     system    19,597 Mar 15 11:04 disk/dsk46c
brw——-   1 root     system    19,599 Mar 15 11:04 disk/dsk46d
brw——-   1 root     system    19,601 Mar 15 11:04 disk/dsk46e
brw——-   1 root     system    19,603 Mar 15 11:04 disk/dsk46f
brw——-   1 root     system    19,605 Mar 15 11:04 disk/dsk46g
brw——-   1 root     system    19,607 Mar 15 11:04 disk/dsk46h
crw——-   1 root     system    19,594 Mar 15 11:04 rdisk/dsk46a
crw——-   1 root     system    19,596 Mar 15 11:04 rdisk/dsk46b
crw——-   1 root     system    19,598 Mar 15 11:04 rdisk/dsk46c
crw——-   1 root     system    19,600 Mar 15 11:04 rdisk/dsk46d
crw——-   1 root     system    19,602 Mar 15 11:04 rdisk/dsk46e
crw——-   1 root     system    19,604 Mar 15 11:04 rdisk/dsk46f
crw——-   1 root     system    19,606 Mar 15 11:04 rdisk/dsk46g
crw——-   1 root     system    19,608 Mar 15 11:04 rdisk/dsk46h
# file rdisk/dsk46a
rdisk/dsk46a:   character special (19/594) SCSI #2 RZ28D disk
#1 (SCSI ID #6) (SCSI LUN #0)
```

### 3.3.3 SCSI Tapes

SCSI tape devices have device names as shown in Table 3.1. In this table, the "x" indicates the device number and the "y" indicates the density code. Generally, lower numbers for "y" are for the higher densities supported by the tape device, and higher numbers are for lower densities. The default tape device on a system is designated by the device tape0. It is used as the first device by many tape-oriented utilities.

**Example:**

This example shows the output from ls –l for a single tape device's device special files. Here we show how the major number stays constant for all the devices, but the minor number is used to specify both the tape device and density code to be used. The density codes will vary greatly depending on the type of tape drive being used. For all tape devices, there are eight density codes. However, not all of these may be used by a particular type of tape device. See the tz(5) reference page for more information on the density codes for supported tape drives on the revision of Tru64 UNIX being used.

```
# cd /dev
#ls -l /dev/*tape/tape0*
crw-rw-rw-   1 root     system    19,258 Mar 22 08:59
   /dev/ntape/tape0
crw-rw-rw-   1 root     system    19,262 Mar 22 08:59
   /dev/ntape/tape0_d0
crw-rw-rw-   1 root     system    19,264 Mar 22 08:59
   /dev/ntape/tape0_d1
crw-rw-rw-   1 root     system    19,266 Mar 22 08:59
   /dev/ntape/tape0_d2
crw-rw-rw-   1 root     system    19,268 Mar 22 08:59
   /dev/ntape/tape0_d3
crw-rw-rw-   1 root     system    19,270 Mar 22 08:59
   /dev/ntape/tape0_d4
crw-rw-rw-   1 root     system    19,272 Mar 22 08:59
   /dev/ntape/tape0_d5
crw-rw-rw-   1 root     system    19,274 Mar 22 08:59
   /dev/ntape/tape0_d6
crw-rw-rw-   1 root     system    19,276 Mar 22 08:59
   /dev/ntape/tape0_d7
crw-rw-rw-   1 root     system    19,260 Mar 22 08:59
   /dev/ntape/tape0c
crw-rw-rw-   1 root     system    19,257 Mar 22 08:59
   /dev/tape/tape0
crw-rw-rw-   1 root     system    19,261 Mar 22 08:59
   /dev/tape/tape0_d0
crw-rw-rw-   1 root     system    19,263 Mar 22 08:59
   /dev/tape/tape0_d1
crw-rw-rw-   1 root     system    19,265 Mar 22 08:59
   /dev/tape/tape0_d2
crw-rw-rw-   1 root     system    19,267 Mar 22 08:59
   /dev/tape/tape0_d3
crw-rw-rw-   1 root     system    19,269 Mar 22 08:59
   /dev/tape/tape0_d4
crw-rw-rw-   1 root     system    19,271 Mar 22 08:59
   /dev/tape/tape0_d5
```

```
crw-rw-rw-    1 root     system     19,273 Mar 22 08:59
   /dev/tape/tape0_d6
crw-rw-rw-    1 root     system     19,275 Mar 22 08:59
   /dev/tape/tape0_d7
crw-rw-rw-    1 root     system     19,259 Mar 22 08:59
  /dev/tape/tape0c
```

**Example:**

This example shows the file(1) output for the tape device from the previous example.

```
#file /dev/*tape/tape0*
/dev/ntape/tape0:        character special (19/258) SCSI #1
   "TZ89" tape #2 (SCSI ID #0) (SCSI LUN #2) offline
/dev/ntape/tape0_d0:     character special (19/262) SCSI #1
   "TZ89" tape #2 (SCSI ID #0) (SCSI LUN #2) offline
/dev/ntape/tape0_d1:     character special (19/264) SCSI #1
   "TZ89" tape #2 (SCSI ID #0) (SCSI LUN #2) offline
/dev/ntape/tape0_d2:     character special (19/266) SCSI #1
   "TZ89" tape #2 (SCSI ID #0) (SCSI LUN #2) offline
/dev/ntape/tape0_d3:     character special (19/268) SCSI #1
   "TZ89" tape #2 (SCSI ID #0) (SCSI LUN #2) offline
/dev/ntape/tape0_d4:     character special (19/270) SCSI #1
   "TZ89" tape #2 (SCSI ID #0) (SCSI LUN #2) offline
/dev/ntape/tape0_d5:     character special (19/272) SCSI #1
   "TZ89" tape #2 (SCSI ID #0) (SCSI LUN #2) offline
/dev/ntape/tape0_d6:     character special (19/274) SCSI #1
   "TZ89" tape #2 (SCSI ID #0) (SCSI LUN #2) offline
/dev/ntape/tape0_d7:     character special (19/276) SCSI #1
   "TZ89" tape #2 (SCSI ID #0) (SCSI LUN #2) offline
/dev/ntape/tape0c:       character special (19/260) SCSI #1
   "TZ89" tape #2 (SCSI ID #0) (SCSI LUN #2) offline
/dev/tape/tape0:         character special (19/257) SCSI #1
   "TZ89" tape #2 (SCSI ID #0) (SCSI LUN #2) offline
/dev/tape/tape0_d0:      character special (19/261) SCSI #1
   "TZ89" tape #2 (SCSI ID #0) (SCSI LUN #2) offline
/dev/tape/tape0_d1:      character special (19/263) SCSI #1
   "TZ89" tape #2 (SCSI ID #0) (SCSI LUN #2) offline
/dev/tape/tape0_d2:      character special (19/265) SCSI #1
   "TZ89" tape #2 (SCSI ID #0) (SCSI LUN #2) offline
/dev/tape/tape0_d3:      character special (19/267) SCSI #1
   "TZ89" tape #2 (SCSI ID #0) (SCSI LUN #2) offline
/dev/tape/tape0_d4:      character special (19/269) SCSI #1
   "TZ89" tape #2 (SCSI ID #0) (SCSI LUN #2) offline
/dev/tape/tape0_d5:      character special (19/271) SCSI #1
   "TZ89" tape #2 (SCSI ID #0) (SCSI LUN #2) offline
/dev/tape/tape0_d6:      character special (19/273) SCSI #1
   "TZ89" tape #2 (SCSI ID #0) (SCSI LUN #2) offline
/dev/tape/tape0_d7:      character special (19/275) SCSI #1
   "TZ89" tape #2 (SCSI ID #0) (SCSI LUN #2) offline
```

```
/dev/tape/tape0c:        character special (19/259) SCSI #1
   "TZ89" tape #2 (SCSI ID #0) (SCSI LUN #2) offline
```

### 3.3.4 CD-ROM devices

Compact Disk Read-Only Memory (CD-ROM) devices are similar to those found on a typical PC these days. The CD-ROM devices use a major number of 19, just like all Tru64 UNIX version 5 devices, and come in both block and character special types. Usually, the device will be off-line until a disk is placed in it, then it will become on-line to the system. The disk will usually start spinning as soon as an attempt has been made to access it. Later on in this chapter, we will discuss how you can read several of the different types of CD-ROM file systems that are available.

**Example:**

This example illustrates how CD-ROM devices look on a Tru64 UNIX system. In this case, they are on a cluster system in which drives located on both systems are concurrently available.

```
# cd /dev
# ls -l *disk/cdrom*
brw——-   1 root     system    19, 33 Nov 30 08:29 disk/cdrom0a
brw——-   1 root     system    19, 37 Nov 30 08:29 disk/cdrom0c
brw——-   1 root     system    19,161 Nov 30 09:38 disk/cdrom1a
brw——-   1 root     system    19,165 Nov 30 09:38 disk/cdrom1c
crw——-   1 root     system    19, 34 Nov 30 08:29
rdisk/cdrom0a
crw——-   1 root     system    19, 38 Nov 30 08:29
rdisk/cdrom0c
crw——-   1 root     system    19,162 Nov 30 09:38
rdisk/cdrom1a
crw——-   1 root     system    19,166 Nov 30 09:38
rdisk/cdrom1c
# file rdisk/cdrom?a
rdisk/cdrom0a:  character special (19/34) EIDE #1 "CD-224E"
disk #1 (SCSI ID #0) (SCSI LUN #0) offline
rdisk/cdrom1a:  character special (19/162) EIDE #1 "CD-224E"
disk #1 (SCSI ID #0) (SCSI LUN #0) offline
```

### 3.3.5 Floppy drives

Floppy devices are used to exchange very small amounts of data between computer systems. The device files on a Tru64 UNIX system are given the name "floppy" along with a specific device number and partition. Unlike regular disks, which have eight possible partitions, floppies only define partitions a and c, both of which represent the entire floppy. The other partitions don't exist, because it really doesn't make sense to subdivide such a small amount of storage space. In addition, Zip™ drives are recognized as floppy drives by Tru64 UNIX.

**Example:**

```
# cd /dev
# ls -l *disk/floppy*
brw-rw-rw-   1 root     system    19,  1 Nov 30 08:29
disk/floppy0a
brw-rw-rw-   1 root     system    19,  5 Nov 30 08:29
disk/floppy0c
brw-rw-rw-   1 root     system    19,129 Nov 30 09:38
disk/floppy1a
brw-rw-rw-   1 root     system    19,133 Nov 30 09:38
disk/floppy1c
crw-rw-rw-   1 root     system    19,  2 Nov 30 08:29
rdisk/floppy0a
crw-rw-rw-   1 root     system    19,  6 Nov 30 08:29
rdisk/floppy0c
crw-rw-rw-   1 root     system    19,130 Nov 30 09:38
rdisk/floppy1a
crw-rw-rw-   1 root     system    19,134 Nov 30 09:38
rdisk/floppy1c
```

## 3.4 Managing Disks

The fixed disk is the most important component of the storage subsystem. In this section, we cover some of the more common tasks of managing the disk subsystem.

### 3.4.1 Adding New Disks to the System

In this section, we cover one of the most important aspects of storage management on a Tru64 UNIX system: adding new devices and making them available to the users and/or applications that require them. It is very important to master this task, because you will likely be doing it frequently as storage requirements change. In this section, we give you the steps required to add new storage to a Tru64 UNIX system. We start with a rough outline, then give details for each step as we go along.

To add a new disk to your Tru64 UNIX system, you must perform the following steps:

- Install the hardware.
- Scan the devices and add any new ones.
- Create the device special files.
- Add a disk label to the device.
- Add the device to LSM (optional).
- Make and mount the file system (optional).

#### 3.4.1.1 Hardware Steps

These are the steps that are required by the storage system you are using. Since Tru64 UNIX can handle almost any standard device that behaves like a SCSI disk, the exact steps taken will depend greatly on the complexity of the devices being connected. There are many things that could be covered here, but here are at least some of the things that you need to consider at this step:

- Ensure the device is cabled to the system properly. This includes using correct cables, following proper cabling distance requirements, and using proper termination on the buses.
- Make sure the external storage shelves are plugged in and operating properly. For example, if a wide device is used, make sure you have a wide shelf, or the devices won't operate as expected.
- For Fibrechannel, some additional steps may be required to program any hubs and other connectivity devices so the correct disks are seen by the correct hosts. The primary and redundant paths should be correctly connected and logically enabled.
- If an intelligent controller (e.g., a SCSI attached or backplane RAID controller) is used, then the units must be set up so they can be seen by the system console before the operating system will be able to access them.

#### 3.4.1.2 Add New Devices to the Device Tables

The tool used to perform this function is hwmgr(8). This is a complex device management tool that can perform many different functions. Here we show how to use hwmgr(8) to scan for and update the device tables for a device without requiring a system reboot.

```
# hwmgr -show scsi
        SCSI                    DEVICE     DEVICE  DRIVER NUM  DEVICE FIRST
 HWID:  DEVICEID HOSTNAME   TYPE       SUBTYPE OWNER  PATH FILE   VALID PATH
-------------------------------------------------------------------------
    0:  5         clu3       disk       none    0      1    (null)
   69:  0         clu3       disk       none    0      1    dsk0   [0/0/0]
   70:  1         clu3       cdrom      none    0      1    cdrom0 [1/0/0]
   71:  2         clu3       disk       none    0      1    dsk1   [5/1/0]
   72:  3         clu3       disk       none    0      1    dsk2   [5/2/0]
   73:  4         clu3       disk       none    0      1    dsk3   [5/3/0]
   75:  6         clu3       disk       none    2      1    dsk5   [5/5/0]
# hwmgr -scan scsi
hwmgr: Scan request successfully initiated
# hwmgr -show scsi
        SCSI                    DEVICE     DEVICE  DRIVER NUM  DEVICE FIRST
 HWID:  DEVICEID HOSTNAME   TYPE       SUBTYPE OWNER  PATH FILE   VALID PATH
-------------------------------------------------------------------------
    0:  5         clu3       disk       none    0      1    (null)
   69:  0         clu3       disk       none    0      1    dsk0   [0/0/0]
   70:  1         clu3       cdrom      none    0      1    cdrom0 [1/0/0]
   71:  2         clu3       disk       none    0      1    dsk1   [5/1/0]
   72:  3         clu3       disk       none    0      1    dsk2   [5/2/0]
   73:  4         clu3       disk       none    0      1    dsk3   [5/3/0]
   75:  6         clu3       disk       none    2      1    dsk5   [5/5/0]
   78:  7         clu3       disk       none    0      1    dsk6   [5/4/0]
```

#### 3.4.1.3 Create the New Device Special Files

Generally, the previous step would also create appropriate device special files along with updating the system tables. However, in some cases it may be necessary to manually create the device special files for a new device. In those cases, you'll have a "(null)" entry for those devices and you will need to explicitly create the device special files using the dsfmgr(8) tool. In Tru64 UNIX 5.0 and higher, the MAKEDEV tool is no longer used for this purpose.

```
# hwmgr -show scsi
        SCSI                    DEVICE     DEVICE  DRIVER NUM  DEVICE FIRST
 HWID:  DEVICEID HOSTNAME   TYPE       SUBTYPE OWNER  PATH FILE   VALID PATH
-------------------------------------------------------------------------
   69:  0         clu3       disk       none    0      1    dsk0   [0/0/0]
   70:  1         clu3       cdrom      none    0      1    cdrom0 [1/0/0]
   71:  2         clu3       disk       none    0      1    dsk1   [5/1/0]
   72:  3         clu3       disk       none    0      1    dsk2   [5/2/0]
   73:  4         clu3       disk       none    0      1    dsk3   [5/3/0]
   75:  6         clu3       disk       none    2      1    dsk5   [5/5/0]
   80:  5         clu3       disk       none    0      1    (null)   [5/4/0]
dsfmgr -K
dsfmgr: NOTE: creating device special files for system at /
    +dsk8a +dsk8b +dsk8c +dsk8d +dsk8e +dsk8f +dsk8g +dsk8h +dsk8a +dsk8b +dsk8c
+dsk8d +dsk8e +dsk8f +dsk8g +dsk8h
# ls /dev/*disk/dsk8*
```

```
/dev/disk/dsk8a    /dev/disk/dsk8e    /dev/rdisk/dsk8a   /dev/rdisk/dsk8e
/dev/disk/dsk8b    /dev/disk/dsk8f    /dev/rdisk/dsk8b   /dev/rdisk/dsk8f
/dev/disk/dsk8c    /dev/disk/dsk8g    /dev/rdisk/dsk8c   /dev/rdisk/dsk8g
/dev/disk/dsk8d    /dev/disk/dsk8h    /dev/rdisk/dsk8d   /dev/rdisk/dsk8h
# hwmgr -sh scsi
        SCSI                DEVICE     DEVICE  DRIVER NUM  DEVICE FIRST
 HWID:  DEVICEID HOSTNAME   TYPE       SUBTYPE OWNER  PATH FILE   VALID PATH
-------------------------------------------------------------------------
   69:  0        clu3       disk       none    0      1    dsk0   [0/0/0]
   70:  1        clu3       cdrom      none    0      1    cdrom0 [1/0/0]
   71:  2        clu3       disk       none    0      1    dsk1   [5/1/0]
   72:  3        clu3       disk       none    0      1    dsk2   [5/2/0]
   73:  4        clu3       disk       none    0      1    dsk3   [5/3/0]
   75:  6        clu3       disk       none    2      1    dsk5   [5/5/0]
   80:  5        clu3       disk       none    0      1    dsk8   [5/4/0]
```

#### 3.4.1.4 Add a Disk Label to the Device

The next step in adding a disk to a Tru64 UNIX system is to add a disk label to the new disk. The function of adding a disk label is to put a default partition table and some other information about the device on the first block of the disk. Each disk on a system may contain a disk label, which provides detailed information about the geometry of the disk, and the partitions into which the disk is divided. It should be initialized when the disk is formatted, and may be changed later with the disklabel(8) command. This information is used by the system disk driver and by the bootstrap program to determine how to program the drive and where to find the file systems on the disk partitions. Additional information may be used by the file system in order to use the disk efficiently and to locate important file system information. The description of each partition contains an identifier for the partition type (standard file system, swap area, etc.).

#### 3.4.1.5 Add Device to LSM (optional)

Many sites choose to manage their storage using the Logical Storage Manager (LSM). This is a powerful system that enables the system administrator to create logical containers that behave like UNIX block and character special devices. There are options for creating RAID level 0, 1, 0+1, and 5 within the LSM subsystem. If your site uses LSM, you would add your disk to the LSM subsystem at this point. If you do not use LSM to manage your storage, you can safely skip this step.

#### 3.4.1.6 Making a File System (optional)

In order to make storage available to your users and applications, you need (in most cases) to add a file system organization to the storage. Without this step, your disk device is a logical association of contiguous blocks. The details of how you make a file system on a new device are covered elsewhere in this text. We simply want you to be aware that this is an optional step that will be accomplished at this point in the process of adding storage to the system. It should be noted that you have two options for making a new file system: the Advanced File System and the UNIX File System. See the later sections of this chapter for more information about the different options available.

### 3.4.2 Disk Partitioning

A characteristic of UNIX disk management is the concept of disk partitioning. Disk partitioning is logically dividing a disk into several (possibly overlapping) areas of varying sizes. The system administrator uses disk partitions to subdivide a disk into manageable pieces for containing the operating system, paging areas, and user applications and data. As the capacity of an individual disk increases, partitioning allows more efficient use of storage. In addition, segregating different types of data prevents system problems. For instance, placing user home directories on a partition other than the one containing the /usr file system prevents user activity from affecting the operating system.

As mentioned earlier, there are eight partitions on a Tru64 UNIX disk, and the partitions are labeled with the letters "a" through "h." The sizes and uses of each of the partitions on a disk are user-definable, and the system administrator is responsible for defining the partition layout. In Tru64 UNIX, only two partitions (a and c) have any particular significance. On a boot disk, the root file system must reside in partition a, which must start at the beginning of the disk (block 0.) Partition c normally refers to the entire disk.

Determining how to partition a disk is often a matter of personal preference. UNIX disk partitioning philosophies range from the practice of not partitioning at all and simply using an entire disk as one large partition, to the other extreme of partitioning each disk into the maximum possible number of partitions. Each strategy has pros and cons and, as with most situations, the best solution is probably somewhere between the two extremes. The main advantage of a single, large partition is that all processes and users have access to the entire disk and are not limited to a single partition that may be only a portion of the total disk space. This, however, is also a disadvantage in that any process or user has the ability to fill the entire disk and possibly impact other processing. The other end of the disk-partitioning spectrum is to create many small partitions. Depending on the disk's intended purpose, this may be exactly what is needed for the most efficient use of the disk space. If, however, one or more of the partitions needs to be resized, the system administrator may find it difficult and time-consuming to manage the disk repartitioning. The best recommendation regarding disk partitioning is to create only enough partitions on a disk to sufficiently isolate different types of users and processes to prevent each from impacting others in the event of an unexpected or inadvertent disk usage increase. For example, in addition to separating partitions for the Tru64 UNIX operating system (the root, /usr, and possibly the /var file systems and the swap partitions), create a separate partition for user home directories.

Compaq provides a default disk partition table, but it is up to the system administrator to decide whether to use this default layout or customize the partition sizes and locations. Most default layouts are similar to that described in Figure 3.1. Using this example, it should be clear that it would be impossible to use all eight of these partitions at the same time, since there would be overlap, which is not permitted. Assuming that the partition sizes were not changed, the following are the possible partition combinations:

- c only
- a, b, d, e, and f
- a, b, g, and h
- a, b, d, and h
- a, b, f, and g

The first three combinations would use the entire disk, while the fourth and fifth would leave some of the disk unallocated. Fortunately, Tru64 UNIX allows partition sizes to be adjusted to suit the system requirements. The tool for adjusting the partition layout of a disk from the command line is disklabel(8) or diskconfig(8), if using a graphics terminal. We will discuss the method using the former tool in the following section.

### 3.4.3 The disklabel(8) Command

The disklabel(8) command is used to display, install, and modify a disk's partition layout, or disk label, as Tru64 UNIX terms it. The disk label is physically located on the disk on one of the first sectors of each disk (located on block 0). In addition to the partition layout, the disk label also contains detailed information about the characteristics of the disk.

#### 3.4.3.1 Writing a Default Disk Label

As we discussed earlier, one of the first steps to follow when working with a disk, especially a new disk, is to write a default disk label to it. Prior to doing this, a disk is unlabeled and, until a label is installed, Tru64 UNIX cannot make use of the disk. Writing a default disk label prepares the disk for use, either using the default partition layout or when planning to configure a custom partition layout. Writing a default disk label is not reserved only for new disks. Occasionally, it becomes necessary to repartition an existing disk; if the entire disk will be redone, it is recommended to rewrite a default disk label onto the disk and repartition it.

Before writing a new default label to a disk, one recommended step is to remove any existing label. This is not entirely necessary, but it is a simple step that will avoid the possible situation where certain existing partitions may persist onto the new label. To clear any existing label, use the following command, specifying the appropriate disk:

```
# disklabel -z dsk8
```

If the following harmless message is returned, the disk was already unlabeled:

**Figure 3.1** *Default Disk Partition Layout*

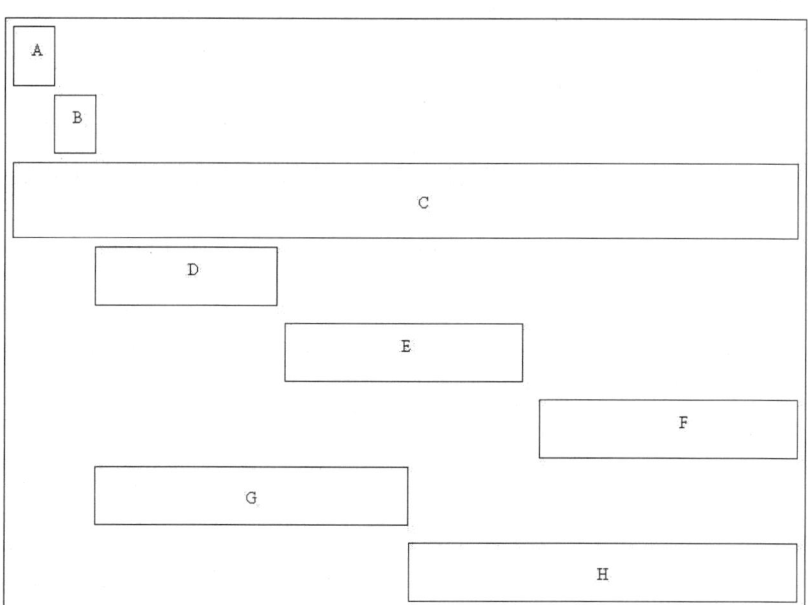

```
Disk is unlabeled or, /dev/rdisk/dsk8c is not in block 0 of the
disk
```

Note that while the simple disk name (dsk8) is specified as the disklabel argument, the disklabel command actually translates that into a full pathname to the character special device file (/dev/rdisk/dsk8c). It is perfectly legal to specify the fully qualified character special device file, but using just the simple disk name is a convenient shorthand. If a particular partition is not specified, the disklabel command uses the first partition that starts at block zero on the disk. Typically, this is the "a" or "c" partition.

The disk label command cannot be used to alter a partition that is open or is in use. This includes the partition used as the "handle", therfore, if you intend to alter the "a" partition's parameters, for example, you must specify the "c" handle or an error will be returned

Once any existing disk label is removed from a disk, use the disklabel command to write a new default disk label. The syntax for writing a new disk label varies, depending on whether the disk to be labeled will be a non-bootable data disk or a bootable system disk. The most common will be for non-bootable disks, but the ability to label a bootable disk is equally important, especially in a recovery situation when the system disk must be relabeled prior to restoring its contents from a backup.

To label a normal (non-bootable) disk, use a command similar to the following:

```
# disklabel -rw dsk8 RZ26N
```

The "-r" flag instructs the disklabel command to write the new label directly to the disk rather than to an in-memory cache. The "-w" flag simply means to write a default label to the disk, in this case, dsk8. The final parameter is the disk type or model number. If known, specify the correct value. In this example, the disk being labeled is a Compaq RZ26N. In the event the disk type is unknown, using a value of "UNKNOWN" will cause the disklabel command to query the disk driver for the disk's geometry. For example:

```
# disklabel -rw dsk8 UNKNOWN
```

To label the disk and configure it as a bootable system disk, an additional command line argument must be specified. This argument, "-t", is used to indicate to disklabel the type of root file system. The disklabel command will write the appropriate bootstrap programs to the boot block area on the disk.

For example, to write a standard disklabel to a disk that will contain an Advanced File System (AdvFS) root file system, use the following command:

```
# disklabel -rwt advfs dsk8 RZ28
```

For a disk with a UNIX File System (UFS) root file system, specify "ufs" as the type rather than "advfs." This is the default value, and UFS boot blocks are written if no "-t" parameter is specified.

#### 3.4.3.2 Displaying a Disk's Label

Issuing a disklabel command with only a disk argument will display the label written on that disk. To ensure that the information displayed is the most current, always use the "-r" flag to instruct the disklabel command to read the label directly from the disk rather than from the in-memory copy of the label. The format of this disk label output is fairly standard regardless of disk type or size. An example of using the disklabel command to display a disk's label follows:

```
# disklabel -r dsk0
# /dev/rdisk/dsk0a:
type: SCSI
disk: RZ28D
label:
flags:
bytes/sector: 512
sectors/track: 99
tracks/cylinder: 16
sectors/cylinder: 1584
cylinders: 2595
sectors/unit: 4110480
rpm: 7200
interleave: 1
trackskew: 8
cylinderskew: 16
headswitch: 0           # milliseconds
track-to-track seek: 0  # milliseconds
drivedata: 0

8 partitions:
#          size     offset    fstype   [fsize bsize   cpg]
# NOTE: values not exact
  a:     262144          0     AdvFS
# (Cyl.    0 - 165*)
  b:     401408     262144      swap
# (Cyl.  165*- 418*)
  c:    4110480          0    unused        0     0
# (Cyl.    0 - 2594)
```

```
  d:   1148976      663552     unused        0      0
# (Cyl.  418*- 1144*)
  e:   1148976     1812528     unused        0      0
# (Cyl. 1144*- 1869*)
  f:   1148976     2961504     unused        0      0
# (Cyl. 1869*- 2594)
  g:   1433600      663552      AdvFS
# (Cyl.  418*- 1323*)
  h:   2013328     2097152      AdvFS
# (Cyl. 1323*- 2594)
```

The first part of the disk's label presents some useful disk characteristic information and the final eight lines show the partition layout of the disk. Probably the most useful piece of disk geometry information displayed is the number of bytes per disk sector. Since the partition size and offset values are displayed in sectors, the bytes per sector value allows conversion of the partition size and conversion of the offset to the more useful bytes, megabytes, or gigabytes.

#### *3.4.3.3 Editing the Disklabel*

After writing a default disk label on a new disk, the next operation is typically to customize the label, adjusting the partitions to meet the requirements. The disklabel program allows easy editing of a disk's label using the "-e" flag. As with displaying a disk's label, always specify the "-r" flag to instruct the disklabel command to edit a copy of the label directly from the disk rather than from the in-memory copy of the label. The following command retrieves a copy of the disk label and invokes an editor specified by the EDITOR environment variable:

```
# disklabel -e -r dsk1
```

If no editor is specified, the vi(1) editor is used, and if vi is not available, the ed(1) editor is used. While in the editor session, only a copy of the disk's label is being modified.

The purpose of editing a disk's label is to modify the partition layout and, as such, to only modify the last eight lines of the disk label. The size and offset values for each of the eight partitions are in sectors, which can be converted to megabytes by dividing the sector value by 2,048. For example, consider the following disk label fragment:

```
#   size    offset     fstype   [fsize  bsize  cpg]
a:  131072  0          unused   0    0    # (Cyl. 0-164*)
b:  262144  131072     unused   0  0  # (Cyl. 164*-492*)
```

```
c:  2050860  0         unused   0  0  # (Cyl. 0-2569)
d:  552548   393216    unused   0  0  # (Cyl. 492*-1185*)
e:  552548   945764    unused   0  0  # (Cyl. 1185*-1877*)
f:  552548   1498312   unused   0  0  # (Cyl. 1877*-2569)
g:  819200   393216    unused   0  0  # (Cyl. 492*-1519*)
h:  838444   1212416   unused   0  0  # (Cyl. 1519*-2569)
```

In this example, partition 'a' starts at the beginning of the disk (sector 0) and is 64 MB (131,072/2,048) in size. Partition 'b' starts immediately after partition a (sector 131072) and is 128 MB (262,144/2,048) in size, and so on. After determining the number of desired partitions and their sizes, convert the sizes to sectors, calculate the appropriate offset values, and update the disk label with the editor. Normally, that is all that is necessary is to change the size and offset values for the desired partitions. The other fields in each of the partition rows are automatically updated, either by disklabel(8) itself or by other utilities when the partitions are used.

Once the desired partition updates are completed, quit the editor, saving the file. The following prompt will be displayed:

```
write new label? [y]:
```

If the changes were satisfactory, simply press the <Return> key to write the updated label to the disk. Otherwise, enter an "n" to discard the changes, and you will be given the opportunity to re-edit the disk label. Note that if the ed(1) editor is used and there is an unexpected error during the editing session, the following message will be displayed:

```
Warning, edit session exited abnormally!
```

If this occurs, do not write the label to the disk. Re-edit the label to ensure that the modifications are made correctly.

As an example, suppose a system administrator has installed a new 1-GB RZ26 disk and wishes to create a 300- and a 500-MB partition on this disk using partitions a and b, respectively. These partition sizes result in the first partition starting at sector zero and being 614,400 sectors in size, and the second partition starting at sector 614,400 and being 1,024,000 sectors in size. The sizes of the partitions in sectors are calculated by multiplying the number of megabytes desired by 2,048.

The following demonstrates this example by clearing any existing disk label, writing a new default label, and then editing the label to change partitions 'a' and 'b':

```
# disklabel -z dsk3
# disklabel -r -w dsk3 RZ26
# disklabel -e -r dsk3C
```

In the editor, the following two lines:

```
a:  131072  0       unused  0  0  # (Cyl. 0-164*)
b:  262144  131072  unused  0  0  # (Cyl. 164*-492*)
```

are changed to:

```
a:  614400   0       unused  0  0  # (Cyl. 0-164*)
b:  1024000  614400  unused  0  0  # (Cyl. 164*-492*)
```

## 3.5 Tru64 UNIX File Systems

Once a disk has been partitioned, it is ready for the creation of file systems, which is the most common use of disk space on a Tru64 UNIX system. A file system is a structure built on a disk partition that allows the partition to contain files and directories in a hierarchical format. The file system is the primary environment of files and directories that most users see when logging onto the system. Tru64 UNIX supports the following types of disk-based file systems:

- UNIX File System (UFS)
- Advanced File System (AdvFS)
- Compact Disk File System (CDFS)
- Digital Versatile Disk File System (DVDFS)

These four file system types make up the majority of all file systems in use on Tru64 UNIX systems, and system administrators should be familiar with their management. The UFS and AdvFS file systems will be discussed in this section; information on the CDFS and DVDFS file systems can be found later in this chapter, in the section on managing these devices.

In addition, Tru64 UNIX also supports the following file system types:

- Memory File System (MFS)
- Process File System (PROCFS),
- File-on-File Mounting File System (FFM)
- File Descriptor File System (FDFS)
- Network File System (NFS)
- Cluster File System (CFS)

The Memory File System is a memory-based file system that appears to the users of a system as disk-based but is not built on disk partitions. The Process File System is a pseudo file system that is used by some system utilities to access memory of the system. The File-on-File Mounting File System and File Descriptor File System are specialized file systems that are not commonly used. The Network File System and Cluster File System are used by systems that wish to share files on remote systems. Refer to the Tru64 UNIX Technical Overview manual for information on these six file system types.

### 3.5.1 The UNIX File System

UFS is Compaq's implementation of the Berkeley Software Distribution (BSD) version 4.3 Fast File System, and is commonly used for both system and user file systems. The maximum file system size for a UFS file system is 512 GB for Tru64 UNIX versions prior to 4.0D, and 1 terabyte for version 4.0D and above. UFS was the first file system type on Tru64 UNIX and, because of its heritage, does not have features such as disk spanning and fast recovery, which exist in more modern file systems such as AdvFS. Nevertheless, UFS is a very robust and well understood file system, and it continues to enjoy great popularity.

### 3.5.2 UFS File System Layout

A UFS file system is made up of 8-kilobyte blocks. Each disk block in a UFS file system is one of four possible types:

- *Boot Block:* The first block (block 0) of every UFS file system is reserved for an initialization, or boot, program. Typically, only a root file system contains such a boot program, but any UFS file system may have one.
- *Superblocks:* The second block (block 1) of every UFS file system contains information that describes the configuration of the file system. This information is called the superblock and is critical to the proper operation of the file system. A UFS superblock contains:

  The total size of the filesystem

  Number of inodes

  List of free inodes

  The beginning of the free-block list

  Date of the last superblock update

  The superblock is so important that when the file system is created, redundant copies of the superblock are distributed across the disk in a pattern that reduces the chances that a single track, cylinder, or platter failure would destroy all copies of it.

- *Inode Blocks:* UFS uses a structure called an inode, or Index Node, to allow random access and multiple file allocations (links). Inodes are simply pointers to a file's data blocks. Inodes are statically allocated when the file system is created, and every file has only one inode associated with it.
- *Data Blocks:* Finally, the majority of disk blocks in a UFS file system are dedicated to the storage of user file and directory data.

### 3.5.3 Creating UFS File Systems

The creation of a UFS file system is the process of formatting a disk partition and building the disk structures to support a hierarchy of directories and files. This task is accomplished with the newfs(8) command, specifying the disk partition as the only required command line argument. For instance, to create a UFS file system on the first partition of the dsk8 disk, use the following syntax:

```
# newfs dsk8a
Warning: 1008 sector(s) in last cylinder unallocated
/dev/rdisk/dsk8a:       131072 sectors in 26 cylinders of 20
tracks, 254 sectors
        64.0MB in 2 cyl groups (16 c/g, 39.69MB/g, 9536 i/g)
super-block backups (for fsck -b #) at:
 32, 81568,
```

This example demonstrates the default use of newfs. Unless additional file system option arguments are specified, the newfs command uses default values along with the geometry values specified in the disk's label to construct the new file system. While newfs actually uses the character disk device file when creating the file system, a simple disk name and partition may be specified in place of either the full character or block disk device name. The newfs command translates any of these disk specifications into the full character disk device.

There are a group of newfs options that override the default method of creating UFS file systems. Most of the default newfs values are normally appropriate for most situations, however, these command options are infrequently used. Refer to the newfs reference page for information on the UFS file system options.

One of the newfs optional flags specifies how many inodes are created in the new file system. This is a particularly important parameter, since the number of inodes determines the maximum number of files the new file system may contain, regardless of disk space. The default is to create one inode for each 4K (4096 bytes) of disk space. This value makes the assumption that the average file size in a new file system will be approximately 4K. If, for instance, the average file size were actually 1K, it would be possible that the file system could run out of inodes before running out of disk space. In this case, the file system should be created with more inodes than the default. On the other hand, if a file system were going to contain fewer, larger files, the recommendation would be to create the file system with fewer inodes. Since each inode takes up a small amount of disk space itself (only 128 bytes), specifying fewer inodes leaves more disk space for user data. The newfs command provides a command line option (-i) to specify a "bytes per inode" value. Simply put, estimate the projected average file size in bytes and create the file system with that value. For example, if a file system will contain relatively large files, averaging approximately 500K, the following newfs command will create that file system specifying 512000 bytes (500 * 1024) per inode:

```
# newfs -i 512000 /dev/rdisk/dsk2c
```

Specifying a value larger than the default of 4096 bytes results in fewer inodes; to create more inodes in the file system, a smaller number should be given. To display the number of inodes configured in a file system, use the df(8) command with the "-i" switch:

```
# df -i /home

Filesystem 512-blocks Used Available Capacity Iused Ifree
%Iused Mounted on

/dev/disk/dsk2c  126462 476  113338  1%  36 16637  0% /home
```

In this example, the file system has 16,637 free inodes, with 36 in use.

Finally, newfs has a special parameter that permits the system administrator to execute a newfs command without actually creating the file system. This parameter, "-N", displays the file system creation parameters that would be used if the file system were actually created. This can be useful for displaying the default file system creation parameters or for trying different options without touching the disk. This is particularly useful for locating the alternate superblocks in case the primary superblock is damaged. For example:

```
# newfs -N -i 12288 dsk8b
Warning: 2016 sector(s) in last cylinder unallocated
/dev/rdisk/dsk8b:        262144 sectors in 52 cylinders of 20
tracks, 254 sectors
        128.0MB in 4 cyl groups (16 c/g, 39.69MB/g, 3200 i/g)
super-block backups (for fsck -b #) at:
 32, 81568, 163104, 244640,
```

### 3.5.4 Mounting File Systems

After creating a file system, the next operation is to mount the file system onto the existing hierarchy. The mount(8) command is used to mount all types of file systems and make them available for use. Only the root user may mount and unmount disk-based, local file systems. Refer to the mount reference page for details on the various file system mount options. The following example will mount the UFS file system on partition b of disk dsk8 onto the /home mount point:

```
# mount /dev/disk/dsk8b /home
```

The mount point parameter of the mount command is simply a directory that must exist. This directory may be empty, but does not have to be. Be aware that any contents of a mount point directory will be unavailable while a file system is mounted "over" that directory. Mount points are often created at the base of the root file system (/), but this is not a requirement. The only issue to be aware of when mounting a file system on a mount point in a non-root file system is that the base file system should be mounted before attempting to mount the secondary file system. For example, if a file system is mounted on /home and a second file system is mounted on /home/tools, ensure that /home is mounted first before attempting to mount /home/tools. Also, if a file system is manually mounted with the mount command and is not listed in the /etc/fstab file, the mount will be temporary and will not persist after a system reboot.

#### *3.5.4.1 The /etc/fstab File*

Permanent file systems are ones that should be automatically mounted when the system is started. The mechanism for doing this is the /etc/fstab file. File systems listed in this file are mounted when the system boots as the file is read from top to bottom. During a Tru64 UNIX installation, any file systems created as part of the installation are added to the fstab file. This includes the root, /usr, and, if created, the /var file systems. In addition, prior to Tru64 UNIX version 5.0, the fstab file contained a record for each swap partition on the system and was consulted when activating the system's swap files. This function is now performed by the sysconfigtab file; see Chapter 4 for a discussion of this function. Following is a sample /etc/fstab file:

```
/dev/disk/dsk0a     /ufs     rw 1 1
/dev/disk/dsk0g     /usr     ufs     rw 1 2
/dev/disk/dsk2g     /var     ufs     rw 1 2
tools#utils     /tools/utils     advfs     rw,userquota,
  groupquota 0 2
```

The format of the /etc/fstab file specifies that each file system be on a separate line and that each field be delimited by space or tab characters. Blank lines or lines that begin with a pound sign (#) are ignored. Each file system line should contain the name of the file system to be mounted, the mount point, the file system type, any special mount options, whether the file system should be backed up with either the dump(8) or vdump(8) commands, and the sequence in which the file system, if UFS, should be checked with the fsck(8) command. The format of the first parameter depends on the file system type. For UFS file systems, the block special device file name should be used, while for AdvFS file systems, the parameter should be in the form filedomain#fileset.

Once a file system is properly listed in the /etc/fstab file, the file system can be mounted by issuing the mount command and specifying just the mount point. For example, assuming the following entry in the /etc/fstab file:

```
/dev/disk/dsk4c     /home     ufs     rw 1 2
```

This file system could be mounted with this command:

```
# mount /home
```

rather than the more verbose:

```
# mount /dev/disk/dsk4c /home
```

### 3.5.5 Unmounting File Systems

The opposite of the mount(8) command is the umount(8) command, which is used to unmount a file system. Unmounting a file system flushes any uncompleted writes to the disk and then disconnects the file system, making it unavailable for use. Only the root user may unmount local file systems with the umount command. Simply specify the mount point as an argument to umount to unmount that file system. For example:

```
# umount /home
```

If any user process is active in a file system, that file system cannot be unmounted and the umount command returns the following error message:

```
<mount point>: Device busy
```

This can occur even if only a single user has changed directories into the file system. If the file system must be unmounted, determine which user or process is using the file system and either shut the process down or, in the case of an interactive user session, have that user cd(1) to another directory outside of the target file system. Tru64 UNIX version 4.0 and greater provides a utility, fuser(8), to quickly identify the processes and/or users occupying a file system. Run the fuser command specifying the mount point of the file system in question. For example:

```
# fuser /home
/home:    608c    879c
```

This output indicates that two processes (PID 608 and 879) are running and they have this directory as their current working directory (See Table 3.2). Search the process table listing with the ps(1) command to identify the processes. A useful fuser option is "-u," which indicates the user name associated with the process identifiers:

```
# fuser -u /home
/home:    608c(jsmith)    879c(jsmith)
```

### 3.5.6 Checking UFS File Systems

The UFS file system, not having the write-ahead logging feature of AdvFS, is somewhat vulnerable to improper system shutdowns or unexpected system failures. Since the UFS file system provides buffering of disk writes, if a file system is not properly unmounted and the buffers flushed to disk, there exists the possibility of corrupting the file system. This is the primary reason a Tru64 UNIX system should be shut down gracefully. However, hardware problems, power problems, and system errors resulting in kernel panics can

**Table 3.2** *fuser(8) Output Explanation*

| Character | Description |
|---|---|
| c | The process with the given process identifier (PID) has this directory as its current working directory. |
| m | The process with the given process identifier has a memory mapped (See mmap(2)) file open. |
| o | The process with the given process identifier has this file open. |
| p | The process with the given process identifier is using this file as the parent of its current directory. |
| r | The process with the given process identifier is using the file as its root directory. |
| t | The process with the given process identifier is using the text file as an executable. |
| y | The process with the given process identifier is using this file as its controlling tty. |

and do occur, and for these situations a file system check utility is provided. The fsck(8) program checks UFS file systems and can correct file system inconsistencies, such as incorrect inode or free block counts, unreferenced inodes, or orphan data blocks. When using fsck to check a UFS file system, the file system must be unmounted and the character disk device name should be specified on the fsck command line. The fsck command then proceeds to check the file system in five passes. If inconsistencies are found, the fsck program prompts before each correction is attempted. This allows the system administrator to answer yes or no. Typically, the answer should always be yes to the questions. For instance:

```
# fsck /dev/rdisk/dsk8a
/sbin/ufs_fsck /dev/rdisk/dsk8a
** /dev/rdisk/dsk8a
** Last Mounted on /mnt
** Phase 1 - Check Blocks and Sizes
** Phase 2 - Check Pathnames
UNALLOCATED  I=3  OWNER=root MODE=0
SIZE=0 MTIME=Dec 31 19:00 1969
NAME=/vmunix
REMOVE? [yn] y
** Phase 3 - Check Connectivity
** Phase 4 - Check Reference Counts
** Phase 5 - Check Cyl groups
FREE BLK COUNT(S) WRONG IN SUPERBLK
SALVAGE? [yn] y
BLK(S) MISSING IN BIT MAPS
SALVAGE? [yn] y
```

```
SUMMARY INFORMATION BAD
SALVAGE? [yn] y
159 files, 1076 used, 61772 free (4 frags, 7721 blocks, 0.0%
fragmentation)
Filesystem '/dev/rdisk/dsk8a' Tru64 UNIX UFS v.3 UFS
***** FILE SYSTEM WAS MODIFIED *****
In this example, a correction was successfully made and the
file system is now ready to be mounted.
```

The fsck command is automatically run in a noninteractive mode when the system boots to check all UFS file systems listed in the /etc/fstab file. For file systems unmounted cleanly, no checking is necessary. However, if a file system was not unmounted properly, fsck silently checks the file system. Any inconsistencies that are discovered are repaired if the correction can be safely completed without risk of data loss. If a severe inconsistency is encountered, the fsck program exits, leaving the system in single-user mode with a recommendation to run fsck manually.

### 3.5.7 Extending UFS File Systems

A new feature of the UFS file system with Tru64 UNIX 5.1 is the ability to extend a file system should the underlying storage size change. Traditionally, if you had a UFS file system in Tru64 UNIX, the only way to increase the size of the file system was to back it up, remake the file system with newfs, and then restore the data. This was a time-consuming process that many administrators were not happy to do. Luckily, this process is no longer required to take advantage of growth in the underlying storage.

The main command used to implement this feature is called extendfs(8). There are at least two ways in which the underlying storage might change. These are:

- Change the partition size with disklabel.
- Grow the LSM volume with volassist(8).

The procedure for performing the UFS file system extend operation is as follows:

- Unmount the file system.
- Change the underlying storage size.
- Extend the file system size.
- Remount the file system.

As an example, we take an existing UFS file system created on a 500,000 block partition, dsk8b.

```
# df /mnt
Filesystem        512-blocks        Used   Available Capacity
Mounted on
/dev/disk/dsk8b    482544          2       434286      0%     /mnt
# umount /mnt
```

At this point, we use the disklabel command to double the size of the dsk8b partition from 500,000 blocks to 1,000,000 blocks. Then, we can continue with the file system extend procedure as follows:

```
# extendfs dsk8b
Warning: 760 sector(s) in last cylinder unallocated
/dev/rdisk/dsk8b:       1000000 sectors in 197 cylinders of 20
tracks, 254 sectors
        488.3MB in 13 cyl groups (16 c/g, 39.69MB/g, 9536 i/g)
super-block backups (for fsck -b #) at: 570784,
 652320, 733856, 815392, 896928, 978464,
# mount /dev/disk/dsk8b /mnt
# df /mnt
Filesystem        512-blocks        Used   Available Capacity
Mounted on
/dev/disk/dsk8b      968048            2       871240      0%
/mnt
```

### 3.5.8 Tuning UFS

The UNIX File System includes a tool for manipulating a few of the dynamic, tunable parameters located in the superblock, known as tunefs(8). The tool does not alter any data on the file system; it only affects the way future writes will be handled. The flags that you specify indicate which parameters are to be changed. The following items can be changed using tunefs:

- The maximum number of contiguous blocks that will be written in one transfer (the cluster size).
- The rotational delay between groups of blocks in a file
- The maximum number of blocks any single file can allocate out of a single cylinder group at one time
- The percentage of free space on the file system held back from use by the non-root users (also known as minfree)
- The optimization preference

This tool works on mounted and active file systems as well as those that are unmounted. However, the superblock for a mounted file system is cached in memory, so changes made while a file system is mounted will be clobbered the next time the buffers are synchronized. If you attempt to make changes to a mounted root file system, the system must be rebooted for those changes to be effective.

Here's an example showing how you can use tunefs to modify the minfree value for a UFS file system.

```
# newfs /dev/vol/rootdg/voltest
Warning: 3808 sector(s) in last cylinder unallocated
/dev/rvol/rootdg/voltest:      500000 sectors in 123 cylinders
of 32 tracks, 1s
        244.1MB in 8 cyl groups (16 c/g, 32.00MB/g, 7680 i/g)
super-block backups (for fsck -b #) at:
 32, 65696, 131360, 197024, 262688, 328352, 394016, 459680,
# tunefs -m 2 /dev/rvol/rootdg/voltest
minimum percentage of free space changes from 10% to 2%
should optimize for space with minfree < 10%
# dumpfs /dev/rvol/rootdg/voltest | grep minfree
minfree 2%      optim    time    maxcontig 8     maxbpg  2048
```

### 3.5.9 The Advanced File System (AdvFS)

The Advanced File System (AdvFS), another local file system supported on Tru64 UNIX, is quickly replacing UFS as the file system of choice, particularly for large file systems. AdvFS provides many modern file system features, such as write-ahead logging for fast file system recovery, on-line backups, disk spanning, and file striping. The AdvFS architecture allows management of file systems while they are mounted. This includes dynamically resizing file systems, defragmenting to make files more contiguous on disk, and cloning of file systems for backup purposes.

The base AdvFS functionality is a licensed part of the Tru64 UNIX operating system and can completely replace UFS on a Tru64 UNIX system, including the root, /usr, and /var file systems. The Tru64 UNIX custom installation option allows the installer to select AdvFS as a file system for the system partitions. (See Chapter 2, "Installation," for details on performing a custom installation.) In addition, an optional set of utilities provides additional capabilities to the AdvFS file system. This optional product, the Advanced File System Advanced Utilities (AdvFS Advanced Utilities), is available as a separately licensed set of commands from Compaq. The AdvFS Utilities provide such features as file undelete capability, on-line file migration, and a graphical user interface (GUI). These utilities are now included with a base installation.

From a system administration standpoint, an AdvFS file system differs significantly from a UFS file system, both in terms of initial creation and ongoing management. Some of the concepts are similar, but it is necessary for a Tru64 UNIX system administrator to understand the unique characteristics of AdvFS to fully utilize its capabilities. This section covers the components of an AdvFS configuration and the details of setting up an AdvFS file system. Two new concepts that characterize the Advanced File System are file domains and filesets.

#### 3.5.9.1 AdvFS File Domains

A file domain is a grouping of one or more volumes into a shared pool of disk storage. In this context, a volume is any physical or logical object that can be referenced as a Tru64 UNIX block special device, for example:

- An entire physical disk
- An individual disk partition
- A logical volume configured with the Logical Storage Manager (LSM)

When creating an AdvFS file domain, the domain initially consists of exactly one volume. If the AdvFS Utilities are licensed, additional volumes may be added to a domain, up to 250 volumes. Volumes may be added to an AdvFS domain immediately after initial file domain creation, or one can wait until the domain requires additional space. Without the AdvFS utilities, however, one is limited to single-volume domains. There is no limit to the total number of AdvFS file domains per system; however, there may only be 100 active file domains at any one time. A file domain is considered active if at least one of its filesets is mounted.

The AdvFS file system automatically creates and updates the /etc/fdmns directory structure, which is used by the various AdvFS utilities to ensure access to file domains. The /etc/fdmns directory contains a subdirectory for each file domain on the system. Within each subdirectory is a symbolic link to a block special device file for each volume in the file domain. This directory is crucial to the healthy operation of the AdvFS file system. Do not edit or remove the /etc/fdmns directory or its subdirectories without fully understanding the implications of the action.

When planning the layout of file domains, the best performance can be achieved by dedicating entire disks to individual file domains. Though splitting a disk's partitions between multiple file domains is permitted, the performance of such a configuration might suffer significantly due to head contention within that disk. In addition, since a single volume failure within a file domain means that the entire file domain fails, avoid large numbers of volumes in single file domains. Compaq has recommended that there should be no more than three volumes in a file domain to reduce the risk of file domain failure.

#### 3.5.9.2 AdvFS Filesets

The second important component of the AdvFS file system is the fileset. A fileset is an object that contains files and directories that can be mounted for use, just like a UFS file system. A fileset differs from a regular file system in one important manner: while a UFS file system resides on a single disk partition, an AdvFS fileset is created inside a file domain, which can be one or more volumes. This means that a fileset can be larger than a single disk partition and is able to span multiple disks. In addition, there can be many filesets within a single file domain. The concept of filesets provides much of the flexibility of the AdvFS file system.

Tru64 UNIX permits an unlimited number of filesets per system; however, the total allowable number of actively mounted filesets is limited to 512 minus the number of active AdvFS file domains. When planning fileset layout, keep in mind that the design philosophy of the Advanced File System encourages multiple filesets per file domain. Since filesets are managed independently, regardless of which file domain they reside in, there is no penalty for a large number of filesets. The most flexible configuration is fewer file domains and more filesets. This allows the system administrator to worry less about disk space, since it is collected into pools larger than individual disks.

#### 3.5.9.3 Creating an AdvFS File Domain

The first step in setting up an AdvFS file system is to create a file domain using the mkfdmn(8) command. The mkfdmn command requires two arguments: the block special device file and the file domain name. A file domain name must be unique, may be up to 31 characters in length, and cannot contain white space characters (space, tab, etc.) or certain special characters (/ # : * ?). An example of creating a new file domain follows:

```
# mkfdmn /dev/disk/dsk3c tools
```

This command creates a new AdvFS file domain named "tools." This file domain is composed of the entire dsk3 disk (partition c). As a result of this file domain creation, a subdirectory with the same name as the new file domain was created in the /etc/fdmns directory:

```
# ls -l /etc/fdmns
total 8
```

```
drwxr-xr-x  2 root  system  8192 Feb 14 12:13 tools
  # ls -l /etc/fdmns/tools
total 0
lrwxr-xr-x  1 root  system  9 Feb 14 12:13 dsk3c ->
  /dev/disk/dsk3c
```

The mkfdmn command has several optional command line arguments to modify how AdvFS file domains are created. Refer to the mkfdmn man page for more information on these options.

#### 3.5.9.4 Creating an AdvFS Fileset

Once an AdvFS file domain has been created, the next step is to create one or more filesets within that domain. For this, use the mkfset(8) command, specifying the file domain name and the name of the fileset to be created. For instance, to create two filesets within the tools file domain, use the following commands:

```
# mkfset tools project1
# mkfset tools project2
```

Each fileset within a file domain must have a unique name no longer than 31 characters. The space character and the / # : * ? characters are invalid for fileset names. A common convention is to name a fileset with its intended mount point. This is not required, but is a helpful organizational practice.

#### 3.5.9.5 Mounting AdvFS Filesets

After creating a file domain and one or more filesets, the filesets must be mounted before they are available for use. As with UFS file systems, the mount(8) and umount(8) commands are used to mount and unmount AdvFS filesets. The main difference is that rather than specifying the full pathname to the block special device file for a UFS file system, an AdvFS fileset is referred to using the "filedomain#fileset" descriptor. For instance, the following commands will create two mount points, then mount our example filesets:

```
# mkdir /tools/project1
# mkdir /tools/project2
# mount -t advfs tools#project1 /tools/project1
# mount -t advfs tools#project2 /tools/project2
```

The pound sign (#) between the file domain name and the fileset is required as part of the syntax representing an AdvFS fileset. Also, the mount command's optional "-t" flag specifies the file system type. If newly created and mounted AdvFS filesets are to be a permanent configuration, add an entry to the /etc/fstab file for each fileset. This will cause the filesets to be automatically mounted when the system reboots.

#### 3.5.9.6 AdvFS Fileset Quotas

When using multiple AdvFS filesets within a single AdvFS file domain, it is important to understand the concept of AdvFS fileset quotas. Fileset quotas are a management tool available to the system administrator to limit the amount of disk space and the number of files consumed by a fileset. This is important since, by default, all the filesets within a file domain have equal access to the domain's disk space. This means that a single fileset could consume all available disk space in a file domain. For example, the following two newly created filesets are in the same file domain:

```
# df -k /tools/project1 /tools/project2
Filesystem   1024-blocks  Used  Available  Capacity  Mounted on
tools#project1  1025424  16  1020952  1%  /tools/project1
tools#project2  1025424  16  1020952  1%  /tools/project2
```

This df(1) output can be somewhat misleading in that it appears that both the tools#project1 fileset and the tools#project2 fileset each have more than 1,000 MB of space available. This is not really the case, however, as the file domain is a fixed pool of disk space. Since there are no fileset quotas on either of these two filesets, each has access to the entire amount of disk space in the file domain.

By setting a fileset quota on one or both of these filesets, each is limited to the amount specified by the quota limit. For instance, suppose that it is decided to set the quota limit on the first fileset (tools#project1) to 400 MB and the second fileset (tools#project2) to 600 MB. The following chfset(8) commands will implement these quotas:

```
# chfsets -b 409600 tools project1
project1
  Id   : 3584af2e.000e8160.1.8001
  Block H Limit: 0 -> 409600
# chfsets -b 611328 tools project2
project2
  Id   : 3584af2e.000e8160.2.8001
  Block H Limit: 0 -> 611328
```

Now, after setting these fileset quota limits, the df(1) output of the two filesets is more understandable:

```
# df -k /tools/project1 /tools/project2

Filesystem  1024-blocks  Used  Available  Capacity  Mounted on
tools#project1  409600  16  409584  1%  /tools/project1
tools#project2  611328  16  611312  1%  /tools/project2
```

The AdvFS fileset quotas are a valuable tool for managing AdvFS filesets. Suppose that a fileset had become full or, more accurately, had reached the configured fileset quota limit. If the file domain where the file set resided still had available disk space, it would be a simple matter to increase the fileset quota limit on the full fileset. This will allow data to be added to the fileset, effectively increasing the size of the fileset. Refer to the chfsets(8) man page for more information on managing AdvFS fileset quotas.

### 3.5.10 Logical Storage Manager (LSM)

Tru64 UNIX supports the Logical Storage Manager (LSM), a robust logical storage manager based on the VERITAS Volume Manager from VERITAS Software. LSM supports all of the following:

- *Disk spanning:* Disk spanning allows you to concatenate entire disks or parts (regions) of multiple disks together to use as a single logical volume. For example, you could combine two RZ28s and have them contain the /usr file system.
- *Mirroring:* Mirroring allows you to write simultaneously to two or more disk drives to protect against data loss in the event of an individual disk failure.
- *Striping:* Striping improves performance by breaking data into segments that are written to several different physical disks in a "stripe set."
- *RAID 5:* As we discussed earlier, this is a mechanism for providing redundancy with a cost of adding only one extra disk. LSM supports RAID 5 in software in Tru64 UNIX 5.0 and later versions.
- *Disk management:* LSM supports disk management utilities that, among other things, change the disk configuration without disrupting users while the system is up and running.

Mirroring, striping, RAID 5, and the graphical interface require a separate, optional license PAK (Product Authorization Key).

For each logical volume defined in the system, the LSM volume device driver maps logical volume I/O to physical disk I/O. In addition, LSM uses a user-level volume configuration daemon (vold) that controls changes to the configuration of logical volumes. The root user can administer LSM either through a series of command-line utilities or via an X Window System graphical interface (dxlsm(8X) or lsmsa(8)).

To help users transform their existing UFS or AdvFS file systems into LSM logical volumes, Compaq has developed a utility that will transform each partition in use by UFS or AdvFS into a nonstriped, nonmirrored LSM volume. After the transformation is complete, the system administrator can mirror the volumes if desired. This feature is known as encapsulation.

In order to utilize a disk under LSM, it must be added to LSM. Devices can be added as one of three types: Sliced, Simple, or Nopriv (encapsulated). Each of these is described as follows:

- *Sliced:* The entire disk is dedicated to LSM. The disk will have two regions shown in the disk label: the public and private regions. The public region contains those blocks that are usable for LSM volumes, and the private region is reserved for use by the LSM subsystem metadata. This is by far the best way to use a disk in LSM.
- *Simple:* Only a single partition is being used by LSM. In this case the public and private regions are combined into one partition on a disk.
- *Nopriv:* This is an encapulated file system. You can take an existing file system and encapsulate the blocks containing the file system's data, making them part of LSM. No private data is used for this type of LSM disk.

To add an entire disk to the LSM subsystem, you have many choices available including several command-line tools, the voldiskadm(8) menu system, or the dxlsm(8) or lsmsa(8) graphical interfaces. The voldiskadd(8) command is the easiest method:

```
# voldiskadd dsk5
```

Note that LSM volumes can be used in conjunction with AdvFS, as components of AdvFS file domains. We've barely scratched the surface of what LSM can do for your site; for more information on LSM, refer to the Tru64 UNIX Logical Storage Manager guide.

### 3.5.11 Managing Free Space

One of the important tasks of a system administrator is to manage the existing free space on the file systems. You can manage the free space in one of two ways:

- Voluntary policy
- Quotas

Which you use at your site will depend upon the system requirements and on how good the users are at policing themselves. Most sites start out with the former and end up putting quotas in place later. Other sites have no need to police users because they don't have any interactive users. Such systems tend to be dedicated to specific applications, such as commercial databases, which are only accessed by other client systems over the network. In such cases, no policy is required.

#### 3.5.11.1 Finding the Disk Hog

Occasionally, it will become necessary to find out why a particular file system is becoming full and try to track down which user is hogging the space. With a voluntary policy, it is up to the system administrator to police the usage periodically. The df(1) command is the most obvious tool for monitoring the current available free space; however, it is not the only tool available. Typically, a system administrator would use one or a combination of the following tools to determine where the blocks have been consumed on a given system.

- df(1)–Displays free space on a per mounted file system basis. The output can be given in 512-byte blocks or in kilobytes.
- vdf(8)–A better df for use with the Advanced File System. This tool will give more accurate information based on output from showfdmn(8), showfsets(8), shfragbf(8), and df(1) to more accurately depict the usage patterns.
- du(1)–Shows usage for all files in all subdirectories under a specified directory. The output can be given in either 512-byte blocks or kilobytes. A useful switch for narrowing a search to a specified file system is "-x", which does not allow the search to cross a mounted file system boundary.
- find(1)–Can be used to display files of a given size or larger and/or that have been created within a specified time period. A useful switch is "-mount" (or "-xdev"), which does not allow the search to cross a mounted file system boundary.

#### 3.5.11.2 Quota Management

Once you've spent many hours performing the method described in the previous section, you will understand the usefulness of quotas. The main benefit of setting quotas is for those cases where you cannot control your users' behavior using the standard methods of peer pressure and intimidation, and their productivity is being affected. There will always be those people who will never take the time to clean up after themselves. The advent of ever larger and cheaper disk farms makes the task of policing more difficult.

Quotas for both AdvFS and UFS are most frequently used to limit usage on a Tru64 UNIX file system on a user-by-user basis. You can apply quotas to file systems to establish a limit on the number of blocks and inodes (or files) that a user or group of users can allocate. You can set a separate quota for each user or group of users on each file system. AdvFS also has the concept of fileset quota that does not exist and has no meaning in the context of a UFS file system. For more information, see our discussion of fileset quotas in Section 3.5.2.6.

File systems can have both soft and hard file limits. When a hard limit is reached, no more disk space allocations or file creations that would exceed the limit are allowed. The soft limit may be exceeded for a period of time known as the grace period. If the soft limit is exceeded for an amount of time greater than the grace period, no more disk space allocations or file creations are allowed until enough disk space is freed or enough files are deleted to bring the disk space usage or number of files below the soft limit.

## 3.6 Managing Tape Devices

The tape devices on a typical Tru64 UNIX system are used for backing up files and restoring from those backups. As such, the system administrator will either be using the tape drive to test and perform backups on a routine basis or restoring files on an emergency basis. It is important to understand how the tape drive works on your system before you need to use the tape drive for restoring backups. We cover backups in greater detail in Chapter 11, and we refer you to that discussion for details on those procedures. In this section, we refer to the operations you may be called upon to perform on the tape drive itself. Since tape drives operate differently from one another, we will necessarily be general in our discussion.

### 3.6.1 Adding a New Tape Device to the System

The steps for adding a new tape drive to a Tru64 UNIX system are similar to those we followed for adding a disk device, so we refer you to that procedure for the particulars on each of the steps. The procedure is generally the following:

- Install the hardware.
- Scan the devices and add any new ones.
- Create the device special files.

### 3.6.2 Manipulating Tape Devices

Typically, manipulation of a tape device is done using whatever archiving tool you plan to use for backing up your data. We don't plan to spend a great deal of time discussing those tools, since they are covered in Chapter 11. However, there is one tool that is indispensable for manipulating a tape device: the mt(1) command. This command is used for locating the tape position, getting status about the tape device, rewinding the tape, and loading and unloading tapes from the device.

**Example:**

The following example shows the kind of information you can get from the mt(1) command about a tape device connected to your system.

```
# mt -f /dev/tape/tape0 status

DEVIOGET ELEMENT         CONTENTS
--------         ----
category                 DEV_TAPE
bus                      DEV_SCSI
interface                SCSI
device                   TZ89
adpt_num                 0
nexus_num                2
bus_num                  1
ctlr_num                 1
slave_num                2
dev_name                 tz
unit_num                 2
soft_count               0
hard_count               0
stat                     0x5
                         DEV_BOM DEV_OFFLINE
category_stat            0x0
                         DEV_85700_BPI

DEVGETINFO ELEMENT       CONTENTS
----------         ----
media_status             0x10001
                         BOM POS_VALID
unit_status              0x122
                         Offline 2_FM_Close Rewind Buffered
record_size              0
```

```
density (current)        85700 BPI
density (on write)       0 BPI
Filemark Cnt             0
Record Cnt               0
Class                    1 - DLT (tk)

MTIOCGET ELEMENT         CONTENTS
________      _____
mt_type                  MT_ISSCSI
mt_dsreg                 0x5
                         DEV_BOM DEV_OFFLINE
mt_erreg                 0x2 Unit is not ready.
mt_resid                 0
mt_fileno                0
mt_blkno                 0
DEV_EEI_STATUS
        version          0x2
        status           0x6400  Device/bus reset occured
        flags            0x1000007
                         CAM_STATUS SCSI_STATUS SCSI_SENSE
CAM_DATA
        cam_status       0x4  CCB request completed with an err
        scsi_status      0x2  SCSI_STAT_CHECK_CONDITION
        scsi_sense_data  (hex)
                         70  0  2  0  0  0  0 16
                          0  0  0  0 3a  0  0  0
                          0  0 82  0  0  0  0 6e
                         52  0  0  0  0  0  0  0
                          0  0  0  0  0  0  0  0
                          0  0  0  0  0  0  0
        ASC/ASQ = 3a/0   Medium not present
```

## 3.7 Managing Direct-Access Removable Media Devices

Tru64 UNIX supports a number of direct-access removable media type devices, which share some characteristics with both the fixed disk and tape types we've been discussing until now. The removable media devices are generally used in a block-oriented fashion, but have a media that is designed to be removed from the drive and taken to another system like a tape device. Tape devices are read and written in a character-oriented manner; thus, they are not random access in nature. The removable devices discussed in this section are designed to provide random access to their data.

The most popular of these type devices on a Tru64 UNIX systems are CD-ROM, DVD-ROM, and floppies, and it is these to which we will confine our discussion. Even though these are the most popular, they are far from the only ones that can be used. There are other types of read-write and read-only optical devices that can be used, as well as third-party devices like the Zip™ drive from Iomega.

## 3.7.1 CD-ROM and DVD-ROM Devices

Tru64 UNIX supports both CD-ROM and DVD-ROM (Digital Versatile Disk, Read-Only Memory) devices. CD-ROM drives come with most Tru64 systems these days. The devices usually come internal to the system and can be used to load new firmware or software, or even play music! As the name implies, they are read-only, which means you can only get data from them but not write data onto them. The capacity of the average CD is around 650 MB, while the DVD-ROM can hold up to 17 GB! The media is also quite inexpensive to mass produce, so they are very useful when produced in quantity for software distributions, video, or music.

### *3.7.1.1 Mounting CD-ROMs*

Tru64 UNIX can read CD-ROMs formatted in a number of industry-standard and proprietary formats. The most popular format today is ISO9660 level II "High-Sierra" standard format. This format can be read by PCs, UNIX, and many other operating systems. Tru64 UNIX sees this format as a CDFS, or CD-ROM File System. CDFS also supports an extension to the ISO9660 format, known as the Rock Ridge extensions. This gives additional "UNIX-like" file system qualities when the disk is mounted, such as extra long file names and support for case-sensitive file names. Without these additions, the CD-ROM would only support 8.3 character upper-case file names. A command similar to the following would be used on a pre-5.0 system to mount a CD-ROM with this format:

```
# mount -r -t cdfs -o noversion,rrip <device> <mount-point>
```

In Tru64 UNIX 5.0 and later, the -t and -o flags can be omitted.

Tru64 can also read CDs created in native UFS format. These can be mounted directly or booted as if they were any other UFS file system. UFS used to be the standard format for the Tru64 UNIX operating system CDs, but has since been replaced with the ISO standard format. Mounting such a CD is a simple matter of issuing a command similar to the following as root:

```
# mount -r <device> <mount-point>
```

where the '-r' flag indicates this is a read-only mount (synonymous with "-o ro").

#### 3.7.1.2 Playing Audio CDs

Another format that can be read on a Tru64 system is the music CD format. This allows the operating system to play music through a set of speakers and sound card, if your system is so equipped. An application program such as xcd is needed along with the necessary hardware to make this work properly. A utility that allows the playing of audio CDs, xmcd, is authored by Ti Tan. Xmcd is a CD Player package that is composed of two utilities: xmcd, a CD player for the X Window System with a Motif graphical interface, and cda, a command-line–driven, text-mode CD player that also features a character-based, screen-oriented mode. Both utilities allow your CD-ROM drive to play music CDs. The xmcd package has a rich feature set including shuffle play and support for CD databases. See the xmcd web page for more information and a link to download a Tru64 UNIX binary distribution:

```
http://sunsite.unc.edu/~cddb/xmcd/
```

DVD-ROM is relatively new and is supported on Tru64 UNIX with the DVDFS, or DVD-ROM File System. This file system supports the Universal Data Format (UDF). Naturally, newer systems will have drives capable of supporting the newer formats taht older CD-ROM drives do not support.

### 3.7.2 Floppy Devices

A floppy is a device that uses removable media, like a CD-ROM. However, the floppy media (known as a floppy disk) can also be written to. Also unlike the CD-ROM, the floppy has a very small number of blocks that you can use to store data. The standard 3.5 inch floppy will store only 1.44 MB of information. Not every Alpha system has a floppy drive, so you may have to purchase one if you wish to use it. In many ways, floppy disks are becoming less and less useful because of the limited amount of data they can hold, but they are still available and can still be used for functions such as the following:

- Moving small files from one system to another when the network is not available
- Updating firmware on some of your hardware controllers
- Running programs from the Alpha system console, such as the SWXCR manager
- Transferring data from PCs to your Tru64 UNIX system

You can use a floppy disk on your Tru64 UNIX system by either putting a UFS file system on it, using it as a raw device with an archive tool such as tar(1), or accessing an MS-DOS formatted floppy created on a PC. Each of these methods has its advantages and disadvantages, which we discuss in the following sections.

### 3.7.2.1 Formatting a Floppy

Before a floppy disk can be used by a Tru64 UNIX system (or any system for that matter), it must be low-level formatted. The formatting process puts a special organization on the disk such that the system can find the correct location to read or write data. Tru64 UNIX can use any DOS-formatted floppy as is, with no other action necessary by the system administrator. Many floppies come pre-formatted from the box, which can save a lot of time later. You can also format your floppies on a typical Windows-based PC with a floppy drive. Once the PC has finished with the format, take the floppy disk over to the Tru64 system and you are ready to use it.

If you don't have a preformatted floppy and don't have access to a Windows-based PC, you can still use the fddisk(8) tool in the following manner to make the floppy usable by the system:

```
# fddisk -fmt <floppy device>
```

---

*Note:* Do not use fddisk with a Zip drive even though the drive is identified by the operating system as a "floppy" device.

---

**Example:**

Here we show an example of how to use the fddisk(8) tool to format a floppy disk on a Tru64 UNIX system.

```
# fddisk -fmt -f /dev/rdisk/floppy0c
NOTE:  Setting interleave factor to ''-i2:4''.
       Use ''-i<nnn>[:<ccc>]'' option to override.
Disk type: 3.50 inch, HD  (1.44MB)
Number of sectors per track: 18
Number of surfaces:   2
Number of cylinders: 80
Sector size:  512
interleave factor:  2:4
Formatting disk...
  Percentage complete: Format complete, checking...
 Quick check of disk passes OK.
```

#### 3.7.2.2 *Using a Floppy as an Archive*

One way in which a floppy can be used for exchanging files with other UNIX systems is to simply use tar(1) or cpio(1) to copy data to or from it. Since tar(1) and cpio(1) formats are fairly standard among different UNIX flavors, this can be used as an interchange mechanism for small amounts of data. You only need a floppy with a low-level format, then simply tar(1) to the raw 'c' partition of the floppy disk. No disk label is required for this operation.

**Example**

Let's say you want to copy the hosts file from one of your Tru64 systems to a Linux system. This example shows how you could use tar to create an archive on a floppy to take over to the Linux machine.

```
# tar cvf /dev/rdisk/floppy0c /etc/hosts
a /etc/hosts 4 Blocks
# tar tvf /dev/rdisk/floppy0c
blocksize = 256
-rwxr-xr-x     3/4     1827 May 18 12:08:29 2001 /etc/hosts
```

#### 3.7.2.3 *Creating a File System on a Floppy*

Creating a file system on a floppy is a simple matter. You only have one choice of file system type, because AdvFS will not create a file system on a space as small as a floppy. Therefore, you must use UFS for your file system on a floppy disk. This is not much of a limitation, since most sites are not likely to need to keep the floppy mounted for an extended period of time, and given the size, fsck(8) will not take very long. Therefore, the standard reasons for choosing AdvFS over UFS don't apply in this case. Keep in mind that since the floppy is a removable media, you don't want to remove the floppy until you have unmounted the file system. Failing to do this could cause severe distress to the system.

The sequence of steps to create a new file system on a new floppy disk is as follows:

- Format the floppy.
- Write a partition table using disklabel(8).
- Create the UFS file system with newfs(8).
- Mount the floppy-based UFS file system.

**Example:**

This example shows how to create a disk label and create a new UFS file system on a floppy using the newfs(8) tool. After creating the file system, you can mount it as you would any other UFS file system.

```
# disklabel -rw floppy0
# newfs /dev/rdisk/floppy0c
/dev/rdisk/floppy0c:    2880 sectors in 80 cylinders of 2
tracks, 18 sectors
        1.4MB in 5 cyl groups (16 c/g, 0.28MB/g, 64 i/g)
super-block backups (for fsck -b #) at:
 32, 640, 1184, 1792, 2336,
# mount /dev/disk/floppy0c /mnt
# df -k /mnt
Filesystem         1024-blocks       Used   Available Capacity
Mounted on
/dev/disk/floppy0c        1303          1        1171      0%
/mnt
```

#### 3.7.2.4 Using MTOOLS

MTOOLS are a collection of useful freeware tools for manipulating files on a DOS-formatted floppy disk from a UNIX-based system. The reason you might want to use a DOS file system on a UNIX system is for transfer of files between the two systems. The DOS file system is widely used on almost any PC-based operating system such as MS-DOS, Windows, or even Linux. This portability can come in handy in a variety of situations. You may want to keep some critical files that need to be loaded on either a Tru64 system or PC. Therefore, the most common denominator would be the DOS-formatted floppy. Most PC-based operating systems will not be able to read a UFS or tar(1) formatted floppy.

The MTOOLS used to be available only from the freeware tools CD-ROM or via download from the Internet. However, due to their popularity and usefulness, they have been packaged for Tru64 installation on the base operating system CD, under the OSFDOSTOOLSxxx subset. The tools are installed into the /usr/bin/mtools directory; thus, you will need to alter your default path or explicitly use the full path name when invoking a tool. See Table 3.3 for a summary of the tools with descriptions of their functions.

Use the following steps to prepare a new floppy disk for use with MTOOLS:

- Format the floppy with fddisk(8).
- Put a DOS file system on the floppy with mformat(8).

**Table 3.3** *MTOOLS and Their Functions*

| Tool | Description |
|---|---|
| dos2unix unix2dos | Converts DOS-formatted text files to UNIX style and vice versa. |
| mattrib | Sets or checks the attributes of a file on a DOS file system. |
| mcd | Changes the current working directory to that which is specified. |
| mcopy | Copies a file from UNIX to DOS or DOS to UNIX. This utility will convert line terminators from DOS to UNIX and vice versa. |
| mdel | Removes a DOS file from a floppy disk. |
| mdir | Lists the files for a single directory on a DOS file system. |
| mdiskcopy | Copies a DOS-formatted floppy disk to another floppy disk. Creates an identical copy of the first floppy onto the second. |
| mformat | Creates a DOS file system on a low-level formatted floppy. |
| mkmanifest | Creates a shell script to restore UNIX file names from DOS. |
| mlabel | Displays and manipulates the label on a DOS-formatted floppy. |
| mmd | Creates a new subdirectory on a DOS file system. |
| mrd | Removes a subdirectory on a DOS file system. |
| mread | Copies the specified DOS file to the named UNIX file, or copies multiple DOS files to the named UNIX directory. |
| mren | Renames an existing file on a DOS file system to another name. |
| mtype | Displays the contents of a file on a DOS file system. |
| mwrite | Copies the specified UNIX file to the named DOS file, or copies multiple UNIX files to the named DOS directory. |

**Example:**

This example illustrates how to initialize a new floppy for use by MTOOLS or any DOS or Windows-based PC on a Tru64 UNIX system.

```
# fddisk -fmt -f /dev/rdisk/floppy0c
NOTE:  Setting interleave factor to ''-i2:4''.
       Use ''-i<nnn>[:<ccc>]'' option to override.
Disk type: 3.50 inch, HD  (1.44MB)
Number of sectors per track: 18
Number of surfaces:   2
Number of cylinders: 80
```

```
Sector size:  512
interleave factor:  2:4
Formatting disk...
  Percentage complete: Format complete, checking...
 Quick check of disk passes OK.
# /usr/bin/mtools/mdir
Probable non-MSDOS disk
mdir: Can't read floppy
# /usr/bin/mtools/mformat a:


Format will erase all file[s] ...
Press any key to continue ...
# /usr/bin/mtools/mdir
 Volume in drive A: has no label
 Directory for A:/
```

## 3.8 Summary

In this chapter, we've explored the mechanisms by which data is stored on a Tru64 UNIX system. This discussion should give you the basics you need to get your system up and manage the available storage on the system. Storage is a complex and highly evolving subject, and new technology will come along that will undoubtedly make the information in this chapter seem out-of-date. Our goal has been to give you a foundation for understanding where we've been and how to manage storage as it is used on a typical Tru64 UNIX system, rather than trying to cover all the details of a particular technology.

# 4

# *System Configuration*

This chapter will cover some of the aspects of Tru64 UNIX system configuration. In the first revision of this book we stated that the configuration of a Tru64 UNIX system is a broad topic that touches every possible system and user subsystem and service, both hardware and software; it continues to be a broad topic with more ingredients thrown into the stew than ever before. But just as the configuration possibilities have become more wide and varied, Tru64 UNIX includes new and improved tools to handle these configuration options.

Since the hardware configuration tools were discussed in Chapter 3, we will cover some of the more common software configuration tools in this chapter. We will start by discussing basic configuration tasks you will need to do after your Tru64 UNIX operating system installation completes using the checklist program (if you're a GUI kinda person) or the setup program (if you're an old-school command-line person). Once the basics are completed, we will discuss how to reconfigure the kernel, install additional software, and load licenses.

## 4.1 Post-Installation Checklist

So you've installed Tru64 UNIX, and you find yourself sitting at the console with the login prompt in front of you.

If you are on a workstation (or a system with a graphics card and monitor), it will look like what you see in Figure 4.1. If you are on a server without a graphical user interface (GUI), it will look a little less glitzy, but nonetheless perfectly functional. For example:

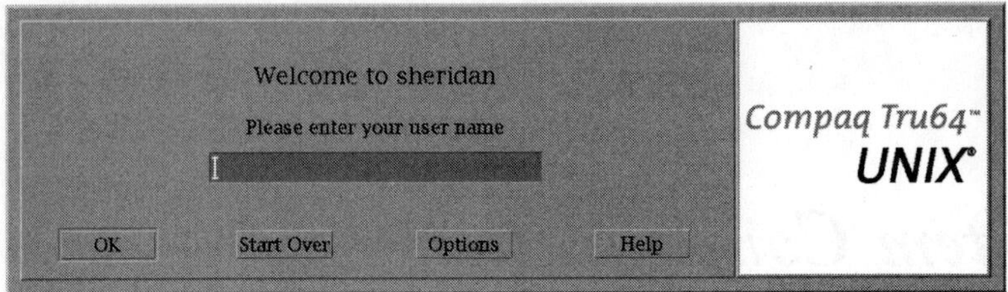


**Figure 4.1**
*CDE Login Screen.*

```
Compaq Tru64 UNIX V5.1 (Rev. 732) (sheridan) console
login:
```

Login using the "root" user name and when prompted for the password, enter the password that you typed when installing the operating the system.

> *Note*: Do not be concerned with the following message, as it is merely informing you that you have not installed your operating system license.
>
> ```
> "can't find an OSF-BASE, UNIX-WORKSTATION, or UNIX-SERVER
> license PAK"
> ```
>
> This message will go away as soon as you register the license product authorization key (PAK) that came with your system (it's probably a nice-looking piece of paper titled, "License PAK" in an 8 ½" by 11" zippered plastic bag), which we will be discussing in a moment.

Once the login process completes, if you are in a GUI environment, you will see the checklist program (Figure 4.2) in the center of your screen; if you are logging into a non-GUI console, you will automatically find yourself in the setup(8) program (Figure 4.3).

The checklist and setup programs are used to configure various operating system components. Both programs offer three options:

- Quick Setup
- Custom Setup
- Cloning Information

We will show the GUI environment for the remainder of this section although the setup program can do the same functions.

**Figure 4.2** *The /usr/sbin/checklist program.*

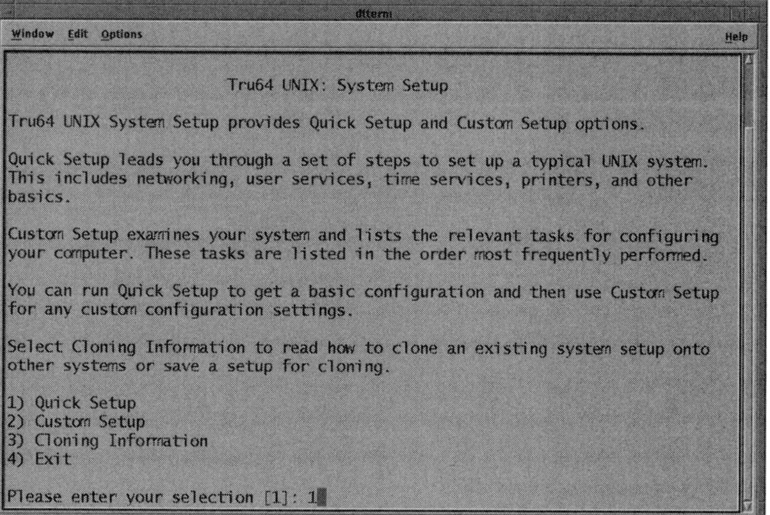


**Figure 4.3** *The /usr/sbin/setup program.*

### 4.1.1 Quick Setup 

Quick Setup is an option to step you through setting up the most common components. The Quick Setup option configures the following components:

- Step 1: Registering the base operating system license
- Step 2: Setting the system's primary network interface card (NIC)
- Step 3: Set up a static network router.
- Step 4: Set up the Domain Name Service (DNS/BIND).[1]
- Step 5: Set up a Network Time Provider (NTP).
- Step 6: Set up the Network Information Service (NIS).
- Step 7: Set up the Network File System (NFS).
- Step 8: Set up a mail server.
- Step 9: Set up a default printer and server.

Some of the steps in the quick setup path can be skipped if you do not want or need to set up a particular component.

In the first step, you register that license PAK that we mentioned in the previous section. The quick setup program will prompt you to enter some of the information listed on the paper PAK. Steps 2–8 will require you to know your site's network configuration. If you have a Network Administrator, now would be a good time to walk down the hall and have a conversation. If your boss informed you that you are going to be the Network Administrator, then you might want to turn to Chapter 7, "Networking," and then curl up in a comfortable chair with the Tru64 UNIX Network Administration guide.[2] If you do not have a hard copy of the guide you can download it from the following Web location:

```
http://www.tru64unix.compaq.com/docs/pub_page/doc_list.html
```

Select the operating system version that you have installed, and then select the "System and Network Management Documentation Bookshelf."

1. Berkeley Internet Name Domain.
2. Starting with V5.1A, the Network Administration guide was split into two guides titled: "Network Administration: Connections" and "Network Administration: Services."

Step 9 will require that you have some information about your printer's configuration so refer to your printer's documentation, and turn to Chapter 8, "Printing."

### 4.1.2 Custom Setup

The Custom Setup option is a little more freeform in its approach. You are not sequentially walked through a series of configuration steps as with the Quick Setup option, but rather given the ability to configure components in the order you choose. The Custom Setup option starts various SysMan services to assist you in your configuration tasks. The SysMan services listed in Table 4.1 are started through the Custom Setup option:

**Table 4.1** *SysMan Services Custom Setup and Further Reading*

| SysMan Service | Additional Information | | SysMan Service | Additional Information | |
|---|---|---|---|---|---|
| | This Book | Compaq | | This Book | Compaq |
| License Manager | License Management on Section 4.6 | System Admin | Mail Configuration | N/A | Network Admin |
| Disk Configuration | Chapter 3 | System Admin | LAT[*] Configuration | N/A | Network Admin |
| Network Setup Wizard | Chapter 7 | Network Admin | UUCP[†] Configuration | N/A | Network Admin |
| DNS (BIND) Configuration | Chapter 7 | Network Admin | Printer Configuration | Chapter 8 | System Admin |
| NIS Configuration | Chapter 7 | Network Admin | Security Configuration | Chapter 6 | Security |
| NFS Configuration | Chapter 7 | Network Admin | Audit Configuration | Chapter 6 | Security |
| File Sharing | Chapter 7 | Network Admin | Configure DOP[‡] privileges | Chapter 6 | System Admin |
| NTP Configuration | Chapter 7 | Network Admin | Configure DOP actions | Chapter 6 | System Admin |
| PPP[§] Configuration | N/A | Network Admin | Prestoserve I/O Acceleration Configuration. | N/A | Guide to Prestoserve |

Table 4.1 *(continued)*

| SysMan Service | Additional Information | | SysMan Service | Additional Information | |
|---|---|---|---|---|---|
| SLIP** Configuration | N/A | Network Admin | GUI Selection | N/A | System Admin |
| Account Manager | Chapter 5 | System Admin | Insight Manager | N/A | System Admin |

* Local Area Transport
† UNIX-to-UNIX Copy Program
‡ Division of Privleges
§ Point-to-Point Protocol
** Serial Line Internet Protocol

SysMan is a suite of applications used to assist you in managing your Tru64 UNIX system. We will introduce you to using SysMan in Section 4.2, "Introducing SysMan."

### 4.1.3 Cloning Information 

This option does not do anything except give you information on how to clone the configuration information for your system (see Figure 4.4). This information is used when cloning systems. Installation Cloning was discussed in Chapter 2.

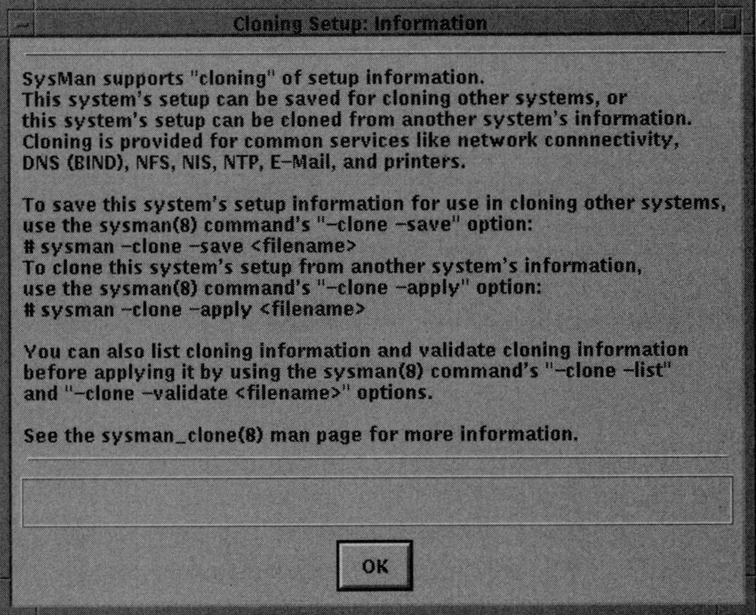


Figure 4.4 *Cloning Information.*

# 4.2 Introducing SysMan

As mentioned earlier in the chapter, SysMan is a suite of applications used to assist you in managing your Tru64 UNIX system. There are currently four interfaces to SysMan (/usr/sbin/sysman) as shown in Table 4.2.

See also sysman(8) and sysman_intro(8) reference pages for additional information.

## 4.2.1 SysMan Components

SysMan currently has 12 main components as shown in Table 4.3:

Of these components there are subcomponents. Associated with each component and subcomponent is an accelerator—an option to the sysman command that will take you directly to the component or subcomponent on which you are interested in browsing and/or modifying.

**Table 4.2** *SysMan Interfaces*

| | | |
|---|---|---|
| SysMan Menu | sysman -menu<br>sysman | sysman_menu(8) |
| SysMan Station | sysman -station | sysman_station(8)<br>smsd(8) |
| SysMan CLI | sysman -cli | sysman_cli(8) |
| SysMan Clone | sysman -clone | sysman_clone(8) |

**Table 4.3** *SysMan Components*

| | | | |
|---|---|---|---|
| Accounts | Table 4.4 | Security | Table 4.10 |
| Hardware | Table 4.5 | Software | Table 4.11 |
| Mail | Table 4.6 | Storage | Table 4.12 |
| Monitoring and Tuning | Table 4.7 | Support and Services | Table 4.13 |
| Networking | Table 4.8 | TruCluster Specific* | Table 4.14 |
| Printing | Table 4.9 | General Tasks | Table 4.15 |

* Requires the TruCluster Server software be installed and configured.

**Table 4.4** *SysMan Component—Accounts*

| **Accounts—sysman accounts** | |
|---|---|
| **Subcomponent** | **Accelerator** |
| Manage local users | sysman users |
| Manage local groups | sysman groups |
| Manage NIS users | sysman nis_users |
| Manage NIS groups | sysman nis_groups |

**Table 4.5** *SysMan Component—Hardware*

| **Hardware—sysman hardware** | |
|---|---|
| **Subcomponent** | **Accelerator** |
| View hardware hierarchy | sysman hw_hierarchy |
| View cluster | sysman hw_cluhierarchy |
| View device information | sysman hw_devices |
| View central processing unit (CPU) information | sysman hw_cpus |

**Table 4.6** *SysMan Component—Mail*

| **Mail—sysman mail** | |
|---|---|
| **Subcomponent** | **Accelerator** |
| Configure Mail | sysman mailsetup |
| Manage users' mail accounts | sysman mailusradm |

**Table 4.7** *SysMan Component—Monitoring and Tuning*

| **Monitoring and Tuning—sysman monitoring** | |
|---|---|
| **Subcomponent** | **Accelerator** |
| View events | sysman event_viewer |
| Set up Insight Manager | sysman imconfig |
| Class Scheduling | sysman class_sched |
| Configure Class Scheduler | sysman class_setup |
| [Re]Start Class Scheduler | sysman class_start |
| Stop Class Scheduler | sysman class_stop |
| View Virtual Memory (VM) statistics | sysman vmstat |
| View Input/Output (I/O) statistics | sysman iostat |
| View Uptime statistics | sysman uptime |

**Table 4.8** *SysMan Component—Networking*

| **Networking—sysman network** | |
|---|---|
| Subcomponent | Accelerator |
| Network Setup Wizard | sysman net_wizard |
| Basic Network Services | sysman networkbasic |
| Set up Asynchronous Transfer Mode (ATM) | sysman atm |
| Set up Network Interface Card(s) | sysman interface |
| Set up static routes (/etc/routes) | sysman route |
| Set up routing services (gated, routed, IP Router) | sysman routing |
| Set up hosts file (/etc/hosts) | sysman host |
| Set up hosts equivalency file (/etc/hosts.equiv) | sysman hosteq |
| Set up remote who services (rwhod) | sysman rwhod |
| Set up the networks file (/etc/networks) | sysman networks |
| Additional Network Services | sysman networkadditional |
| Domain Name Service (DNS(BIND)) | sysman dns |
| Configure system as a DNS server | sysman dns_server |

**Table 4.8** *(continued)*

| **Networking—sysman network** | |
|---|---|
| Configure system as a DNS client | sysman dns_client |
| Deconfigure DNS on this system | sysman dns_deconfigure |
| Serial Line Networking | sysman serial_line |
| Point-to-Point Protocol (PPP) | sysman ppp |
| Create option files | sysman ppp_options |
| Modify pap-secrets file | sysman pap |
| Modify chap-secrets file | sysman chap |
| Configure system for UNIX-to-UNIX copy (uucp) connections | sysman uucp |
| Network Time Protocol (NTP) | sysman ntp |
| Configure system as an NTP client | sysman ntp_config |
| View status of NTP daemon | sysman ntp_status |
| {Re}start NTP daemon | sysman ntp_start |
| Stop NTP daemon | sysman ntp_stop |
| Network File System (NFS) | sysman nfs |
| View NFS configuration status | sysman nfs_config_status |
| Configure system as an NFS client | sysman nfs_client |
| Deconfigure system as an NFS client | sysman nfs_deconfig_client |
| Configure system as an NFS server | sysman nfs_server |
| Deconfigure system as an NFS server | sysman nfs_deconfig_server |
| View NFS daemon status | sysman nfs_daemon_status |
| {Re}start NFS daemons | sysman nfs_start |
| Stop NFS daemons | sysman nfs_stop |
| Configure Network Information Service (NIS) | sysman nis |
| Configure Local Area Transport (LAT) | sysman lat |
| Set up the system as a DHCP Server (joind) | sysman joind |
| View network daemon status | sysman dmnstatus |
| {Re}start network services | sysman inet_start |
| Stop network services | sysman inet_stop |

**Table 4.9** *SysMan Component—Printing*

| **Printing—sysman printers** | |
|---|---|
| **Subcomponent** | **Accelerator** |
| Configure line printers | sysman lprsetup |

**Table 4.10** *SysMan Component—Security*

| **Security—sysman security** | |
|---|---|
| **Subcomponent** | **Accelerator** |
| Configure Division of Privileges (DOP) | sysman dopconfig |
| Manage DOP Actions | sysman dopaction |
| Security Configuration | sysman secconfig |
| Audit Configuration | sysman auditconfig |

**Table 4.11** *SysMan Component—Software*

| **Software—sysman software** | |
|---|---|
| **Subcomponent** | **Accelerator** |
| Installation | sysman install |
| Install software | sysman setldload |
| List installed software | sysman setldlist |
| Remove installed software | sysman setldd |
| Cleanup after an OS update (updadmin) | sysman updadmin |
| Register license data | sysman lmfsetup |

**Table 4.12** *SysMan Component—Storage*

| **Storage—sysman storage** | |
|---|---|
| Subcomponent | Accelerator |
| Manage DRD Storage* | sysman drdmgr |
| File Systems Management Utilities | sysman filesystems |
| General File System Utilities | sysman generalfs |
| Dismount a File System | sysman dismount |
| Display Currently Mounted File Systems | sysman df |
| Mount File Systems | sysman mount |
| Manage Cluster File System (CFS)* | sysman cfsmgr |
| Share Local Directory (/etc/exports) | sysman export |
| Mount Network Directory (/etc/fstab) | sysman net_mount |
| Advanced File System (AdvFS) Utilities | sysman advfs |
| Manage an AdvFS Domain | sysman domain_manager |
| Manage an AdvFS File | sysman file_manager |
| Defragment an AdvFS Domain | sysman defrag |
| Create a New AdvFS Domain | sysman mkfdmn |
| Create a New AdvFS Fileset | sysman mkfset |
| Recover Files from an AdvFS Domain | sysman salvage |
| Repair an AdvFS Domain | sysman verify |
| UNIX File System (UFS) Utilities | sysman ufs |
| Create a New UFS File System | sysman newfs |
| Logical Storage Manager (LSM) Administration | sysman lsm |
| Initialize the Logical Storage Manager (LSM) | sysman volsetup |
| Logical Storage Manager (LSM) Administrator | sysman lsmmgr |
| Create a Bootable Tape | sysman boot_tape |

* Requires the TruCluster erver software be installed and configured

**Table 4.13** *SysMan Component—Support and Services*

| **Support and Services—sysman support** | |
|---|---|
| **Subcomponent** | **Accelerator** |
| Create escalation report | sysman escalation |
| Create configuration report | sysman config_report |

**Table 4.14** *SysMan Component—TruCluster Specific*

| TruCluster Specific*—sysman clusters | |
|---|---|
| Subcomponent | Accelerator |
| Cluster Application Availability (CAA) Management | sysman caa |
| Manage Cluster File System (CFS) | sysman cfsmgr |
| Manage DRD Storage | sysman drdmgr |
| Cluster Alias Manager | sysman clu_aliases |

* Requires that the TruCluster Server software be installed and configured

**Table 4.15** *SysMan Component—General Tasks*

| **General Tasks—sysman general_tasks** | |
|---|---|
| **Subcomponent** | **Accelerator** |
| Shutdown the system | sysman shutdown |
| Quick Setup | sysman quicksetup |
| Configure Prestoserve software | sysman presto |
| Configure X Display Manager | sysman xsetup |
| Cloning setup information | sysman cloneinfo |
| Command line interface information | sysman sysmancli |

### 4.2.2 SysMan Menu

SysMan Menu is the primary SysMan interface. There are two user interfaces to SysMan Menu: GUI (Figure 4.5) and CUI[3] (Figure 4.6).

The GUI is an OSF/Motif-style graphical interface (actually, it's Tcl/Tk[4]) and the CUI is a cursor-style interface.

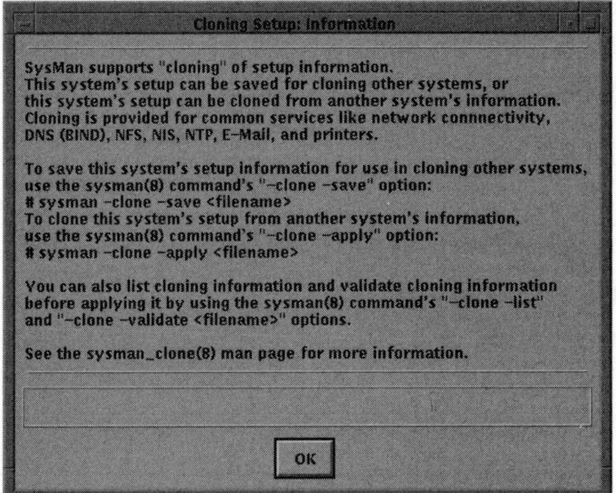


**Figure 4.5** *SysMan Menu (GUI).*

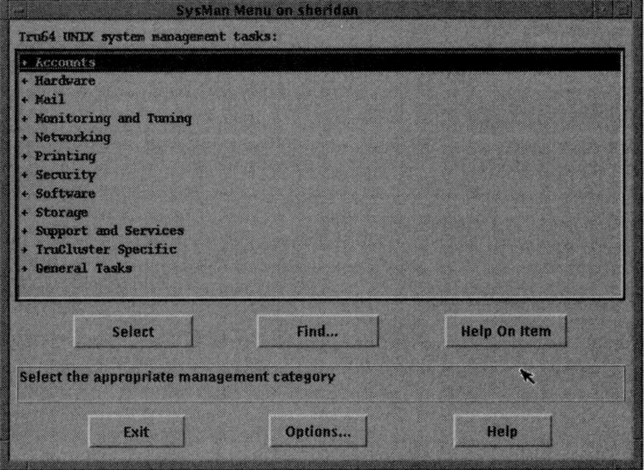


**Figure 4.6** *SysMan Menu (CUI).*

3. Command-line user interface.
4. Tcl is a general-purpose scripting language written by Dr. John K. Ousterhout. Tk is an X Windows System toolkit based on Tcl. For more information see the Tcl Developer's Site at http://dev.scriptics.com/.

What interface starts is dependent on whether or not you have defined your DISPLAY shell environment variable.

### 4.2.3 SysMan Station

SysMan Station (Figure 4.9) is a monitoring and management interface. The SysMan Station can be started on the command line by typing "/usr/sbin/sysman -station" or /usr/sbin/sms, or from the CDE Front Panel, by clicking on the SysMan Station icon (Figure 4.7).

SysMan Station provides a monitoring facility where you can visually see the status of file systems, storage devices, and the network. In a TruCluster Server environment SysMan Station also monitors the cluster as well as any application resources registered with the Cluster Application Availability (CAA) subsystem. Figure 4.8 shows the possible status icons for SysMan Station.

You can launch SysMan Menu and/or SysMan Services from SysMan Station as well. One of the coolest features of SysMan Station, though, is its ability to show you, graphically, the physical hierarchy (Figure 4.10) of the hardware on your system.

### 4.2.4 SysMan CLI

If you are the kind of System Administrator who likes to automate as many tasks as you possibly can, then SysMan CLI is something you may want to

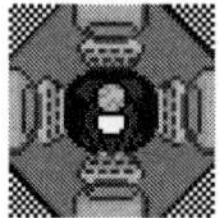

**Figure 4.7** *SysMan Station Icon.*

**Figure 4.8** *SysMan Station Status Indicators.*

| | | |
|---|---|---|
| | GREEN | This indicates that everything is okay. |
| | YELLOW | This indicates a potential problem, an event has occurred. |
| | RED | This indicates a serious problem has occurred. |

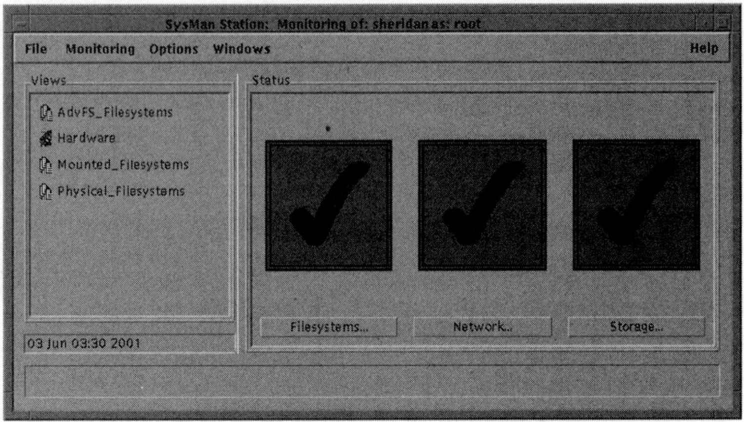


**Figure 4.9**
*SysMan Station.*

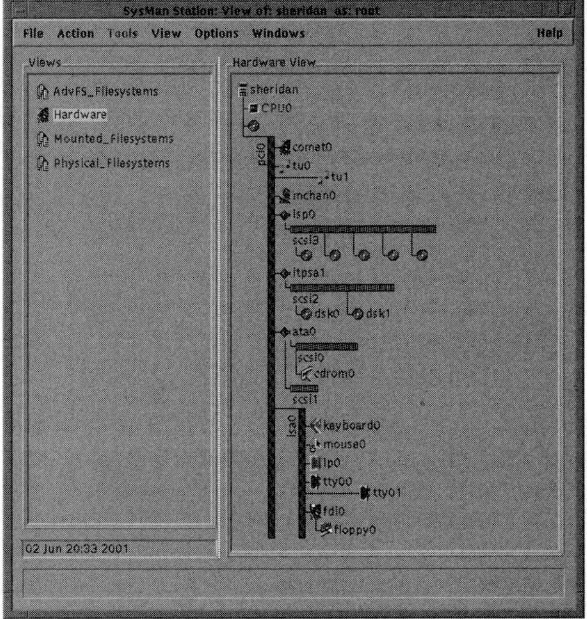


**Figure 4.10**
*SysMan Station—Hardware Hierarchy.*

spend some time checking out. The SysMan CLI is the command-line interface to SysMan and is particularly suited to modifying your configuration via scripting.

You can get or set values for just about every component. To see the available components, type:

```
# sysman -cli -list components
Component(s):
  Imconfig
  account_management
  atm
  auditconfig
  bindconfig
...
  mailusradm
  networkAdapters
  networkServices
  networkedSystems
  networks
...
  shutdown
  storage
  syscheck
```

Once you have determined the component, you can find out what attributes are associated with the component by typing:

```
# sysman -cli -list attributes -comp networkAdapters
Component: networkAdapters
  Group: interfaces
    Attribute(s):
      action
      alternateNetAddr
      debug
      devName
      hasDynamicNetAddr
      hasRCInfo
      hopCountMetric
      ifaceNum
      maxTransUnit
      networkAddress
      netMask
      operational
      receiveAll
      receiveMulticast
      speed
      systemName
      type
      useArp
      change_hostnameifprim
  Group: componentid
    Attribute(s):
      manufacturer
      product
      version
      serialnumber
      installation
      verify
```

```
  Group: digitalmanagementmodes
    Attribute(s):
      deferredcommit
      cdfgroups
```

So, let's list the values for some of the attributes for our network adapters.

```
# sysman -cli -list value -comp networkAdapters \
> -group interfaces \
> -attr devName,type,networkAddress,netMask
Component: networkAdapters
  Group: interfaces
    tu0 ETHERNET 192.168.0.69 255.255.255.0
    tu1 ETHERNET 10.0.0.69 255.255.255.0
```

You can get more granular by specifying a key. To determine what keys are available for the networkAdapters groups, type:

```
# sysman -cli -list keys -comp networkAdapters \
Component: networkAdapters
  Group: interfaces                                   Key: devName
  Group: componentid                                  Key: <NONE>
  Group: digitalmanagementmodes                       Key: <NONE>
```

There appears to be one valid key for the interfaces group, the device name. We can therefore choose to list only attributes for a particular network adapter.

```
# sysman -cli -list value -comp networkAdapters
> -group interfaces -key1 tu0
Component: networkAdapters
  Group: interfaces
    Key: 'tu0'
      Attribute: action                   Value: none
      Attribute: alternateNetAddr         Value:
      Attribute: debug                    Value: false
      Attribute: devName                  Value: tu0
      Attribute: hasDynamicNetAddr        Value: false
      Attribute: hasRCInfo                Value: true
      Attribute: hopCountMetric           Value: 0
      Attribute: ifaceNum                 Value: 0
      Attribute: maxTransUnit             Value: 1500
      Attribute: networkAddress           Value: 192.168.0.69
      Attribute: netMask                  Value: 255.255.255.0
```

```
Attribute: operational              Value: false
Attribute: receiveAll               Value: false
Attribute: receiveMulticast         Value: false
Attribute: speed                    Value: not_applicable
Attribute: systemName               Value: sheridan
Attribute: type                     Value: ETHERNET
Attribute: useArp                   Value: true
Attribute: change_hostnameifprim    Value: no
```

While this may seem like the long way around for casual browsing, if you want to control the behavior of a component from a script, this is powerful feature. We have shown only how to list information from the SysMan CLI interface, but in Chapter 6, "Security," we will show you how to use SysMan CLI to create a DOP privilege group and a couple of DOP actions as well as set a value.

### 4.2.5 SysMan Clone

Tru64 UNIX provides a method to clone a system's configuration. This is particularly useful if you are attempting to set up a lot of systems with the same configuration. We discussed cloning briefly in Chapter 2, "Installation." You may also want to check out the Tru64 UNIX Installation Guide—Advanced Topics or the sysman_clone(8) reference page for more information regarding configuration cloning.

## 4.3 Runtime Configuration

When the Tru64 UNIX system boots, along the way from the console (SRM) prompt to the login screen, many things happen to prepare the system for use. While we will not endeavor to give you all of the gory details of the boot process, we will tell you that once the kernel is loaded, it starts a very important daemon known as init(8).

### 4.3.1 The init(8) daemon

The init daemon is responsible for the runtime configuration of your system. Tru64 UNIX has four run levels by default (although more can be configured), and it is the job of the init daemon to configure the system to operate in these run levels.

**Table 4.16** *Tru64 UNIX Run Levels*

| Run Level | Script | Description |
|---|---|---|
| 0 | /sbin/rc0 shutdown | Shuts down and halts the system. |
| s | /sbin/rc0 off | Single-user Mode |
| 2 | /sbin/rc2 | Multi-user Mode sans Networking |
| 3 | /sbin/rc3 | Multi-user Mode with Networking |

When the init daemon is started it reads the /etc/inittab file. The /etc/inittab file is an ASCII file that tells the init daemon what to run. Each line in the file is colon delimited and has the following format:

Identifier:Runlevel:Action:Command[5]

Here is a typical example of the /etc/inittab file.

```
is:3:initdefault:
ss:Ss:wait:/sbin/rc0 shutdown < /dev/console > /dev/console 2>&1
s0:0:wait:/sbin/rc0 off < /dev/console > /dev/console 2>&1
lsmr:s:sysinit:/sbin/lsmbstartup -b </dev/console >/dev/console  2>&1 ##LSM
lsm:23:wait:/sbin/lsmbstartup </dev/console >/dev/console 2>&1  ##LSM
vol:23:wait:/sbin/vol-reconfig -n </dev/console >/dev/console  2>&1 ##LSM
fs:23:wait:/sbin/bcheckrc < /dev/console > /dev/console 2>&1
kls:Ss:sysinit:/sbin/kloadsrv < /dev/console > /dev/console  2>&1
hsd:Ss:sysinit:/sbin/hotswapd < /dev/console > /dev/console  2>&1
sysconfig:23:wait:/sbin/init.d/autosysconfig start < /dev/console > /dev/console 2>&1
update:23:wait:/sbin/update > /dev/console 2>&1
smsync:23:wait:/sbin/sysconfig -r vfs smoothsync-age=30 >  /dev/null 2>&1
smsyncS:Ss:wait:/sbin/sysconfig -r vfs smoothsync-age=0 >  /dev/null 2>&1
it:23:wait:/sbin/it < /dev/console > /dev/console 2>&1
kmk:3:wait:/sbin/kmknod > /dev/console 2>&1
s2:23:wait:/sbin/rc2 < /dev/console > /dev/console 2>&1
s3:3:wait:/sbin/rc3 < /dev/console > /dev/console 2>&1
cons:1234:respawn:/usr/sbin/getty console console vt100
cms:s:sysinit:/sbin/sysconfig -o cms 100 > /dev/null 2>&1
```

5. See the inittab(4) reference page for a description of each field.

**Table 4.17** *Run Levels in the inittab File*

| Identifier* | Runlevel | Action† | Command |
|---|---|---|---|
| ss | Ss | wait | /sbin/rc0 shutdown < /dev/console > /dev/console 2>&1 |
| s0 | 0 | wait | /sbin/rc0 shutdown < /dev/console > /dev/console 2>&1 |
| s2 | 23 | wait | /sbin/rc2 < /dev/console > /dev/console 2>&1 |
| s3 | 3 | wait | /sbin/rc3 < /dev/console > /dev/console 2>&1 |

* A fourteen-character field used to uniquely identify the entry. This identifier is optional.

† Valid actions are: respawn, wait, once, boot, bootwait, powerfail, powerwait, off, initdefault, and sysinit. See the inittab(4) reference page for more information.

Among the lines in /etc/inittab are lines informing init to execute rc scripts that in turn run other scripts to ultimately start all the services you have configured.

Here's what happens when the system boots to multi-user mode without networking services configured (runlevel 2):

- The kernel (typically, /vmunix) starts the init daemon.
- The init daemon reads /etc/inittab.
- The init daemon runs many programs including the /sbin/rc2 script.
- The rc2 script executes all the scripts that start with an "S" in /sbin/rc2.d.

If you look in the rc?.d directories, you will see files that either start with a "K" or an "S." If you look a little closer, you will see that these files are symbolic links to scripts in /sbin/init.d. For example:

```
# file /sbin/rc2.d/S12evm
/sbin/rc2.d/S12evm:      symbolic link to ../init.d/evm
```

Exploring further still, you will see that there appears to be a method to this rc madness in that the links start with a "K" or an "S" followed by a number, and then a name.

```
# ls /sbin/rc2.d
K00lpd          K16timed        K48route        K56niffd        S19security
K03lat          K20cron         K49gateway      K57quota        S20sia
K04dhcp         K30sendmail     K50syslog       K89desta        S25enlogin
K05inetd        K35nfs          K51uucp         S00savecore     S35streams
K08collect      K36presto       K52write        S05paging       S45atm
K09snmpd        K40nfsmount     K53binlog       S06mfsmount
K12envmon       K43nis          K54.50ip6host   S10recpasswd
K12insightd     K45named        K55inet         S12evm
K15xntpd        K47rwho         K56netrain      S15uucp
```

The links are named in the order that they are to be run.

So what's with the "K" and "S"? Well, the "S" scripts are run when moving from a lower run level to higher run level (like during system startup), while the "K" scripts are run when moving from a higher run level to a lower run level.

If you install an application that you would like to have started every time the system boots, you can place the application's init script in the /sbin/init.d directory and then create a symbolic link to the rc?.d directory that corresponds to the run level where you would like the application started/stopped. It should be noted that these scripts have a consistent calling standard:

```
scriptName start|stop
```

The scripts are not restricted to only start and stop options, but all will have at least these two. Therefore, it is important that any init scripts you create handle the start and stop arguments appropriately. As an example, we suggest you take a look at the existing scripts in the /sbin/init.d directory and note how they deal with the arguments. Once you are comfortable with these, you can become fancier according to your needs.

For more information see the Tru64 UNIX System Administration guide and the init(8), inittab(4), rc0(8), rc2(8), and rc3(8) reference pages.

### 4.3.2 rc.config, rc.config.common, and rcmgr too

If we continue digging into this configuration mystery, one of the next things that you may notice is that out of the nearly 70 scripts in the /sbin/init.d directory, more than 40 of the scripts reference either the rcmgr(8) command [33], the rc.config(8) file [19], or both (9).

Located in /etc, the rc.config file contains runtime configuration variables that the init scripts use to properly configure the system or application. To get, set, or delete a runtime configuration variable, always use the rcmgr command. There is nothing preventing you, as the system administrator, from editing this file with your favorite editor. However, this is not recommended due to the possibility for mistakes or multiple accesses to corrupt this critically important file. A simple mistake could render your system unbootable. The rcmgr(8) reference page states:

```
"Caution
You should always use rcmgr to make changes to the files.  This
will preserve the correct syntax in the files. A lock file,
/etc/rcmgr.lock prevents multiple access to the data files."
```

In preparation for clustering, the rc.config file was split into two files in Tru64 UNIX version 5.0: rc.config and rc.config.common. In a standalone environment, this makes little difference, but in a cluster, rc.config contains the member-specific runtime configuration variables, whereas rc.config.common contains all cluster-common runtime configuration variables.

The rc.config script executes the rc.config.common script before doing anything else, so any variables set in the rc.config.common file will be overridden by the same variables in the rc.config file. There is an optional third file, rc.config.site, which if it exists should be executed by the rc.config.common file before it does anything else so that any variables set in rc.config.site will be overridden by the same variables set in the rc.config.common file.

For additional information see the Tru64 UNIX System Administration guide or the rcmgr(8) reference page.

## 4.4 Kernel Configuration

On occasion you may find yourself needing to reconfigure the kernel in order to add or remove support for some type of hardware or software. The design of the device driver or subsystem you have installed will determine whether or not the kernel has to be reconfigured statically (a kernel rebuild), or can be configured dynamically. Table 4.18 shows the tools that can be used for kernel configuration.

If you build a new kernel, a reboot is required for the modifications to take effect.

**Table 4.18** *Kernel Configuration Tools*

| | | |
|---|---|---|
| **Static** | doconfig(8) | Builds a new kernel as described by the system configuration files located in the /usr/sys/conf directory. |
| | sizer(8) | Displays information about the system or kernel. Creates a system configuration file. |
| **Dynamic** | autosysconfig(8) | Maintains the list of dynamic kernel subsystems that are automatically configured. |
| | dxkerneltuner(8) | Modifies or displays kernel subsystem attributes. Can modify the in-memory configuration database or the sysconfigtab(4) configuration database. |
| | sysconfig(8) | Maintains the kernel subsystem configuration. Modifies the in-memory configuration database. |
| | sysconfigdb(8) | Manages sysconfigtab(4), the subsystem configuration database. |

## 4.4.1 Static Kernel Configuration

When a new kernel subsystem is installed it may be necessary to modify the kernel configuration file and build a new kernel. The configuration file is located in /usr/sys/conf and is the name of your unqualified hostname in uppercase. The configuration file is in ASCII and therefore can be modified using your favorite text editor. Once the configuration file has been edited, build the kernel using the doconfig command. Once the kernel has been built, copy the old kernel as a precaution in case the new kernel does not boot, copy the new kernel to the root (/) directory, and optionally delete the kernel in the build directory.

### *4.4.1.1 Kernel Build Example*

1. Build the kernel.

```
# doconfig -c SHERIDAN

*** KERNEL CONFIGURATION AND BUILD PROCEDURE ***

Saving /sys/conf/SHERIDAN as /sys/conf/SHERIDAN.bck
Do you want to edit the configuration file? (y/n) [n]: n

*** PERFORMING KERNEL BUILD ***
        Working....Thu Jun  7 00:21:53 EDT 2001
The new kernel is /sys/SHERIDAN/vmunix
```

2. Back up the old kernel.

```
# cp /vmunix /vmunix.save
```

3. Copy the new kernel to the root directory.

```
# cp /sys/SHERIDAN/vmunix /vmunix
```

4. Delete the kernels in the build directory.

```
# cd/sys/SHERIDAN; rm -i vmunix vmunix.sys vmunix.SHERIDAN
rm: remove vmunix? y
rm: remove vmunix.sys? y
rm: remove vmunix.SHERIDAN? y
```

5. Reboot the system.

```
# shutdown -sr +15 "System shutdown to install a new kernel"
```

*Important:* Do not use the mv(1) command to move the new kernel to the root (/) directory; use the cp(1) command.

In Tru64 UNIX version 5.0, the Context Dependent Symbolic Link (CDSL) was introduced. A CDSL is a symbolic link with a "{memb}" variable inserted into the link.

```
# file /etc/rc.config
/etc/rc.config: symbolic link to ../cluster/members/{memb}/etc/rc.config
```

This variable is replaced by the Virtual File System (VFS) when the system resolves the link to the file to which it points. This "{memb}" will resolve to the system's memberid (a generic kernel subsystem attribute) added to the word "member." A standalone system is always member0. For example, let's look at the /etc/rc.config file's serial number and then look at the serial number of the rc.config file in /cluster/members/member0/etc. It is the same file.

```
# cd /etc && ls -iL rc.config
 2204 rc.config
```

```
# cd /cluster/members/member0/etc && ls -iL rc.config
 2204 rc.config
```

This change was necessary for the TruCluster Server product in order to maintain member-specific files without modifying the perceived location of operating system files. While /vmunix is not a CDSL on a standalone system, it is a CDSL in a cluster.

The mv command will delete the link and replace it with the file whereas the cp command will follow the link. Removing this link with a file could render some systems in the cluster unbootable, so care should be followed.

#### 4.4.1.2 New Hardware Kernel Build Example

In certain instances, when you install new hardware in the system, you can boot the generic kernel (/genvmunix) and then run the sizer(8) command to create a new kernel configuration file. The Tru64 UNIX operating system is getting smarter with every release, and as a result you will rarely have to use this procedure in the future. But we document it here just in case. When will this procedure be needed? This procedure may be needed when you add a new Compaq hardware device of a type that has not heretofore been installed. For example, if you already have a Fibre Channel adapter (e.g., a KGPSA) then you can install another KGPSA without building a new kernel. If, however, you bought a new card of a type not previously installed in the system, you will need this procedure. For example, you have decided to prepare your system to be added into a cluster, so you purchase and install a MEMORY CHANNEL card.

1. Boot to single-user mode using the generic kernel.

   ```
   >>> boot -fl s -fi genvmunix
   ```

2. Mount the local file systems.

   ```
   # bcheckrc
   ```

3. Run the sizer command to build a new kernel configuration file.

   ```
   # sizer -n SHERIDAN-MCHAN
   ```

4. Determine the differences between the current kernel configuration file and the new kernel configuration file.

```
# diff /tmp/SHERIDAN-MCHAN /sys/conf/SHERIDAN
1c1
< ident          "SHERIDAN-MCHAN"
--
> ident          "SHERIDAN"
...
config_driver mchan
```

5. Edit the current kernel configuration file.

   Add in the "config_driver mchan" line to the /sys/conf/SHERIDAN.
6. Build the kernel.

   See Section 4.4.1.1, "Kernel Build Example."

## 4.4.2 Dynamic Kernel Configuration

More often than not, today's Tru64 UNIX can be reconfigured dynamically (i.e., no kernel build required). But dynamic can mean different things depending on your point of view. A subsystem may be dynamically loadable but may or may not be dynamically unloadable, for example. Subsystem attributes may be dynamically configured when the system boots but not configurable while the system is running; other subsystem attributes can be reconfigured while the system is running, but in only one direction (e.g., proc:maxusers can be raised, but not lowered). And finally, if you're really lucky, a growing number of subsystem attributes are fully configurable while the system is running.

### 4.4.2.1 *Automatically Load and Configure a Dynamic Subsystem*

If you want to automatically load and configure a dynamic subsystem at boot time, use the autosysconfig command to add the subsystem to its list of subsystems to load. For more information see the autosysconfig(8) reference page.

### 4.4.2.2 *Manually Load and Configure a Dynamic Subsystem*

If you have a dynamic subsystem that you would rather not load and configure on system startup, you can use the sysconfig command to load and configure it on the fly.

For example, we will load and configure the CD-ROM file system subsystem (cdfs), which by default is unloaded.

```
# sysconfig -s cdfs
cdfs: unloaded

# sysconfig -c cdfs

# sysconfig -s cdfs
cdfs: loaded and configured
```

To unload the subsystem you can use the following command.

```
# sysconfig -u cdfs

# sysconfig -s cdfs
cdfs: unloaded
```

At this point you may be asking yourself, "How do I determine what subsystems are static or dynamic?" You can use the "-m" option to the sysconfig command.

```
# sysconfig -m
cm: static
hs: static
ksm: static
psm: static
generic: static
io: static
ipc: static
proc: static
...
envmon: dynamic
```

#### 4.4.2.3 Reconfiguring Subsystem Attributes with sysconfig(8)

As was demonstrated in the previous section, the sysconfig program can be used to configure, unconfigure, and query subsystems; however, that is not the extent of the sysconfig command's abilities.

> *Note:* Before we get too far along with configuring attributes, you may be curious as to where you can get more information on what attributes are in each subsystem and what they do. To find out more information on the attributes of a particular subsystem, read the reference page for that

subsystem. All of the subsystem reference pages have a name beginning with "sys_attrs_" and end with the subsystem name. So the reference page name for the proc subsystem would be sys_attrs_proc. Of course you can also list all the subsystem reference pages by typing, "man -k sys_attrs_".

Table 4.19 shows the more common sysconfig command options. For a list of all the options see the sysconfig(8) reference page.

As is noted in Table 4.19, the sysconfig command with the "-r" option can reconfigure a subsystem attribute, but how can you determine which subsystem attributes can be reconfigured? You can query the subsystem for attribute information using the "-Q" option as shown in Figure 4.11. An attribute with an "R" in the op field can be reconfigured while the system is running.

If the attribute has a "C" in the op field, it can only be configured on system boot. In order for the system to configure an attribute at boot time, the attribute must be in the sysconfigtab file.

#### 4.4.2.4 Configuring Subsystem Attributes at Boot Time

The sysconfigdb program is used to maintain the sysconfigtab file. The sysconfigtab file, located in the /etc directory, is the kernel subsystem configuration file. It is an ASCII file in a stanza(4) file format. The sysconfigtab file is

**Table 4.19** *Common sysconfig(8) Command Options*

| | | | |
|---|---|---|---|
| Query | Attribute Configuration Information | -Q | sysconfig -Q subsystem [attribute...] |
| | Attribute Values (Current) | -q | sysconfig -q subsystem [attribute...] |
| | Attribute Values (Saved) | -d | sysconfig -d subsystem [attribute...] |
| | Subsystem Mode | -m | sysconfig -m [subsystem...] |
| | Subsystem State | -s | sysconfig -s [subsystem...] |
| Modify | Reconfigure an Attribute Value | -r | sysconfig -r subsystem attribute=value |
| Configure | Load and Configure a Dynamic Subsystem | -c | sysconfig -c subsystem |
| Unconfigure | Unconfigure and Unload a Dynamic System | -u | sysconfig -u subsystem |

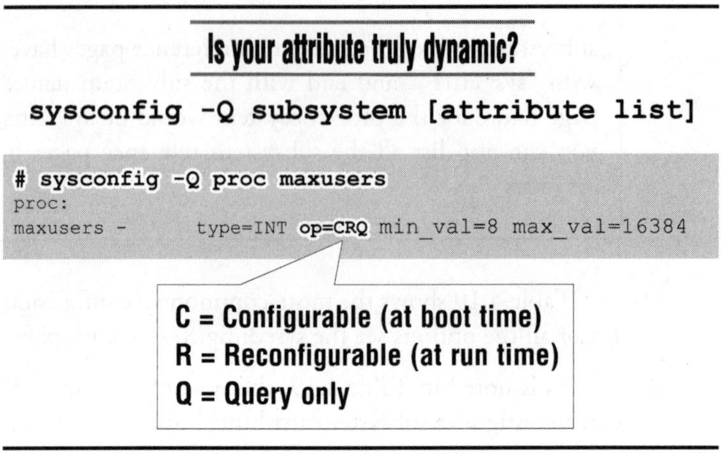

**Figure 4.11** *Subsystem Attribute Information*

**Is your attribute truly dynamic?**

```
sysconfig -Q subsystem [attribute list]
```

```
# sysconfig -Q proc maxusers
proc:
maxusers -      type=INT op=CRQ min_val=8 max_val=16384
```

**C = Configurable (at boot time)**
**R = Reconfigurable (at run time)**
**Q = Query only**

read by the kernel, extremely early in the boot process and uses the information contained within to configure kernel subsystems and device drivers. If you make a mistake in modifying the sysconfigtab file, it can render the system unable to boot. For this reason (and the fact that the sysconfigtab may not remain an ASCII file in the future Tru64 UNIX release), you should always use the sysconfigdb (or dxkerneltuner—see Section 4.4.2.5) command to modify subsystem parameters.

For more information see the sysconfigdb(8), sysconfigtab(4), and stanza(4) reference pages.

**Table 4.20** *Command Options for sysconfigdb(8)*

| | | |
|---|---|---|
| Add a subsystem entry. | -a | sysconfigdb -a-f stanzafile subsystem |
| Update a subsystem entry. | -u | sysconfigdb -u-f stanzafile subsystem |
| Merge subsystem attributes. | -m | sysconfigdb -m-f stanzafile [subsystem] |
| Remove the subsystem entries listed in the stanzafile. | -r | sysconfigdb -r-f stanzafile [subsystem] |
| Delete a subsystem entry. | -d | sysconfigdb -d subsystem |
| Synchronize the in-memory configuration database so that it matched the sysconfigtab file. | -s | sysconfigdb -s |
| List subsystem entries. | -l | sysconfigdb -l [subsystem…] |

#### 4.4.2.4.1 Modifying Subsystem Attributes with sysconfigdb(8)

Let's run through an example to illustrate how to use the sysconfigdb command to add (or modify) an attribute to the sysconfigtab file. In this example we will add a secondary swap device to the system.

1. List the saved subsystem attribute values and make a backup copy as well.

   When you are considering modifying a subsystem attribute it is a good idea to check to see if the attribute is currently in the sysconfigtab file. It is also a good idea to create a directory to store your stanza files for later use.

```
[/]
# mkdir stanza && cd stanza

[/stanza]
# sysconfigdb -l vm | tee vm.stanza.preSwap2

vm:
        swapdevice = /dev/disk/dsk0b
        vm-swap-eager = 1
```

   You should also backup your /etc/sysconfigtab file, just to be on the safe side.

2. Create a stanza file (or copy the backup and edit it).

   In order to add an attribute to sysconfigtab, you must create a stanza file. A stanza file has the following format (see the stanza(4) reference page for more information):

```
"The syntax for a stanza file entry is as follows:

entry_name:
         Attribute1_name = Attribute1_value
         Attribute2_name = Attribute2_value
         Attribute3_name = Attribute3_value1,
Attribute3_value2"

[/stanza]
# cat > swap2.stanza
vm:
        swapdevice = /dev/disk/dsk0b,/dev/disk/dsk6c
^D
```

> *Important:* Verify that the device or partition you plan to use for your secondary swap device does not have data on it you want to keep. You can check the disklabel using the disklabel(8) command.

3. Update the sysconfigtab file.

```
# sysconfigdb -m -f swap2.stanza

Warning: duplicate attribute in vm: was swapdevice =
   /dev/disk/dsk0b, now swapdevice =
   /dev/disk/dsk0b,/dev/disk/dsk6c
```

4. Verify the change has occurred.

```
# sysconfigdb -l vm

vm:
        swapdevice = /dev/disk/dsk0b,/dev/disk/dsk6c
        vm-swap-eager = 1
```

5. Finish

Normally, the next step would be to schedule a reboot so the new attribute values will take effect, but in this case you can dynamically add the swap partition using the swapon(8) command.

#### 4.4.2.5 *The dxkerneltuner(8) Utility*

The dxkerneltuner program is a CDE GUI that can be used to modify subsystem attributes. This tool combines several of the features from both sysconfig and sysconfigdb as well some enhancements.

For more information see the dxkerneltuner(8) reference page, or better yet, click on the help button or pulldown menu (Figure 4.13).

#### 4.4.2.6 *If Things go Wrong...*

If you make a change to an attribute in your sysconfigtab file and upon reboot find your system (or yourself) in a state of confusion (the system won't boot), you may have inadvertently made a mistake. If you can boot to single-user mode (boot -fl s) and put things back the way they were, great! But if not, you might want to boot your system without the sysconfigtab file. To boot the system without the sysconfigtab file, type the following command at the >>> prompt.

```
>>> boot -fl sc
```

Once the system boots. Replace the sysconfigtab file with the backup you made or remove the attribute modifications you made, and reboot. If this

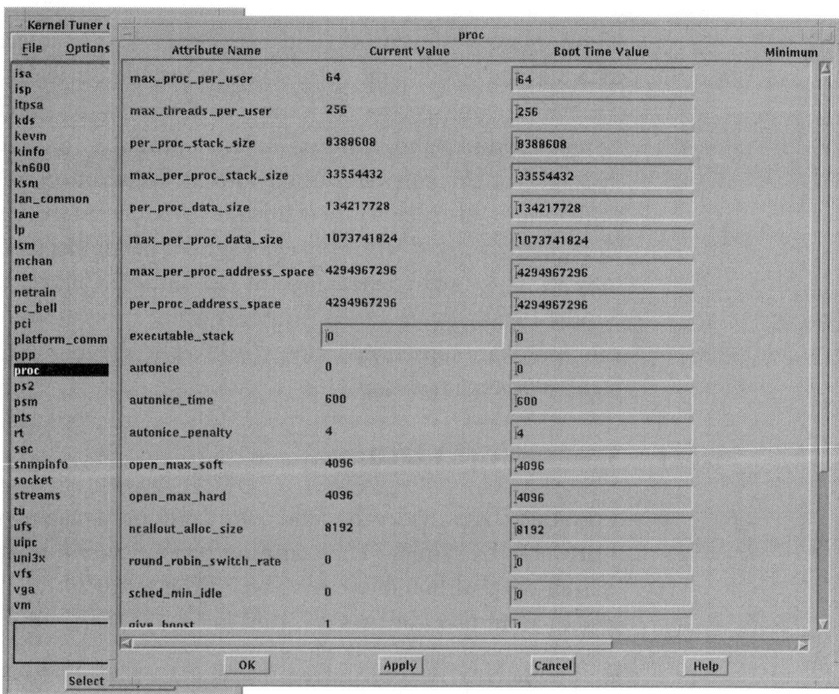


**Figure 4.12** *The dxkerneltuner(8) program*

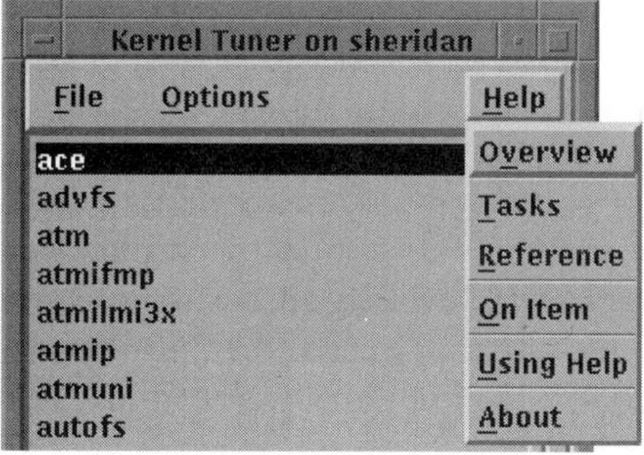


**Figure 4.13** *The dxkerneltuner(8) Help Pulldown Menu.*

does not solve your problem it is probably time to log a call with the Compaq Customer Support Center.

## 4.5 Software Subset Management

A system running Tru64 UNIX is actually composed of a collection of individual software pieces, each providing a different type of functionality. These software pieces, called Software Subsets, are packaged to provide ease of installation, removal, inventory, and validation. A software subset is composed of data and script files and is basically an installation kit for an individual software product or service. All Tru64 UNIX software—both the base operating system products and optional, layered products, produced by Compaq—is packaged in this software subset format. In addition, some third-party software vendors also deliver their software products in this subset format. Finally, all regular Tru64 UNIX operating system patch kits are also provided in this format. This broad acceptance of the software subset facility means that a Tru64 UNIX system administrator must be familiar with the process of managing software subsets in Tru64 UNIX. The key to the software subset facility is the setld(8) command.

### 4.5.1 The setld(8) Utility

Tru64 UNIX provides the setld command for managing software subsets on a Tru64 UNIX system. The common pronunciation of the setld command is "set-ell-dee," although we have heard the term "set-load" used as well. The system administrator uses this tool to:

- Display installed software subsets.
- Load software subsets.
- Delete installed software subsets.
- Verify installed software subsets.
- Configure an installed software subset.
- Extract software subsets.

Each of these functions is executed by running the setld command with the necessary argument(s). Invoking setld with no arguments displays a usage message showing the syntax of each of the functions. Each of the setld functions either requires, or can optionally accept, one or more software subset names as arguments. The software subset names are displayed with all letters in the name capitalized, but the setld command is case insensitive and will accept subset names in all lower, all upper, or mixed case. All but the display function of setld requires root access to execute.

### 4.5.2 Subset Inventory

Probably the most common use of the setld command is to display an inventory of all software subsets loaded on a Tru64 UNIX system. To perform this function, simply execute the following command:

```
# setld -i
Subset        Status       Description
------        ------       -----------
...
CXLLIBA510    installed    DEC C++ Class Archive Libraries
CXLSHRDA510   installed    DEC C++ Class Shared Libraries
CXXBASE620    installed    Compaq C++ Version 6.2 for Tru64 UNIX Systems
CXXHTML620    installed    Compaq C++ HTML documentation
CXXOLD620     installed    Compaq C++ V5.7 (-oldcxx) compiler
...
```

Typical Tru64 UNIX installations have many software subsets installed, and this inventory output may run on for hundreds of lines. Note that the setld command displays three pieces of information for each software subset: Subset Name, Status, and Description. The Subset Name has a length of seven or more characters, is normally a combination of capital letter and numbers, is usually an abbreviation of the subset name, and contains some version number information. The Status field displays the current status of the subset. The Status will always be one of four possible values:

1. installed

   The "installed" status indicates the subset is correctly loaded and installed.

2. incomplete

   A value of "incomplete" indicates that at the time this subset was loaded, the subset kit was incorrect or incomplete.

3. corrupt

   A "corrupt" subset most likely means that the installation of the subset failed.

4. not installed

   The "not installed" status indicates that either the subset was installed in the past but has been deleted, the subset installation was canceled, or simply that the subset control files are in the /usr/.smdb. directory.

The Description field is normally the software product's name as described in the Software Product Description (SPD) issued with the product.

In addition to displaying the entire software subset inventory, the setld command can display a listing of all the files in a particular software subset. Specify one or more software subsets after the "-i" flag for the subset inventory:

```
# setld -i OSFBASE510
./.new...cshrc
./.new...login
./.new...profile
./.new..DXsession
./bin
./dev
./dev/SYSV_PTY
./etc
./etc/.new..TIMEZONE
./etc/.new..autopush.conf
...
```

Individual software subsets can have from only a few component files to many hundreds of files. Note that the files in an inventory listing are displayed relative to the root path, which, by default, is /. The inventory for a software subset may be displayed regardless of the status of the subset, that is, if the subset is listed in the master inventory.

### 4.5.3 Subset Installation

The most important role of the setld command is as a software subset installer. Every Tru64 UNIX and third-party software product that is packaged as a software subset is installed via the setld utility. The process of installing a software subset is much more than just copying software onto a system. The setld utility does the following during a software load operation:

- Validate dependencies and prerequisites
- Execute preinstallation procedures, if any
- Copy subset components into place
- Register the product in the system software subset inventory
- Execute post-installation procedures, if any

In addition, the setld utility can load software subsets from three possible sources: a disk distribution (a CD-ROM or simply a kit in a directory on a file system), directly from a tape or floppy disk, or from a Remote Installation Server (RIS) across the network.

The most common software subset distribution media is probably CD-ROM. Most Compaq software, especially the Tru64 UNIX operating system and layered products, is shipped on CD-ROM. After inserting a Software Distribution CD-ROM into a system's local CD-ROM drive and mounting the CD-ROM, issue the setld command to commence the load operation. For example, the following session demonstrates mounting the

Tru64 UNIX Associated Products, volume 2, distribution CD-ROM and running the setld command to display a menu of available software subsets, in this case, the TruCluster Server software subsets:

```
# mount /dev/disk/cdrom0c /mnt

# setld -l /mnt/TruCluster/kit
The subsets listed below are optional:
```

There may be more optional subsets than can be presented on a single screen. If this is the case, you can choose subsets screen by screen or all at once on the last screen. All of the choices you make will be collected for your confirmation before any subsets are installed.

```
*** Enter subset selections ***

The following subsets are mandatory and will be installed
automatically unless you choose to exit without installing any
subsets:

      * TruCluster Base Components

The subsets listed below are optional:

     There may be more optional subsets than can be presented
on a single
     screen. If this is the case, you can choose subsets screen
by screen
     or all at once on the last screen. All of the choices you
make will
     be collected for your confirmation before any subsets are
installed.

 - TruCluster(TM) Software :
     1) TruCluster Migration Components
     2) TruCluster Reference Pages

-- MORE TO FOLLOW --
Enter your choices or press RETURN to display the next screen.

Estimated free diskspace(MB) in root:89.5 usr:524.7

Choices (for example, 1 2 4-6):


Or you may choose one of the following options:

     3) ALL mandatory and all optional subsets
```

```
        4) MANDATORY subsets only
        5) CANCEL selections and redisplay menus
        6) EXIT without installing any subsets

Estimated free diskspace(MB) in root:89.5 usr:524.7

Enter your choices or press RETURN to redisplay menus.

Choices (for example, 1 2 4-6): 3
```

This menu of software subsets is a feature of the setld utility and is displayed whenever specific subsets to be loaded are not specified on the setld command line. Only subsets not currently installed are listed as menu choices. Also, individual subsets are designated as either mandatory or optional by the software subset producer. This distinction is used to ensure that certain required subsets are loaded, and the setld menu enforces this by requiring the user to load mandatory subsets. Alternatively, the software load may be aborted by selecting the EXIT menu choice.

Select the desired software subsets for installation by entering the menu choice(s). Either enter individual menu choices separated by a space (e.g., 1 2 3) or select a range of menu choices (e.g., 1-3). Also, the menu contains a menu choice for "ALL of the above." Select this to install all listed subsets. After choosing the software subsets to load, a prompt similar to the following is displayed as a final confirmation:

```
You are installing the following mandatory subsets:

        TruCluster Base Components

You are installing the following optional subsets:

 - TruCluster(TM) Software :
        TruCluster Migration Components
        TruCluster Reference Pages

Estimated free diskspace(MB) in root:89.5 usr:522.9

Is this correct? (y/n): y
```

Simply enter a "y" if the list is correct to proceed with the subset installation.

While the setld menu interface provides an interactive interface to the installation of software subsets, it is occasionally desirable to quickly load individual software subsets in a noninteractive fashion. An example of this would be to load a single subset from a disk distribution without scrolling through a menu containing possibly hundreds of unnecessary subsets. To load one or more individual subsets, simply specify the subset name(s) on the command line. For multiple subsets, separate the subset names with spaces. The following example demonstrates this method using tape as the install media:

```
# setld -l /dev/tape/tape0_d0 CXXBASE620 CXXHTML620 CXXOLD620
```

This noninteractive setld subset load does not prompt for confirmation and immediately begins the installation.

### 4.5.4 Subset Deletion

The opposite of software subset installation is subset deletion, and the setld command can quickly remove individual subsets from a Tru64 UNIX system. In order to remove a subset, the subset must be installed and the user must know the subset's name. Use setld's inventory flag (-i) to determine a particular subset's name. Once this is known, run the setld command to remove the subset:

```
# setld -d OSFLEARN425
Deleting "Computer Aided System Tutor" (OSFLEARN510).
```

Be aware that no confirmation is requested and the subset is immediately deleted from the system. If a subset is inadvertently removed, simply reinstall it from the distribution media.

### 4.5.5 setld(8) Activity Logging

The setld utility conveniently logs all operations (installs, deletes, inventories, etc.) along with a time/date stamp in a log file for future reference. This log file (setld.log) is located in the /var/adm/smlogs directory. Refer to this log file for information on a past setld transaction.

### 4.5.6 The fverify(8) Command

The fverify(8) command is useful for checking the state of the files installed on the system. It checks for inconsistencies in the file size, checksum, user ID, group ID, permissions, and file type. It also checks for missing files.

The fverify command appends all errors and informational messages to the /var/adm/smlogs/fverify.log file.

The setld program uses the fverify program when installing subsets to guarantee correct installation. You can use the fverify command if you suspect a file has become corrupt, deleted, or you suspect that someone has tampered with the file.

---

*Note:* If a patch kit has been installed on the system, the fverify command will report errors. You can call the Compaq Customer Support Center (CSC) for a copy of allverify2, which is a "patch friendly" verification script that uses the fverify program. The allverify2 script is an unsupported tool, but is frequently used by CSC Specialists.

---

### 4.5.7 Restoring a File from a Subset

If a file or program is accidentally deleted from the system and a backup is not readily available, the file can be either copied from the installation CD or extracted from a subset on the installation CD.

For example, the awk and convauth programs are inadvertently removed from the system. Here are the steps that can be taken to replace the files:

1. Locate the subset.

```
# grep -E "/awk|/convauth" /usr/.smdb./*.inv
/usr/.smdb./OSFBASE510.inv:0     164496  35436   3        4        100755  8/24/005
10       f        ./usr/bin/awk    none     OSFBASE510
/usr/.smdb./OSFBASE510.inv:0     164496  00000   3        4        100755  8/24/005
10       l        ./usr/bin/nawk   ./usr/bin/awk    OSFBASE510
/usr/.smdb./OSFC2SEC510.inv:0    26      00000   0        0        120777  8/25/005
10       s        ./tcb/bin/convauth      ../../usr/tcb/bin/convauth      OSFC2SEC
510
/usr/.smdb./OSFC2SEC510.inv:0    1983    34555   3        4        100644  8/24/005
10       f        ./usr/lib/nls/msg/en_US.ISO8859-1/convauth.cat  none    OSFC2SEC
510
/usr/.smdb./OSFC2SEC510.inv:0    26      00000   0        0        120777  8/25/005
10       s        ./usr/sbin/convauth     ../../usr/tcb/bin/convauth      OSFC2SEC
510
/usr/.smdb./OSFC2SEC510.inv:0    32944   50838   6        11       100110  8/24/005
10       f        ./usr/tcb/bin/convauth  none    OSFC2SEC510
...
```

The awk command is in the OSFBASE subset. The convauth program is in OSFC2SEC510.

2. Mount the Tru64 UNIX Operating System CD.

```
# mount /dev/disk/cdrom0c /mnt
```

3. Determine is the subset is in the ALPHA/BASE directory on the Tru64 UNIX Operating System CD.

```
# cd /mnt/ALPHA/BASE ; ls OSFBASE510 OSFC2SEC510
ls: OSFBASE510 not found
OSFC2SEC510
```

If the subset is not in the ALPHA/BASE directory, then the program is actually in the directory on the CD indicated in the inventory file. In this case, the awk program (in OSFBASE510) is in /usr/sbin.

- Copy the program from the location on the CD.

```
# cp /mnt/usr/bin/awk /usr/bin/awk
```

- Set the user, group, and permission bits.

```
# ls -l /mnt/usr/bin/awk
-rwxr-xr-x   2 bin  bin   164496 Aug 24  2000 /mnt/usr/bin/awk
# chown bin:bin /usr/bin/awk
# chmod 755 /usr/bin/awk
```

If the subset is in the ALPHA/BASE directory, the program must be extracted from the subset. The subset is in a compressed, tar(1) format.

- Make a link to the subset.

```
# cd /
# ln -s /mnt/ALPHA/BASE/OSFC2SEC510 OSFC2SEC510.tar.Z
```

- Extract the file from the subset.

  Since the convauth program is actually located in /usr/tcb/bin/convauth and contains two symbolic links to it as indicated by the "s" in the second field of the line in the inventory file, we need to extract the file and both symbolic links. This can be verified as follows:

```
# grep -E "/usr/tcb/bin/convauth" /usr/.smdb./*.inv

/usr/.smdb./OSFC2SEC510.inv:0   26     00000   0       0       120777  8/25/005
10      s       ./tcb/bin/convauth      ../../usr/tcb/bin/convauth     OSFC2SEC  510
/usr/.smdb./OSFC2SEC510.inv:0   26     00000   0       0       120777  8/25/005
10      s       ./usr/sbin/convauth     ../../usr/tcb/bin/convauth     OSFC2SEC  510
/usr/.smdb./OSFC2SEC510.inv:0   32944  50838   6       11      100110  8/24/005
10      f       ./usr/tcb/bin/convauth  none    OSFC2SEC510
```

Extract the files with the following command:

```
# zcat OSFC2SEC510.tar.Z \
 | tar xvpf - ./tcb/bin/convauth ./usr/sbin/convauth ./usr/tcb/bin/convauth
```

```
blocksize = 16
lrwxrwxrwx     0/0       0 Aug 24 22:17:36 2000 ./tcb/bin/convauth symbolic lin
k to ../../usr/tcb/bin/convauth
lrwxrwxrwx     0/0       0 Aug 24 22:17:36 2000 ./usr/sbin/convauth symbolic li
nk to ../../usr/tcb/bin/convauth
--x-x--     6/11   32944 Aug 24 21:11:27 2000 ./usr/tcb/bin/convauth
```

## 4.6 License Management

The Tru64 UNIX operating system and many of the Tru64 UNIX layered products are licensed to the end user rather than sold. This means that the vendor, Compaq Computer Corporation in this case, has sold only an authorization to use a particular software product. The license agreement between the software vendor and the end user specifies the terms of the license. These license terms typically specify each party's responsibilities regarding the use of the software product. A system administrator should be aware of the licensing terms to ensure that the organization honors the terms of the license. If that was all there were to licensing, a system administrator's responsibility would be minimal and would consist mostly of administrative paperwork. However, certain software products produced by Compaq have special licensing characteristics and requirements.

### 4.6.1 Types of Licensing

Two types of software licenses are issued by Compaq, and a software product might be licensed only one way or the other, or optionally both ways, depending on the product itself. A product's licensing type is indicated on the license information provided with the software media and documentation.

#### *4.6.1.1 Availability Licensing*

A software application might be licensed to allow unlimited use of the product, but only on certain specific models of processors. This type of license is called an availability license or, occasionally, a traditional license. An availability license is purchased based on the model and size of the Alpha system on which the software product will be run. For example, an availability license sized for a small server such as an AlphaServer DS10L could not be run on a large AlphaServer GS320. However, an availability license purchased for the AlphaServer GS320 would run fine on the AlphaServer DS10L. Since the price of the license is proportional to the price of the computer, a license for a GS320 is usually significantly more than the same license for a DS10L. While it would be foolish to purchase more licenses than necessary, the ability to move a "larger" license to a "smaller" system may be useful when planning for a "backup" system. In the event that a main server is unavailable, it is possible to move a software product and its license to a smaller (and less expensive) system so the product is still available to its users.

#### *4.6.1.2 Activity Licensing*

Other products may be licensed to allow only a certain number of users to run the product simultaneously. This type of license is called an activity license, or a per-user or concurrent use license. For example, consider a software development software product such as a compiler that is used by many users, but not on a constant basis. Analyzing the usage of the compiler may indicate that no more than five users are ever actively compiling at any one time. An availability license providing unlimited use for such a product may be prohibitively expensive and unnecessary, but an activity license for five concurrent users would be very economical and would likely be sufficient. If, in this example, the number of developers was increased and the new concurrent use average was eight users, all that would be necessary would be to purchase three additional per-user licenses to increase the size of the activity license.

While all software products are licensed, only certain software licenses are enforced that is, the product will only run with proof of a license. Since software is usually a source of revenue for a company such as Compaq Computer Corporation, the vendor must take measures to protect that software development investment and prevent illegal use of software licenses. For this purpose, Digital (now Compaq) created the License Management Facility for Tru64 UNIX.

### 4.6.2 The License Management Facility (LMF)

The License Management Facility (LMF) for Tru64 UNIX was developed as a way for software products to validate licensing information. The LMF maintains a list of licensed software products on a particular system in a database. The system administrator is responsible for managing this license database to ensure that all LMF licensed products are registered. Every Tru64 UNIX system will have at least two, and probably more, LMF licenses as the operating system itself is a licensed product. Licensed software products will call license-checking functions to check that a valid license is registered with the LMF before making the product available for use. In addition to meeting the legal responsibility of licensing, properly administering the license database ensures that users are able to log in to the system and run the software products necessary to doing their job.

In addition to the License Management Facility, there are other types of license managers available that run on Tru64 UNIX. Most of these license managers are third-party products that independent software developers have used for license management with their applications. These other license managers, FLEXlm by GLOBEtrotter Software is an example, typically ship with the particular software product and are not part of Tru64 UNIX. This section will only concern itself with Compaq's LMF and the software products that support LMF. If it becomes necessary to install and manage a third-party license manager, consult the documentation that came with the product for assistance. Regardless, any such third-party license manager will run in conjunction with Compaq's LMF and understanding the operation of LMF is still a requirement.

If a software product's licensing information is in the form of a Product Authorization Key (PAK), the software product supports the LMF, and the PAK must be registered with the LMF in order for the software to be used. A PAK is a special document incorporating security printing that makes it difficult to forge or copy and, as formal proof of purchase of software license, should be retained indefinitely in a secure place. See Table 4.21 for description of the fields on a license PAK. In addition to these fields, a PAK usually provides the following one or more of the following useful pieces of information, none of which are entered into LMF:

- Customer P.O.—This field may contain the purchase order number used to purchase this license.
- License Issue Date—This is the date the PAK was actually produced by Compaq.
- Descriptive Product Name—Since the PAK PRODUCT NAME field is limited in length, this field usually contains a more readable description of the licensed software product.
- License Type—This field indicates whether the license is a Traditional (Availability) or Concurrent (Activity) license type.

**Table 4.21** *License PAK Fields Explained*

| Field | Explanation |
|---|---|
| Issuer: | The Issuer is the vendor licensing the software product. For Compaq Computer Corporation (formerly Digital Equipment Corporation) products, this is typically the string "DEC." |
| Authorization Number: | The Authorization Number is a unique string that the PAK issuer assigns to a specific PAK. The combination of the Issuer and the Authorization Number uniquely identifies a PAK. |
| Product Name: | The name used by the LMF to distinguish among different software products. |
| Producer: | The name of the company that produced the licensed software. This is typically DEC. |
| Number of Units: | The Number of Units indicates how many license units are supplied by the PAK. If this field is zero (0), the PAK provides unlimited use of the product on any type of processor. |
| Version: | The Version field is used if the PAK applies only to certain versions of the software product. If a version is specified, the PAK will work with that version and earlier of the software. If this field on the PAK is empty, the PAK is not restricted to a specific version of the software. |
| Product Release Date: | The Product Release Date is used if the PAK is restricted to only versions of the software product released before the specified date. If this field on the PAK is empty, the PAK is not restricted to a specific release date of the software. |
| Key Termination Date: | The Key Termination Date is the date when the PAK expires. Once this date passes, LMF no longer allows users to invoke the software product. If this field on the PAK is empty, the PAK will function indefinitely. |
| Availability Table Code: | The Availability Table Code represents the number of units required to give unlimited use of a product on a particular hardware system model.<br><br>A letter represents a value from the License Unit Requirement Table (LURT) that specifies the number of units necessary for the product to run on a specific hardware model. The LURT is internal to LMF and cannot be displayed or modified.<br><br>If the field specifies "CONSTANT=integer," the integer value indicates the number of units necessary to run the software product, regardless of the hardware model in use. |
| Activity Table Code: | The Activity Table Code represents the number of units required for each concurrent user of the product. This field may either be a single letter or the string "CONSTANT=integer."<br><br>A letter represents a value from the License Unit Requirement Table (LURT) that specifies the number of units necessary for each concurrent user to run the product on a specific hardware model. The LURT is internal to LMF and cannot be displayed or modified. |

**Table 4.21** *(continued)*

| | |
|---|---|
| | If the field specifies "CONSTANT=integer," the integer value indicates the number of units necessary for each concurrent user to run the software product, regardless of the hardware model in use. |
| Key Options: | The Key Options field may contain one or more of the following options delimited by commas:<br>MOD_UNITS<br>This option indicates that the system administrator is able to modify the value specified in the NUMBER OF UNITS field. See the lmf(8) modify command for more information.<br>ALPHA<br>This option indicates that the PAK is valid only on the Alpha family of computers.<br>NO_SHARE<br>This option indicates that the license cannot be combined with another license for the same software product on the same computer. |
| Product Token: | The Product Token field is not currently used by LMF. However, if a PAK contains data in this field, you must enter the specified string when registering the PAK. |
| Hardware-Id: | The Hardware-Id is not currently used by LMF. However, if a PAK contains data in this field, you must enter the specified string when registering the PAK. |
| Checksum: | The Checksum is a string generated from a sum of the values of the other PAK fields. This string is used to verify the accuracy and integrity of the entered PAK data. |

Finally, a PAK has a box labeled "For Customer Use," which contains two fields that the system administrator may want to complete in pencil after registering the PAK:

- CPU Serial No
- Node Id

#### 4.6.2.1 PAK Units

The LMF concept of license units is the key to the operation of LMF. A license unit is the basic unit of measurement that Compaq uses to specify how much product use a license provides. The producer of a software product determines the number of units that are required to run the application on a particular system. This value is tied to the License Unit Requirement Table (LURT), which is a part of the Tru64 UNIX operating system. The LURT specifies a series of license unit requirements, essentially performance ratings, for each model of processor. Processors that provide more performance (more or faster CPUs, for instance) have greater license unit requirements. The LURT is internal to the LMF and cannot be displayed or modified. Suffice it to say that larger and more powerful server systems have higher license unit requirements than smaller workstations and servers. To see how many units your system requires see the "Alpha License Rating Table" at the Compaq website—as of this writing, the URL is:

```
http://www.compaq.com/products/software/info/refmat/
  swl_alpha.html
```

#### 4.6.2.2 LMF Database Files

The LMF database files are located, by default, in /var/adm/lmf and consist of two files:

- ldb—The actual LMF database file
- ldb_history—The license management history file, which is a record of all LMF maintenance commands that have been issued on the system

The LMF database files are binary files and should not be edited or modified except via the utilities provided by the LMF. However, the database files can be safely copied using the cp command as long as no LMF activities are occurring. Once the LMF database is populated with a system's licenses, the database files are normally only accessed at the system startup to copy the license information into the system's license cache. This cache, not the database files on disk, is what is accessed by a software product when verifying that a valid license is registered. To maintain license database consistency, always copy both files (ldb and ldb_history) together when backing them up, whether to tape or to another directory.

#### 4.6.2.3 The lmf(8) Utility

The principal tool provided by Tru64 UNIX to manage and manipulate the license database is the lmf(8) command. The lmf command is used to register new licenses, delete existing licenses, list registered licenses, update the system's license cache, and carry out other license maintenance tasks. The lmf command is, by default, executable by all users. However, the LMF database files are normally only readable and writable by the root user. The effective result of this is that the lmf command is only usable by root, as probably should be the case. Do not change the ownership of the LMF database files.

The lmf command has two modes: command line arguments and an interactive environment. Both modes provide identical functionality, and the use of one mode over the other is normally a matter of personal preference. The exception to this is if you wish to place lmf commands into a script. In this case, use the lmf command line arguments for the desired functionality. Actually, the lmf commands themselves are identical, and the mode differs only in the invocation. To run an lmf command from the command line, simply execute the lmf utility followed by the desired command. For example:

```
# lmf help
Usage : lmf [ -d <directory> ] [ <command> <arguments> ]
   help [<command>]
   exit
   register [ - | <template> ]
   delete <product> [ <producer> [ <authorization> ] ]
   amend <product> [ <producer> [ <authorization> ] ]
   modify <product> [ <producer> [ <authorization> ] ]
   enable <product> [ <producer> [ <authorization> ] ]
   disable <product> [ <producer> [ <authorization> ] ]
   cancel <date> <product> [ <producer> [ <authorization> ] ]
   issue <file> <product> [ <producer> [ <authorization> ] ]
   list [ full ] [ ldb|cache|all ] [ for <product> [ <producer> ] ]
   history [ short|full ] [ from <date> ] [ for <product> [ <producer> ] ]
   load <users> <product> [ <producer> [ <authorization> ] ]
   unload <users> <product> [ <producer> ]
   reset [ cpus [ n ] ]
```

This will execute the command and then return to the shell prompt.

The interactive mode of the lmf utility is entered by simply typing lmf followed by a return. This will present an lmf> prompt where lmf commands may be executed by entering just the command (without prefacing "lmf"). To exit from interactive mode, type exit or a Ctrl-D. For example:

```
# lmf
lmf> help
Usage :     [ -d <directory> ] [ <command> <arguments> ]
    help [<command>]
    exit
    register [ - | <template> ]
    delete <product> [ <producer> [ <authorization> ] ]
    amend <product> [ <producer> [ <authorization> ] ]
    modify <product> [ <producer> [ <authorization> ] ]
    enable <product> [ <producer> [ <authorization> ] ]
    disable <product> [ <producer> [ <authorization> ] ]
    cancel <date> <product> [ <producer> [ <authorization> ] ]
    issue <file> <product> [ <producer> [ <authorization> ] ]
    list [ full ] [ ldb|cache|all ] [ for <product> [ <producer> ] ]
    history [ short|full ] [ from <date> ] [ for <product> [ <producer> ] ]
```

```
    load <users> <product> [ <producer> [ <authorization> ] ]
    unload <users> <product> [ <producer> ]
    reset [ cpus [ n ] ]

lmf> exit
#
```

In the following examples, the command line mode of the lmf command will be used for brevity.

Additionally, there is a command line flag that can be specified regardless of the execution mode. This flag, "-d", allows an alternative location for the LMF database files to be specified. By default, the database files are located in the /var/adm/lmf directory, and lmf will use this directory if another directory is not specified. The "-d" flag is useful when experimenting with the LMF configuration on a system. By copying the LMF database files (ldb and ldb_history) to another directory, then specifying that alternate directory, one can manipulate a backup copy of the database without affecting the primary copy.

#### 4.6.2.4 Listing Licenses

The most basic LMF command is "list". This command provides the ability to query and display either the LMF database files, the kernel license cache, or both. At its simplest, list without any modifiers displays a one-line summary of the PAK data for each product in the license database:

```
# lmf list
Product          Status            Users: Total      Active
OSF-USR          active                   10         0
OSF-USR          active, multiple         10         0
OSF-BASE         active                   unlimited
LSM-OA           active                   unlimited
ADVFS-UTILITIES  active                   unlimited
```

The list command also has modifiers to provide more complete information on individual PAKs, and allows listing only specific PAKs based on product name and producer. These options provide a fair amount of flexibility when listing a system's PAKs. To display all PAK fields except for the checksum, plus several additional fields related to the current status of the PAK, use the following list command:

```
# lmf list full
```

To list just a specific product's PAK, use the following syntax:

```
# lmf list full for osf-base
             Product Name: OSF-BASE
                 Producer: DEC
                   Issuer: DEC
     Authorization Number: ALS-NQ-1998JAN31-130
          Number of units: 15
                  Version:
     Product Release Date:
     Key Termination Date:
  Availability Table Code: A
      Activity Table Code:
              Key Options: MOD_UNITS, ALPHA
            Product Token:
              Hardware-Id:
           License status: active
        Cancellation Date:
          Revision Number: 0
                  Comment:
        Cache Total Units: 15
          Activity Charge: 0
```

#### 4.6.2.5 Registering Licenses

One of the first tasks after installing the Tru64 UNIX operating system is to register the operating system PAKs (OSF-USR and possibly OSF-BASE). Registering a PAK is the process of copying the PAK data into the LMF for use by the product licensed by the PAK. Since the fields containing license data varies from PAK to PAK, the registration process prompts for all possible fields. When registering a PAK, enter data into a field only when the corresponding field on the PAK has data. Simply hit <Return> to skip unnecessary fields. Also, entry of data from a PAK is case-insensitive. Usually the characters on a PAK are all uppercase; however, it is not necessary to enter the characters in uppercase—lowercase or mixed case is fine.

The simplest way to register a PAK is to use the lmfsetup(8) command. This command is actually a shell script that prompts the user for each PAK field, then registers the PAK after all the fields have been entered. The following is an example lmfsetup session:

```
# /usr/sbin/lmfsetup
Register PAK (type q or quit to exit) [template]
                     Issuer : DEC
       Authorization Number : ARS-MT-1998JAN31-249
               Product Name : OSF-USR
                   Producer : DEC
            Number of units : 1050
                    Version :
       Product Release Date :
       Key Termination Date :
    Availability Table Code : H
        Activity Table Code :
                Key Options : MOD_UNITS,ALPHA
              Product Token :
                Hardware-Id :
                   Checksum : 2-YABA-DABA-DOOO-BEDO
PAK registered for template successfully
Register PAK (type q or quit to exit) [template] quit
```

Alternatively, a PAK can be registered by issuing the following lmf command:

```
# lmf register
```

This will open an editor containing an empty PAK template allowing the license data to be added to the appropriate fields. The lmf utility runs the editor specified by the EDITOR environment variable, or if the environment variable is undefined, the vi editor is run. After completing the template, simply exit the editor and the completed PAK will be validated by the LMF. If the PAK does not validate, the user is given the opportunity to reenter the editor to correct any mistakes. Once all the PAK fields are correctly entered into the template, the PAK is successfully registered into the LMF.

Occasionally, a PAK may be supplied in electronic format, such as in an e-mail message or as a text file. Rather than typing in the data to register the PAK, the lmf command provides a simple method of registering such PAKs. To register a PAK from a file that contains valid license data, issue the following command:

```
# lmf register - < PAK.txt
```

The dash (-) instructs the lmf command to take registration data from standard input, which is redirected in from the PAK.txt file via the less than symbol (<).

#### 4.6.2.6 *Updating the Kernel License Cache*

Once a PAK is registered in the LMF database file, the next step is typically to enable that newly entered license. Until the PAK data is copied to the system's kernel license cache, the license is unavailable to users. To update the system's license cache, simply issue the following command:

```
# lmf reset
```

This reset can be done at any time without disturbing active users or processes. Note that an "lmf reset" is executed as part of the system startup to initially copy the license data from the LMF database file to the active license cache.

#### 4.6.2.7 *Transferring Licenses*

Occasionally it may be desirable to move a software product from one system to another. This may be because the original system is going to be taken down for maintenance, or perhaps an organization is upgrading or downgrading to a different system. Whatever the reason, such a move would also require moving the license information in addition to the software product itself. Obviously, the system administrator could simply reregister the PAK(s), but Compaq has provided a way to remove a license from a system and produce a file containing the removed PAK data in one step. This process is called issuing a PAK and is done with the following syntax:

```
lmf issue <file> <product> [ <producer> [ <authorization number> ]]
```

Replace <file> with a filename to contain the reconstructed PAK data, and specify the product name in place of <product>. If there is more than one PAK with the same product name, it is necessary to specify the producer and authorization number to identify what specific PAK is to be issued. For example, the following command will issue a specific OSF-USR PAK to the file /tmp/OSF-USRPAK.txt:

```
# lmf issue /tmp/OSF-USRPAK.txt OSF-USR DEC ARS-MT-1998JAN31-249
```

To load this issued PAK on another system, transfer the PAK.txt file to that system and issue the following register command:

```
# lmf register - < OSF-USRPAK.txt
```

Note that using the "lmf issue" command to illegally copy license PAKs is against the terms of the license agreement and is forbidden. Refer to the license terms on the back of the license PAK for more information.

#### 4.6.2.8 Fixing a "Not enough units to load OSF-BASE DEC" Error

The OSF-BASE license is an availability license. When an AlphaServer is purchased it ships with a license of the appropriate capacity.

If a CPU is added to the AlphaServer it is possible that the capacity of the license will be exceeded and the following error message will be displayed:

```
"Not enough units to load OSF-BASE DEC"
```

The following actions can be taken to solve this problem:

Check the OSF-BASE for MOD_UNITS in the "Key Options" field. If it exists you can increase the number of units.

```
# lmf list full for OSF-BASE | grep MOD_UNITS
                 Key Options: MOD_UNITS, ALPHA
```

If MOD_UNITS exists, check the LURT table for appropriate number units necessary for the AlphaServer/CPU combination. See section 4.2.6.1.

- Increase the number of units to value specified in LURT table.

  ```
  # lmf modify OSF-BASE
  ```

  Note, you will be placed in the editor specified by the your EDITOR environment variable or vi(1) if EDITOR is undefined.

  Edit the "Number of units" field to the appropriate number.

  ```
  # lmf reset
  ```

If the MOD_UNITS attribute does not exist, call Compaq to request a temporary OSF-BASE PAK and purchase an additional PAK.

Note any license with MOD_UNITS can have its units increased or decreased.

#### 4.6.2.9 The OSF-USR "UNIX-SERVER-IMPLICIT-USER" License

Tru64 UNIX includes a four-user OSF-USR PAK, known as the "implicit-user" license because the value of the "Authorization Number" field is "UNIX-SERVER-IMPLICIT-USER". Remove this license when adding a larger capacity OSF-USR PAK to allow more than four users to log into the system.

# 5

# User Accounts

## 5.1 User Account Management

User account management is, if not the most important job of a system administrator, certainly one of the most visible. An individual's login account defines the overall system to the user. When the system administrator configures the login environment appropriately by determining the command path, setting an informative shell prompt, defining helpful aliases and necessary environment variables, and assigning group memberships, the users can immediately become productive.

Actually, creating user accounts and the eventual removal or retirement of user accounts is just the beginning, and end, of user account management. In between is the day-to-day support of your user community. This includes account modifications, such as resetting passwords and adjusting group memberships, ensuring that users are aware of upcoming system changes or outages, and managing security to allow users to get their work done while protecting the system from accidental or intentional harm. Behind the scenes, the administrator should define user and group IDs (UIDs and GIDs) to avoid collisions, create appropriate default account "dot" files, create and monitor home directory file systems, and perform a variety of other tasks necessary for the smooth operation of a Tru64 UNIX system.

This chapter covers the details of adding and removing user accounts, plus other aspects of user account management. In addition, some administrative strategies to be aware of are presented.

## 5.2 Base Security vs. Enhanced Security

Before moving on to the particulars of user account management in Tru64 UNIX, the two levels of security available in Tru64 UNIX must be explained, since the system's security level impacts account management in a variety of ways. The two levels are:

- Base security
- Enhanced security (also called C2 security)

Base security is the default security level when installing Tru64 UNIX, and is distinguished by traditional UNIX passwords. Base security is often sufficient for single-user workstations or less critical systems.

Enhanced security provides a rich set of password and login controls. The password controls include shadow passwords, configurable password length (both minimum and maximum), and password usage history. The login controls include per-terminal settings for delays between consecutive successful or failed login attempts, the ability to retire or lock accounts, and logging of successful and unsuccessful login attempts. Enhanced security is the recommended security level for Tru64 UNIX systems deemed sensitive due to the type of data they contain, and especially for any systems connected to the Internet.

The command to determine the current system security level is:

```
# /usr/sbin/rcmgr get SECURITY
```

If the string "BASE" or no output is returned, you are running Base security. If, however, the string "ENHANCED" is returned, Enhanced security is enabled on your system. See Chapter 6, "Security," for instructions on enabling and configuring Enhanced security on your system.

## 5.3 Account Management Tools

Tru64 UNIX provides several tools to add, remove, and modify user accounts. These are:

- The Account Manager (dxaccounts)
- The Accounts option in the SysMan menu (sysman accounts)
- Command line utilities (useradd, usermod, userdel, groupadd, groupmod, and groupdel)

- User management scripts (adduser and removeuser)
- The ability to manually edit system files

The following sections discuss the features and advantages of each of these tools.

## 5.3.1 Account Manager

The Tru64 UNIX Account Manager, dxaccounts(8X), is the recommended utility for managing user accounts. Account Manager is an X Window System graphical user interface (GUI) that can be used to add, modify, and delete user accounts and groups. For systems running Enhanced security, Account Manager is also used to modify individual and system-wide security parameters, such as password aging and length.

Account Manager is invoked through the CDE Application Manager, which is opened by selecting the Application Manager icon from the CDE Front Panel, followed by selecting System_Admin, then DailyAdmin, and finally Account Manager. Once you double-click on the Account Manager icon, you will be prompted via a Get Password dialogue box for the root password, unless you're already logged in as root. The initial Account Manager window is shown in Figure 5.1.

Optionally, you can start Account Manager from the command line:

```
# /usr/bin/X11/dxaccounts
```

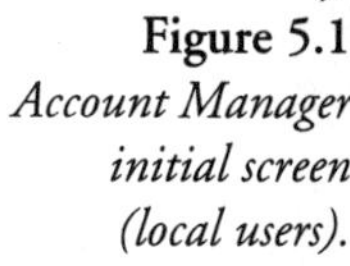

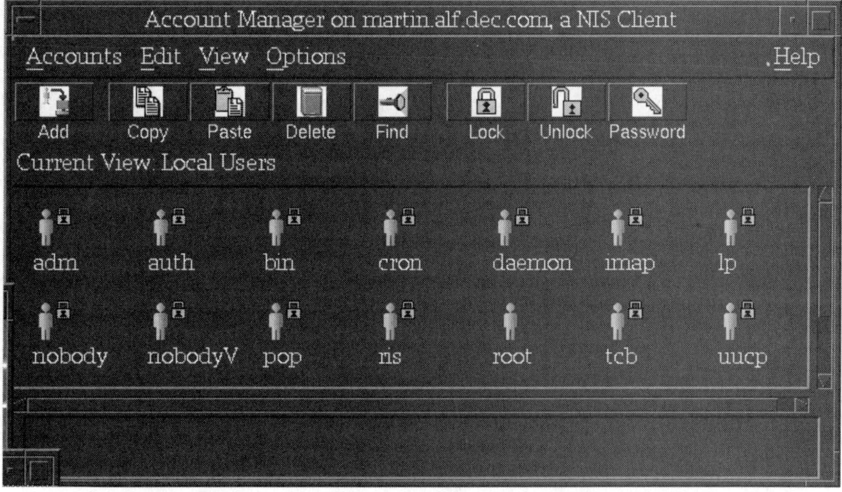


**Figure 5.1** *Account Manager initial screen (local users).*

The buttons at the top of the screen in Figure 5.1 make it easy to perform account management functions. For example, you can lock an account simply by selecting the icon for that account and then clicking on the Lock button. Locked accounts are indicated by a small lock symbol next to the account. To add a new user, click on the Add button, and Account Manager will display an account template (Figure 5.2). Fill in the template with the appropriate information and click Apply or OK, and the user account is added to the system.

You can also use Account Manager to set the general account management options for your system. This screen (Figure 5.3) is accessible from the Options menu on the initial screen. You can optionally allow duplicate UIDs (in Base security only) and duplicate GIDs. In general, duplicate UIDs are a bad idea; file permissions and most system activities are tracked by UID, not user name, so it becomes nearly impossible to distinguish between multiple users with the same UID. The same argument is true for duplicate GIDs, although this is a less serious issue than duplicate UIDs.

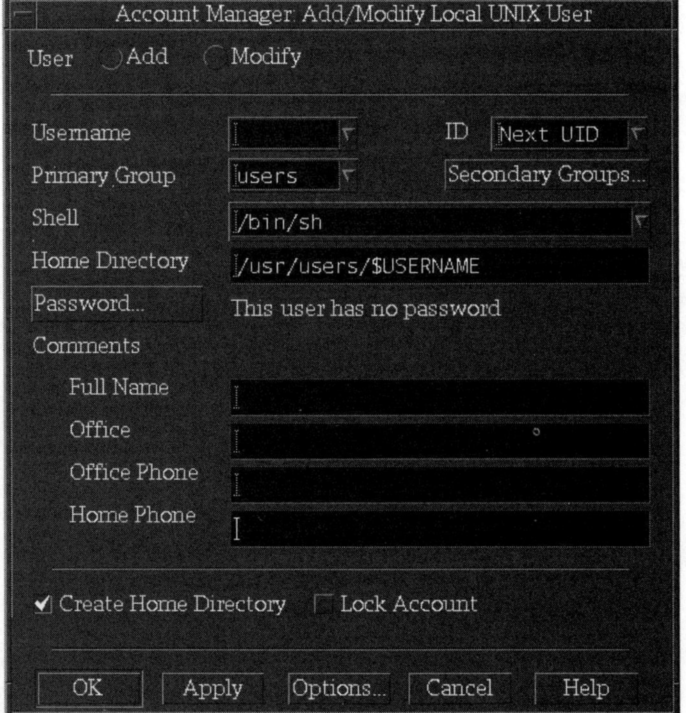


**Figure 5.2**
*Adding a user in Account Manager.*

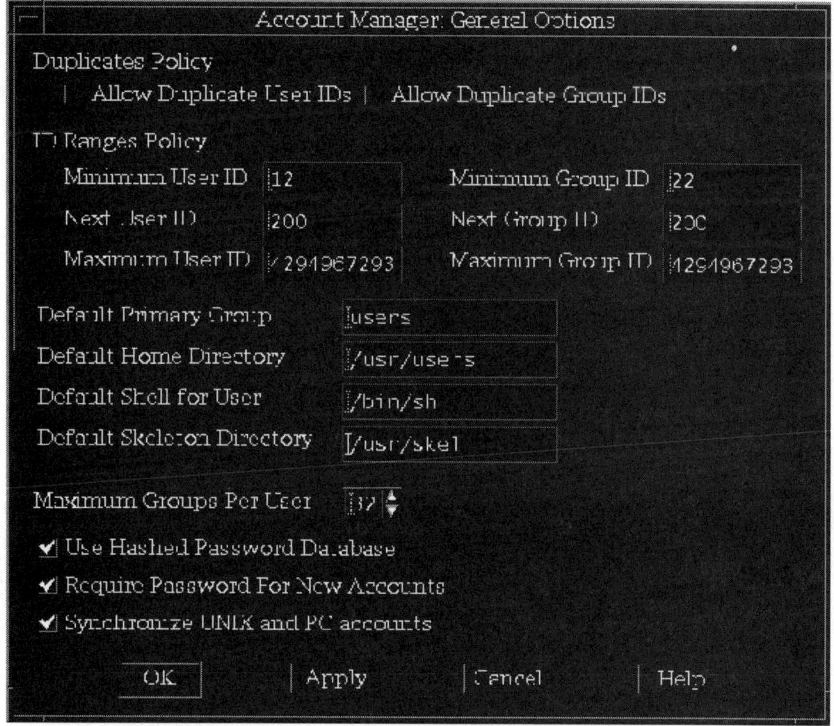


**Figure 5.3**
*Account Manager general options.*

The "Use Hashed Password Database" box should be checked for any system with more than a handful of users. The hashed password database allows faster lookups of account information; without the hashed database, the system must perform a sequential search of the password file. This can cause a serious performance degradation on systems with large password files.

If you find yourself changing the Account Manager defaults (such as default shell, primary group, or home directory) each time you create an account, it is easy to permanently change the defaults that Account Manager uses. To do so, select the Save Options choice from the Options drop-down menu in the initial Account Manager window. This saves a configuration file with the unusually straightforward name of Account_defaults in a subdirectory of your home directory ($HOME/.sysman). Simply edit this file and change the defaults you wish to modify, and restart Account Manager to cause the new defaults to take effect.

For example, this Account_defaults file specifies the default base directory (base_dir) for new users as /usr/users:

```
max_uid 65535
min_uid 12
next_uid 200
max_gid 65535
min_gid 22
next_gid 200
dup_uid 0
dup_gid 0
max_groups_per_user 32
base_dir /usr/users
distributed 0
local 1
lock 0
local_first 0
primary_group users
skel_dir /usr/skel
shell /bin/sh
```

To change the default base directory for new accounts to /home, replace the string "/usr/users" with "/home" in $HOME/.sysman/ Account_defaults and restart Account Manager. You can also do this with the usermod command (see Section 5.3.3) as follows:

```
# usermod -D -d /home
```

Account Manager, along with most of the other account management tools, ensures that only one privileged user can modify the password database at a time. It does this by creating a lock file called /etc/.AM_is_running. If this file already exists when Account Manager starts, it exits with the message "The password and group files are currently locked by another user." If Account Manager doesn't exit normally (e.g., if the system crashes while Account Manager is running), the file will not be deleted, and subsequent attempts to run Account Manager will fail with the "locked by another user" message. If this happens, make sure that there really are no other users running Account Manager, then remove /etc/.AM_is_running. In addition, there are a few other files whose existence can lock out some or all of the account management utilities:

```
/etc/passwd.dir.new
/etc/passwd.pag.new
/etc/passwd.ptmp
/etc/ptmp
/etc/ptmp.dir
/etc/ptmp.pag
/var/yp/src/passwd.AM_orig
/var/yp/src/passwd.ptmp
```

If you receive the "locked" message and /etc/.AM_is_running does not exist, check for the existence of the files listed above and remove any of them that you find.

### 5.3.2 The SysMan Accounts Option

The Accounts option of the SysMan menu provides capabilities similar to the Account Manager. Although the Accounts option is somewhat more limited than dxaccounts, it has the advantage of running in either a graphical or character-cell environment. You can invoke the Accounts option from the CDE Application Manager or with the following command line:

```
# sysman accounts
```

The Accounts Menu has the following options:

- Manage local users
- Manage local groups
- Manage NIS users
- Manage NIS groups

Selecting one of these options brings up a list of users or groups, as shown in Figure 5.4. Selecting Add or Modify brings up a template similar to the one shown in Figure 5.2.

### 5.3.3 Command Line Utilities

Although the Account Manager is a useful interface for system management, there are times when a nongraphical tool is preferable. Some systems do not have graphics capability (either attached to the system or via the network), while other system administrators prefer to use command line tools whenever possible. In addition, command line utilities can be used in customized scripts tailored to your particular environment—something that graphical interfaces don't allow.

Tru64 UNIX provides a number of command line utilities to manage user accounts and groups. These are divided into two groups:

- User account management utilities (useradd, usermod, and userdel)
- Group management utilities (groupadd, groupmod, and groupdel)

The useradd, usermod, and userdel utilities, as the names indicate, are used to add, modify, and delete user accounts. Similarly, groupadd,

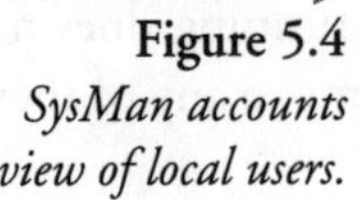

**Figure 5.4**
*SysMan accounts view of local users.*

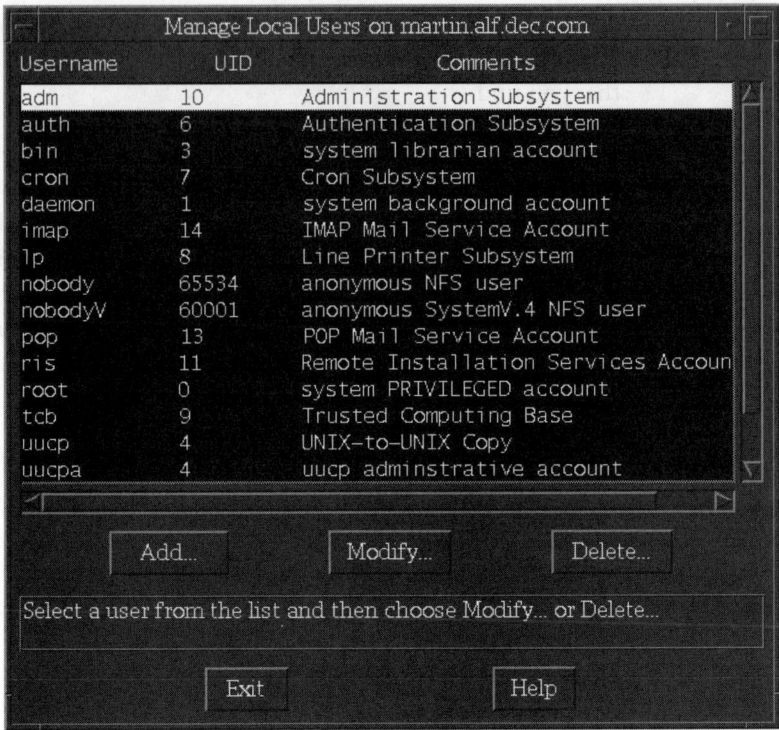


groupmod, and groupdel are used to add, modify, and delete user groups. These commands are very flexible and allow as much customization as desired. For example, to add a new user account named beth, using all default values, the command is simply:

```
# useradd beth
```

Any of the default values can be overridden on the command line; see the useradd man page for details. To give Beth a nondefault home directory and shell, the command would be:

```
# useradd beth -H /usr/staff/beth -m -s /usr/bin/csh
```

Using the –D switch with useradd or usermod will display or change the system defaults used by the account management utilities. These are the same defaults used by Account Manager and described in Section 5.3.1. For example, usermod –D with no other arguments displays the current defaults:

```
# usermod -D
Minimum User ID                  = 12
Next User ID                     = 200
Maximum User ID                  = 4294967293
Duplicate User ID                = 0
Use Hashed Database              = 1
Max Groups Per User              = 32
Base Home Directory              = /usr/users
Administrative Lock              = 1
Primary Group                    = users
Skeleton Directory               = /usr/skel
Shell                            = /bin/sh
Inactive Days                    = 0
Expire Date                      = Never
```

Note that usermod –D displays only those defaults related to user accounts, not groups. To see the group-related defaults, use groupmod –D:

```
# groupmod -D
Local                            = 1
Distributed                      = 0
Minimum Group ID                 = 22
Next Group ID                    = 200
Maximum Group ID                 = 4294967293
Duplicate Group ID               = 0
```

### 5.3.4 User Management Scripts

Tru64 UNIX has historically provided a set of Korn shell scripts (adduser, removeuser, addgroup, and removegroup) for adding and removing user accounts and groups. In version 5, these scripts are little more than front-end interfaces to the command line utilities discussed in the previous section. The older scripts are considered obsolete, and are likely to disappear from Tru64 UNIX in the near future. If you are using any of these scripts for account management, it would be advisable to migrate to one of the other tools described above.

### 5.3.5 Manually Editing Files

Of the possible account management methods, the least desirable is manually editing the necessary system files. For example, to add a new user with this method, you would have to add an entry to the /etc/passwd file and possibly the /etc/group file, create the user's home directory, and copy in default "dot" files (.profile, .exrc, etc). In addition, if you have Enhanced security enabled, you must create an appropriate protected password authentication database file, which, among other things, contains the actual encrypted password. This method is discouraged unless you have a thorough understanding of all the details of the security database files.

If you absolutely have to manually edit the password file, use the vipw(8) utility instead of a standard editor such as vi. vipw has several useful features:

- It locks the password file to prevent multiple users from making changes at the same time.
- It performs consistency checks on the root entry in the password file.
- If the hashed password database is in use, vipw automatically updates it.

A common mistake in manually editing the password file is to use vi or another common editor on a system where the hashed password database is in use. Although the password file is modified, the hashed database is not updated with the changed information, so system utilities (which access the hashed database) do not see the changes. If this happens, you can manually re-create the hashed database with the mkpasswd(8) utility:

```
# cd /etc
# rm passwd.dir passwd.pag
# mkpasswd passwd
```

### 5.3.6 Verification Tools

Tru64 UNIX provides three programs to verify the consistency and integrity of your password database. The pwck(8) and grpck(8) utilities check the password and group files, respectively, while authck(8) checks the Enhanced security authentication database. For example, pwck checks each entry in the password file for the proper number of fields; verifies that the user name, UID, and GID are valid; and checks for the existence of the user's home directory and default shell. These utilities can be extremely helpful in tracking down user login problems. It's also a good idea to run them periodically as part of your regular system maintenance.

## 5.4 User Account Creation

Any of the tools described above can be used to add new user accounts. Which one you choose to use will depend on your system environment and personal preferences; however, in most cases, the Account Manager is the recommended method. When you use it to add a user account, the Account Manager performs several useful tasks for you:

- Ensures that the new user name and user ID do not already exist
- Adds the user to specified secondary groups
- Updates /etc/passwd and (if necessary) Enhanced security authentication databases
- Creates the home directory (optional)
- Copies default configuration files from a skeleton directory (optional)
- Configures password aging and quality parameters (optional, if using Enhanced security)
- Sets parameters to limit system resource usage (optional, if using Enhanced security)
- Forces a password change at initial login (optional, if using Enhanced security)

To add an account from the main Account Manager window (Figure 5.1), click the Add icon or use the Accounts pull-down menu to select Add New User. The Add/Modify User window (Figure 5.2) will be displayed with default values in certain fields. If these defaults are acceptable for the user being added, all you need to do is enter a user name and password, and select either Apply or OK. Alternatively, you can create a new account by cloning an existing account. Click on an existing user, then use the Copy and Paste buttons to create a copy of the account, then double-click on the new account to add the required information (user name, UID, and password.)

You may optionally enter comments for a new account, such as the user's full name, phone number, and location. This information is helpful in identifying users via the finger command, especially on systems with more than a few accounts. In addition, this information can show up as the "From:" information in outgoing mail.

## 5.5 User Account Removal or Retirement

When the time comes to remove a user account—for example, when a user leaves the organization or simply no longer needs access to the system—you have two options: completely remove the account from the system, including the home directory and all files owned by that account, or retire the account. Retiring an account is an option if the system is using Enhanced security; retirement permanently locks the account, preventing reuse of that account's user ID and name. Once an account is retired, it cannot be reenabled without manually editing the Enhanced security authentication database (see Chapter 6 for details.)

Whether to remove or retire an account depends on two factors:

- The local security policy
- The current security level (Base or Enhanced)

Your locally defined security policy may specify the procedure to follow when an account is no longer needed. This may include disabling the account but not removing any of the account's files for a specifed time period, or archiving the files owned by an account prior to removing it. In addition, if your organization is using Enhanced security and is required to conform to the more stringent C2 account requirements, you may have to retire accounts rather than remove them.

Generally speaking, you can use any of the account management tools to delete an account. However, if you're running Enhanced security on a version of Tru64 UNIX older than V5.1, Account Manager will only allow you to retire an account, not delete it. Deleting an account with Account Manager is a straightforward process. Select a user account icon to be deleted, and then choose Delete from the Edit menu or click the Delete (trash can) icon. Retiring an account is similarly straightforward: select the account, and then click the Retire ("no" symbol) icon. A dialogue box is presented, giving you the option to remove the user's files.

When an account is retired, the icon for that user remains in the user account view of the Account Manager, but it is marked as retired with the international "no" symbol (a red circle crossed by a diagonal line.) You can still select a retired account icon and view its account information, but you can't modify any of the fields.

### 5.5.1 Locking Accounts

There may be times when you wish to temporarily disable or "lock" a user account without going as far as removing or retiring the account. For example, this might be desirable if a user goes on an extended leave of absence or is suspected of improper activity. The account management tools all provide an option to lock a user account. The capability to lock an account exists in both Base and Enhanced security, although the underlying method for locking an account is different for each level.

Using either of the graphical interfaces (Account Manager or SysMan Accounts), select a user account by clicking on its icon, then choose the Lock option from the menu. Similarly, to unlock a locked account, select the account and then choose Unlock. You can also use the usermod utility to accomplish this from the command line. For example, to lock the account for user jsmith, the command would be:

```
# usermod -x administrative_lock_applied=1 jsmith
```

To unlock the account, change the value to 0:

```
# usermod -x administrative_lock_applied=0 jsmith
```

## 5.6 User Account Modification

Modifying user accounts is an ongoing activity that includes actions such as changing a user's default shell, adding a user to additional groups, and similar tasks. All of the account management utilities described above can be used to modify user accounts. For example, from the Account Manager display shown in Figure 5.1, simply click on the desired account icon and select Modify... from the Edit pull-down menu. This opens the familiar Add/Modify User window. Select and change the desired fields and click the OK or Apply button to complete the edit.

In some cases, users may be able to make their own modifications. For example, users can change their own passwords using the passwd(1) command or, in NIS environments, the yppasswd(1) command. If you are using Enhanced security, you can optionally restrict the ability of users to choose their own passwords; see the Tru64 UNIX Security Manual for details.

Similarly, users can change the descriptive information in the comments or "gecos" field of their /etc/passwd entry by using the chfn(1) command. This information is displayed in the output of the finger(1) command. Users can also choose a new default shell from the list of available shells with the chsh(1) command. Interestingly, passwd(1), chfn(1), and chsh(1) are all hard links to a single executable program; the commands "passwd –f" and "passwd –s" may be substituted for chfn and chsh, respectively.

## 5.7 Managing User Account Resources

There are several types of resources that a system administrator needs to consider when managing user accounts:

- User Names
- UID Numbers
- User Groups
- User Disk Space

These resources are finite and a system administrator must ensure that they are allocated properly. On a system with few accounts, these resources probably don't need to be tended as closely as on a system with hundreds or thousands of users. Frequently, user accounts are created shortly after initial system installation, with little thought given to the long-term management of these resources. Some strategic planning prior to turning your users loose on the system will be worthwhile in the long run, either by reducing your day-to-day "fire fighting" or by eliminating massive and painful system reorganizations. Of course, you must know something about your users' workload patterns and disk space requirements, both now and in the future, to make adequate plans. This is sometimes impossible or unrealistic, and sometimes you may just have to make your best estimate. Experience will have to guide you in these situations.

### 5.7.1 User Names

User account names have only a few format restrictions:

- One to eight characters in length
- Cannot begin with a hyphen (-)
- Cannot contain a colon (:)

The eight-character limit is partially relaxed in Tru64 UNIX version 5. The Tru64 UNIX kernel supports longer user names (up to the value of parameter login_name_max in the generic subsystem), but most system utilities still observe the eight-character limit. However, it appears likely that a future version of Tru64 UNIX will fully support longer names.

In addition, it is recommended that user names be unique and not contain either capital letters or periods. Beyond this, there is no universal standard or convention. User account names are, by their very nature, often a personal choice; on systems with just a handful of users, this is probably fine. However, as the number of user accounts and/or the number of systems increases, the need for a local convention or two becomes obvious. For example, if the local convention is the user's first initial, followed by up to seven characters of the last name, the likelihood of more than one "jsmith" is proportional to the size of the organization. A less desirable solution is to select a naming convention based on semi-random strings. While this might guarantee uniqueness, many users and administrators prefer to have account names that bear some relationship to the user's real name. For example:

```
$ who
mcheek    ttyp1    Jun 4 09:35
p5mpc7    ttyp2    Jun 4 15:19
```

The administrator should select a reasonable standard and expect to make exceptions for name conflicts (for instance, the second and subsequent jsmith's might use their first and second initials plus last name) or individual user resistance, as longtime UNIX users occasionally become very possessive of their chosen account names. The name of the game with user account names is consistency, both on a single system and across multiple systems that users share.

### 5.7.2 UID Numbers

The User ID (UID) is a unique number between 0 and 4,294,967,293 (the largest number that can be represented with 32 bits) that the system uses to identify a user and determine file access permissions. (If you are running an older version of Tru64 UNIX, the maximum UID may be limited to 65,535 or 262,143.) The UID should be unique across a system (or group of systems) to avoid UID collisions. File access permissions are checked by UID, not user name, so two users with the same UID will automatically have access to each other's files. For this reason, uniqueness across multiple systems becomes crucial if you are using the Network File System (NFS) to share file systems. If two different users on two different systems have the same UID, each user would have access via NFS to the other user's files, depending on how the file systems are mounted. The Network Information Service (NIS) can be used to solve this problem; with NIS, you can share common user and group definitions among your systems, ensuring that a specific UID or GID always represents the same user or group across your systems.

The root or superuser account is always UID zero (0). By convention, UIDs from 0 to 99 are considered "system" UIDs, and you should avoid creating accounts with UIDs in this range. One important reason to not use these system UIDs is to avoid UID conflicts if future releases of Tru64 UNIX create new system-required accounts. Simply create your accounts with UIDs starting at 100 and you will have no problems. If you wish to be cautious, start at 1000 instead.

One final recommendation regarding UIDs is to select ranges of UIDs for different types of users. For instance, you could place system administrators and operators in the range 100–999, developers in the range 1000–1999, application testers in the range 2000–2999, and so on. Categorizing your users and placing them in appropriately sized UID ranges is a helpful way to organize your user community.

### 5.7.3 User Groups

Along with UIDs, you should plan your user groups and group IDs (GIDs). Groups provide a mechanism to allow users with similar needs or responsibilities to share resources based on group memberships. A user account must belong to at least one group, which is specified by the GID field of the /etc/passwd file entry. This group is called the account's primary group. Additional group memberships, which are called secondary groups, are specified in the /etc/group file.

A Tru64 UNIX account may belong to up to 32 groups. This may cause a problem in environments using a mix of servers from different vendors, because some variants of UNIX support only 8 or 16 groups per user. For example, if you have an NFS server that supports only 16 groups per user, but you have a user on your Tru64 UNIX system who belongs to more than 16 groups, that user may not be able to access file systems mounted from that NFS server. If this is likely to be a problem in your environment, you can change the maximum number of groups per user on your system with the following command:

```
# usermod -D -x max_groups_per_user=16
```

Group IDs (GIDs) are unique numbers between 0 and 4,294,967,293 (65,535 in older versions) that the system uses to identify a specific group. Like UIDs, GIDs should be unique across a system (or group of systems) to avoid GID collisions. If you are using NFS to share file systems across the network, this GID uniqueness is doubly important to avoid security holes. For example, suppose that system A has a user group named payroll with a GID of 2001. The members of the payroll group can access the accounting system containing the company's salary data. Now suppose that system B has a group named clerks, also with a GID of 2001. Because the GIDs are the same, the clerk accounts will have the same group access as the payroll group to any NFS-mounted file systems. If the salary data is on an NFS-mounted file system, a clerk could possibly read or (even worse) change or delete company salary information. This is an extreme example, but the potential for this type of exposure is significantly reduced by ensuring unique GIDs (with NIS, for example) across your systems.

Only members of group 0 (the system group) are permitted to become the superuser (root) by using the su(1) command. It is especially important to add those individuals who need the ability to become the superuser to group 0 if remote root logins are disabled. If this is not done, the only way to become the superuser is to log in as root on the system console.

Groups are used by the system administrator to provide shared access to files and directories to users with similar responsibilities or jobs. For instance, all developers who need access to the source code for an ongoing development project would likely be placed in the same group, and the source files would be group-owned with the permissions set to provide group-read and possibly group-write access. This would allow all members of the developer group to read or write the files, regardless of who created or currently owns the files. Determining the number and membership of groups on your system requires some level of knowledge about your user community and their work. Group management is frequently an ongoing task that, if planned and set up intelligently early on, can be a minor responsibility.

### 5.7.4 User Home Directories and Other Disk Space

Management of disk space can involve considerable effort. Users have a seemingly unlimited appetite for disk space, and they always seem to have an urgent case for needing more, no matter how many gigabytes you have at your disposal. By having an idea of your users' needs and requirements, you are a step closer to successfully managing the disk resources at your disposal.

The first area to focus on is your users' home directories. The file systems containing home directories are often the most active, and are probably where you will spend the most time and energy fighting disk space shortages. Small systems, or systems with small user communities, usually have only one file system for users' home directories. Some common names for the users' file system are /home, /users, and /u. The important thing to note about these common names is that they should be separate file systems, and not simply subdirectories of either the root file system (/) or /usr. The Tru64 UNIX account creation tools all default to a home directory for new accounts of /usr/users/$HOME. It is not a good idea to create your user home directories in /usr/users, either as a separate file system mounted on /usr or, worse, actually as a subdirectory of the /usr file system. There is nothing technically wrong with mounting a separate file system on the /usr/users mount point, but it can be confusing to some users due to the similarity of "usr" and "users". Even worse is actually putting your users' home directories in the /usr file system. The first time your system grinds to a halt because an active user has filled up the /usr file system, you will quickly understand that the best strategy is to isolate the users on their own file systems to prevent this kind of impact on your system.

This leads to the idea of segregating your users onto different file systems in order to isolate an active user group from a less active group of users. For example, if you have a team of developers actively compiling, linking, and debugging on a large development effort, and another group of users who simply run a canned accounting package, it would make sense to place the developers' home directories on one large file system, and the accounting staff on a separate file system sized appropriately for their needs. Then if one or two busy developers fill up their home file system, neither the accounting staff nor the rest of the system will be impacted.

A tip to help manage multiple user file systems is to create a directory, such as /u, that contains symbolic links to the users' true home directories, which could reside on different file systems. This allows you to specify any user's home directory as /u/<user name>. Specify this symbolic link in the home directory field of the /etc/passwd file, and you will be able to transparently relocate user home directories by simply changing the link after physically moving the directory. By educating your users to use either this symbolic link or the $HOME environment variable in their scripts and aliases, you will have the flexibility to reorganize your file systems when needed, with little or no impact on your users.

#### 5.7.4.1 Disk Quotas

Another mechanism for managing user disk space is disk quotas. The Tru64 UNIX file systems, UFS and AdvFS, allow you to set quotas on a per-user and per-group basis to limit the amount of disk space that a specific user or group can use on a particular file system. Quotas can limit both the amount of disk space and the total number of files that a user or group can consume. By setting quotas, you can ensure that each user or group uses no more space than is reasonable, and prevent them from impacting other users by filling up an entire file system.

Disk quotas can have both "hard" and "soft" limits. A hard limit is an absolute limit; when it is reached, no more disk space can be consumed. A soft limit is a lower limit that a user is allowed to exceed for a specified time known as the grace period. During the grace period, the user receives warnings, but may still allocate space, up to the hard limit. If the grace period expires before the user frees enough space to get below the soft limit, the effect is the same as reaching the hard limit: no more disk space can be consumed.

The details of configuring and managing quotas vary slightly depending on the type of file system (UFS or AdvFS) and the operating system version. For more information, the Tru64 UNIX System Administration Manual and the quota(1) reference page are good starting points.

## 5.8 Managing the User Account Environment

Configuring user accounts with appropriate environments is an important task for system administrators. Accounts should have certain environment variables set with suitable default values, and there may be site-specific commands or programs that every user should run during the login process. Experienced users will tailor their personal login files and reset environment variables to suit their preferences, but you, as the system administrator, can ensure that every user starts out with the minimum necessary environment.

There are two primary ways to ensure that your user accounts are properly "provisioned" before a user logs on for the first time:

- A skeleton account
- Global default shell login files

### 5.8.1 Skeleton Account Setup

A skeleton account is simply a directory that serves as a template for new account home directories. In Tru64 UNIX, the default skeleton directory is /usr/skel, which contains files named .profile, .cshrc, and .login, plus a bin subdirectory. During account creation, the contents of the skeleton directory are copied to the new account's home directory. If you construct a default .profile or .cshrc/.login pair containing site-specific environment variables and aliases, they will be placed in every new user account's home directory.

In addition to the typical shell initialization or "dot" files, such as .profile and .cshrc, the skeleton directory is also the place for any type of user default or configuration files, such as the vi editor initialization file (.exrc), e-mail auto-forwarding file (.forward), or .hushlogin file to suppress the message of the day. Any file or directory that you normally have to copy into newly created user home directories is a good candidate for the skeleton directory.

If you are using the Account Manager to create user accounts, you can have several different skeleton directories for different types of users. Account Manager makes it easy to select which skeleton directory to use when creating a new user account. Click on the Options... button at the bottom of the

Add/Modify User window to open a dialogue box where you can specify, or even browse for, the desired skeleton directory.

As your users' needs evolve and your experience and knowledge increases, you will probably add to or modify the files in your skeleton directory. Changes to your skeleton directory will, of course, take effect for subsequent new user accounts, but will not automatically be applied to existing user accounts. If you wish to update your existing accounts to reflect any skeleton directory changes, you will have to manually perform the updates yourself. At first glance, this is a straightforward task, especially when you have a small user community. However, as both the size and proficiency of your users increases, you may run into resistance trying to standardize the user account environment. For this reason, it's best to keep the shell initialization files (.profile, .cshrc, .login) stored in your skeleton directory reasonably generic, and use the global default shell login files for most of your shell environment standardization.

## 5.8.2 Global Default Shell Login Files

As part of the login sequence, all shells read a global default initialization file containing environment variables and commands before they run the user's local shell initialization file, which is usually located in the user's home directory. For example, the Bourne shell (/bin/sh) and the Korn shell (/bin/ksh) read the /etc/profile initialization file at login before running the user's local $HOME/.profile. In the case of the C shell (/bin/csh), the /etc/csh.login initialization file is read at login before running the user's $HOME/.cshrc and $HOME/.login files. This shell behavior means that you, the system administrator, can force your users to have certain desired environment variables and aliases. Of course, a user can override your definition of a variable or alias via their local initialization file, but the purpose of defining global defaults is not to interfere with your knowledgeable users, but to provide a default environment for the majority of users who never concern themselves with customizing their personal environments.

By placing the desired default configuration into a global file that only root can change, you avoid having to edit each user's local shell initialization files when you need to add a new environment variable or change an alias. Since these global default shell login files are read by several different shells (e.g., /etc/profile is read by sh, ksh, and bash), ensure that any commands you add are generic enough for all the shells that may execute those commands. For example, to set an environment variable in /etc/profile, use the following syntax:

```
MANPATH=/usr/man:/usr/local/man; export MANPATH
rather than:
export MANPATH=/usr/man:/usr/local/man
```

In the Korn and BASH shells, both formats produce the same result. However, since the latter is not a valid command in the Bourne shell, setting and exporting environment variables in one statement will cause an error at login and, more importantly, not achieve the desired result of setting the MANPATH environment variable. Table 5.1 contains a list of common environment variables. Some of these are set by the shell when the user logs in, but you may wish to set the others in your global default files.

**Table 5.1** *Common Shell Environment Variables*

| Environment Variable | Description |
|---|---|
| DISPLAY | Default display for X-Windows applications |
| EDITOR | Default editor |
| HOME | Home directory |
| LOGNAME | Login name |
| MAIL | Primary incoming mailbox (/usr/spool/mail/<username> by default) |
| MAILCHECK | How often (in seconds) the shell checks for new mail |
| MAILPATH | List of colon-separated file names that the shell monitors for new mail |
| MANPATH | List of directories that the man(1) command searches for man pages |
| PAGER | The default file viewer, e.g., more(1) or pg(1) |
| PATH | List of directories to search for command executables |
| PS1 | Primary shell prompt ($ by default) |
| PS2 | Secondary shell prompt (> by default) |
| SHELL | Pathname of the shell |
| TERM | Terminal type |
| TIMEOUT | Bourne shell idle timeout (in minutes) |
| TMOUT | Korn shell idle timeout (in seconds) |
| TZ | Time zone |
| USER | User name |
| VISUAL | Default visual (full-screen) editor, e.g., vi(1) |

## 5.9 Communicating with Users

A system administrator frequently needs to communicate important information to both the general user community and to individual users. Tru64 UNIX provides several mechanisms for you to communicate with your users:

- The message of the day (/etc/motd)
- The system identification file (/etc/issue)
- System news
- talk
- write and wall (Write All)

### 5.9.1 Message of the Day

When you have something that is not particularly urgent to tell your users, such as when the next scheduled reboot will occur, the message of the day (motd) is a useful mechanism. Simply edit (or create) the file /etc/motd with a text editor such as vi, and enter the text that you want your users to see. This file is displayed to each user, every time they log in to the system. The main drawback to using the motd as a communication channel is that a user can suppress the display of the motd simply by placing a .hushlogin file in the user's home directory:

```
$ touch $HOME/.hushlogin
```

Because the motd does not change often, users become accustomed to its contents and will tend to ignore or miss important information. As such, it's best to place only reasonably static information in the /etc/motd file: the Tru64 UNIX version, the system host name and IP address, and the standard legalese disclaimer required by local policy. This way, experienced users can safely ignore the motd, but the information is there for new users.

### 5.9.2 System Identification File

While the contents of the message of the day file (/etc/motd) are displayed after a user successfully logs in, Tru64 UNIX provides a mechanism to identify the system before the login prompt is presented. Simply edit (or create) the /etc/issue file with a text editor, and insert the text you wish to be displayed. If /etc/issue exists, the getty(8) command writes its contents to the screen prior to starting the login dialogue. Typically, a system administrator may want to display identification information such as host name, location, or contact instructions. Other sites may be required to present a standard disclaimer to warn against unauthorized system access.

The /etc/issue file is primarily for serial terminal connections, including a serial console. Tru64 UNIX provides a second file, /etc/issue.net, which works identically to /etc/issue, except that the contents of the /etc/issue.net file are displayed by the telnetd(8) daemon for a new telnet connection prior to starting the login dialogue. If /etc/issue exists and /etc/issue.net does not, the telnetd daemon displays the contents of the /etc/issue file.

### 5.9.3 System News

System news, not to be confused with USENET News, is a little-used mechanism that is handy for presenting information to your users. News consists of two pieces: the news program itself (/usr/bin/news), and the news directory (/usr/news). To set up news on your system, add the following command to your global default shell login files:

```
/usr/bin/news
```

This command will have no effect until you create one or more news items. A news item is a text file placed in the /usr/news directory. For example:

```
This system will be unavailable for two hours on Friday, June
29, starting at 01:00 for the installation of a new disk array.
A full system backup will be taken immediately prior to the
shutdown. Your friendly system administrator.
```

The next time a user logs in, the following will be displayed immediately after the message of the day:

```
root (root) Mon Jun 25 18:39:36 2001
This system will be unavailable for two hours on Friday, June
29, starting at 01:00 for the installation of a new disk array.
A full system backup will be taken immediately prior to the
shutdown. Your friendly system administrator.
```

One nice feature of news is that each particular news item will be displayed only once for each user. The news program keeps track of which items have been seen by placing a file in each user's home directory ($HOME/.news_time) that is used as a time-stamp to determine whether a particular news item has been seen.

A user can see all news items at any time, regardless of whether they have already been seen, by issuing this command:

```
$ news -a
```

Finally, news is not just for the system administrator. To allow non-root users to place news items in the news directory, change the permissions of the news directory to allow world-writable access:

```
# chmod 1777 /usr/news
```

The “1” in the permission bits sets the sticky bit (1000 octal) on the /usr/news directory. Setting the sticky bit is recommended for any world-writable directory; it prevents users from deleting other users’ files in the directory—in this case, other users’ news items.

### 5.9.4 talk, write, and wall

The message of the day, the /etc/issue file, and system news are passive communication mechanisms, i.e., you as the superuser create messages to be seen at a later time as users log in. A more immediate method is required when you are logged in and need to communicate immediately with other logged-in users. There are three commands that provide this kind of immediate communication.

The talk(1) program allows you to have a two-way conversation with another user. In its simplest form, the command is:

```
# talk username
```

where username is the account name of the user you wish to talk to. If the target user is logged in, the screen of the user who initiates the talk session displays a split-screen talk interface with the following status line:

```
[Waiting for your party to respond]
```

and the target user will see the following invitation:

```
Message from Talk_Daemon@pluto at 19:17 ...
talk: connection requested by root@pluto.
talk: respond with: talk root@pluto
```

If the target user chooses to accept the invitation and join the talk session, all the user needs to do is respond with the suggested command:

```
$ talk root@pluto
```

At this point, the target user's screen also displays the same split-screen talk interface, and the two users are now connected. Whatever each user types (including typos and backspaces) in the top half of this display is simultaneously displayed on the bottom half of the other user's screen. If either user's screen becomes disrupted, say by additional talk invitations, pressing Ctrl-L will refresh the screen. Finally, either user can end the talk session by pressing either the interrupt key sequence, which is usually Ctrl-C, or the end-of-file key sequence, typically Ctrl-D.

If the target user is logged on more than once, there is an additional command line argument to talk, tty-name, to specify which tty the initiating user would like to send the talk invitation to. To determine which tty you need, issue the who(1) command, and the second column of the output specifies the tty for each login session. For example:

```
# who
root     console    Jun 6 09:34
mcheek    ttyp4     Jun 6 15:45 <- This session is the most recent
mcheek    ttyp3     Jun 3 09:35
mcheek    ttyp1     Jun 3 09:35
# talk mcheek ttyp4
```

write(1) is similar to talk in that it is directed to only one active user account. The difference is that write is only one-way rather than interactive. The syntax of write is similar to talk:

```
# write username [tty-name]
```

After issuing the write command, any text you type is immediately displayed on the target user's screen, one line at a time, preceded with an identifying header, regardless of what they are doing or which application they are currently running. Since each line is not sent until a carriage return is entered, keep lines short if a multi-line message is being sent. This avoids frustrating the target user with long delays between lines of the message. Sending continues until the sending user enters the end-of-file key sequence, usually Ctrl-D.

write should be used sparingly, as users will become annoyed if uninvited messages or talk invitations are constantly appearing on their screens, possibly disrupting their work. UNIX even provides a command that users can use to block incoming talks or writes: the mesg(1) command. By default, incoming talk requests and writes are enabled. The mesg command acts as a toggle to enable or disable them. The "n" argument blocks incoming communications:

```
$ mesg n
```

When a user has blocked incoming messages in this manner, other users attempting to talk or write to that user receive the following error message:

```
[Your party is refusing messages]
```

Similarly, "mesg y" enables incoming talks and writes, and issuing the mesg command with no arguments reports the current message permission setting (yes or no.) The superuser account (root) can issue talk invitations and send write messages to any terminal regardless of the user's mesg setting.

wall(1) is nearly identical to write, with one important exception: the text is sent to *all* logged-in users. Running wall with no command line arguments behaves like write in that any text you type, including carriage returns, is immediately displayed on all logged-in users' screens, preceded with a broadcast header, regardless of what they are doing. wall also has the ability to read from a prepared file, which can be useful for broadcasting prepared statements concerning periodic events such as system reboots. For example, to broadcast the contents of a file, issue the following command:

```
# wall /tmp/shutdown.txt
```

All logged-in users will see the following on their screen:

```
Broadcast Message from root@pluto (console) at 19:50 ...
The system will be shut down in 10 minutes to perform a cold
backup. Please save your work and log off. The system will be
available in approx. 1 hour.
```

# 6

# Security

## 6.1 Tru64 UNIX Security

This chapter describes several important aspects of Tru64 UNIX system security. As a system administrator, you are responsible for the overall security of your system, which includes both physical system security and Tru64 UNIX operating system security. By default, Tru64 UNIX is installed with a minimal security configuration, which may be sufficient for a noncritical, single-user workstation. For a system that supports a mission-critical application or is connected to the Internet, however, the default minimal security configuration may be inadequate. The purpose of this chapter is to address ways to improve system security with the goal of a more secure Tru64 UNIX system. The following topics will be covered:

- Physical security
- Resetting passwords
- Login controls
- The trusted host facility
- Enhanced security
- Auditing
- Access control lists
- Division of privileges

Prior to beginning our discussion, it is important to understand the history and implications of implementing security on a UNIX system. UNIX was originally developed in a research environment with little thought given to security. Scientists at Bell Labs created UNIX for their own use, and such facilities as passwords and file permissions were avoided. This was the origin of the belief that UNIX is an inherently insecure operating system. UNIX can be configured to be completely insecure, of course, but so can any other computer operating system. Conversely, most modern implementations of UNIX, including Tru64 UNIX, provide facilities and tools to secure the system as tightly as necessary.

## 6.2 Physical Security

The issue of physical security should be covered before moving on to operating system security. The reason for this is that, given physical access to a Tru64 UNIX system, it is possible to circumvent operating system security measures such as passwords and permissions. The physical security of a Tru64 UNIX system simply means restricting physical access to the system itself, usually by placing the computer in a secure, locked room or area. This is especially important for mission-critical systems containing important data and programs. The console or console port of a system should also be secured. This, of course, precludes connecting a modem to the console port and allowing unrestricted dial-in access to the console. A secure computer room or data center with secure power feeds and climate controls is ideal, but a locked office or closet is usually adequate.

The two vulnerabilities of a physically insecure Tru64 UNIX system are:

- The ability to simply turn the system off, preventing use
- The ability to "break in" to the system as the root user

### 6.2.1 Unauthorized Power Removal

The first vulnerability is a denial-of-service type of attack. If someone turns the system off, either accidentally or intentionally, the system obviously becomes unavailable for use. Some Tru64 UNIX systems also have halt buttons on the front panel that cause the operating system to halt, leaving the system at the console prompt. The Ctrl-P key sequence on some Tru64 UNIX system consoles will also halt the system. Halting a system is as bad as removing power, for the system is no longer running Tru64 UNIX.

### 6.2.2 Unauthenticated Root Access

The second vulnerability of a physically insecure Tru64 UNIX system is the potential ability to halt and reboot the system in single-user mode. In the default security configuration, single-user mode provides a root login on the system console without prompting for a password. At this point, the system is completely compromised and an intruder can view any file, change passwords, create new accounts, or simply destroy files or data. Tru64 UNIX provides this automatic root login to allow resetting of the root password in the event that this important password is forgotten or lost. However, for systems that require more security, an optional secure console mode is available (see Section 6.2.3.)

Physically securing a Tru64 UNIX system should be the first step in developing a system security strategy. The environment, the criticality of the system, and the available physical resources are all important factors in deciding where and how to physically secure a system. Obviously, an individual desktop workstation would not be very useful locked in a computer room, and probably belongs on a user's desk. But a workstation may be impossible to secure in a cubicle environment. In this situation, the best strategy may be to ensure that critical or confidential data is stored on a physically secure remote server rather than on the workstation's local disks. This reduces the vulnerability of having an individually unsecured workstation. On the other hand, it relies on the remote file server to provide proper security safeguards.

Additional security at the Tru64 UNIX system console can be obtained by selecting the secure console mode in Tru64 UNIX and/or by setting a console password at the firmware level. This ensures that a person with access to the system console can't perform certain actions, such as booting the system into single-user mode, without entering the root password or a special console password. However, even these methods do not provide complete security, since there is ultimately a way to reset the console password, just as there is a way to reset the root password.

### 6.2.3 Secure Console Mode

By default, a Tru64 UNIX system entering single-user mode provides a root login on the system console without requiring a password. If the console is not physically secure, this obviously provides an opportunity for unauthorized root access. If you wish to prevent this possibility, Tru64 UNIX provides an optional secure console mode to help prevent such unauthorized access. When secure console mode is enabled, the system will print the message "Single user root login" and prompt for the root password whenever single-user mode is entered. The user must enter the root password to continue.

To enable secure console mode, set the environment variable SECURE_CONSOLE in /etc/rc.config to YES. The command to do this is:

```
# rcmgr set SECURE_CONSOLE YES
```

Similarly, to disable secure console mode, set the variable to NO:

```
# rcmgr set SECURE_CONSOLE NO
```

If SECURE_CONSOLE is not set in /etc/rc.config, the operating system will try to determine whether the system is in secure console mode based on the presence or absence of a console password at the firmware level (see Section 6.2.4). If the system determines that a console password has been set, it will assume that secure console mode is desired, and will prompt for the root password when it enters single-user mode.

### 6.2.4 Setting a Console Password

In addition to secure console mode, which is a capability of the Tru64 UNIX operating system, the firmware on many Compaq Alpha systems has the ability to set a separate password for console access. If such a password is set, a person with access to the console must enter this password before performing certain activities at the console, such as booting the system to single-user mode or from a device other than the default system disk.

Not all Alpha systems provide the console password feature. Consult the hardware documentation for your system to see whether it provides this feature and for details on how to activate it.

## 6.3 Resetting Passwords

A frequent request to a system administrator is to reset a user's forgotten password. Since Tru64 UNIX stores user account passwords in a one-way encrypted format, it is not possible to determine the actual password from an encrypted password string. The only option is to reset the password to a new value. This is a simple operation that requires superuser privileges. First, either become the root user via the su(1) command or log in as root. Then issue the passwd(1) command for the account you are resetting. For example, to reset the password for jsmith:

```
$ su -
# passwd jsmith
Changing password for jsmith.
New password: <enter the new password>
Retype new password: <enter it again for confirmation>
```

If no username is specified on the passwd command line, the password of the currently logged-in user is changed.

If the root password is forgotten or lost, the only recourse is to "break in" to the system and reset the root password. This requires access to the system console and the ability to halt and reboot the system to single-user mode. It is necessary to halt the system, since only the superuser can gracefully shut down the system and, in this situation, the root account is inaccessible. If the system is in secure console mode, the process of breaking in becomes more difficult. Secure console mode requires the root password when the system enters single-user mode. Since the root password is unknown, we cannot simply boot to single-user mode and change the password. In this case, it is necessary to boot from another device, such as a Tru64 UNIX Installation CD-ROM, mount the normal root filesystem, disable secure console mode, and then boot (from the regular root disk) to single-user mode.

The procedure to reset the root password is as follows:

1. Halt the system, either by pressing the HALT button or, on some system types, typing the Ctrl-P (^P) key combination from the console. This should bring the system to the console prompt, which is usually something like ">>>".
2. If the system console is secured with a password, enter the console password:

   ```
   >>> LOGIN
   ```

   Please enter the password: <enter the console password>
3. If you know that the system is not in secure console mode, proceed to step 10. If you're not sure, go ahead and proceed to step 10 anyway; if you get a password prompt when the system reaches single-user mode, you'll know that the system is in secure console mode, and you can then return to step 4.
4. Insert a Tru64 UNIX Installation CD-ROM in the CD-ROM drive and boot the system from that device. Substitute the appropriate device name for DKA400 in the following command:

   ```
   >>> BOOT DKA400
   ```
5. When the installation software starts up, exit to a shell window. If you are using a serial terminal as the console, select option 3 (Exit

Installation). If you are using a graphics console, pull down the File menu and select Shell Window.

6. Mount your root filesystem. If the root filesystem type is UFS, enter the following command (substitute the appropriate device name for dsk1a):

```
# mount /dev/disk/dsk1a /mnt
```

7. If the root filesystem type is AdvFS, you may need to create a temporary domain subdirectory and link it to the appropriate device. (If the installation process has already created the directory and device name link shown below, just skip those steps.) Again, substitute the appropriate device name for dsk1a:

```
# cd /etc/fdmns
# mkdir root_domain
# cd root_domain
# ln -s /dev/disk/dsk1a
# mount root_domain#root /mnt
```

8. Edit the rc.config file on the root filesystem and change the value of the SECURE_CONSOLE setting to NO. If there is no SECURE_CONSOLE definition in /mnt/etc/rc.config, add the following line:

```
SECURE_CONSOLE="NO"
```

9. Unmount the root filesystem and halt the system to return control to the console:

```
# cd /
# umount /mnt
# halt
```

10. Boot the system to single-user mode:

```
>>> BOOT -FL S
```

11. When the system reaches single-user mode, mount the local filesystems:

```
# /sbin/bcheckrc
```

12. Change the root password:

```
# passwd
New password: <enter the new password>
Retype new password: <enter the password again>
```

13. Resume booting the system to multi-user mode by typing "exit" or the Ctrl-D (^D) key combination.
14. Log in as root using the newly changed password to verify success.
15. If you changed the value of SECURE_CONSOLE in step 8 above, change it back to YES if you wish to continue using secure console mode.

## 6.4 Login Controls

Tru64 UNIX provides a variety of mechanisms to control login access and restrict the abilities of user accounts once they are successfully logged in. These login and account controls include the following:

- Restricting root logins to the system console
- Restricting File Transfer Protocol (FTP) access
- Specifying approved shells or command interpreters
- Restricting the ability to su(1) to root
- A restricted shell to provide an environment with limited capabilities

### 6.4.1 Restricting Root Logins

The root account on a Tru64 UNIX system is, by its very nature, a shared login account. In other words, the account may be used by multiple people. Because the root account is all-powerful, access and use of the root account should be restricted to only those individuals who are trained, knowledgeable, and, most importantly, authorized. The root account should normally be accessed by logging into the system using a user's individual user account, then using the su(1) command to "switch" to the root account. If you have more than one person with access to the root account, this allows you to track the actions performed by each privileged user. By default, Tru64 UNIX restricts direct root logins to the console, or the primary display on a system with a graphics console.

The mechanism to control direct root logins is the file /etc/securettys. This file specifies the locations from which root is permitted to log in. The default /etc/securettys file contains the following lines:

```
/dev/console
local:0
:0
```

In order to allow direct root logins from across the network (via telnet), add a line to /etc/securettys containing the string "ptys". If you have a terminal or modem connected to a serial port on the system and wish to allow direct root logins from that port, add a line containing the serial port's device name, for example, "/dev/tty00".

Unless there is a special requirement for nonconsole direct root logins, it is best to restrict root logins to the console. The root account is obviously a prime target for remote attacks, and by preventing network and non-console terminal root logins, you effectively block such attacks.

### 6.4.2 Restricting File Transfer Protocol (FTP) Access

Tru64 UNIX provides the ability to block incoming FTP connections on a per-account basis. This functionality is, by default, used to prevent remote users from logging into a system via ftp(1) as either root or the uucp account, but any system or user account can be blocked. The FTP server ftpd(8) consults the /etc/ftpusers file when authenticating inbound FTP connections. If a user account is specified in this file, that inbound connection is rejected, as the following example illustrates:

```
% ftp jupiter
Connected to jupiter.
220 jupiter FTP server (Compaq Tru64 UNIX Version 5.60) ready.
Name (jupiter:martin): root
530 User root access denied.
Login failed.
```

Accounts to be restricted are listed, one to a line, in the /etc/ftpusers file. The ftpusers file can have no white space, and account names must exactly match user account names in the /etc/passwd file. If this syntax is not adhered to, the FTP server may incorrectly parse the ftpusers file and possibly allow undesired FTP access. If the /etc/ftpusers file does not exist, no FTP security checks are done. A representative /etc/ftpusers file is:

```
root
daemon
bin
uucp
cron
adm
jsmith
```

In this example, the six listed system accounts and the regular user account jsmith are all prevented from logging in via FTP.

In general, all of the system accounts listed in /etc/passwd should be added to the /etc/ftpusers file. These accounts are rarely used interactively and should never be accessed via FTP. A common break-in strategy is to attempt to FTP into a system using a known system account, and listing these accounts in /etc/ftpusers effectively removes this vulnerability.

### 6.4.3 Specifying Approved Shells

The Tru64 UNIX FTP server (ftpd) also validates inbound FTP connections by checking whether the shell of the account being logged into is an approved shell. The shell, or command interpreter, is specified in the seventh field of the /etc/passwd file entry for each system account, and is typically the Korn shell (ksh) or C shell (csh) for interactive users. The FTP server determines if a shell is valid by consulting the /etc/shells file, which is simply a list of the acceptable shells on the system. If an account's shell is not found in the /etc/shells file, the FTP login session is rejected.

The /etc/shells file should be maintained by the system administrator and should contain, in addition to the standard system shells, any additional shells or command interpreters used on the system. For example, this /etc/shells file also lists two common public domain shells, bash and tcsh:

```
/usr/bin/sh
/usr/bin/csh
/usr/bin/ksh
/usr/bin/posix/sh
/bin/sh
/bin/csh
/bin/ksh
/usr/local/bin/bash
/usr/local/bin/tcsh
```

Note that each entry is the full path name of the shell executable, and that all possible paths for a given shell are listed. Blank lines and all characters after a pound sign (#) are ignored. When troubleshooting FTP access–denied issues, ensure that the /etc/shells file exists and that it contains all appropriate shells.

### 6.4.4 Restricting the Ability to su to Root

The su(1) command requires the password of the account being specified and, upon providing that account's password, changes to that user and invokes that user's shell. There is no restriction, other than having to provide the password, to becoming non-root users with the su command. However, su does restrict the ability to become the root user. Only users who belong to group number 0, the system group, can issue the su command to become root, even if they possess the root password.

To allow a user to become root via the su command, simply add that user to the system group. To do so, either specify the system group as one of an account's groups when creating the account, or add an existing account to the system group in the /etc/group file. For example, given the following /etc/group file, only user martin is permitted to su to root:

```
# head -1 /etc/group
system:*:0:root,martin
```

### 6.4.5 The Restricted Shell

The designers of UNIX recognized the need to occasionally create user accounts whose abilities are more controlled than those running standard shells. For this purpose, the Restricted Shell, Rsh, was created. Rsh is a derivative of the standard Bourne shell (sh), and has all the capabilities of the Bourne shell except for the following, which are not allowed:

- Changing directories with the cd command
- Setting the value of the environment variables PATH and SHELL
- Specifying pathnames or command names containing /
- Redirecting output (with > and >>)

The Restricted Shell is invoked for an account by specifying /usr/bin/Rsh as the login shell when creating the account, or by placing /usr/bin/Rsh in the last field of the /etc/passwd file entry for an existing account. Upon logging into an account running Rsh, the $HOME/.profile for that account is executed before the above restrictions are enforced. For this reason, the creator of a restricted account's $HOME/.profile has complete control concerning which commands are executed, which environment variables are set, and which directory the restricted user is left in after the login. Ideally, the final directory should not be the login directory, but rather a directory not owned by the restricted user.

Rsh is ideal for novice or risky users, because you, as the system administrator, can restrict their PATH and prevent them from running undesirable commands. Rsh is not a complete security solution, especially for technically savvy users; but for certain low-risk situations, it is a useful tool to restrict a user's activities on the system.

## 6.5 The Trusted Host Facility

UNIX has a set of commands typically referred to as the "r-commands," due to the fact that the name of each begins with the letter "r" for "remote." These commands are rlogin(1), rsh(1), and rcp(1), and are used to log in to, execute commands on, and copy files to remote hosts. For example, the following command will log in to the host pluto:

```
$ rlogin pluto
```

The rsh command is usually used to execute a command on a remote system. For instance, this command will return the process status of the remote system pluto:

```
$ rsh pluto ps -ef
```

Finally, the rcp command will copy a file from the local system to a remote system:

```
$ rcp /tmp/file.txt pluto:/tmp/file.txt
```

These r-commands will fail unless the remote host specified in each command is configured to allow these operations. This configuration, in which one system allows a second system to connect via the r-commands, is known as trusted—the first system trusts the second system. This trusted relationship must be managed carefully by the system administrator, especially if two systems in such a relationship are not managed by the same department, organization, or company. Depending on the level of trust granted, a user on one system could, either inadvertently or maliciously, compromise or damage another system that the user may not normally be able to access.

There are two mechanisms to specify trusted relationships on a Tru64 UNIX system:

- $HOME/.rhosts file(s)
- /etc/hosts.equiv file

### 6.5.1 The .rhosts File

The .rhosts file, a user-specific file located in a user's home directory, contains a list of remote hosts, and, optionally, accounts on those remote hosts, that are not challenged for a password when they execute the rcp, rlogin, or rsh commands. The permissions of a .rhosts file, if it exists, must be set to 600 (read and write by the owner only), and the file must be owned by the owner of the home directory it is located in or by the root user.

The format of the .rhosts file is:

- host [user]

where host is the name of the remote system. If the remote system is in a different domain than the local system, the fully qualified domain name must be specified.

The second field, user, is the login name of a remote user. This field is optional; if it is not specified, any user on the remote system is exempt from providing a password, and is assumed to have the same account name on both the local and remote systems. Entries in the .rhosts file are either positive or negative. A positive entry allows access, while a negative entry denies access. Negative entries are specified by prefacing either a host name or a user name with a minus sign. Positive entries are the default and have no special indicator. In addition, a plus sign (+) can be used in place of either a host name or a user name. In place of the host name, it means any remote host, and in place of the user name, it means any user on the specified host.

For example, the first entry in the following /home/styler/.rhosts file on a system named jupiter allows user jsmith on remote host pluto to log in to jupiter as user styler without providing a password. The second entry prevents user tlee on pluto from logging in to jupiter as styler, while the third entry allows any user on remote host saturn to log into jupiter as styler:

- pluto jsmith
- pluto –tlee
- saturn +

Obviously, as the last entry shows, the .rhosts file is potentially a large vulnerability. The worst entry a user can have in an .rhosts file is a single plus sign (+). This allows any user from any remote system to log in as that user without being challenged for a password. If the root user has such an .rhosts file, it is only a matter of time before this vulnerability is discovered and exploited. A system administrator responsible for systems connected to a network, and especially to the Internet, must be diligent in examining any user-created .rhosts files for such entries.

### 6.5.2 The /etc/hosts.equiv File

The second configuration file that defines trusted relationships with remote systems is /etc/hosts.equiv. This file is similar to an individual user's .rhosts file, except that /etc/hosts.equiv specifies trusted relationships for the entire system. In addition, the /etc/hosts.equiv file is checked before the local .rhosts file, and if a match is found in the hosts.equiv file, the validation ends. The syntax of the hosts.equiv file is identical to the .rhosts file, with one notable addition. By specifying the keyword "NO_PLUS" in /etc/hosts.equiv, the use of the plus character (+) to match any host or user is disallowed on a system-wide basis. Because of the security implications of users specifying a plus sign in local .rhosts files, the NO_PLUS entry should be added to the /etc/hosts.equiv file to close the vulnerability made possible by the plus sign.

In addition, when an r-command is run against the root account on a remote system, only the root account's .rhosts file, if it exists, is checked for permission. The /etc/hosts.equiv file does not apply when validating remote access to the root account.

Similar to the .rhosts file, the contents of the /etc/hosts.equiv file are critical for ensuring system security. An incorrectly placed plus sign could open up a system to unauthorized access. Carefully manage the individual entries in both the /etc/hosts.equiv file and any individual user's .rhosts file.

## 6.6 Enhanced Security

There are two levels of security in Tru64 UNIX: Base security and Enhanced security. Base security is the default security level when installing Tru64 UNIX and is distinguished by traditional UNIX passwords. Enhanced security provides "shadow" passwords and a rich set of password and login controls. Enhanced security is frequently called C2 security, because its capabilities allow a system to be configured to the C2 security level defined by the U.S. Computer Security Center's "Orange Book." When running Enhanced security, the available password controls include configurable password length, both minimum and maximum; password usage history; and many other features. The login controls include per-terminal settings for delays between consecutive successful or failed login attempts, the ability to retire or lock accounts, and logging of successful logins and unsuccessful login attempts.

Shadow passwords are encrypted user passwords that are stored in a location inaccessible to unprivileged users. In a standard UNIX system, the encrypted passwords are stored in the default password file, /etc/passwd, which must be world-readable for certain system utilities to function properly. Although the encrypted passwords are one-way encrypted (it's not possible to determine the original password by decrypting the encrypted password string), having them readable by any user makes them vulnerable to so-called "crack" attacks. Such attacks involve encrypting every word in the dictionary, along with other plausible passwords, and comparing each resulting string to a user's encrypted password. If the encrypted strings match, the original password is revealed.

Although this is somewhat of a brute-force approach, the speed of modern computers makes it eminently practical. One way to defend against crack attacks is to ensure that user passwords do not include words from the dictionary or other plausible strings, such as variations on the user's name, or to require that passwords include both letters and numbers, both upper and lower case, or similar restrictions. Enhanced security provides ways to enforce such password restrictions. Shadow passwords provide a different line of defense against crack attacks by the simple method of removing the encrypted passwords from /etc/passwd and placing them in an inaccessible location.

Historically, Tru64 UNIX systems have typically been configured to use Base security. In part, this is due to the perceived complexity of Enhanced security, particularly in older versions of the operating system, as well as the fact that Base security is the default level on a newly installed system. Running Enhanced security can be more complex than Base security from a system administration viewpoint, but Enhanced security provides so many useful capabilities that the additional effort is worthwhile. Managing Enhanced security has become progressively easier in successive versions of Tru64 UNIX. In particular, starting with version 5, it is possible to quickly and easily enable shadow passwords without having to configure any other Enhanced security features.

There is also a perception among some administrators that Enhanced security degrades the performance of a Tru64 UNIX system. The only area in which performance can be significantly affected has to do with the recording of successful login times and unsuccessful login attempts for each user and each terminal. If many users are constantly logging in and out (for example, in a large university system with thousands of student users), the recording of login information creates a bottleneck on the files where the information is recorded. If performance is more of a concern than recording login information, this feature can be partially or completely disabled (see Section 6.6.1.3). When it is disabled, Enhanced security should have no significant impact on system performance.

If you have multiple systems in a TruCluster configuration, all systems must be at the same security level. If you are planning to use Enhanced security in a version 5 cluster, it is easiest to configure Enhanced security on the initial cluster member, before the cluster is actually created. When the cluster is created and additional members are added, the Enhanced security configuration will be automatically copied to the new members. If you have an existing cluster running Base security, it is still possible to convert it to Enhanced security; however, this is somewhat trickier and requires that each cluster member be rebooted.

If you are distributing passwords with the Network Information Service (NIS), you must take extra care in configuring Enhanced security. The interaction between NIS and Enhanced security can be tricky to set up and manage. Consult the Tru64 UNIX Security Manual for details on configuring and managing Enhanced security in an NIS environment.

### 6.6.1 Enabling Enhanced Security

The first step in successfully implementing Enhanced security is deciding on the global defaults for the password and login controls. Some of these can be configured during the process of enabling Enhanced security (Section 6.6.1.3), while others can be customized later by editing the system authentication database (see Section 6.6.3).

Once reasonable values have been selected for the system defaults, the process of enabling Enhanced security can begin. The steps are:

1. Log in as root.
2. Install the Enhanced security subsets, if not already installed.
3. Run the secconfig(8) utility to select the Enhanced security level and configure its features.
4. Reboot the system.

5. Test your applications.

In order to enable Enhanced security, you must have the ability and opportunity to reboot your system(s). Coordinate a time that is convenient with your users so as not to disrupt their work. The subsections that follow present detailed instructions for enabling Enhanced security.

#### 6.6.1.1 Log in as Root

This process can be done from either the system console logged in directly as root, or logged in from a terminal or across the network as a regular, non-privileged user who has become the root user via the su(1) command. Before proceeding, check the system's current security level with the following command:

```
# /usr/sbin/rcmgr get SECURITY
```

If the string "BASE" or no output is returned, you are running Base security and can proceed to enable Enhanced security. If, however, the string "ENHANCED" is returned, Enhanced security is already enabled. In this case, you can modify the current security configuration by running the secconfig utility and making the appropriate choices.

#### 6.6.1.2 Install the Enhanced Security Subsets

Before you can enable Enhanced security, two Enhanced security Software Subsets must be loaded. These subsets are named OSFC2SECxxx and OSFXC2SECxxx. (The "xxx" specifies a numeric subset version corresponding to your version of the operating system; for Tru64 UNIX V5.1, this value is 510.) To determine if these subsets are already installed, run the following command:

```
# /usr/sbin/setld -i | grep -i c2
OSFC2SEC510  installed  C2-Security (System Administration)
OSFXC2SEC510 installed  C2-Security GUI (System Administration)
```

In this example, both subsets are installed. If you do not receive any output, or if the "installed" keyword in the second column is absent, you must install the subsets from the operating system installation media. For assistance in installing Tru64 UNIX subsets, see Chapter 4, "System Configuration."

#### 6.6.1.3 Run the secconfig Utility

The secconfig(8) utility, which replaces the secsetup utility used in earlier versions of Tru64 UNIX, is used to set the system security level and configuration. To run secconfig, enter "sysman secconfig". The security configuration GUI will start up and ask you to select either BASE or ENHANCED security. Select ENHANCED and click the Next button.

After selecting ENHANCED security, you will be asked to select one of three options:

- SHADOW
- UPGRADE
- CUSTOM

SHADOW enables shadow passwords, but does not configure any of the login or password controls available in Enhanced security. This option is available for system administrators who desire to protect their users' passwords from a password-cracking attack, but don't want any of the extra features provided by Enhanced security.

UPGRADE is used only during a rolling migration of a TruCluster from Base to Enhanced security. After all members have been rebooted, SHADOW or CUSTOM must be selected.

CUSTOM sets standard default values for certain Enhanced security features and allows you to customize all of its features to your desired values. The standard defaults set by CUSTOM are as follows:

- Logging of successful logins and unsuccessful login attempts is enabled.
- Null passwords are not allowed.
- Password expiration time is set to 6 months.
- Password lifetime is set to 1 year.

When CUSTOM is selected, secconfig brings up a screen (Figure 6.1) that allows you to customize some of the most commonly used Enhanced security features. Additional features may be customized by editing the authentication database; see Section 6.6.3 for details.

Password expiration is the maximum time that can occur between password changes. A user who fails to change his password in this amount of time is forced to change it on the next login. Password lifetime is slightly different; if a user fails to change his password in this amount of time, the account is

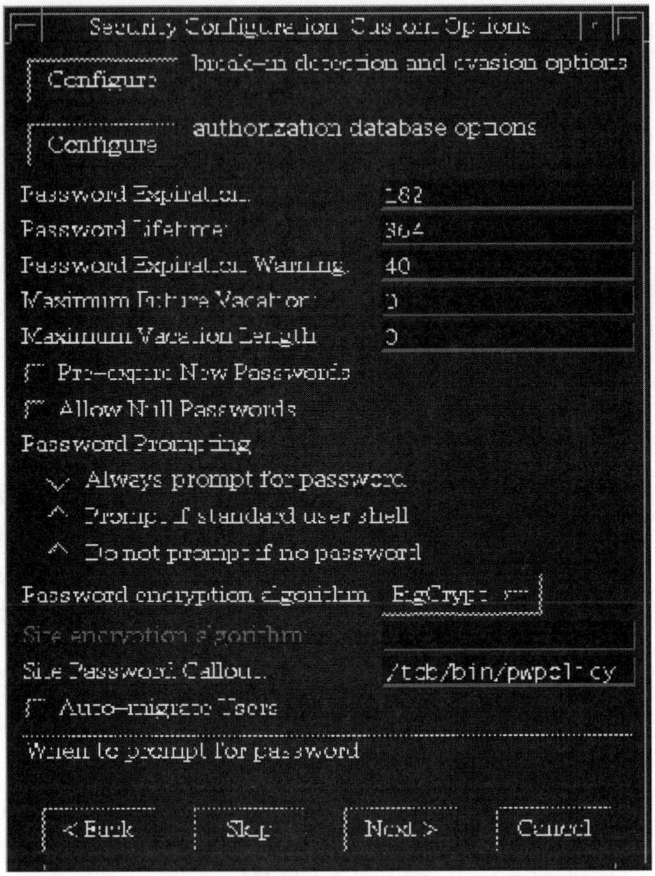

**Figure 6.1** *Configuring Enhanced security options.*

automatically disabled, and must be re-enabled by the superuser. Password lifetime should always be greater than or equal to password expiration time.

Selecting the first Configure button (break-in detection and evasion options) brings up an additional menu that lets you selectively enable or disable the logging of the following:

- Successful and unsuccessful logins on each terminal device
- Successful logins for each user
- Unsuccessful login attempts for each user

Disabling some or all of these options may improve performance on a system with a large number of interactive users. However, disabling them will also disable the system's ability to automatically detect and evade break-in attempts.

The site password callout is a program or script that checks possible passwords for conformance to site-specific security policies. You can write your own program and specify its full pathname here, or modify the system-provided script, /tcb/bin/pwpolicy. See the acceptable_password(3) man page for more information on this topic.

Next, secconfig will offer you a menu to enable or disable the following system configuration options. These choices are available in both Base and Enhanced security, so this menu is presented regardless of the security level that you chose earlier.

- Segment sharing
- Execute bit set only by root
- Enable Access Control Lists (ACLs)

Segment sharing is enabled by default, and you should leave it enabled unless you have special requirements. See the Tru64 UNIX Security manual for information on this option. ACLs are also enabled by default; they are discussed in more detail in Section 6.8. The middle option is disabled by default. When this option is enabled, ordinary users may not set any of the execute permission bits on any file, even files they own. This minimizes the likelihood of a deceptive program such as a "Trojan horse" being introduced to the system.

Next, you have an opportunity to set a new root password. It's a good idea to do this if you're changing from Base to Enhanced or vice versa; this helps ensure that you will still be able to log in after rebooting at the new security level. If you're just using secconfig to change some of the custom security parameters or options, without changing the security level, there is no need to change the root password.

#### 6.6.1.4 Reboot the System to Enable Enhanced Security

The system must be rebooted to make the new security level take effect. The simplest way to accomplish this is:

```
# /sbin/shutdown -r +2 "Enabling Enhanced Security."
```

This shuts down and reboots the system with two minutes grace time and displays an informative message to all logged-in users.

#### 6.6.1.5 Test Your Applications

At this point, your system is running Enhanced security, and you should conduct whatever testing of your applications is deemed appropriate before declaring success. In addition, there is an issue related to passwords on newly enabled Enhanced security systems that bears mentioning. In Base security, the maximum password length is eight characters, but if a user attempts to use a longer password string, the system simply truncates it to eight characters without an error message. As such, users may believe their passwords are longer than eight characters, but the system is actually encrypting only the first eight. When Enhanced security is enabled and the user attempts to use the longer password, only the first eight characters will be accepted as the valid password. For example, if the user was used to entering "toogood2be" for a password, the user must enter only "toogood2" (the first eight characters) to successfully log in. This anomaly is an issue only until the user changes the password under Enhanced security, at which point the global password control defaults (or user defaults if different) dictate the password length. Ensure that your users are aware of this password issue prior to logging into the system at the Enhanced security level.

### 6.6.2 Disabling Enhanced Security

If you decide to disable Enhanced security and return to Base security, the steps are:

1. Log in as root.
2. Run the secconfig utility to select the BASE security level.
3. Reboot the system.

This will quickly revert the system back to Base security and copy the encrypted passwords from the authentication database into the /etc/passwd file. Rebooting the system completes the process. This will leave all of the Enhanced security files in place if you decide to re-enable Enhanced security at a future date.

### 6.6.3 The Authentication Database

Tru64 UNIX Enhanced security stores all security information in a set of five databases that are collectively known as the authentication database. The five component databases, and the types of information they contain, are shown in Table 6.1.

**Table 6.1** *Components of the Enhanced Security Authentication Database*

| Database Name | File Name | Field prefix |
|---|---|---|
| Protected Password | /tcb/files/auth.db and /var/tcb/files/auth.db | u_ |
| Terminal Control | /etc/auth/system/ttys.db | t_ |
| System Default | /etc/auth/system/default | d_ for system-wide defaults; t_, u_, and v_ may also appear |
| Device Assignment | /etc/auth/system/devassign | v_ |
| File Control | /etc/auth/system/files | f_ |

Each component database contains a set of entries; for example, the protected password database contains one entry for each user account on the system. Each entry consists of an entry name, followed by a set of one or more fields, followed by the field "chkent," which indicates the end of the entry. The fields are separated, and the chkent field is terminated, by a colon. Fields can be strings, integers, or Boolean values. A string field has the form "field_name=value". Integer fields have the form "field_name#value". Boolean fields have the form "field_name" if they have a true value, and "field_name@" if they have a false value; in other words, the "@" at the end of the field acts as a negation operator. It is not mandatory for every possible field to be present in every entry. When a particular field is not specified in an individual entry, the corresponding field value from the system defaults database is used for that entry.

Many of the authentication database fields indicate time values, either a duration (e.g., password lifetime) or an absolute time (e.g., time of last successful login). All time values are represented in seconds. For an absolute time, the value is the number of seconds since the standard UNIX time epoch, which is the beginning of the year 1970. The value zero has a special meaning in many of the integer fields, generally indicating an infinite value or a check that will not be performed. For example, the field "u_exp#0" indicates that the password expiration time is infinite (i.e., the password will never expire).

A typical protected password database entry for user "test1" looks like this:

```
test1:u_name=test1:u_id#200:u_pwd=L3Nx804.OGaQo:
  u_succhg#982007788:\
:u_pwdict=1BES4y3QfDW62:u_oldcrypt#2:u_suclog#982009033:
  u_suctty=INET#robot.alf.dec.com:\
:u_unsuctty=\:0:u_unsuclog#982008362:u_lock@:chkent:
```

The backslash characters at the end of the first two lines indicate that the entry is continued onto the following lines. The continuation lines must be indented by a single tab character.

Table 6.2 shows a set of some of the more useful field definitions in the authentication database. For a complete list of possible fields, see the authcap(4), prpasswd(4), ttys(4), default(4), devassign(4), and files(4) reference pages.

**Table 6.2** *Selected Authentication Database Fields*

| Field Name | Type | Value |
|---|---|---|
| d_admin_preexpire_psw | Boolean | Passwords set by the superuser must be changed the first time a user logs in. |
| d_pw_expire_warning | Integer (duration) | Time before password expiration during which to warn user of impending expiration |
| d_skip_fail_login_log | Boolean | Logging of login failures for each user is disabled. Setting this and the following two fields may improve login performance. |
| d_skip_success_login_log | Boolean | Logging of successful logins for each user is disabled. |
| d_skip_ttys_updates | Boolean | Logging of logins per terminal is disabled. |
| t_devname | String | Terminal device name |
| t_failures | Integer | Number of consecutive login failures from this terminal |
| t_lock | Boolean | Terminal is locked by administrator |
| t_login_timeout | Integer (duration) | Maximum time for a login attempt to be completed |
| t_logindelay | Integer (duration) | Minimum time allowed between login attempts |
| t_logtime | Integer (absolute time) | Time of last successful login from this terminal |
| t_maxtries | Integer | Number of consecutive login failures allowed before terminal is disabled |

**Table 6.2** *(continued)*

| Field Name | Type | Value |
|---|---|---|
| t_uid | Integer | UID of last user to successfully log in from this terminal |
| t_unsuctime | Integer (absolute time) | Time of last unsuccessful login attempt from this terminal |
| t_unsucuid | Integer | UID of last user to unsuccessfully log in from this terminal |
| u_exp | Integer (duration) | Password expiration time; after this time, password must be changed at next login |
| u_expdate | Integer (absolute time) | Account expiration time; when this date is reached, the account is automatically retired. |
| u_life | Integer (duration) | Password lifetime; if password not changed in this time, account is disabled. |
| u_lock | Boolean | Account is locked by administrator |
| u_max_login_intvl | Integer (duration) | Maximum login interval; if no login during this time, account is disabled. |
| u_maxchosen | Integer | Maximum length of user-chosen passwords |
| u_maxlen | Integer | Maximum length of system-generated passwords |
| u_maxtries | Integer | Number of consecutive unsuccessful login attempts that will disable the account |
| u_minchg | Integer (duration) | Minimum time between password changes |
| u_minchosen | Integer | Minimum length of user-chosen passwords |
| u_minlen | Integer | Minimum length of system-generated passwords |
| u_numunsuclog | Integer | Number of consecutive unsuccessful login attempts |
| u_pickpw | Boolean | User may choose own password. |
| u_psw_change_reqd | Boolean | Password change required at next login |
| u_pwd | String | Encrypted password string |
| u_pwdepth | Integer | Number of previous passwords to retain to prevent reuse |
| u_pwdict | List of comma-separated strings | Old encrypted passwords to be checked for password reuse |
| u_restrict | Boolean | Perform triviality checks on user-chosen passwords. |

**Table 6.2** *(continued)*

| Field Name | Type | Value |
|---|---|---|
| u_retired | Boolean | Account is retired |
| u_succhg | Integer (absolute time) | Time of last successful password change |
| u_suclog | Integer (absolute time) | Time of last successful login |
| u_suctty | String | Terminal or host from which last successful login occurred |
| u_unlock | Integer (duration) | Time period that disabled accounts will be locked out |
| u_unsuclog | Integer (absolute time) | Time of last unsuccessful login attempt |

The authentication database can be manipulated manually via the edauth(8) program. An entry in any of the component databases can be viewed, edited, or removed using the edauth command. For example, the following command displays the protected password entry for the root account:

```
# edauth -g root
```

To edit the entry for the root account:

```
# edauth root
```

This second command invokes the editor specified by the EDITOR environment variable, or /usr/bin/ex by default, with the protected password entry for the specified account.

Another useful command is authck(8), which checks the integrity and consistency of the authentication database. If you encounter difficulties with your Enhanced security configuration, one of the first actions you should take is to run authck to see if there are any problems with the authentication database. If so, you can repair the problems using edauth.

### 6.6.4 Account Management

One of the primary responsibilities of a UNIX system administrator is user account management. This includes account creation, modification, and removal. Unlike earlier versions of Tru64 UNIX, version 5 uses a common set of account management tools for both Base and Enhanced security. The primary tool is the CDE Account Manager GUI, dxaccounts. Account management can also be performed using the SysMan Accounts menu, or command-line utilities such as useradd, userdel, and usermod. The command-line utilities are sometimes necessary due to an inability to run X Window System applications, or in non-interactive situations such as site-specific scripts to automate the addition of user accounts. See Chapter 5, "User Accounts," for details on account and group creation, deletion, and modification in both Base and Enhanced security.

The Account Manager is also used to edit the new user account template, which specifies the default account parameters used when a new account is created. These default parameters, which can be overridden on a per-account basis, include password length, account expiration date, time-of-day restrictions, and so on. These parameters are stored in the authentication database and can be modified by the superuser using the methods discussed above.

The Account Manager has several functions that are specific to Enhanced security:

- Locking and unlocking accounts
- Re-enabling disabled accounts
- Retiring accounts

Locking a user account is an administrative function. The superuser explicitly locks the account so that it cannot be used until it is unlocked by the superuser. This might be done if a user is on a leave of absence, suspected of improper activity, or for any other reason requiring the account to be temporarily unusable. The Account Manager displays a small lock symbol next to the name of a locked account.

A disabled account is slightly different from a locked account. Locking is an explicit action on the part of the superuser, but disabling occurs automatically when a user violates one of the thresholds specified in the login controls (for example, too many consecutive unsuccessful login attempts.) A locked account can't be used until it is explicitly re-enabled by the superuser. Disabled accounts can be re-enabled by the superuser, but they will also automatically unlock after a period of time determined by parameter u_unlock. For example, if a user account is disabled due to excessive login failures, and the account has a u_unlock value of 86400 (the number of seconds in one day), then the account is disabled for 24 hours; the user will not be able to log in during that interval, even with the correct password. After 24 hours, the user will have another chance to try and log in—but if he fails again, it will be a further 24 hours before he can try again.

Beginning with Tru64 UNIX version 5.1, the Account Manager indicates disabled accounts with a new symbol: a white X on a red circle. (In earlier versions, disabled accounts were indicated by a lock symbol, making it impossible to distinguish between locked and disabled accounts.)

Retiring a user account, rather than simply deleting the account, is a requirement of C2 security. Prior to version 5.1, the Account Manager could not simply delete an account from a system with Enhanced security. (In V5.1 and up, however, it can delete accounts.) Retiring an account locks the account permanently, preventing reuse of that account's user ID. A retired account is indicated by the international "No" symbol (a red circle crossed by a diagonal line), and cannot be re-enabled by the Account Manager. You can "unretire" an account by manually editing the user's protected password entry and removing the "u_retired" or "u_retired@" field. The following command line unretires the account for user fred, using sed to remove the key field:

```
# edauth -g fred | sed 's/:u_retired@\{0,1\}:/:/' | edauth -s
```

Figure 6.2 shows the Account Manager view of user accounts. Account "novatest" has been retired (the red "No" symbol may be difficult to distinguish in the figure.) Account "test1" has been disabled due to login failure; this is indicated by the X-in-circle symbol. The lock symbol next to "wnn" indicates that this account has been deliberately locked by the superuser.

Existing account security characteristics can be viewed and changed via the Modify User Accounts dialog box of the Account Manager. You can spec-

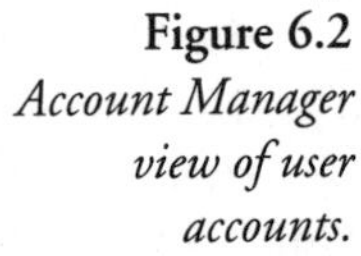

**Figure 6.2** *Account Manager view of user accounts.*

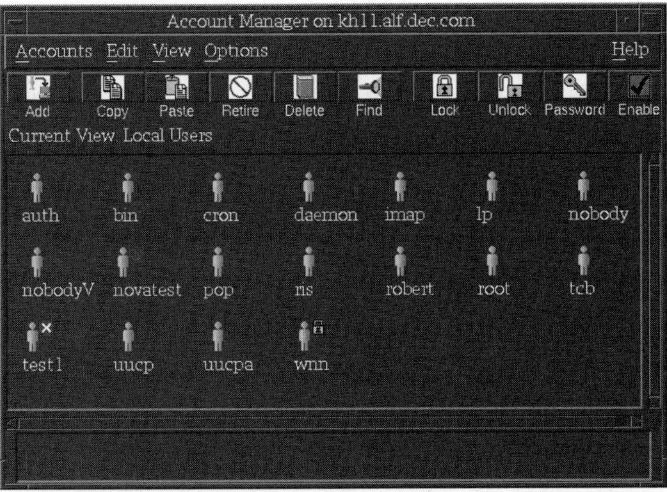

ify the groups that the account belongs to, its login control parameters, and its password length and aging parameters. These parameters are stored in the authentication database.

### 6.6.5 Security Logging

One unique feature of Tru64 UNIX is a consolidated security authentication mechanism called the Security Integration Architecture (SIA). This SIA layer isolates the security-related commands such as login, su, and passwd from the specific security mechanisms, which include, in addition to Base and Enhanced security, optional products such as the Distributed Computing Environment (DCE). You do not need to be concerned with this SIA layer unless you wish to take advantage of the centralized logging that it provides via the sialog file. This log will record all security events, including the success and failure results of logins, password changes, and su(1) commands. To enable the sialog, simply create the log file:

```
# touch /var/adm/sialog
```

and the SIA will start writing to this log. The recommended permissions for the sialog are 600. As a general rule, you should prevent non-privileged users from viewing the contents of security logs such as the sialog. An excerpt from the sialog shows the types of events recorded:

```
SIA:ERROR Wed Feb 14 15:12:13 2001
Failure on authentication for su from martin to root
SIA:EVENT Wed Feb 14 15:12:17 2001
Successful authentication for su from martin to root
SIA:EVENT Wed Feb 14 15:12:17 2001
Successful launching of session
```

Because this log will continue to grow without bounds, it must be manually truncated periodically. To stop logging of SIA events, remove the sialog file. Since the SIA is part of the Tru64 UNIX operating system, the sialog can be used whether the security level is Base or Enhanced.

### 6.6.6 Application Issues

As the system administrator, you will usually be responsible for installation and configuration of Commercial Off The Shelf (COTS) software. Prior to enabling Enhanced security, you must ensure that any applications currently installed are compatible with Enhanced security. If an application that relied on the system for user authentication, such as a database or security tool, were not aware of Enhanced security, user authentication into the application would most likely fail. In the event that the application vendor does not know if enabling Enhanced security will affect its product, proceed slowly with implementing Enhanced security, and test the application as much as possible prior to going into production.

An additional responsibility you may have is to support software development efforts, both in-house and commercial applications. Coordinate the implementation of Enhanced security with any software developers you support on your system(s). The Compaq Tru64 UNIX Security manual includes a "Programmer's Guide to Security" section that details programming techniques and provides coding examples that would be invaluable to your development staff.

As you can see, successfully implementing Enhanced security requires a thorough knowledge of your environment and requirements, careful planning, and a significant amount of ongoing administrative responsibility, both in account management and general system maintenance. However, the benefits of Enhanced security, such as comprehensive auditing of security events and more robust identification and authentication features, far outweigh the possible disadvantages of the Enhanced security level.

## 6.7 Auditing

Tru64 UNIX provides the ability to audit all events that occur on the system. Every activity that occurs on the system can generate an "audit record" that describes what the activity was, when it occurred, who caused it, and other information. As system administrator, you decide which activities will generate audit records. This is a powerful tool to monitor activity on your system. Auditing can help you to:

- Detect security violations, such as system break-ins or break-in attempts.
- Assess the damage and restore system integrity if a break-in does occur.
- Discourage attempts to violate security (for fear of being detected).
- Evaluate and debug application software.
- Troubleshoot, in some cases, system or application performance problems.

Auditing may be used in both Base security and Enhanced security mode. You can audit individual system calls and trusted events (logins, logouts, and events that affect the audit subsystem itself). You can also define your own audit events.

Managing the auditing capability consists of the following tasks:

- Configuring the audit subsystem
- Selecting activities to be audited
- Producing audit reports
- Managing disk space used by auditing
- Archiving audit logs

The audit subsystem is configured by the auditconfig utility (sysman auditconfig). Other audit management tasks are performed via the Audit Manager (dxaudit), which is available from the Daily Administration subset of the CDE System Applications menu.

The auditconfig utility provides several basic auditing profiles that are appropriate for different types of systems. These are shown in Table 6.3. You can also customize your audit configuration exactly as needed for your system, down to the level of specific system calls to be audited. For details on customizing the audit subsystem, consult the Tru64 UNIX Security Manual.

## 6.8 Access Control Lists

The traditional UNIX file permission scheme allows the owner of a file to specify three types of access (read, write, and execute) for three classes of users: the file owner, members of the file's group, and all other users. This scheme is somewhat limited in scope, and there is often a need for more granularity in

**Table 6.3** *Basic Auditing Profiles*

| Auditing Profile | Appropriate System Type |
|---|---|
| Desktop | Single-user workstation |
| NIS Server | NIS server |
| Networked System | Networked workstation |
| Server | Server for network-based applications |
| Timesharing | System with multiple interactive users |
| Timesharing_extended_audit | Extended auditing for timesharing system |

granting file access to particular users or groups. Access Control Lists (ACLs) allow the file owner to define access for the three classes of users described above, but also allow access to be individually granted or denied to specific users or groups.

ACLs can be enabled or disabled dynamically on a Tru64 UNIX system, and are independent of other security options. It is not necessary to be at the Enhanced security level in order to enable ACLs. In version 5 of Tru64 UNIX, ACLs are enabled by kernel parameter acl_mode, which is part of the sec (security) subsystem. Use the sysconfig command to determine whether ACLs are enabled:

```
# sysconfig -q sec acl_mode
acl_mode = enable
```

There are three ways to enable or disable ACLs:

1. Change the parameter value in /etc/sysconfigtab by using the sysconfigdb utility. Then reboot the system.
2. Run the secconfig utility and select or deselect the "Enable Access Control Lists (ACLs)" option (see Section 6.6.1.3).
3. Because acl_mode is a dynamic kernel parameter, you can change it on a running system with the sysconfig utility. However, the change will last only until the next system reboot unless you use one of the other two methods as well. The command to enable ACLs in this manner is:

```
# sysconfig -r sec acl_mode=enable
```

The output of ls(1) provides no information about a file's ACL, even such basic information as whether or not the file has one! To see whether a file has an ACL, you must use the getacl(1) command. To add, remove, or change an ACL, use the setacl(1) command. In addition, the dxsetacl utility provides a GUI to view and change ACLs. dxsetacl can be invoked from the command line (/usr/bin/X11/dxsetacl) or from the CDE Application Manager Menu.

An ACL consists of a number of access control entries, each of which consists of three colon-separated fields:

- The entry type (user, group, or other)
- A user or group name or numeric UID, or a null field

- A permission specification, similar to the permission bits displayed by ls(1)

A user entry without a name or UID defines the access permissions of the user who owns the file. This is always identical to the user permission bits displayed by "ls –l". Every ACL must contain one (and only one) such entry. Similarly, a user entry containing a name or UID defines the access permissions of the specified user; an ACL may contain zero or more such entries.

Group entries are similar to user entries. There must be exactly one group entry without a name or ID field; this defines the access permissions for members of the group that owns the file, and is identical to the group permission bits displayed by "ls –l". An ACL may also contain zero or more group entries that contain a group name or GID. These entries define the access permissions for members of those groups.

Finally, each ACL must contain exactly one "other" entry, which always has a null second field. This entry defines the permissions for all users not included in any of the other entries in the ACL. It is identical to the "other" permission bits displayed by "ls –l".

A typical ACL looks like this:

```
# file: test
# owner: martin
# group: system
#
user::rw-
user:steve:rw-
user:joe:--
group::r–
group:staff:r–
other::--
```

In this example, the file owner (martin) has read and write access; user steve also has rw access; and user joe has no access to the file. The owning group (system) has read access only, the "staff" group also has read access, and all other users have no access to the file. The output of "ls –l" for this file would show the permission bits as "-rw-r– – – – –". This is reflected in the "user::", "group::", and "other::" entries.

What happens if a user is defined in more than one access entry? In the above example, suppose that user joe is in the staff group. The staff group has read access, but the entry for user joe denies all access. In such a case, a user entry takes precedence over a group entry, so user joe would be denied all access. Another possibility is that a user is a member of multiple groups that have entries defining different access permissions. In this case, the user is granted the union of all of the applicable group permissions. For example, if the entry for group staff was "– – x", a user who belongs to both the staff and system groups would have read *and* execute permission on the file: read from the owning group (system) entry, and execute from the staff group entry.

Regular files may have only one ACL, which defines access to the file. A directory may have up to three ACLs: an access ACL, a default access ACL, and a default directory ACL. The access ACL defines access permissions to the directory, as we have already discussed. The default access ACL is inherited by newly created files in the directory; that is, new files receive an access ACL that is identical to the default access ACL. Similarly, the default directory ACL is inherited by newly created subdirectories. For more details on ACL inheritance, see the acl(4) man page or the Tru64 UNIX Security manual.

In order for ACLs to be effective on NFS filesystems, ACLs must be enabled on both the NFS server and clients. In addition, the NFS server must run the property list daemon, proplistd, and NFS clients must mount the filesystem with the proplist option. The client's /etc/fstab entry for such a filesystem would contain proplist in the options field, for example:

```
students:/home /nfs_home nfs rw,proplist 0 0
```

## 6.9 Division of Privileges

By default, UNIX has an "all or nothing" view of privileged accounts. The root account is all-powerful, while other accounts have no special privileges. This scheme fails to consider the usefulness of accounts that have a few specific privileges, but not the universal privileges of the root account. For example, it may be desirable to create an operator account able to backup and restore files, shutdown the system for maintenance, or similar functions. The traditional UNIX privilege model provides no easy way to accomplish this.

Prior to version 5, Tru64 UNIX had no mechanism for division of privileges, although there were outside products that could perform this function, such as the open source program "sudo." Version 5.0 introduced the Division of Privilege utility, dop(8). This utility allows the superuser to assign privileges to perform system administration tasks (or classes of tasks) to specific users or groups. These users are able to perform the specified task without knowing the root password, which would otherwise be required.

Tru64 UNIX provides a number of useful privileges (see Table 6.4). These privileges enable specified users to perform one or more related tasks. For example, the Security privilege allows a user to change the system security level, configure the audit environment, and use the dop utility to grant privileges to other users. In addition to the predefined privileges, it is possible to define your own privileged actions.

**Table 6.4** *Division of Privileges*

| Privilege Group | Actions Allowed |
|---|---|
| SuperUsers | All privileges (root) |
| AccountManagement | Add, modify, and delete user accounts and groups |
| CDEConfiguration | Configure CDE (dtsetup) |
| ClusterConfiguration | Configure cluster-related services |
| ClusterManagement | Administer cluster-related services |
| EventConfiguration | Configure event-related services |
| EventManagement | View and monitor event-related services |
| FileManagement | Archive, restore, and copy files |
| HostManagement | Perform host management tasks (dxhosts) |
| KeyboardConfiguration | Customize keyboard settings and mapping |
| MailConfiguration | Configure mail services (sendmail, IMAP, POP) |
| MailManagement | Administer and monitor mail services |
| NetworkConfiguration | Configure networks, interfaces, routes, etc. |
| NetworkManagement | Monitor network status |
| PowerManagement | Power management tasks (dxpower) |
| PrinterConfiguration | Printer setup and configuration |
| PrinterManagement | View print queues, add/remove print jobs, etc. |
| ProcessManagement | Process management (e.g., allocate CPU resources) |
| Security | Configure and manage security, auditing, DOP |
| SoftwareManagement | Install/remove software subsets and licenses |
| StorageConfiguration | Configure disks, add/remove filesystems |
| StorageManagement | Monitor disks, mount/unmount filesystems |
| SystemManagement | Build kernel, shutdown/reboot, etc. |

There are a number of different ways to invoke the dop utility. From a shell command line, type "/usr/sbin/dop" followed by the desired command options. You can also invoke dop via the CDE Application Manager: select the Configuration folder, then click on the DOP icon to invoke dop. Finally, dop can be invoked via the SysMan menu. You can either type "sysman dopconfig" at the command line, or select Configure Division of Privileges (DOP) from the SysMan Menu security option list.

### 6.9.1 Defining a Custom Privilege

To define your own custom privileges, you must use the command line interface (/usr/sbin/dop) to do the following:

- Define the new privilege
- Define the users who have the privilege
- Define the actions allowed to the privilege

We'll describe this process by means of an example. The following paragraphs show you how to add a custom privilege named "cdusers" with the authority to mount and unmount CD-ROM disks.

First of all, if you're running a version of Tru64 UNIX older than V5.1A, you may have an error in one of dop's resource files. If so, attempting to add a privilege group will fail with the following error message:

```
couldn't compile regular expression pattern: invalid character
range
```

To fix this error:

```
# cd /usr/share/sysman/mcl
# cp doprc.mcl doprc.mcl.orig
# vi doprc.mcl
```

Search for the following:

```
[regexp — {[^]&a-zA-Z0-9._$- - - []} $newval]
```

and replace it with:

```
[regexp — {[^]&a-zA-Z0-9._$- - []} $newval]
```

That is, the sequence of three consecutive hyphens has one too many; remove one of the hyphens.

Now add the new privilege. The following command is split into two lines due to its length; the backslash at the end of the first line indicates the command is continued on the next line.

```
# sysman -cli -add row -comp doprc -group dopinfo -data \
"{cdusers} {} {} {} {Users who can mount/umount the CD-ROM}"
```

Now add a list of users to the privilege. The user names in the list should be separated by white space.

```
# sysman -cli -set values -comp doprc -group dopinfo \
-key1 cdusers -attr users="fred wilma barney"
```

Verify that the group and users have been added successfully:

```
# sysman -cli -list values -comp doprc -group dopinfo \
-key1 cdusers
Component: doprc
  Group: dopinfo
    Key: 'cdusers'
      Attribute: resource                    Value: cdusers
      Attribute: users                       Value: fred wilma
barney
      Attribute: groups                      Value:
      Attribute: catalog                     Value:
      Attribute: description                 Value: Users who can
mount/umount the CD-ROM
```

Now define the "mountcd" and "umountcd" commands belonging to the new privilege:

```
# dop -a cdusers mountcd "/sbin/mount -r /dev/disk/cdrom0c *"

# dop -a cdusers umountcd "/sbin/umount /dev/disk/cdrom0c"
Verify that the addition of the commands succeeded:
# sysman -cli -list values -comp doprc -group dopActions \
-key1 mountcd
Component: doprc
  Group: dopActions
    Key: 'mountcd'
      Attribute: action                      Value: mountcd
      Attribute: privs                       Value: cdusers
      Attribute: paths                       Value: { /sbin/mount -r
/dev/disk/cdrom0c * }

# sysman -cli -list values -comp doprc -group dopActions \
-key1 umountcd
Component: doprc
```

```
Group: dopActions
  Key: 'mountcd'
    Attribute: action                    Value: umountcd
    Attribute: privs                     Value: cdusers
    Attribute: paths                     Value: { /sbin/umount
/dev/disk/cdrom0c }
```

Now all that remains is to verify that it all works. Place a CD-ROM in the drive, and give it the acid test:

```
# dop mountcd /mnt

# df -k /mnt
# ls -l /mnt
# dop umountcd
```

# 7

# *Networking*

## 7.1 Networking

A network is a collection of computers connected by hardware and software to allow the sharing of data and resources. In order for the computers on a network to communicate, they must all speak the same language, or protocol. Today, it is a rare Tru64 UNIX system that is not a member of a network of some sort. Tru64 UNIX, like all other flavors of UNIX, supports Transmission Control Protocol/Internet Protocol (TCP/IP) networking natively, which is the networking protocol of the Internet. In addition, Tru64 UNIX also supports Compaq's DECnet, the native networking protocol of Compaq's OpenVMS operating system, though only as an extra cost option. Due to the almost universal acceptance of TCP/IP, that is the only networking protocol that will be covered. This chapter is intended as a guide to configuring and managing basic TCP/IP networking on Tru64 UNIX systems. The first part of the chapter is an introduction to the requirements of TCP/IP networking on a Tru64 UNIX system. This includes Internet Protocol (IP) addresses, subnets and subnet masks, and gateways and routing.

We will then cover the configuration process and provide examples of both the character-based setup sequence and the graphical SysMan utility available on Tru64 UNIX version 5.0 and above. Following this, the different network interfaces available on a Tru64 UNIX system will be outlined, along with any special requirements or considerations. Next, some basic network troubleshooting tips will be demonstrated. Finally, several common network services for sharing resources across a network, such as the Domain Name Service (DNS) and File Transfer Protocol (FTP), will be covered.

## 7.2 Network Configuration

There are several prerequisites to configuring TCP/IP networking on a Tru64 UNIX system. The first, of course, is that the system has a network interface and is connected to a network. Tru64 UNIX supports several different network interfaces, including Ethernet, Token Ring, Fiber Distributed Data Interface (FDDI), Asynchronous Transfer Mode (ATM), and both Serial Line Internet Protocol (SLIP) and Point-to-Point Protocol (PPP) for TCP/IP networking across serial lines, particularly dial-up modems. Since most, if not all, Tru64 UNIX systems have at least one Ethernet interface, we will use Ethernet as an example.

There are two popular Ethernet network layouts, or topologies, and the determining factor in which topology is used is the way a computer is physically connected to the network. The first, and by far the most common, is a star topology (Figure 7.1), in which each host is connected to a central hub via a direct cable. A star network is so termed because of the use of a central hub with each host radiating out on an individual spoke. This type of network is commonly referred to as a 10BaseT, a UTP (Unshielded Twisted-Pair), or simply a Twisted-Pair network and is readily identified by the distinctive RJ-45 connector on the host network interface. This RJ-45 connector looks like a jumbo U.S.-style phone jack and snaps into the jack with an audible click. The identifier "10BaseT" is an IEEE designator that includes three pieces of information. The first part, "10," indicates the media speed in megabits per second—in this case, 10 megabits per second (Mbps). The word "Base" stands for "Baseband," a type of network signaling whereby Ethernet signals are the sole signals carried across the wire. The last piece, "T," stands for "Twisted-Pair" and simply designates the cable type. A Fast Ethernet network, which is the most popular type today, an interface using twisted-pair

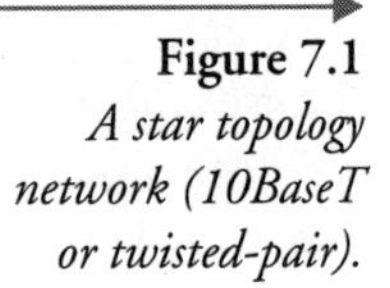

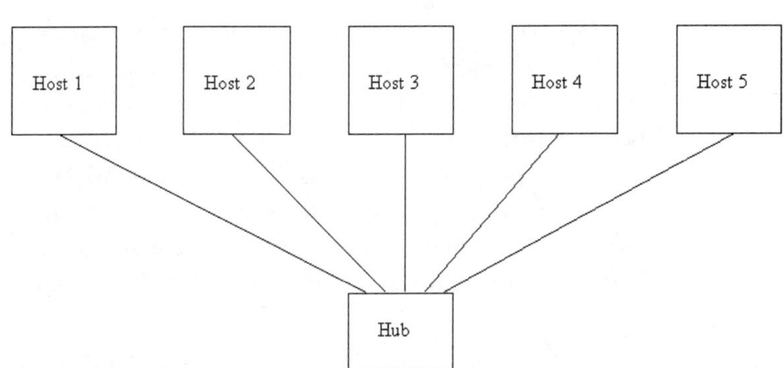


**Figure 7.1** *A star topology network (10BaseT or twisted-pair).*

cabling, would be termed "100BaseT" to indicate a media speed of 100-Mbps. A switchable regular and Fast Ethernet network interface is frequently referred to as a "10/100BaseT" card. One big advantage of a star topology network is that a cable break or cut affects only one host; the remaining hosts are not impacted. Troubleshooting a star network can be simpler since each segment, or spoke, supports only a single host. A disadvantage is the additional requirement for a hub. Ethernet hubs are available in sizes ranging from very small five-port units to large rack-mounted units with hundreds of ports.

The second type of network topology is a bus layout (Figure 7.2), in which each host is attached to a single cable, or bus, via tee connectors. This type of network is commonly referred to as a 10Base2, Thinnet, or Thin Coax network, and is characterized by the coaxial connector on the host network interface. This connector is typically termed a BNC (Bayonet Nut Coupling) and requires a tee connector for insertion into the main bus cable. The identifier "10Base2" indicates that the media speed is 10- Mbps and uses Baseband signaling. The "2" is an indicator of segment length and is rounded up from the 185 meter maximum length for individual thin coaxial segments. The main disadvantage to a bus topology network is that a single cable cut or break can disable the entire network if it occurs on the main bus cable. In addition, a bus network requires tee connectors for each host, and 50Ω terminators to be attached to each end of the coaxial segment. However, if the network is small, consisting of just a few hosts physically close to one another, a bus network may be the simplest type of network to configure. There is also a 10Base5 type of Ethernet bus topology, also known as Thick-wire Ethernet. This used to be very popular but has lost favor in recent years to the 10BaseT topology.

Once a system is properly connected to a network, the next step is to configure and enable TCP/IP networking on the system. This requires at least two and possibly three pieces of Address information:

- An IP address
- A Subnet Mask
- A Gateway Address or Default Route (optional)

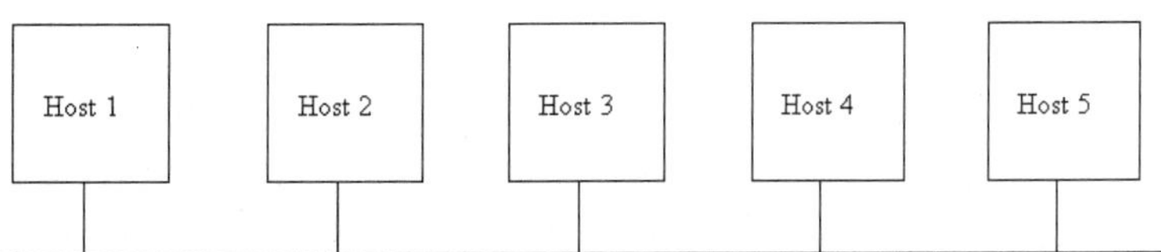


**Figure 7.2**
*A bus topology network (10Base2 or thin coax).*

## 7.3 Addressing

Every host on a network must have a unique address. This uniqueness is necessary to allow one host to contact and communicate with any other host on the network. There are actually three layers of addressing, each serving a specific purpose, and each referring to the layer below it and ultimately to a distinct network interface:

- Host name
- Internet Protocol (IP) Address
- Hardware Address

We discuss each of these in the sections that follow.

### 7.3.1 Host Name

A system's host name is simply a convenient name for use by people and programs. It is much easier to remember and use a name such as "saturn" rather then referring to a system by its IP address. A system's host name is configured at system installation time and is fairly arbitrary. Obviously, though, the networking software cannot directly use a host name when attempting to communicate with another host on the network and must translate a host name into the next lower type of address—an IP address. The mechanism that does this translation is called the Resolver, and in the simplest configuration, it consults the /etc/hosts file for the corresponding IP address for a given host name. More complex configurations can also use either the Network Information Service (NIS) or the Internet Domain Name Server (DNS), which are both network services that perform network name to IP address translation. NIS uses a local networking model that distributes a number of different system administration data to client systems, whereas the DNS is an Internet-wide distributed database of host names and their associated IP addresses. The NIS was originally developed by Sun Microsystems along with its Network File System (NFS) to maintain a single security domain among a group of local UNIX systems for the purpose of sharing files among them. Later in this chapter, the DNS implementation supported by Tru64 UNIX is discussed (see Section 7.10).

The host name is only one name that can be associated with a host on a network to which a network connection can be made. A Tru64 UNIX system can have a large number of different names and IP addresses associated with an individual network interface. These additional names associated are also known as "aliases." If an alias is properly associated to the interface on a host, then that host can accept connections from both the host name and those aliases.

### 7.3.2 IP Address

An IP address is a unique 32-bit number that is assigned to identify a particular network interface. The IP address notation is normally written as four numbers separated by periods: for example, 192.168.4.100. Each of the four period-delimited numbers, or octets, represents 8 bits of the IP address. An IP address is not arbitrary and must be selected carefully based on the network on which the computer will reside and in coordination with the other hosts on that network. An IP address is actually composed of two pieces: a Network number and a Host number. The Network number must be identical for all hosts on the same network. Consider that the Network number is like the area code of a telephone number. All phone numbers in the same geographic region have the same area code. The Host number must be unique within a network. Continuing the telephone number analogy, all telephone numbers must be unique within a given area code. As you can imagine, if this weren't the case, it would be impossible for a call to be correctly dispatched to a single individual. The phone number is nothing more than the network-addressing scheme for the global telephone network, similar to the IP address for the global Internet.

The designers of TCP/IP networking anticipated differing sized networks and partitioned the network space defined by an IP address into three main categories:

- Class A—For this type of network, the first octet of the IP address specifies the network number and the remaining three octets define the host number. There are 126 Class A networks, each able to have up to 16,777,214 hosts. Class A networks are in the range 1.0.0.0 through 126.0.0.0 (the 0.0.0.0 and 127.0.0.0 ranges are reserved). Only very large organizations or companies can justify a Class A network, and in fact, there are no longer any available Class A addresses. As an example, Compaq Computer Corporation has a Class A network.
- Class B—A Class B network uses the first two octets of the IP address to specify the network number and the remaining two octets to define the host number. There are 16,384 Class B networks, each able to have up to 65,534 hosts. Class B networks are in the range 128.1.0.0 through 191.254.0.0. Class B networks are frequently used in medium-sized companies and universities.

- Class C—A Class C network uses the first three octets of the IP address to specify the network number and the remaining octet to define the host number. There are 2,097,151 Class C networks, each able to have up to 254 hosts. Class C networks are in the range 192.0.1.0 through 223.255.254.0. Class C networks are the most common and, in some ways, the most versatile networks because they are the smallest grouping of hosts available and there are so many Class C addresses available. Organizations unable to justify the larger Class B networks will frequently obtain multiple Class C addresses in order to meet their needs.

Table 7.1 shows some example IP addresses and their logical division based on which Class they are. Note that these sample addresses assume no subnetting, a topic that is covered below (see Section 7.4).

Additionally, there are also Class D and Class E networks. Class D networks are numbered starting at 224.0.0.0 and are used for multicasting. Class E networks start at 240.0.0.0 and are currently used only for experimental and research purposes.

If a network is either currently connected to the Internet or is anticipated to be connected to the Internet, contact the The Internet Corporation for Assigned Names and Numbers (ICANN) Registration Service (or equivalent) to apply for a block of IP addresses for your network from the IP address space. Most organizations that connect their systems to the Internet will receive their IP network addresses from their upstream Internet Service Provider (ISP). If your company or organization is large enough, you may have to contact the ICANN directly using the contact information below.

The Internet Corporation for Assigned Names and Numbers
4676 Admiralty Way, Suite 330
Marina del Rey, CA 90292
USA

**Table 7.1** *Example IP Addresses*

| IP Address | Class | Network Number | Host Number |
|---|---|---|---|
| 18.131.55.75 | A | 18 | 131.55.75 |
| 138.12.70.190 | B | 138.12 | 70.190 |
| 216.196.23.17 | C | 216.196.23 | 17 |

Phone: +1.310.823.9358
FAX: +1.310.823.8649
General Email: icann@icann.org
Web site: http://www.icann.org/

This block of IP addresses could be one or more Class C addresses or simply a subset of a Class C block depending on the size of the network. For a private network, one completely isolated from the Internet, it is not necessary to register addresses with the ICANN. However, it is still recommended that IP addresses be applied for to avoid having to renumber the network in the event a connection to the Internet is added later. As an alternative, three blocks of IP addresses have been reserved for private networks:

10.0.0.0–10.255.255.255
172.16.0.0–172.31.255.255
192.168.0.0–192.168.255.255

The advantages of using IP addresses from these ranges are that no coordination with the ICANN is necessary to use these addresses; in the event that a network that is numbered in this range is connected to the Internet, there will be no conflict with registered hosts.

### 7.3.3 /etc/hosts File

The /etc/hosts file is a network configuration file that can contain a list of host names, their IP addresses, and, optionally, one or more host name aliases for systems reachable via the network. At a minimum, an individual system's /etc/hosts file should contain an entry (host name and IP address pair) for the system itself and for the system's loopback or localhost interface, which always has the IP address "127.0.0.1." For small networks or on systems that communicate with only a few remote hosts, it is probably reasonable to keep all host information in local /etc/hosts files on all the systems. However, as the number of systems increases, the process of managing this large list of host names and associated IP addresses and aliases quickly becomes impractical. For anything more than just a handful of hosts, a distributed host name database such as the Domain Name Service (DNS) is almost a necessity. When using DNS, the /etc/hosts file becomes a backup for when the name server is not running. In this case, it is suggested that only a few hosts be included in this file. These should include addresses for the local interfaces that ifconfig(8) needs at boot time.

The format of the /etc/hosts file is one entry per host, each entry on a single line. Each host's record should have the following information:

```
IP_Address Canonical_Host name [Alias_1,...,Alias_n] [#
Comments]
```

The fields in the /etc/hosts file are separated by white space. Therefore, any number of spaces and/or tab characters separates items. A pound sign (#) indicates the beginning of a comment, and any characters between the pound sign and the end of the line are ignored. The following is a fragment of an /etc/hosts file:

```
# /etc/hosts
127.0.0.1 localhost
192.168.171.78 saturn prod # Production Server
192.168.171.80 jupiter
```

The localhost entry is essential and must always exist in the hosts file. This has historically been used by the resolver to respond to requests for the loopback device, but is no longer used for that purpose.

## 7.4 The Subnet Mask

Frequently, a network is subdivided into smaller segments. For instance, while a Class A network can support more than 16 million hosts, it simply is not practical and definitely not recommended to have that many hosts on one segment. Dividing or subnetting a network into smaller sections is done for a variety of reasons, including network performance efficiency; ease of management, such as decentralization of network administration and overcoming physical cable distance limitations. The mechanism for subnetting is the Subnet Mask, a modifier that is used to determine how the network is subdivided. Every network configuration requires a subnet mask in addition to the IP address. The subnet mask is a 32-bit number specified in the same dotted decimal format as an IP address and, together with the IP address, is used to specify which part of the address is the network and which is the host. One minor disadvantage of subnetting is that in each subnet, the first number and last subnet number is reserved. Additionally, the first and last host number of each subnet is also reserved and cannot be used as a host address.

For networks that are not subnetted, the default subnet mask is specified:

```
Class A—255.0.0.0
Class B—255.255.0.0
Class C—255.255.255.0
```

For a subnetted network, the subnet mask specifies a further logical subdivision of the host part of the IP address into a subnet number and a smaller host number. When the subnet mask is represented in binary, each bit that is a one indicates that the corresponding bit in the IP address is the network number and the subnet number; each zero bit in the subnet mask indicates the host number in the in the IP address. For instance, consider the following Class B IP address:

```
172.30.12.75
```

Converting each octet of this address to binary results in the following representation:

```
10101100   00011110   00001100   01001011
```

If this IP address were part of a network that is not subnetted, the subnet mask, and its binary representation, would be used as shown in Figure 7.3.

This would result in the first two octets (172.30) representing the network number and the second two octets (12.75) representing the host number.

If this IP address is part of a network that is subnetted with the following subnet mask, the resulting division would be as you can see in Figure 7.4.

This would result in the first two octets (172.30) representing the network number, the third octet (12) representing the subnet number, and the fourth octet (75) representing the host number. This subnets the Class B network into 254 (256-2 reserved) subnets, each capable of supporting 254 hosts.

Finally, if the Class B network needed to be logically divided into more subnets, each with few hosts, the following subnet mask might be used as shown in Figure 7.5.

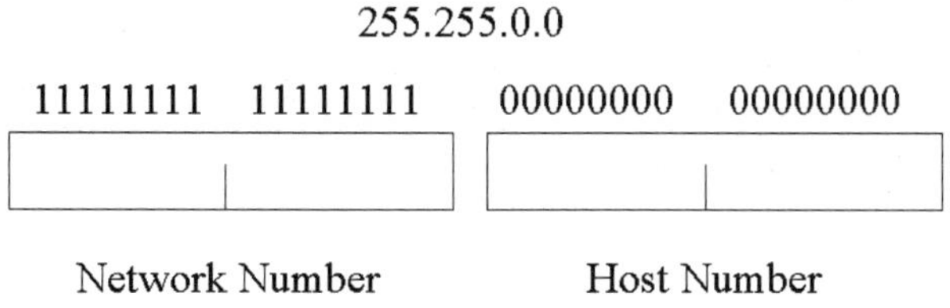

255.255.0.0

11111111 11111111 00000000 00000000

Network Number Host Number

**Figure 7.3** *Binary representation of nonsubnetted IP address.*

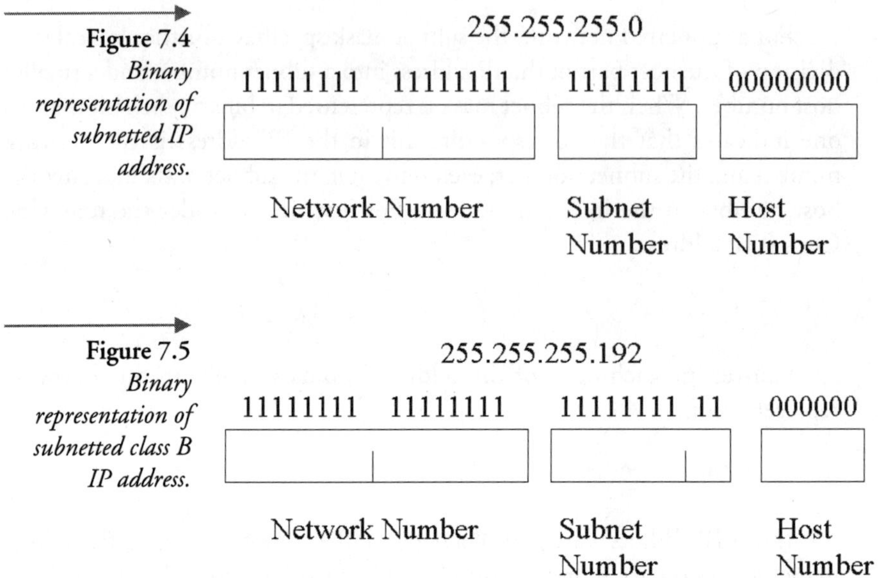


**Figure 7.4** *Binary representation of subnetted IP address.*

**Figure 7.5** *Binary representation of subnetted class B IP address.*

As this example shows, the subnet does not necessarily have to be on a byte boundary and can be at any bit position in the host part of the IP address. This subnet mask would result in the first two octets (172.30) representing the network number; the third octet (12) and two bits of the fourth octet representing the subnet number; and the last six bits of the fourth octet representing the host number. This subnets the Class B network into 1022 (1024-2 reserved) subnets, each capable of supporting 62 hosts.

See Table 7.2 for the results of different subnet masks on Class B and Class C networks. Note that two has already been subtracted from the resulting subnet and host quantities to take into account the reserved subnet and host numbers.

## 7.5 Hardware Address

Once a host name has been translated into an IP address, the next step for the networking subsystem to do is identify which physical computer on the network is assigned that IP address. The third and final address is the hardware or Media Access Control (MAC) address. Every network interface (Ethernet, Token Ring, FDDI, etc.) has a unique hardware address, and this address is typically burned into a read-only memory (ROM) chip and is unchangeable. A system's MAC address is displayed from the SRM console prompt with the "show device" command:

**Table 7.2** *The Results of Subnetting on Class B and C Networks*

| **Class B Subnetting** | | |
|---|---|---|
| **Subnet Mask** | **Number of Subnets** | **Number of Hosts** |
| 255.255.192.0 | 2 | 16382 |
| 255.255.224.0 | 6 | 8190 |
| 255.255.240.0 | 14 | 4094 |
| 255.255.248.0 | 30 | 2046 |
| 255.255.252.0 | 62 | 1022 |
| 255.255.254.0 | 126 | 510 |
| 255.255.255.0 | 254 | 254 |
| 255.255.255.128 | 510 | 126 |
| 255.255.255.192 | 1022 | 62 |
| 255.255.255.224 | 2046 | 30 |
| 255.255.255.240 | 4094 | 14 |
| 255.255.255.248 | 8190 | 6 |
| 255.255.255.252 | 16382 | 2 |
| 255.255.255.192 | 2 | 62 |
| 255.255.255.224 | 6 | 30 |
| 255.255.255.240 | 14 | 14 |
| 255.255.255.248 | 30 | 6 |
| 255.255.255.252 | 62 | 2 |

```
>>> show device | grep ew
ewa0.0.0.11.0    EWA0    00-00-F8-01-42-5F
```

In this example, the Ethernet interface (EWA0) has a hardware address of "00-00-F8-01-42-5F". The TCP/IP networking software must know the hardware address of a destination host in order to communicate with that host. Translating an IP address into a hardware address is accomplished with the Address Resolution Protocol or ARP. This basically broadcasts a request across the network asking if any other host knows the location of the system with the target IP address. Once the hardware address of the destination host has been identified, network communication can commence.

## 7.6 Routing

Routing is the process whereby network packets are routed or directed to and from different networks. The TCP/IP networking subsystem on a system is able to accomplish the routing of information by consulting a list that contains instructions on where to send any particular packet based on the packet's destination address. This list, the routing table, is basically a list of destination networks or hosts, the corresponding network interface, and the next stop on the way to the final destination. For instance, consider the following routing table:

```
# /usr/sbin/netstat -nr
Routing tables
Destination      Gateway            Flags  Refs  Use   Interface
default          192.168.171.254 UGS    0     44    tu0
127.0.0.1        127.0.0.1          UH     3     4294  lo0
192.168.171/24   192.168.171.78     U      4     1166  tu0
```

Note that there are three records in this table, each providing routing instructions for a different destination. Every network packet has coded within it a destination address, and the networking software takes that destination address and compares it with the destination value of each routing table entry, starting at the bottom, looking for a match. For example, a packet destined for IP address 172.31.12.75 does not match the third destination, which is for hosts in the range of 192.168.171.0 to 192.168.171.254. This route is for systems on the local network, and packets for this destination are sent out the local Ethernet interface (192.168.171.78). The second destination (127.0.0.1) matches packets intended for services on the local system, and this route is to keep internal packets from ever getting out onto the network. The route is the loopback interface that "loops" the packets right back into the system. The first and final destination is labeled "default." Since our imaginary packet destination (172.31.12.75) does not match any other destination in the routing table, this final default route is applied. This instructs the networking software to pass the packet onto the gateway at 192.168.171.254, which will accept the packet and then repeat the process, comparing the packet's destination address to its own routing table. See Section 7.7 for information on Gateways. This simple example shows how network packets are routed from host to host until they arrive at their final destination. Each step, or hop, gets the packet a little closer to its destination.

There are three ways of managing the routing table on a Tru64 UNIX system: minimal, static, and dynamic. Determining which routing configuration to use depends on the size and type of the network a system is connected to. The three types of routing configuration are explained as follows.

### 7.6.1 Minimal

A minimal routing configuration is one that contains only the routes created when the ifconfig(8) command activated the networking system. Typically, this means only a single route that corresponds to each network interface in use, plus the loopback route. This configuration is sufficient for small networks that are not connected to any other networks or are subnetted. For this configuration, no additional steps are necessary to manage the routing table. Here is an example of a minimal routing table:

```
Destination  Gateway  Flags  Refs  Use  Interface
127.0.0.1  127.0.0.1  UH  3  4294  lo0
192.168.171/24  192.168.171.78  U  4  1166  tu0
```

### 7.6.2 Static

A static routing configuration is characterized by a routing table that contains, in addition to the routes present in a minimal configuration, one or more routes added manually by the system administrator. The simplest static routing table has one additional route: a Default route that points to a gateway where all nonlocal network traffic should be directed. Additionally, there may be other, special static routes added in order to route certain packets to specific hosts or networks. These static routes are managed manually with the route(8) command. The following example demonstrates adding a static route to a network to the routing table:

```
# /usr/sbin/netstat -nr
Routing tables
Destination  Gateway  Flags  Refs  Use  Interface
default  192.168.171.254  UGS  0  44  tu0
127.0.0.1  127.0.0.1  UH  3  4294  lo0
192.168.171/24  192.168.171.78  U  4  1166  tu0
# /usr/sbin/route add -net 192.168.159 192.168.171.101
# /usr/sbin/netstat -nr
Routing tables
Destination  Gateway  Flags  Refs  Use  Interface
default  192.168.171.254  UGS  0  44  tu0
127.0.0.1  127.0.0.1  UH  3  4294  lo0
192.168.159/24  192.168.171.101  UGS  0  0  tu0
192.168.171/24  192.168.171.78  U  4  1166  tu0
```

The first netstat command displays the routing table showing a default route, a loopback route to the local host, and a route to network 192.168.171 through interface tu0. The route add command adds a static route to another network (192.168.159) through interface tu0, with the next destination being the host at IP address 192.168.171.101. The second netstat command again displays the routing table, and the newly added static route is now displayed immediately after the loopback route.

### 7.6.3 Dynamic

In a dynamic routing configuration, the routing table is dynamically updated by a program using one or more routing protocols to determine the "best" route to a destination. The program is able to dynamically react and reroute around temporary or permanent network outages. Dynamic routing should be used on a network, which has more than one possible route to a destination. Tru64 UNIX provides two routing daemons, routed (pronounced "route d") and gated ("gate d"). The routed routing daemon is the older of the two daemons and also the least flexible, for it understands only one routing protocol, RIP (Routing Information Protocol). RIP is well suited for small local area networks and is therefore very commonly used. The gated routing daemon is a more modern program and understands RIP as well as several other routing protocols. The gated daemon is normally considered a replacement for routed. You can run either gated or routed on a system but not both. If the only routing protocol in use is or will be RIP, it is generally recommended to run routed, though gated will also do RIP. If, however, the network is running a routing protocol different from RIP, you must run gated. It is beyond the scope of this text to explore IP routing and routing protocols. Refer to one of the recommended references on TCP/IP networking in Appendix B for further information on configuring routing daemons and routing protocols.

## 7.7 Gateway

A system is able to communicate directly with other systems located on the same network or subnet. In order to reach a system on a different network, however, a system must go through a gateway. A gateway is typically a dedicated piece of hardware, either a repeater, a bridge, or a router, but a computer system may also function as a gateway if it has more than one network interface.

The simplest types of gateways are repeaters and bridges, which are used to connect distinct network cable sections to overcome network cable distance limitations. Repeaters and bridges extend a single network rather than connecting different networks together. A repeater simply passes all network traffic transparently between the two network segments without any type of filtering or modification. A bridge is an intelligent repeater and has the ability to filter traffic based on various criteria.

The most common type of gateway is known as a router, so named because it "routes" network traffic between different networks. A router has connections simultaneously on multiple networks. All network traffic originating on a specific network and destined for systems on remote networks must travel through this router, which is also called a default route. A router is usually a stand-alone device with sophisticated software that has the ability to examine individual network packets and make a determination, based on source, destination, or type, whether to forward the packet on to another network.

When configuration TCP/IP networking on a Tru64 UNIX system, it is usually not necessary to know what type your gateway is. Simply knowing the IP address of the gateway is sufficient. For example, Figure 7.6 shows two networks connected by a Gateway. Host 1 is able to communicate to Host 2 directly without traveling through the gateway, but in order for Host 1 to communicate with Host 3, the network traffic must be routed through the gateway between the two networks. Providing the gateway's address instructs

**Figure 7.6** *A gateway connecting two networks.*

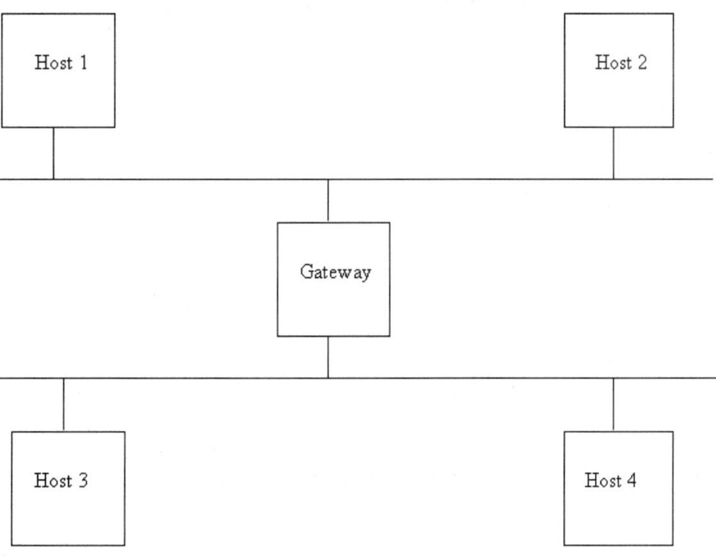

the TCP/IP software where to send network packets destined for hosts not on the local network.

## 7.8 Activating Networking

Once a system's network parameters are in hand, the next step is to actually configure and start the Tru64 UNIX TCP/IP networking subsystem. Compaq has historically provided a character cell utility for configuring networking at all levels of Tru64 UNIX. This utility, netsetup(8), works in the same way, regardless of the version of Tru64 UNIX, and provides a text-only menu-driven interface for configuring individual network interfaces, starting and stopping certain network daemons, entering gateway information, and adding and deleting remote host information. Starting at Tru64 UNIX version 5.0, Compaq retired the netsetup tool and added a new TCP/IP network configuration tool providing more flexibility then the netsetup. This tool, SysMan, defaults to an X Window System graphical user interface, but can also be run from a character-cell menu interface, or from the command line specifying configuration options. This section will only cover the use of the Network Setup Wizard and SysMan tool for basic TCP/IP network configuration.

### 7.8.1 SysMan network

The SysMan(8) network utility provides a simple, menu-driven method of configuring or reconfiguring the TCP/IP network subsystem on Tru64 UNIX. Run the SysMan network utility as root,

```
# sysman network
```

and on a character cell terminal, the main menu (Figure 7.7) will be presented.

As you can see, the SysMan menu is rather intuitive. The system administrator can choose from one of six different options shown. The first option, "Network Setup Wizard," brings up the step-by-step–oriented tool to configure simple networking on the system, This tool is discussed in greater detail in Section 7.8.3. The following two options, "Basic Network Services" and "Additional Network Services" will bring up other menu options, if selected. The basic configuration option menu is shown in Figure 7.8.

The basic network services are those that are required to get a simply configured Tru64 UNIX system onto an existing network of other systems. Those tasks are setting the network interface cards; configuring simple, static

**Figure 7.7** *The SysMan network main menu.*

```
                              Networking
Tru64 UNIX system management tasks:
+------------------------------------------------------------------------------+
|>| Network Setup Wizard                                                       |
|  + Basic Network Services                                                    |
|  + Additional Network Services                                               |
|  | View network daemon status                                                |
|  | (Re)start network services                                                |
|  | Stop network services                                                     |
|                                                                              |
+------------------------------------------------------------------------------+
                 Select                            Help On Item

         ================ <CTRL-G> FOR KEYBOARD HELP =================
              Exit                   Options...              Help
```

**Figure 7.8** *Basic Network Services Configuration menu.*

```
                              Networking
Tru64 UNIX system management tasks:
+------------------------------------------------------------------------------+
| | Network Setup Wizard                                                       |
|>- Basic Network Services                                                     |
|      | Set up Asynchronous Transfer Mode (ATM)                               |
|      | Set up Network Interface Card(s)                                      |
|      | Set up static routes (/etc/routes)                                    |
|      | Set up routing services (gated, routed, IP Router)                    |
|      | Set up hosts file (/etc/hosts)                                        |
|      | Set up hosts equivalency file (/etc/hosts.equiv)                      |
|      | Set up remote who services (rwhod)                                    |
|      | Set up the networks file (/etc/networks)                              |
|  + Additional Network Services                                               |
|  | View network daemon status                                                |
|  | (Re)start network services                                                |
|  | Stop network services                                                     |
|                                                                              |
+------------------------------------------------------------------------------+
                 Select                            Help On Item
 Select the appropriate management category

              Exit                   Options...              Help
```

or dynamic routing; managing the hosts, hosts.equiv, and networks databases; and configuring the remote who daemon.

The additional network services (Figure 7.9) are those services used to configure a Tru64 UNIX system on a more complex network containing DNS, NIS, and NFS hosts and services. You can also have your system participate in a network time protocol to synchronize the time on your system to very accurate clocks on the Internet or intranet. If you want your system to be

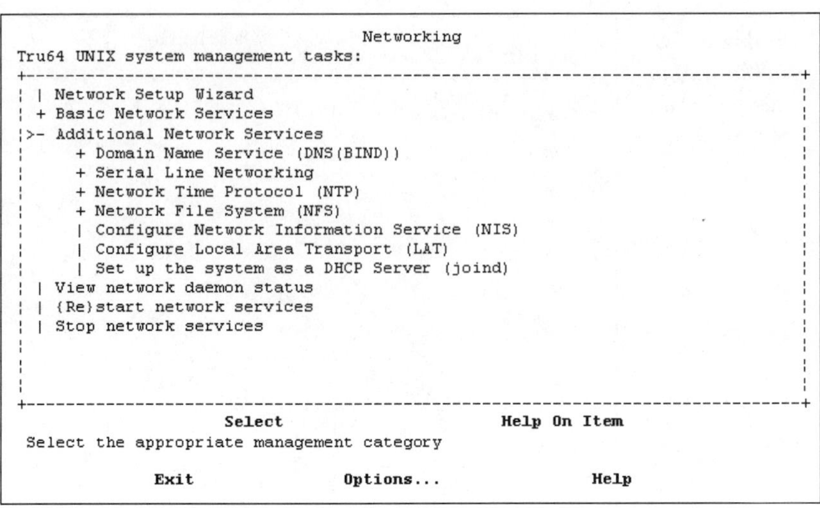
```
                                 Networking
Tru64 UNIX system management tasks:
+----------------------------------------------------------------------------+
| | Network Setup Wizard                                                      |
| + Basic Network Services                                                  |
|>- Additional Network Services                                             |
|     + Domain Name Service (DNS(BIND))                                      |
|     + Serial Line Networking                                               |
|     + Network Time Protocol (NTP)                                          |
|     + Network File System (NFS)                                            |
|     | Configure Network Information Service (NIS)                          |
|     | Configure Local Area Transport (LAT)                                 |
|     | Set up the system as a DHCP Server (joind)                           |
| | View network daemon status                                              |
| | (Re)start network services                                              |
| | Stop network services                                                   |
|                                                                            |
+----------------------------------------------------------------------------+
                  Select                         Help On Item
 Select the appropriate management category

              Exit              Options...              Help
```

**Figure 7.9** *Additional Network Services Configuration menu.*

configured with the Local Area Transport (LAT) or as a Dynamic Host Configuration Protocol (DHCP) server, you would also use this menu. If you are not familiar with these services and options, we recommend you contact the network administrator at your site or read the Compaq Tru64 UNIX documentation for more information.

### 7.8.2 netconfig

The Network Configuration Manager, netconfig, is an X Window System/Motif application on Tru64 UNIX pre–version 5.0 systems that can be used to initially configure and modify the TCP/IP network configuration. The Network Configuration Manager is invoked through the CDE Application Manager, which is opened by selecting the Application Manager icon from the CDE Front Panel, followed by selecting the System_Admin application group icon, then the Configuration application group icon, and finally the Network icon. Once you double-click on the Network icon, if you are not logged in as root, you will be prompted via a Get Password dialog box for the root password.

Optionally, you can start the Network Configuration Manager from the command line:

```
# /usr/sbin/netconfig
```

This application provides all the configuration options available in the older netsetup(8) utility in pre-5.0 systems. In Tru64 UNIX 5.0 and higher, typing netconfig, will automatically bring up a step-by-step–oriented networking setup tool called the Network Setup Wizard. This tool is covered in Section 7.8.3.

### 7.8.3 The Network Setup Wizard

The Network Setup Wizard is a menu-based, step-by-step tool for configuring networking on a Tru64 UNIX system. It is simple and intuitive as you can see from the main menu shown in Figure 7.10.

In order to configure your system, you simply follow the steps in sequence, until you have completed them all. Once you have completed all the steps, your system will be configured on an existing TCP/IP network with many of the options available to you. You start up the Network Setup Wizard from the comand line in one of three ways:

- Type "netconfig".
- Type "sysman net_wizard".
- Type "sysman network," and select the first option off the menu. (See Figure 7.7.)

**Figure 7.10** *The Network Setup wizard menu.*

```
                          Network Setup Wizard
Network Setup helps you set up the network configuration for your UNIX
system.

It leads you step-by-step through the following networking tasks:
 ---------------------------------------------------------------------------
Step 1: Set up Network Interface Card(s)
Step 2: Set up static routes (/etc/routes)
Step 3: Set up routing services (gated, routed, IP router)
Step 4: Set up hosts file (/etc/hosts)
Step 5: Set up hosts equivalency file (/etc/hosts.equiv)
Step 6: Set up remote who services (rwhod)
Step 7: Set up the system as a DHCP server (joind)
Step 8: Set up networks file (/etc/networks)
 ---------------------------------------------------------------------------
No action is performed until you select finish at the end of Network Setup.

Select "Details..." to see the information Network Setup requests.

Select "Next >" to start setting up this system.


        =============== <CTRL-G> FOR KEYBOARD HELP =================
        [Next >]          Details...          Cancel          Help
```

## 7.9 Network Troubleshooting Tools

When a problem arises on a network of systems, it can initially be overwhelming due to the range of possible sources of trouble. Trying to determine whether the problem is hardware (a computer, hub, or router, or cables or connectors, etc.) or software (an improperly configured network interface, incomplete or incorrect routing table information, or invalid or missing host information) can be difficult. The best approach is to understand the symptoms of the issue and then methodically try to isolate the actual problem. Tru64 UNIX (and most other UNIX implementations) provides several troubleshooting utilities, each with a special purpose or focus. Knowing each tool's specialty and what can be learned from its output is important in knowing where to start troubleshooting.

A network problem will probably manifest itself in a connectivity loss between systems. Typically, an individual system or group of systems is unable to communicate with some other system or group of systems. The very first thing that should be done is to attempt to define the problem. Initially this may be something as vague as a user reporting that he or she cannot connect to the company Web site using the browser on his or her workstation. Using this example, the system administrator should be able to refine and bound the problem by asking questions or trying variations of the problem. For instance:

- "Are you able to connect to other Web sites?"
- "Do any of your co-workers have the same problem?"
- "Are any other network services (telnet, FTP, printing) also not working?"
- "Have there been any recent hardware or software configuration changes?"

After collecting further information, the system administrator is able to determine the following:

- The user who raised the issue appears to be the only one impacted.
- The user is experiencing network time-outs regardless of which Web site is attempted.
- All other network services are also failing.
- The networking configuration of the user's workstation was recently changed, but the user does not know what was done.

From this description, it appears that the user's system is no longer a part of the network. More than likely, the recent network reconfiguration has introduced a problem preventing the system from communicating with the rest of the network. The following is an example of a plan of attack and introduces the UNIX network troubleshooting utilities.

The first thing that should be checked is the basic connectivity. Ensure that the system is physically still connected to the network. For a thinnet or coax cable Ethernet network, check that the tee connector is firmly attached to the coax connector of the system's network interface card. For a 10BaseT Ethernet, token ring, or FDDI network, make sure that the connectors on each end of the system's cable run are properly attached to the system and to the network hub or concentrator. Some network interface cards provide a "link" light, frequently green in color, that glows when there is solid network connectivity.

Assuming that the physical connectivity is fine, the next place to investigate is the network configuration on the affected system. The four utilities described in the following subsections are listed in a recommended order of use. Each has a specific purpose and is used in a troubleshooting situation to either confirm or deny that a particular process or system is part of the problem.

### 7.9.1 ifconfig

Normally, the ifconfig(8) utility is used by the system at startup to configure and activate network interfaces (Table 7.3). However, ifconfig is handy for quickly displaying a system's interface configuration. The three most pertinent pieces of information for each network interface are:

**Table 7.3** *Network Interface Types and Device Names*

| Network Interface Type | Network Interface Device Name |
|---|---|
| Loopback | lo |
| Ethernet | tu, le, ln, xna |
| Token Ring | tra |
| FDDI | fta, faa, fza |
| ATM | lta |
| Serial Line Interface | sl |

*Note:* The Network Interface Device Name will be followed with a number designating a particular device (for example, tu0, fta1).

- Interface State (Up or Down)
- IP Address
- Subnet Mask

Simply run the following command to display the information about all the network interfaces on a system:

```
# /usr/sbin/ifconfig -a
tu0:
flags=c63<UP,BROADCAST,NOTRAILERS,RUNNING,MULTICAST,SIMPLEX>
   inet 192.168.171.78 netmask ffffff00 broadcast
192.168.171.255 ipmtu 1500

lo0:
flags=100c89<UP,LOOPBACK,NOARP,MULTICAST,SIMPLEX,NOCHECKSUM>
inet 127.0.0.1 netmask ff000000 ipmtu 4096
```

In this example, there are two interfaces, an Ethernet interface (tu0) and the loopback interface (lo0). Each interface's status is listed as the first field in the "flags=" string. In both of these cases, the status is "UP." The absence of the string "UP" indicates that the interface is down. An interface must be up, otherwise the system does not transmit messages through that interface. If the interface is not up, the following command (using tu0 as an example) will activate the interface:

```
# ifconfig tu0 up
```

The second line of each interface's ifconfig output lists the IP address (inet), the subnet mask (netmask) and the maximum transfer unit value (ipmtu). While the IP address is displayed in a dotted decimal format, the subnet mask is displayed as a hexadecimal value that must be converted to decimal. Ensure that the IP address and subnet mask displayed reflect the correct address information for each interface. If the incorrect IP address and/or subnet mask are shown, reconfigure the interface via the netstat(8) or netconfig(8X) command and restart the networking services.

## 7.9.2 netstat

Once the network interface(s) have been confirmed as correctly configured, the next item to examine is the routing table. The netstat command is primarily a tool to display network statistics; however, it also can be used to display a system's routing table:

```
# /usr/sbin/netstat -nr
Routing tables
Destination  GatewayFlags  Refs  Use  Interface
Netmasks:
Inet  255.255.255.0
Route Tree for Protocol Family 2:
default  192.168.171.254  UGS  0  32551  tu0
127.0.0.1  127.0.0.1  UH  3  955  lo0
192.168.171/24  192.168.171.78  U  4  19110  tu0
```

If the system is on a network that requires a gateway to reach other networks, ensure that the proper gateway(s) are listed in the routing table. Also make sure that there is an entry for the loopback route and any specific static routes that should exist. If the system is using dynamic routing (routed or gated), check that the routes listed are correct. If the routing table is incomplete or has incorrect entries, check that the /etc/routes file contains the correct static routes or, if using dynamic routing, verify the configuration of the routing daemon in use. The following describes the route flags displayed in the netstat output:

- U Up, or available.
- G This route is to a gateway
- H This route is to a host
- S This is a static route that was created by the route command

### 7.9.3 ping

The next step is to check some network connectivity. The tool for this purpose is ping(1). The ping command is used to send one or more ICMP (Internet Control Message Protocol) ECHO_REQUEST packets to a specific host, which should respond back to the pinging host with a matching ICMP ECHO_RESPONSE packet.

To use the ping command, specify the host target name or IP address as a command line argument. Another common flag is "-c" for "count" to specify the number of ICMP packets to send before terminating. If the "-c" argument is omitted, the ping command continuously sends packets until interrupted with Ctrl-C. For example, the following example sends five ICMP packets to the host jupiter and displays the results of each ping, followed by a summary of the entire sequence:

```
# /usr/sbin/ping -c 5 jupiter
PING jupiter (192.168.171.80): 56 data bytes
64 bytes from 192.168.171.80: icmp_seq=0 ttl=128 time=2 ms
```

```
64 bytes from 192.168.171.80: icmp_seq=1 ttl=128 time=0 ms
64 bytes from 192.168.171.80: icmp_seq=2 ttl=128 time=0 ms
64 bytes from 192.168.171.80: icmp_seq=3 ttl=128 time=0 ms
64 bytes from 192.168.171.80: icmp_seq=4 ttl=128 time=0 ms
—jupiter PING Statistics—
5 packets transmitted, 5 packets received, 0% packet loss
round-trip (ms) min/avg/max = 0/0/2 ms
```

In this example, connectivity between the pinging host and jupiter is fine. This can be determined both by the low round-trip times of each ping (<=2ms) and that the fact there was 0% packet loss; that is, all five packets successfully reached the destination (jupiter) and returned.

To show the results of a ping where there is a connectivity problem, consider this similar example to a different host:

```
# /usr/sbin/ping -c 5 192.168.171.81
PING 192.168.171.81 (192.168.171.81): 56 data bytes
—192.168.171.81 PING Statistics—
5 packets transmitted, 0 packets received, 100% packet loss
```

This ping demonstrates the outcome when the pinging system does not receive the ECHO_RESPONSE packets from the remote host. One thing to be aware of is that a ping resulting in 100% packet loss could mean one of several things. The ECHO_REQUEST packets may never have reached their destination, or possibly the ECHO_REQUEST packets did reach the destination, but the ECHO_RESPONSE packets were not able to successfully return. Another possibility is that the network between the source and destination is fine, and the destination host is simply down or unavailable.

Note that this example used an IP address rather than a host name on the ping command line. One recommendation is to always use specific IP addresses rather than host names when troubleshooting using the ping command, to ensure that there is no ambiguity about which host is the target of the ping. However, even if a host name is specified, the ping output displays the resolved IP address.

The best strategy to use when attempting to isolate a network connectivity problem is to ping first the local interface on the system to ensure that a system's own interface is up and running. Next, attempt to ping hosts and gateways further away to try to identify where the fault lies. The most complete picture of a network fault is best drawn through a combination of pings and the output of the next utility, traceroute.

### 7.9.4 traceroute

While the ping command will indicate a loss of basic connectivity between two systems, its output cannot identify where the connectivity may be breaking down. For this, the traceroute(8) command is used. Except for very simple connections, the route between two systems may be through a variety of routers, gateways, or hosts. Any one of the nodes along the path may in fact be the issue. The traceroute command displays the route that network packets travel to reach a remote system. If one of the intermediate stops along the way is down or otherwise not forwarding packets further downstream, it is immediately obvious from the traceroute output.

The traceroute command is run specifying the target destination on the command line. For example, the following is a successful traceroute to the Compaq Web site:

```
# /usr/sbin/traceroute www.compaq.com
traceroute to www.compaq.com (192.208.46.158), 30 hops max,
   40 byte packets
 1 903.Hssi9-0-0.GW1.DEN1.ALTER.NET (157.130.162.57) 6.3 ms
   6.9 ms 7.4 ms
 2 125.Hssi4-0.CR2.KCY1.Alter.Net (137.39.59.214) 30.8 ms
   37.5 ms 31.8 ms
 3 126.ATM10-0-0.CR2.EWR1.Alter.Net (137.39.59.89) 68.5 ms
   168.3 ms 66.1 ms
 4 112.ATM10-0-0.XR2.EWR1.ALTER.NET (146.188.176.22) 70.9 ms
   70.7 ms 66.9 ms
 5 192.ATM11-0-0.XR2.BOS1.ALTER.NET (146.188.176.158) 109.5 ms
   111.3 ms 82.8 ms
 6 190.ATM5-0-0.SR1.BOS1.ALTER.NET (146.188.177.13) 73.0 ms
   73.3 ms 74.6 ms
 7 boston1-br2.bbnplanet.net (4.0.2.73) 74.1 ms 77.7 ms 77.8 ms
 8 cambridge2-br1.bbnplanet.net (4.0.1.186) 82.1 ms 84.4 ms
   81.1 ms
 9 cambridge2-cr3.bbnplanet.net (192.233.33.10) 73.7 ms 76.2 ms
   73.8 ms
10 dec.bbnplanet.net (131.192.95.2) 107.0 ms 79.0 ms 78.5 ms
11 199.93.199.4 (199.93.199.4) 78.5 ms 77.0 ms 78.8 ms
12 www.compaq.com (192.208.46.158) 87.1 ms 82.6 ms 88.9 ms
```

This example indicates that the distance from the source to the destination is 12 steps or hops. For each gateway, the traceroute command launches three small probe packets and listens for a specific response from the gateway. Each line in the traceroute output shows the gateway's IP address (and host name, if the name can be resolved) and the round-trip time for each of the three probe packets.

Below is an example of a traceroute sequence to a host that the ping command indicates is unreachable. As this output shows, the packets do not even reach the destination system, which may be working perfectly fine. If the traceroute command does not receive a response from the next gateway within a three-second time-out interval, an asterisk (*) is printed for that probe.

```
$ /usr/sbin/traceroute jupiter.somedomain.com
traceroute to jupiter.somedomain.com (192.168.171.80), 30 hops
max, 40 byte packets
 1 903.Hssi9-0-0.GW1.DEN1.ALTER.NET (157.130.162.57) 6.3 ms
   6.9 ms 7.4 ms
 2 125.Hssi4-0.CR2.KCY1.Alter.Net (137.39.59.214) 30.8 ms
   37.5 ms 31.8 ms
 3 126.ATM10-0-0.CR2.EWR1.Alter.Net (137.39.59.89) 68.5 ms
   168.3 ms 66.1 ms
 4 112.ATM10-0-0.XR2.EWR1.ALTER.NET (146.188.176.22) 70.9 ms
   70.7 ms 66.9 ms
 5 192.ATM11-0-0.XR2.BOS1.ALTER.NET (146.188.176.158) 109.5 ms
   111.3 ms 82.8 ms
 6 190.ATM5-0-0.SR1.BOS1.ALTER.NET (146.188.177.13) 73.0 ms
   73.3 ms 74.6 ms
 7 * * *
 8 * * *
 .
 .
 .
30 * * *
```

By default, traceroute shows a maximum of only 30 hops and so, unless interrupted with Ctrl-C, traceroute will stop after 30 probes. The number of hops can be adjusted by specifying a value with the "-m" command line flag. In the preceding example, the problem appears to actually be between the source and destination hosts. If you have control over the entire network path, the next step is to identity which gateway is not responding and why. If, as in this case, the nonresponsive gateway is somewhere out on the Internet, the next course of action is to attempt to locate the responsible party and notify that party of an apparent issue.

As you may well understand, being familiar with the "normal" output of these tools on a system properly connected and configured can be helpful in identifying problems. Experiment and explore these troubleshooting tools to become comfortable with their switches, options, and output. Refer to their man pages for more information.

## 7.10 Domain Name System (DNS)

The main reason UNIX systems have host names is to provide a convenient name for use by people. An IP address is simply not an easily remembered identifier, and the future of IP promises even longer IP addresses. However, the TCP/IP software cannot use a host name directly. As discussed earlier, the networking software must convert, or resolve, a host name to an IP address to initiate communication. The simplest mechanism for providing this host name to IP address correlation is the /etc/hosts file, which is a text file listing IP addresses and their corresponding host name(s). The sole use of hosts files may be appropriate for small networks with a limited number of systems. However, as the size of a network grows, or even more pertinent, if a network is connected to the Internet, it becomes unfeasible to include every possible host in the /etc/hosts file. Considering that the Internet is many millions of systems, the lack of scalability of the /etc/hosts file is apparent. The answer to this need is the Domain Name System or DNS.

DNS is a distributed host-name-to-IP and vice versa database that is used as the primary host name resolution environment by most networked systems. The Tru64 UNIX stock DNS is an implementation of the Berkeley Internet Name Domain (BIND). Knowing this is probably not relevant, since most DNS implementations on the Internet are also based on BIND. A system running BIND can be configured to be a primary server, a secondary server, a slave server, a caching server, or simply as a client.

It is beyond the scope of this text to detail the configuration of the different types of DNS servers. Refer to one of the recommended references on TCP/IP networking and DNS in Appendix B for further information on configuring this complex network facility.

## 7.11 File Transfer Protocol

The File Transfer Protocol (FTP) is a mechanism for transferring files between computers across a network. FTP was designed to support straightforward file transfers between different computer system types. For instance, there are FTP clients available for MS-DOS, Microsoft Windows, Compaq's OpenVMS, IBM mainframes, and just about any other type of computer in addition to every flavor of UNIX. When transferring files, FTP can also do translations between different types of systems. For example, FTP can convert a text file to the appropriate format while transferring it between a Tru64 UNIX system and an MS-DOS system.

In this section, we will cover the configuration of FTP on Tru64 UNIX, including the FTP client and server. By default, FTP is enabled on a Tru64 UNIX system, but understanding what configuration options are available is important to managing this facility. In addition, a special variant of FTP, Anonymous FTP, will be discussed. Anonymous FTP, which allows FTP access to a system without user authentication, will be covered.

The ftp(1) command is the Tru64 UNIX interface to the File Transfer Protocol. This command is a character-cell utility for connecting to remote systems and transferring files. For its simplest form, specify the remote system's name on the FTP command line. An FTP login to the remote system will be attempted and, if successful, you will be prompted for a user name and password on the remote system. For example:

```
# ftp saturn
Connected to saturn.
220 saturn FTP server (Tru64 UNIX Version 5.60) ready.
Name (saturn:root): jsmith
331 Password required for jsmith.
Password:
230 User jsmith logged in.
Remote system type is UNIX.
Using binary mode to transfer files.
ftp>
```

This example demonstrates a successful login to the remote system saturn. The ftp> prompt is then displayed indicating that FTP commands may now be entered. These commands include moving around the remote and local directory hierarchy, listing the contents of subdirectories, and getting and putting files to and from the remote system. For example, the following example resumes where the previous example left off, and it demonstrates changing to a particular directory on the remote system and downloading a specific file:

```
ftp> pwd
257 "/" is current directory.
ftp> cd /pub/data
250 CWD command successful.
ftp> ls -l
150 Opening ASCII mode data connection for /bin/ls
   (10.0.0.1,1030).
total 3
-rw-r—r—  1 root   system   1019 Jan 6 12:08 file1
-rw-r—r—  1 root   system   1201 Jan 6 13:54 file2
-rw-r—r—  1 root   system   3772 Jan 6 13:58 file3
226 Transfer complete.
ftp> get file1
200 PORT command successful.
```

```
150 Opening BINARY mode data connection for file1
    (10.0.0.1,1031) (1019 bytes).
226 Transfer complete.
1019 bytes received in 0.0029 seconds (3.4e+02 Kbytes/s)
ftp> bye
221 Goodbye.
#
```

Such an FTP dialog is actually carried out by two pieces, the client ftp(1) utility on the local system and an FTP server daemon on the remote system. This FTP server, ftpd(8), is invoked only when an incoming FTP connection is detected by inetd(8), the system's network server. One ftpd process is started for each inbound FTP connection and exists only for the duration of that particular FTP session.

The ftpd program has two types of configuration options available to the system administrator:

- Debugging and logging switches
- Security and authentication options

The default values of these options, which will be outlined, are usually sufficient for most situations and configurations. However, when troubleshooting problems or looking to increase security, the FTP server does provide this additional configurability. These options are specified and maintained in several configuration files.

### 7.11.1 FTP Debugging and Logging

By default, the Tru64 UNIX FTP server, ftpd(8), does not do any logging of FTP connections or file transfers. If additional information about incoming FTP connections is needed, either for the purpose of debugging problems or as a historical record of connections and file transfers, there are two ftpd command line switches that each instruct ftpd to log additional information via the system logger facility (syslog).

The first of these switches is –d, which provides debugging and output detailing inbound FTP connections. The information logged by ftpd includes the date and time of the FTP connection, which user account was used to log in, whether the log-in was successful or not, and an indication of which commands were issued during the session. Here is an example log of a simple FTP log-in and file transfer session:

```
Jan 14 12:33:47 saturn ftpd[824]: <-- 220 saturn FTP server
    (Digital UNIX Version 5.60) ready.
```

```
Jan 14 12:33:48 saturn ftpd[824]: command: USER root
Jan 14 12:33:48 saturn ftpd[824]: <-- 331 Password required for
   root.
Jan 14 12:33:52 saturn ftpd[824]: command: PASS XXXX
Jan 14 12:33:52 saturn ftpd[824]: <-- 230 User root logged in.
Jan 14 12:33:52 saturn ftpd[824]: command: SYST
Jan 14 12:33:52 saturn ftpd[824]: <-- 215 UNIX Type:
   L8 Version:  Tru64 UNIX V4.0 (Rev. 878)
Jan 14 12:33:54 saturn ftpd[824]: command: CWD /pub/data
Jan 14 12:33:54 saturn ftpd[824]: <-- 250 CWD command
   successful.
Jan 14 12:33:57 saturn ftpd[824]: command: TYPE I
Jan 14 12:33:57 saturn ftpd[824]: <-- 200 Type set to I.
Jan 14 12:33:57 saturn ftpd[824]: command: PORT 10,0,0,1,4,13
Jan 14 12:33:57 saturn ftpd[824]: <-- 200 PORT command
   successful.
Jan 14 12:33:57 saturn ftpd[824]: command: RETR file1
Jan 14 12:33:57 saturn ftpd[824]: <-- 150 Opening BINARY mode
   data connection for file1 (10.0.0.1,1037) (1019 bytes).
Jan 14 12:33:57 saturn ftpd[824]: <-- 226 Transfer complete.
Jan 14 12:33:59 saturn ftpd[824]: command: QUIT
Jan 14 12:33:59 saturn ftpd[824]: <-- 221 Goodbye.
```

Note that the actual commands the user typed at the ftp> prompt are not listed; instead, the FTP requests themselves are displayed. For instance, while the user typed "get file1", the log displays "command: RETR file1". This may require some amount of interpretation in order to determine what exactly the user did during the FTP session. Refer to the man page for ftpd(8) for a list of FTP server requests supported by the Tru64 UNIX FTP server.

The second FTP server command line switch is –l, which simply logs each FTP session's login success and failures along with file transfer operations. The output of the –l log is fairly sparse, but may be sufficient if all that is desired is a record of logins and file transfers. For example, this log is a record of the exact same operation logged in the previous example:

```
Jan 14 12:34:53 saturn ftpd[833]: connection from saturn at Wed
   Jan 14 12:34:531998
Jan 14 12:34:57 saturn ftpd[833]: FTP LOGIN FROM saturn, root
Jan 14 12:35:04 saturn ftpd[833]: retrieve /pub/data/file1
   succeeded, 1019 bytes.
Jan 14 12:35:05 saturn ftpd[833]: FTP LOGOUT, root
```

Finally, each of these two FTP server switches can be specified together (-dl) to generate the absolute maximum amount of log output. If both switches are used, the log generated is simply the combination of the output produced by each of the individual switches; that is, no additional information is generated. As this produces the greatest volume of log data, use the –dl switch combination sparingly on a system with high FTP activity to avoid filling the file system where the log resides, typically /var. Below is an example of an FTP connection and file transfer logged with the –dl switch combination:

```
Jan 14 12:35:38 saturn ftpd[841]: connection from saturn at Wed
   Jan 14 12:35:381998
Jan 14 12:35:38 saturn ftpd[841]: <-- 220 saturn FTP server
   (Tru64 UNIX Version 5.60) ready.
Jan 14 12:35:39 saturn ftpd[841]: command: USER root
Jan 14 12:35:39 saturn ftpd[841]: <-- 331 Password required for
   root.
Jan 14 12:35:42 saturn ftpd[841]: command: PASS XXXX
Jan 14 12:35:42 saturn ftpd[841]: <-- 230 User root logged in.
Jan 14 12:35:42 saturn ftpd[841]: FTP LOGIN FROM saturn, root
Jan 14 12:35:42 saturn ftpd[841]: command: SYST
Jan 14 12:35:42 saturn ftpd[841]: <-- 215 UNIX Type:
L  8 Version: Tru64 UNIX V4.0 (Rev. 878)
Jan 14 12:35:47 saturn ftpd[841]: command: CWD /pub/data
Jan 14 12:35:47 saturn ftpd[841]: <-- 250 CWD command
   successful.
Jan 14 12:35:51 saturn ftpd[841]: command: TYPE I
Jan 14 12:35:51 saturn ftpd[841]: <-- 200 Type set to I.
Jan 14 12:35:51 saturn ftpd[841]: command: PORT 10,0,0,1,4,21
Jan 14 12:35:51 saturn ftpd[841]: <-- 200 PORT command
   successful.
Jan 14 12:35:51 saturn ftpd[841]: command: RETR file1
Jan 14 12:35:51 saturn ftpd[841]: <-- 150 Opening BINARY mode
   data connection for file1 (10.0.0.1,1045) (1019 bytes).
Jan 14 12:35:51 saturn ftpd[841]: <-- 226 Transfer complete.
Jan 14 12:35:51 saturn ftpd[841]: retrieve /pub/data/file1
   succeeded, 1019 bytes.
Jan 14 12:35:52 saturn ftpd[841]: command: QUIT
Jan 14 12:35:52 saturn ftpd[841]: <-- 221 Goodbye.
Jan 14 12:35:52 saturn ftpd[841]: FTP LOGOUT, root
```

By default, this FTP server log information is placed in the file daemon.log in a date-stamped directory under the /var/adm/syslog.dated directory. For instance, the previous ftpd log output was copied from the following file:

```
/var/adm/syslog.dated/current/daemon.log
```

See the section on the syslog daemon in Chapter 12 for details on the syslog facility.

Since the FTP server is actually started by the inetd(8) process, it is necessary to edit the inetd configuration file, /etc/inetd.conf, to specify command line switches to ftpd(8). After any changes to /etc/inetd.conf, simply send the inetd process a hang-up signal to force the inetd to reread its configuration file. For example, to run ftpd with the –dl switch combination, follow these steps:

1. Edit /etc/inetd.conf
2. Locate the entry in /etc/inetd.conf for ftpd. By default, the line is similar to:

```
ftp stream tcp  nowait root  /usr/sbin/ftpd   ftpd
```

3. Add the desired command line argument(s) to the end of the line. For example:

```
ftp stream tcp  nowait root  /usr/sbin/ftpd   ftpd -dl
```

4. Save the file and exit the editor.
5. Signal inetd(8) to reread the /etc/inetd.conf file to cause the updates to take effect:

```
# kill -HUP 'cat /var/run/inetd.pid'
```

All future FTP connections will then be logged as specified by the ftpd command line arguments in the /etc/inetd.conf file. To change the logging or stop FTP logging altogether, edit /etc/inetd.conf and modify or remove any ftpd command line arguments and signal inetd(8) to reread the configuration file.

### 7.11.2 FTP Security Configuration

The Tru64 UNIX FTP server, ftpd(8), has the ability to deny access to particular user accounts based on the contents of two configuration files. The first, /etc/ftpusers, is checked by the FTP server when a user attempts to log in via FTP. If the account name is listed in /etc/ftpusers, that user is not permitted to log in. In addition, the FTP server verifies that the login shell specified in the seventh field of the /etc/passwd file is listed in the /etc/shells file. When troubleshooting a problem where a user is unable to log in to a system via FTP, ensure that the user's account name is not listed in /etc/ftpusers and the user account's log-in shell is contained in /etc/shells. See Section 6.4., "Login Controls" in Chapter 6, "Security," for details on the format of these two ftpd configuration files.

```
root:*:0:1:system PRIVILEGED account:/:/bin/sh
bin:*:3:4:system librarian account:/bin:
ftp:*:1001:15:ftp Account:/var/ftp:/bin/sh
```

**Figure 7.11** *Example of an anonymous FTP passwd(4) file.*

```
system:*:0:root
bin:*:4:bin
users:*:15:bin
```

**Figure 7.12** *Example of an anonymous FTP group(4) file.*

### 7.11.3 Anonymous FTP Configuration

A special FTP server configuration that is commonly used on the Internet as a means of allowing the public to download and upload files is called Anonymous FTP. This configuration does not require an individual account but rather allows anyone to log in via FTP using a commonly known user account, typically "anonymous" or "ftp." A password is prompted for, but the convention is for the user logging in to specify his or her e-mail address, though this convention is not enforced with the Tru64 UNIX FTP server. Because Anonymous FTP allows FTP connections without any authentication, it is critical that Anonymous FTP is configured properly to avoid compromising the security of your system, especially if the system is accessible via the Internet. Following are the minimal steps necessary to securely configure Anonymous FTP on a Tru64 UNIX system.

1. Create an "ftp" user account specifying an appropriate home directory, such as /var/ftp. Note that the remaining steps assume /var/ftp. If another location was selected, substitute that home directory in the following commands.
2. Create several subdirectories in the ftp home directory:

```
# mkdir /var/ftp/bin
# mkdir /var/ftp/etc
# mkdir /var/ftp/pub
```

3. Change the ownership and permissions of the ftp home and subdirectories:

```
# chown root:system /var/ftp
# chown root:system /var/ftp/bin
```

```
# chown root:system /var/ftp/etc
# chown ftp /var/ftp/pub
# chmod 755 /var/ftp
# chmod 755 /var/ftp/bin
# chmod 755 /var/ftp/etc
# chmod 777 /var/ftp/pub
```

4. Copy the statically linked ls(1) executable from /sbin into the ftp $HOME/bin subdirectory:

   ```
   # cp /sbin/ls /var/ftp/bin
   # chown bin:bin /var/ftp/bin/ls
   # chmod 111 /var/ftp/bin/ls
   ```

   This step is necessary to provide the ls(1) command to anonymous FTP users. Ensure that you copy /sbin/ls, which is statically linked, rather than the dynamically linked /usr/bin/ls executable.

5. Create minimal passwd(4) and group(4) files in the ftp $HOME/etc subdirectory:

   ```
   # cp /etc/passwd /var/ftp/etc
   # cp /etc/group /var/ftp/etc
   # chmod 444 /var/ftp/etc/passwd
   # chmod 444 /var/ftp/etc/group
   ```

   Edit these new files to remove all unnecessary entries. The password field in the passwd file is not used and should not contain real encrypted passwords. Replace any encrypted password strings with an asterisk (*). See Figures 7.11 and 7.12 for sample passwd(4) and group(4) files suitable for anonymous FTP.

6. Copy the Tru64 UNIX SIA (Security Integration Architecture) subdirectory into the ftp $HOME/etc subdirectory:

   ```
   # cp -R /etc/sia /var/ftp/etc/sia
   ```

Steps 5 and 6 are necessary to allow the ls(1) command to be able to display file owner and group names rather than user and group ID numbers.

Once Anonymous FTP has been set up, test the configuration by attempting to log in to the system anonymously. Specify either anonymous or ftp as the login name. The following example demonstrates a successful anonymous FTP login:

```
# ftp saturn
```

```
Connected to saturn.
220 saturn FTP server (Tru64 UNIX Version 5.60) ready.
Name (saturn:root): ftp
331 Guest login ok, send ident as password.
Password:
230 Guest login ok, access restrictions apply.
Remote system type is UNIX.
Using binary mode to transfer files.
ftp> dir
200 PORT command successful.
150 Opening ASCII mode data connection for /bin/ls
(10.0.0.1,1046).
total 24
drwxr-xr-x  2 root    system   8192 Mar 15 14:21 bin
drwxr-xr-x  3 root    system   8192 Mar 25 18:53 etc
drwxrwxrwx  2 ftp   users    8192 Mar 15 14:22 pub
226 Transfer complete.
ftp>
```

## 7.12 Summary

In this chapter, we have discussed some of the details of the network services available to the average Tru64 UNIX system. Since most systems today must participate with other systems on an intranet or over the Internet this is a critical part of the average system administrator's job. You should understand enough about how a Tru64 UNIX system is networked given the information presented here to set up basic services and allow the system to participate properly on the network. There are excellent books available for the details of some of the more complex networking daemons and services such as NFS/NIS, gated or sendmail found in Appendix B of this book.

# 8

# Printing

## 8.1 Introduction

Tru64 UNIX supports the ability for users to print both to local printers connected directly to a system's parallel or serial ports and to remote printers via the network. A remote printer can be either another computer's locally connected printer or a standalone network printer. In addition, it may be necessary to provide printing services for other remote clients. Tru64 UNIX supports this print-server ability through the lpd(8) print daemon.

This chapter covers the following Tru64 UNIX printing topics:

- The printer daemon and spooling system
- Local printing
- Remote printing
- Utilities and commands to configure and manage the print services
- Advanced printing

## 8.2 The Tru64 UNIX Printing Subsystem

The printing subsystem on a Tru64 UNIX system is primarily BSD UNIX–based, with the main characteristic being the /etc/printcap configuration file. The BSD UNIX–style print commands include lpr(1), lprm(1), lpq(1), and lpc(8). In addition, Tru64 UNIX supports UNIX System V printing commands such as lp(1) and lpstat(1). Either version of the print commands is acceptable. For instance, these two commands to submit a print job to the draft print queue are equivalent:

```
# lpr -P draft memo.txt
# lp -d draft memo.txt
```

The Tru64 UNIX printing subsystem is managed by the lpd printer daemon. This daemon is typically started when the system enters multiuser mode (run level 3) and runs continuously. Any queued print jobs that were not printed when the system was last shut down are printed when lpd starts up. When a user submits a print job via the lpr or lp command, the following sequence of events occurs:

1. The master lpd printer daemon copies the requested file(s) to the specified printer's spooling directory. If a printer was not specified when the job was submitted, lpd uses the printer specified by the LPDEST[1] or PRINTER environment variable if defined, or else the system default printer is selected. The /etc/printcap file is scanned to determine the spooling directory.
2. The master lpd printer daemon forks a copy of itself to handle the print job, then returns to silently waiting for another print request.
3. The newly forked, or child, lpd printer daemon then perfoms the following operations:
   - The child lpd reads the /etc/printcap file to determine the printer's characteristics.
   - If the printer is remote, the child lpd contacts the master lpd printer daemon on the remote system, transfers the print job to the remote system, and deletes the local copy from the spool directory.
   - If the printer is local, the child lpd checks the spool directory for a lock file. The existence of a lock file usually indicates that another child lpd is already processing this print queue. The lock file contains the process ID (PID) of the existing child lpd process and the name of the file currently being printed. If the lock file exists and the PID contained in the lock file is an actively running lpd process, the newly forked lpd printer daemon exits, since the existing lpd process will take care of printing the submitted job. The purpose of the lock file is to prevent more than one child lpd daemon from processing the same print queue. The results would be unpredictable if this synchronization was not in place and multiple lpd child daemons were essentially fighting over incoming print requests.

1. Only if the Common Desktop Environment (CDE) is in use.

- If, however, the lock file does not exist or the PID in the lock file does not correspond to a running lpd process, the child lpd process creates or overwrites the lock file, inserting its own PID and the name of the first file in the spooling directory. Then the child lpd begins sending the file(s) to the device special file supporting the actual printer.
- As files are printed, the child lpd daemon updates the status file contained in the spool directory. This status file describes the current status of the printer.
- Once the print job has been printed, the child lpd daemon removes the local copy of the file(s) from the spool directory and updates the status file. If additional print jobs have been spooled for this printer, this child lpd will submit them in turn to the printer.
- This child lpd daemon will exit when there are no more files to be printed in this spool directory.

## 8.3 Adding a Local Printer

Configuring local print services on a Tru64 UNIX system includes the following administrative tasks:

- Ensuring the Tru64 UNIX Local Printer Support subset is installed
- Connecting a printer to a port on a Tru64 UNIX system
- Collecting printer information
- Adding an entry for the printer to the /etc/printcap file
- Creating the required printer device file and directories in the spooling area
- Starting the lpd printing daemon if it is not already running
- Testing the printer

### 8.3.1 Required Printing Environment Software

The first step is to verify that the optional Tru64 UNIX "Local Printer Support" software subset is loaded. This subset is named OSFPRINTxxx, where the "xxx" specifies the version of the subset. It contains lpd, the line printer daemon; the various configuration and management utilities; and the spooling system directory structure. To determine if this subset is loaded, execute the following command:

```
# /usr/sbin/setld -i | grep -i osfprint
OSFPRINT510   installed    Local Printer Support (Printing
   Environment)
```

Based on this output, the subset is installed. If you do not receive any output, or if the "installed" keyword in the second column is absent, you must install the subset from the Tru64 UNIX operating system installation media using the setld command. For assistance in installing Tru64 UNIX subsets, see Chapter 4, "System Configuration."

### 8.3.2 Physically Connecting the Printer

Once the required OSFPRINT software subset is installed, the next step to configuring a local printer is to physically connect the printer to the appropriate port. Tru64 UNIX supports both directly connected serial and parallel printers. Connect a printer to the system using the appropriate cable, turn the power on to the printer, and ensure that the printer is online and ready to print as described in the printer owner's documentation.

### 8.3.3 Collecting Printer Information

Before adding the printer to the Tru64 UNIX printing subsystem, it is necessary to gather information about the printer. Most of this information will be added to the /etc/printcap entry for this printer. The /etc/printcap file defines a system's printers. The following information is needed to configure a local printer:

- Printer name
- Alternative printer name(s)
- Printer type (manufacturer) and model
- Connection type (dev, LAT, or tcp)
- Baud rate (for serial printers only)
- Device special file
- Spool directory
- Error log file

The details on how to determine this information follow.

#### *8.3.3.1 Printer Name*

The printer name is more accurately the queue name, and is the name that users will specify when sending print jobs to this printer. A print queue can have multiple names, or aliases; the only limitation on number and length is that the sum total of characters in all the names be less than 80 characters. The selection of a printer name is almost completely arbitrary, with one exception. The name "lp" is special in that it signifies the system default printer. If a print destination is not specified, the print daemon sends the job to the print queue with the name or alias of "lp." The lprsetup(8) utility, discussed later in this chapter (see Section 8.3.4.2), uses a numbering scheme from 0 to 99 for the primary printer name. The first printer configured will be named printer 0, the second will be printer 1, and so on. This strategy is perhaps a good one to follow, even when not using lprsetup to configure printers. Printer aliases are then used for more descriptive printer names.

#### 8.3.3.2 Printer Aliases

It is common to also name a print queue something significant that describes the type, location, or function of the printer. For example, an HP4 laser printer that supports PostSscript printing located in room A5 might be named "hp4," "laser," "room-a5," and "postscript." All of these aliases are acceptable and can coexist, all referring to the same print queue and physical printer. To print to this printer, a user must specify any one of these printer names, unless this printer also has an alias of "lp," in which case it is also the system default printer and specifying a printer name is unnecessary. Thus, all of these print commands are equivalent:

```
# lpr -Plaser letter.txt
# lpr -Proom-a5 letter.txt
# lpr letter.txt
```

Printer aliases are completely optional. The only requirement for configuring a printer is the initial printer name.

#### 8.3.3.3 Printer Type

The printer type is typically the manufacturer and/or the model number of the printer. Tru64 UNIX directly supports a variety of common (and not so common) printer types. Refer to the file /etc/lprsetup.dat for the list of supported printers at that specific release. Supported printers already have default values for many of the parameters. Three special printer types are:

- remote
- unknown
- xf

The remote printer type should be specified when configuring a printer that is not directly connected to the system. Two examples of a remote printer are a printer connected to another Tru64 UNIX system acting as a print server and a network printer directly connected to the network. When configuring a remote printer, two additional pieces of information are required: the host name of the remote system and the printer name on the remote system.

If you are connecting a printer that is not directly supported by Tru64 UNIX, you can specify a printer type of "unknown." When configuring an unknown printer type, you will be asked a series of printer characteristic questions that should be answerable by consulting the printer's owner's manual. Occasionally, a printer not listed as supported has multiple modes, one of which may be supported. For instance, a printer may have an HP LaserJet–compatible mode or an Epson Fx80-compatible mode, both of which are supported. Simply switch the mode of the printer to one of these compatible modes and specify the printer type as that emulated by the compatibility mode.

Finally, if a printer is unsupported and does not have any supported emulation modes, select "xf" as the type. This configures any printer generically and sends output with no formatting or filtering. This is usually only worthwhile when printing plain text to an ASCII printer.

#### 8.3.3.4 Connection Type

The connection type refers to how the printer will be connected to the system. There are three valid connection types: dev, LAT, and tcp. Local printers will be connected to the system either through a serial port or a parallel port, and since these physical ports are accessed by Tru64 UNIX through device special files in the /dev directory, a local printer's connection type is "dev." A networked printer's connection type is "tcp." Finally, for printers accessed via the Local Area Transport (LAT), the connection type is "LAT." The connection type itself is important only in indicating where further information is needed. For instance, when configuring a printer whose connection type is "dev," you will need to know the device special file name for the particular port.

#### 8.3.3.5 Baud Rate

The baud rate is applicable only for locally connected serial printers. Simply determine the baud rate of the printer you are configuring. This value will often be a number such as 4,800 or 9,600. If the printer is a supported type, a default value will be presented by the setup program and, unless the setting has been changed on the printer itself, it is often enough to accept this default baud rate.

#### 8.3.3.6 Device Special File

For a locally connected serial or parallel printer, there will be a device special file located in the /dev directory that the system uses to access the port and thus the printer. The parallel port's device special file is /dev/lpn, and the serial ports are /dev/ttynn, where n and nn specify the number of the port. For instance, the first (or only) parallel port is /dev/lp0; the first serial port is /dev/tty00, and the second serial port is /dev/tty01. This device file is specified in the /etc/printcap file by the "lp" option. For example:

```
lp=/dev/lp0
```

#### 8.3.3.7 Spool Directory

The spool directory is where the lpd print daemon temporarily places print jobs after submission by the user. In addition, the spool directory is used by the print daemon to store several important files used in managing the print queue. For instance, lpd keeps a file named .seq in the spool directory that contains the sequence number of the next print job. The print daemon also stores a file named status that contains the status of the print queue. Because lpd uses the spool directory for more than just storing submitted print jobs, each print queue should have a unique spool directory. Typically, spool directories are located in /usr/spool (usually linked to /var/spool) and have somewhat arbitrary names. By default, the first printer added will have a spool directory of /usr/spool/lpd, the second printer's spool directory will be /usr/spool/lpd1, and so on. A better name for a spool directory would be the printer's name; for instance, for a printer named "draft," name the spool directory /usr/spool/draft. One point to be aware of is that, by default, the /usr/spool directory is contained in the /usr file system. If a user submits a very large print job, the job will be stored in the specified printer's spool directory, and the potential exists to fill the /usr file system if there is limited free space in the /usr file system. If your /usr file system has limited free space and users frequently print many or large files, you should consider either adding space to your /usr file system or possibly locating printer spool directories on another file system with sufficient free space. The spool directory is specified in the /etc/printcap file by the "sd" option. For example:

```
sd=/usr/spool/lpd
```

#### 8.3.3.8 Error Log File

The error log file is simply the location where the lpd print daemon logs printer errors. The type of errors that could be logged include printer errors, such as out-of-paper alerts and printer-offline messages. The error log file is appended to and persists across reboots. For this reason, this error log file grows without bounds and must be manually examined and truncated. The default location for these error log files is in the /usr/adm directory with the name lperr for the first printer, lp1err for the second, and so on. If an error log file is not specified when a printer is configured, any error messages that would have been sent to a log file are instead displayed on the system console. The error log file is specified in the /etc/printcap file by the "lf" option. For example:

```
lf=/usr/adm/lperr
```

Additionally, printing error messages are written to the /var/adm/syslog.dated/<date>/lpr.log files. See Chapter 12, "System Logging and Troubleshooting," for more information on these log files.

#### 8.3.3.9 Insert Escape Sequence

Sometimes there is a requirement to send a special escape sequence to the printer to set up a special function such as changing the pitch or switching to landscape mode. One way to do this is to redefine the form feed and have it sent whenever the device is opened. For example, to send the escape sequence to change the pitch to 16.5 CPI on certain printers you send "<ESC>[4w" to the printer each time it is opened for printing. To make it happen, insert these two lines in that printer's printcap entry:

```
:ff=^[[4w:\
:fo:\
```

Note that the "^[" is the escape character (single ASCII character) and can be inserted using vi(1) by quoting the escape character with this sequence: Ctrl/v followed by Ctrl/[. Using this technique redefines the form feed to the desired escape sequence and enables the form feed character.

### 8.3.4 The /etc/printcap File

The main configuration file for the print subsystem is /etc/printcap. This file is simply a text file that contains the characteristics of each printer configured on the system. This file is read by the lpd print daemon each time a print job is submitted. This means that the lpd print daemon does not have to be signaled or restarted when the /etc/printcap file is modified. The /etc/printcap file consists of options (See Table 8.1) in individual, contiguous entries.

Each entry, which describes a single printer, can be broken into multiple lines with a backslash ("\"). Each option is preceded and followed by a colon (":"). If the entry is broken into multiple lines, a colon and a backslash are required at the end of each line; each continuation line must begin with a colon, and continuation lines are indented by a tab. Comments can be included on lines beginning with the pound sign (#). The following is an example /etc/printcap entry:

```
laser|lp|lp0|0:\
   :af=/usr/adm/lpacct:\
   :if=/usr/lbin/hplaserof:\
   :lf=/usr/adm/lperr:\
   :lp=/dev/lp0:\
   :mx#0:\
   :of=/usr/lbin/hplaserof:\
   :pl#66:\
   :pw#80:\
   :sd=/usr/spool/lpd:\
   :xf=/usr/lbin/xf:
```

Options can have string, numeric, or boolean values. String options have the format "name=string," where string is zero or more characters. Numeric options have the format "name#num." Boolean options are set true by their presence in the /etc/printcap entry and are set false by their absence. If an option is not explicitly included in a printer entry, the option assumes the default value specified in Table 8.1. Refer to the printcap(4) reference page for a full description of all the options.

**Table 8.1** */etc/printcap Options*

| Name | Type | Default | Description |
|---|---|---|---|
| af | string | NULL | Name of accounting file |
| br | number | none | For serial printers, sets the baud rate |
| cf | string | NULL | The cifplot data filter |
| ct | string | dev | The connection type. Only valid when up=psv4.0. The choices are: dev, LAT, and remote. (Required for LAT printers) |
| df | string | NULL | The tex data filter (DVI format) |

**Table 8.1** *(continued)*

| Name | Type | Default | Description |
|---|---|---|---|
| fc | number | 0 | For serial printers, clear flag bits |
| ff | string | \f | String to send for a form feed |
| fo | boolean | false | Print a form feed when the device is opened |
| fs | number | 0 | Like fc, but set bits |
| gf | string | NULL | The graph data filter (plot format) |
| hl | boolean | false | Print the burst header page last |
| ic | boolean | false | Driver supports (nonstandard) ioctl to indent printout |
| if | string | NULL | Name of text filter that does accounting |
| lf | string | /dev/console | Error logging file name |
| lo | string | lock | Name of lock file |
| lp | string | /dev/lp | Device name to open for output. (Required for LAT and remote printers) |
| mj | number | 1000 | Maximum number of jobs that can be submitted to a print queue |
| mx | number | 1000 | Maximum file size (in BUFSIZ blocks). Zero=unlimited |
| nf | string | NULL | The ditroff data filter (for device independent troff) |
| of | string | NULL | Name of output filtering program |
| on | string | NULL | For clusters only. Localhost or comma-separated list of cluster member names |
| pl | number | 66 | Page length (in lines) |
| pw | number | 132 | Page width (in columns) |
| px | number | 0 | Page width in pixels (horizontal) |
| py | number | 0 | Page length in pixels (vertical) |
| rf | string | NULL | Filter for printing FORTRAN style text files |
| rm | string | NULL | Machine name for remote printer. (Required for remote printers) |
| rp | string | lp | Remote printer name. (Required for remote printers) |
| rs | boolean | false | Restrict remote users to those with local accounts |
| rw | boolean | false | Open the printer device for reading and writing |
| sb | boolean | false | Short banner (one line only) |

**Table 8.1** *(continued)*

| Name | Type | Default | Description |
|---|---|---|---|
| sc | boolean | false | Suppress multiple copies |
| sd | string | /usr/spool/lpd | Spool directory. (Required for LAT and remote printers) |
| sf | boolean | false | Suppress form feeds |
| sh | boolean | false | Suppress printing of burst page header |
| st | string | status | Status file name |
| tf | string | NULL | The troff data filter (for the cat photo-typesetter) |
| tr | string | NULL | Trailer string to print when queue empties |
| vf | string | NULL | The raster image filter |
| xc | number | 0 | For serial printers, clear local mode bits |
| xf | string | NULL | Pass-through filter |
| xs | number | 0 | Like xc, but set bits |
| ya | string | NULL | Additional parameters for print filter (I18N) |
| yd | string | NULL | Secondary device name for font faulting (I18N) |
| yp | string | NULL | Printer ID conforming to Wototo standard (I18N) |
| ys | number | 0 | Size of SoftODL character cache (I18N) |
| yt | string | "fifo" | SoftODL character replacement strategy (I18N) |

#### 8.3.4.1 Adding a Printer Entry to /etc/printcap

There are several ways to add, delete, or modify entries in the /etc/printcap file:

- Manually, with an editor such as vi
- With the lprsetup utility
- With the Print Configuration application

Of these three methods, the least desirable is manually, since both lprsetup and the Print Configuration application will also automatically create spool directories and/or error log files in addition to updating the /etc/printcap file. However, manually adding or updating entries in /etc/printcap is perfectly acceptable and can be quicker once you are familiar with the format of the file. Since /etc/printcap is a plaintext file, it can be edited using vi or any other editor.

#### 8.3.4.2 lprsetup

The lprsetup utility is an interactive character-based program that prompts you for printer characteristics and updates /etc/printcap. To see a sample lprsetup in action, see Section 8.6.5 (although that example is actually printconfig, it is identical to lprsetup).

Compaq has indicated that the lprsetup program is to be retired in a future release of Tru64 UNIX. When running Tru64 UNIX V4.0 and later, the recommended method of managing printers is the Printer Configuration application, which has both a graphical and character cell interface.

#### 8.3.4.3 The Printer Configuration Application

The Tru64 UNIX Printer Configuration application, printconfig, is the recommended utility for managing printers on Tru64 UNIX V4.0 and later systems. The Printer Configuration application has both an X Window System/Motif interface and a character-cell interface almost identical to that of the lprsetup utility. This application can be used to add, modify, and delete printers from your system. The Printer Configuration application can be invoked through the CDE Application Manager, which is opened by selecting the Application Manager icon from the CDE Front Panel, followed by selecting System_Admin, then Configuration, and finally the Print application. Once you double-click on the Print application icon, you will be prompted via a Get Password dialog box for the root password. The initial Printer Configuration application window is shown in Figure 8.1.

Optionally, you can start the Printer Configuration application from the command line:

```
/usr/sbin/printconfig [ -ui gui | menu ]
```

Specifying "printconfig" without a command line option causes printconfig to examine the DISPLAY environment variable. If it is defined, the X Window System user interface starts up. If it is not defined, the character cell user interface starts up (as if you had used printconfig –ui menu). Since the lprsetup utility will be retired in a future release of Tru64 UNIX, Compaq recommends using printconfig to manage printers. Doing so will avoid any dependencies on the lprsetup utility.

To see an example of the character-based printconfig command, see Section 8.6.5. The lprsetup and printconfig character cell utilities are identical in behavior.

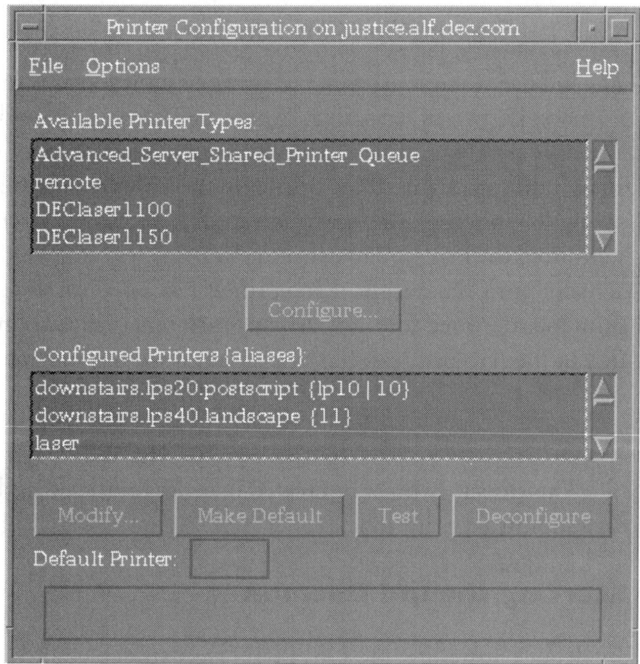


**Figure 8.1** *Initial Printer Configuration window.*

### 8.3.5 Printer Device Files

If either lprsetup or the Printer Configuration application is used to add a printer, the device special file and spooling directories are created if needed. The device file is the special file in the /dev directory that the lpd printer daemon uses to communicate with a local I/O port. Typically, the device special files for the serial ports and parallel port were created when the system was installed. If, however, these files are missing or were removed, use the following steps to recreate them.

To recreate /dev/tty00 and /dev/tty01 (for serial ports one and two):

```
# cd /dev
# ./MAKEDEV ace0  # Serial device is usually ace0 but not
   always
MAKEDEV: special files(0) for ace0:
tty00 tty01
```

To recreate /dev/lp0 for the primary parallel port:

```
# cd /dev
# ./MAKEDEV lp
MAKEDEV: special file(s) for lp:
lp0
```

#### 8.3.5.1 Creating Spooling Directories

The lpd daemon manages the printing of multiple jobs to the same printer by a process known as "spooling." Spooling is saving each submitted print job in a temporary area on disk, typically under the /usr/spool directory hierarchy, and sending each job to the printer in the order in which it was received. This saving, or spooling, of a print job to disk allows the user or application that submitted the print job to continue working without waiting for the printer to actually print the output. Each printer has a dedicated spool directory where print jobs destined for that particular printer are saved. This directory is specified in the /etc/printcap file by the "sd" option. For example:

```
sd=/usr/spool/lpd
```

This directory must be created in order for the print daemon to be able to save submitted print jobs.

### 8.3.6 Starting the lpd Daemon

By default, installing the OSFPRINTxxx subset enables automatic startup of the lpd printer daemon, even if no printers are configured. This subset configures lpd to start when the system is booted. You can determine if the lpd print daemon is currently running by issuing the following command:

```
# ps -ef  |grep lpd
root       637      1  0.0 15:35:39 ??           0:00.01
/usr/lbin/lpd
```

If the lpd print daemon is not running and the OSFPRINTxxx subset is installed, start lpd by issuing the following command:

```
# /sbin/init.d/lpd start
```

### 8.3.7 Testing the Printer

Once a printer has been connected and configured, you should test that the printer was successfully added to the print system. Tru64 UNIX provides a utility, lptest(8), that writes a test pattern to standard output. This pattern contains all 96 printable ASCII characters, staggered to display each character in each column position of the line. To use this utility, simply pipe its output to the lpr command. For instance:

```
# lptest | lpr -Plaser
```

By default, the lptest command displays 200 lines, each 79 characters wide. To specify a different line width and number of output lines, use lptest's two optional command line arguments. The following command displays 10 lines, each 60 characters wide:

```
# lptest 60 10
!"#$%&'()*+,-./0123456789:;<=>?@ABCDEFGHIJKLMNOPQRSTUVWXYZ[\
"#$%&'()*+,-./0123456789:;<=>?@ABCDEFGHIJKLMNOPQRSTUVWXYZ[\]
#$%&'()*+,-./0123456789:;<=>?@ABCDEFGHIJKLMNOPQRSTUVWXYZ[\]^
$%&'()*+,-./0123456789:;<=>?@ABCDEFGHIJKLMNOPQRSTUVWXYZ[\]^_
%&'()*+,-./0123456789:;<=>?@ABCDEFGHIJKLMNOPQRSTUVWXYZ[\]^_'
&'()*+,-./0123456789:;<=>?@ABCDEFGHIJKLMNOPQRSTUVWXYZ[\]^_'a
'()*+,-./0123456789:;<=>?@ABCDEFGHIJKLMNOPQRSTUVWXYZ[\]^_'ab
()*+,-./0123456789:;<=>?@ABCDEFGHIJKLMNOPQRSTUVWXYZ[\]^_'abc
)*+,-./0123456789:;<=>?@ABCDEFGHIJKLMNOPQRSTUVWXYZ[\]^_'abcd
*+,-./0123456789:;<=>?@ABCDEFGHIJKLMNOPQRSTUVWXYZ[\]^_'abcde
```

When troubleshooting printing problems, especially local printers, it is often difficult to isolate the source of a problem. The problem could be with the printer itself, the configuration of the device special file for the port the printer is connected to, or the print service configuration. The first step is to ensure that the printer itself is powered on, has sufficient paper, is connected to the appropriate port (parallel or serial) of the Tru64 UNIX system with the correct cable, and is online. Once these items have been checked, send some output directly to the printer via the device special file. For instance, to output a test pattern to a parallel printer, use the following command:

```
# lptest > /dev/lp0
```

If this test pattern is successfully printed, you can be reasonably sure that the printer itself is configured and cabled correctly. The next step is to check the error log file, which is specified by the "lf" option in the /etc/printcap file entry for the printer. If this error file is nonexistent or empty, then it is possible the printer was not added correctly. Delete the printer and re-add it using the Printer Configuration application.

## 8.4 Adding a Remote Printer

Configuring a Tru64 UNIX system to print to a remote printer is similar to adding a local printer, except that configuring a remote printer requires two additional pieces of information:

- Print server host name

- Print queue name on the print server

### 8.4.1 Print Server Host Name

When configuring a remote printer, it is necessary to know the host name of the print server that is hosting the printer. This host name is usually another computer accessible via the network. This may be another Tru64 UNIX system, a system running a different implementation of UNIX, or a non-UNIX system altogether. In the case of a standalone network printer, this host name may refer to the printer itself. You must be able to resolve the remote system, whether another computer or a network printer, by specifying the host name. This means that the host name and the IP address for the remote system must either be in the local /etc/hosts table or registered with the Domain Name Server (DNS). To test if this is the case, use the ping(1) command. For example, if the remote print server's host name is jupiter, enter the following command:

```
# /sbin/ping -c 3 jupiter
PING jupiter.company.com (192.168.5.2): 56 data bytes
64 bytes from 192.168.5.2: icmp_seq=0 ttl=62 time=2 ms
64 bytes from 192.168.5.2: icmp_seq=1 ttl=62 time=1 ms
64 bytes from 192.168.5.2: icmp_seq=2 ttl=62 time=1 ms
—— jupiter.company.com PING Statistics——
3 packets transmitted, 3 packets received, 0% packet loss
round-trip (ms) min/avg/max = 1/1/2 ms
```

In this example, the host name jupiter resolved to the IP address 192.168.5.2, and the system responded to pings, indicating that it is accessible via the network.

### 8.4.2 Print Queue Name on the Print Server

In addition to the host name of the print server, it is necessary to know the printer or queue name of the printer you wish to access. Contact the system administrator of the remote system for this information. If you have login access to the remote system, simply display the queues on that system with the following command:

```
# lpc status
laser:
       printer is on device '/dev/lp0' speed -1
       queuing is enabled
       printing is enabled
       no entries
       no daemon present
```

In this example, there is a single printer with a print queue name of "laser." In addition, there may be some configuration necessary on the remote print server host to allow remote clients to print to its print queue. These configurations are detailed in Section 8.5.3.

When adding a remote printer, specify a printer type of "remote" in the the Printer Configuration application. The remote printer type is special in that it assumes that the true printer type is managed by the remote print server. When configuring a remote printer, you are prompted for two additional pieces of information: the remote system name and the remote system printer name. This information is specified in the /etc/printcap file by the "rm" and "rp" options, respectively. For example:

```
rm=jupiter.company.com
rp=laser
```

Given a printer with these /etc/printcap entries, print jobs submitted to this printer will be sent to the print queue "laser" on the remote system jupiter.company.com.

## 8.5 Providing Remote Print Services

Once one or more local printers are added to a Tru64 UNIX system, the system can be configured to support remote print services. Rather than installing printers on many systems, frequently a single system is selected to act as a print server. This print server system can then be configured with sufficient print spool space to support many systems' print activity. There are three requirements in order for a Tru64 UNIX system to act as a print server:

- The print server and the print clients must be reachable via the network.
- The print server and the print clients must each be able to resolve the host name of the other.
- Authorized print clients' host names must appear in the print server's /etc/hosts.lpd or /etc/hosts.equiv file.

### 8.5.1 Network Access

The first requirement is fairly obvious. The remote print client systems must be able to reach the print server system across the network. The simplest way to validate this requirement is to telnet from the client to the print server. If the print server's login prompt is presented, the necessary network connectivity is present. If, however, you are unable to reach the print server from the print client, the network may not be correctly configured on either or both of the systems. See Chapter 7, "Networking," for details on configuring the network.

### 8.5.2 Name Resolution

Name resolution is a fancy way of saying, "Can one system determine the IP address of another system given only the host name of the remote system?" The most expedient way to ensure successful name resolution is to place an entry for every remote system in the /etc/hosts file. This is a requirement for both the print server and for any remote print clients. For example, in the following /etc/hosts file fragment, jupiter is the print server host name, and saturn and pluto are print client host names:

```
192.168.5.2  jupiter
192.168.5.3  saturn
192.168.5.4  pluto
```

In addition to the local /etc/hosts file, there is also the Domain Name System (DNS) as a way of resolving IP addresses. DNS is also known as the Berkeley Internet Name Domain, or BIND. DNS is a distributed database that contains information used to translate system host names into IP address and vice versa. To see if a host is known to DNS, use a command like this:

```
$ nslookup jupiter
Server:  fathom.company.com
Address:  192.168.24.6

Name:    jupiter.company.com
Address:  192.168.5.2
```

Here fathom is a DNS server and returns the IP address for jupiter. In this case there is no reason to include a manual entry for jupiter in your /etc/hosts file.

### 8.5.3 Authorizing Remote Print Access

Tru64 UNIX, by default, disallows remote print access. Allowing users on remote systems to submit print jobs to another system is a capability that you, the system administrator, must explicitly enable. When the lpd print daemon on a client system contacts the lpd daemon on a remote system with a print request, the remote lpd daemon determines if remote print access is permitted by searching the /etc/hosts.lpd and the /etc/hosts.equiv files for the name of the system making the print request. If the host name of the requesting system is contained in either of these system files, the remote print request is accepted. Otherwise, the request is rejected and the following message is displayed when querying the status of the queue:

```
# lpq -P draft
saturn:
Warning: saturn.company.com does not have access to remote
printer draft
```

The /etc/hosts.lpd and /etc/host.equiv files have similar formats. Each line is a single entry of the form:

```
[-]host name.
```

To allow a user from another system to print on a local system, that foreign host name must be an entry in one of the files. Preceding a host name with a dash (-) explicitly denies print access from that system. The lpd print daemon searches first the /etc/hosts.equiv file, then the /etc/hosts.lpd file when determining print access control, so the definitions in /etc/hosts.equiv take precedence over /etc/hosts.lpd. However, since the /etc/hosts.equiv file is also used to specify trusted host relationships for remote command execution, /etc/hosts.equiv should not be used to define remote print access. Use /etc/hosts.lpd only to specify this print access. This will avoid confusion and inadvertent trusted host access.

As an example, the following /etc/hosts.lpd file allows remote lpd print access to the systems saturn and pluto, and explicitly denies print access to the system neptune. The absence of an entry for neptune would also indicate denial of print access to the lpd print daemon. Note that lines beginning with a pound sign character (#) and blank lines are ignored.

```
#
# /etc/hosts.lpd
#
saturn
-neptune
pluto
```

## 8.6 Managing the Local Printing System

Tru64 UNIX provides a set of commands to manage the print system after printers have been installed and configured. These commands allow submitting print jobs, canceling submitted print jobs, viewing the status of printers and print queues, enabling and disabling printers, and adjusting the order and priority of individual jobs in the print queue. These commands include:

- lpr(1) and lp(1)
- lpq(1) and lpstat(1)
- lprm(1) and cancel(1)
- lpc(8)

### 8.6.1 lpr and lp

The lpr and lp commands are the BSD UNIX and System V UNIX commands, respectively, used to submit print jobs to the Tru64 UNIX print system. The two commands do the same thing, but have different syntax. Deciding which flavor command to use is purely a personal preference. Both lpr and lp can be invoked with just a single argument specifying the file to be printed. For example, each of these commands will print the file "program.c" on the system default printer:

```
# lpr progra.c
# lp program.c
```

The most common additional argument to these commands specifies the printer to use. For the lpr command, the flag to use is "-P" for Printer; for the lp command, use the flag "-d" for Destination:

```
# lpr -P draft program.c
# lp -d draft program.c
```

### 8.6.2 lpq and lpstat

The lpq and lpstat commands are used to display the status of print queues. Issuing either of these commands with no arguments displays the status of the system default print queue. For instance, the following example shows that there are three entries in the default printer queue, and one of them (job #91) is actively being printed:

```
# lpq
Sat Feb 17 16:59:20 2001: Attempting to print dfA091saturn
Rank    Pri  Owner  Job  Files              Total Size
active  0    root   91   /etc/hosts         1107 bytes
1st     0    aey    93   /home/aey/main.c   21987 bytes
2nd     0    cjy    94   /home/cjy/memo     2151 bytes
```

The lpq command has the ability to display the status of an individual print job, a particular printer (the "-P" flag), or print requests from individual users. The lpq command is primarily for displaying the status of print queues. See the lpq man page for more information on its options.

The lpstat command is a more general status utility. In addition to displaying the status of individual print queues, lpstat can display the status of the lpd printer daemon, the name of the system default destination, and which device special files correspond to which printers. A useful switch of the lpstat command is "-t," which displays the status of the entire print system including all defined printers:

```
# lpstat -t
System default destination: lp
Scheduler is running
Output for printer draft is sent to /dev/lp0
draft:
  printer is on device '/dev/lp0' speed -1
  queuing is enabled
  printing is enabled
  3 entries in spool area
  no daemon present
Requests on draft:
Sat Feb 17 16:59:20 2001:
Rank   Pri  Owner  Job  Files              Total Size
Active 0    root   91   /etc/hosts         1107 bytes
1st    0    aey    93   /home/aey/main.c   21987 bytes
2nd    0    cjy    94   /home/cjy/memo     2151 bytes
```

Refer to the lpq and lpstat man pages for more information on these commands.

### 8.6.3 lprm and cancel

The opposite of the lpr/lp pair, which submit print jobs, is the lprm/cancel utility pair. These programs delete print requests that have already been queued. While the lprm command is a BSD UNIX utility and the cancel command is a System V UNIX utility, either can be used on a Tru64 UNIX system to delete queued print jobs. Both utilities allow deletion of individual print jobs and removal of all jobs from a particular print queue; however, the lprm command also supports deleting all print jobs submitted by a particular user.

To remove individual print jobs, simply issue the command specifying the print job request ID on the command line. The request ID for a particular print job can be determined from the output of the lpq or lpstat command.

Only users with superuser privileges can remove print jobs submitted by other users. For example, to remove request ID 83, issue either of the following commands:

```
# lprm 83
# cancel 83
```

Removing all print jobs spooled for a particular printer is easily done by specifying the printer name as an argument to lprm or cancel. The lprm command has a similar syntax to the lpr command, in that you specify the printer with the "-P" flag. The cancel command, on the other hand, has no special command line flag. As an example, to remove all pending print requests from the printer named "draft," use either of the following commands:

```
# lprm -P draft
# cancel draft
```

Finally, the lprm command has the ability to remove all print requests submitted by a particular user. Specifying one or more users on the command line removes any requests belonging to those users. This works only for a user with superuser authority. For example, the following command removes all queued print jobs submitted by the aey account:

```
# lprm aey
```

A variation on specifying user accounts to the lprm command is the "-" flag. If a non-root user issues the following command, all requests from the user issuing the command are removed:

```
$ lprm -
```

However, if the root user issues the same command, the entire print queue is emptied.

### 8.6.4 lpc

The lpc (line printer control) utility is a tool used to manage printers on a Tru64 UNIX system and provides a system administrator with the ability to:

- Disable and enable printers
- Disable and enable print queues

- Change the order of jobs in a print queue
- Display the status of printers, print queues, and the printer daemon

The lpc utility has two modes of operation, command driven and interactive. The mode is determined by how the utility is invoked. If lpc is run with no arguments, it assumes that the user desires the interactive mode and displays an "lpc>" prompt, waiting for input. When arguments are supplied from the command line, lpc executes the command provided as the argument and exits. See the reference page for lpc for a list of the lpc commands.

The following is an example of an interactive lpc session:

```
# lpc
lpc> status
draft:
  printer is on device '/dev/lp0' speed -1
  queuing is enabled
  printing is enabled
  no entries
  no daemon present
lpc>
```

Part of a system administrator's role is to manage printers and print queues. If, for instance, a particular printer needs repair and will be unavailable for a period of time, you can use the lpc command to mark the printer as "down," which disables printing. The lpc "down" command expects a message that should indicate the cause of the printer unavailability and perhaps an estimated outage duration. For example, the following command will accomplish this:

```
# lpc down draft "Draft printer down for repair until 3pm
  Monday."
draft:
  printer and queuing disabled
# lpq -P draft
Warning: draft is down:
Warning: draft queue is turned off
Draft printer down for repairs until 3pm Monday.
no entries
```

Notice that the lpq command reports that the printer is down and the queue is disabled, and the message entered with the "lpc down" command is also displayed. Once the printer is repaired, simply cancel the printer "down" operation with the following command:

```
# lpc up draft
```

### 8.6.5 TCP Printing

Another method of printing is TCP Printing. This is used when the printer has an IP address and listens on a particular port for incoming print jobs. These printers are necessarily remote printers, and are most likely standalone printers with network interfaces and some modest intelligence. A TCP printer can be configured using the techniques discussed previously, with a couple of minor modifications.

First, the printer must have an IP address and the host must be able to reach the printer. The IP address could be added to the /etc/hosts file or to DNS. Next, consult the printer documentation to determine on which port the printer will listen. Once the printer is connected to the network and its IP address is assigned, the printer is ready to be configured on the Tru64 UNIX host.

In this example, an LN17 PostScript printer is configured. According to the printer's documentation, this printer listens on port 2501. To verify that port 2501 is correct, simply telnet to that port and check for a successful connection.

```
# telnet unln17c 2501
Trying 192.168.24.139...
Connected to 192.168.24.139.
Escape character is '^]'.
^]
telnet> quit
Connection closed.
```

This shows a successful connection to the port, as opposed to the following failure:

```
# telnet unln17c 2502
Trying 192.168.24.139...
telnet: Unable to connect to remote host: Connection refused
```

Once the printer is configured and the port number is known, add an entry to the /etc/services file to indicate what that port is. In this example, it will look like this:

```
tcpprt      2501/tcp            # TCP printing for the LN17
```

Finally, run printconfig to configure the printer. The only difference from this point forward is that the "lp", or device path, is a bit different than previously seen. The "lp" device path will be of the form

"@<hostname>/<servicename>"; in the example below, this path is "@unln17c/tcpprt":

```
# printconfig

Tru64 UNIX Printer Setup Program

Command  < add modify delete exit view quit help >: add

Adding printer entry, type '?' for help.

Enter printer name to add [lp1] :

For more information on the specific printer types
Enter 'printer?'

Enter the FULL name of one of the following printer types:

DEClaser1100 (ln07)   escp_a4_12cpi   hp61     la380k   lg12
  ln17ps
DEClaser1150 (ln07r)  fx1050          hp61_a4  la400
  lg12plus  ln17ps_a4
DEClaser2100 (ln05)   fx80            hp8000   la424
  lg14plus  ln20
DEClaser2150 (ln05r)  generic_ansi    hpIIID   la50     lg31
  ln20_a4
DEClaser2200 (ln06)   generic_ansi_a4 hpIIIP   la600
  lg104plus ln32
DEClaser2250 (ln06r)  generic_text    hpIIP    la70
  lg105plus ln40
DEClaser2300 (ln05ja) generic_text_a4 hpIV     la75
  lg108plus ln40_a4
DEClaser2400 (ln10ja) hp1120c         ibmpro   la84
  lg109plus ln82r
DEClaser3200 (ln08)   hp1120c_a4      la100    la86     lj250
  lnc02
DEClaser3250 (ln08r)  hp4000tn        la120    la88     lj252
  lnc02_a4
DEClaser3500 (ln14)   hp4000tn_a4     la210    la88c    ln03
  nec290
DEClaser5100 (ln09)   hp4050          la280    la90     ln03ja
  ps_level1
HPLaserJet4LC/4VC     hp4mplus        la30n    lf01r    ln03r
  ps_level2
clientps              hp4mplus_a4     la30n_a4 lg02     ln03s
  remote
clienttxt             hp5000          la30w    lg04plus ln15
  unknown
cp382d                hp5simx         la30w_a4 lg05plus ln15_a4
  wwpsof
dl510ka               hp5simx_a4      la324    lg06     ln16
  xf
```

```
ep1050+              hp680c          la380    lg08plus ln17
escp_a4_10cpi        hp680c_a4       la380cb  lg09plus ln17_a4


or press RETURN for [unknown] : ln17ps

Enter printer synonym: laser01

Enter printer synonym:

Set device pathname 'lp' [] ?  @unln17c/tcpprt

Do you want to capture print job accounting data ([y]|n)?

Set accounting file 'af' [/usr/adm/lp1acct] ?

Set spooler directory 'sd' [/usr/spool/lpd1] ?

Set printer error log file 'lf' [/usr/adm/lp1err] ?

Enter the name of the printcap symbol you wish to modify.
Other
valid entries are:

        'q'     to quit (no more changes)

        'p'     to print the symbols you have specified so far

        'l'     to list all of the possible symbols and
   defaults
The names of the printcap symbols are:


 af  br  cf  ct  df  dn  du  fc  ff  fo  fs  gf  ic  if  lf  lo

 lp  mc  mj  mx  nc  nf  of  on  op  os  pl  pp  ps  pw  px  py

 rf  rm  rp  rs  rw  sb  sc  sd  sf  sh  st  tf  tr  ts  uv  vf

 xc  xf  xn  xs  ya  yd  yj  yp  ys  yt  Da  Dl  It  Lf  Lu  Ml

 Nu  Or  Ot  Ps  Sd  Si  Ss  Ul  Xf

Enter symbol name: q

        Printer #1
        ------
Symbol  type  value
----  --  ---
  af    STR    /usr/adm/lp1acct
  if    STR    /usr/lbin/pcfof +Cln17ps.pcf
  lf    STR    /usr/adm/lp1err
  lp    STR    @unln17c/tcpprt
```

```
  mx    INT    0
  of    STR    /usr/lbin/pcfof +Cln17ps.pcf
  pl    INT    66
  pw    INT    80
  rw    BOOL   on
  sd    STR    /usr/spool/lpd1
  xf    STR    /usr/lbin/xf

Are these the final values for printer 1 ? [y]


Adding comments to printcap file for new printer, type '?' for
help.
Do you want to add comments to the printcap file [n] ? :

Set up activity is complete for this printer.
Verify that the printer works properly by using
the lpr(1) command to send files to the printer.


Command  < add modify delete exit view quit help >: exit
From this point you can print to and manage this printer in
much the same way that you would print to and manage a local
printer.
```

## 8.7 Advanced Printing

Advanced Printing is a distributed, client/server, standards-based print subsystem available from Compaq as an Associated Product. It provides a logical queue layer between the user and the physical printers themselves. The printers in the previous sections are all considered physical queues, since they are associated with a specific physical printer. The Advanced Printing Software allows a user to specify a printer type or a logical printer, rather than a particular physical printer, and provides a framework where the user can query types of printers. The print system is based on the ISO/IEC 10175 and POSIX 1387.4 standards. To understand how this new printing environment works, consider its components. Advanced Printing is composed of servers, clients, spoolers, supervisors, and logical and physical printers.

Clients make requests of servers, by way of interprocess communication (IPC), and the servers perform an action, usually associating the job to a printer and printing it. The client programs include the command line interface (CLI), the graphical user interface (GUI), and the LPD inbound gateway. Primarily, the clients will request to print a job or get the status of a printer. The servers consist of the spoolers and supervisors: a system that is an Advanced Printing Server will have at least one spooler and at least one supervisor. The spooler directs print jobs to print queues and schedules them to be printed. The supervisor takes the jobs from spooler queues and matches up job requirements to printer capabilities, then prints the jobs and reports status to the spooler and clients.

Logical and physical printers are connected by queues; users print to logical printers. By using this approach, the physical printers can be changed with little or no impact to users, and the users can specify their requirements based on printer capabilities rather than specifying a particular printer at a particular location. Also, the system administrator can set up the logical-physical printer relationship to be fan-in or fan-out. Fan-in means several logical printers point to a single physical printer; fan-out is just the opposite, with a small number of logical printers pointing to a number of physical printers. Consider this example: if you had four equally capable laser printers, you might consider creating one logical printer called "laser" that feeds all four physical printers. There are several benefits to this approach, not the least of which are load balancing and the ability to take one of the physical printers offline for maintenance. Taking a printer offline can be done with no impact to the user whatsoever, provided the remaining printers can keep up with the printing demand.

## 8.7.1 Installing

Before installing the Advanced Printing subsets, make sure the installation requirements are met. For a print server, the requirement is 64 MB of memory, while clients need at least 32 MB. Also, consideration should be given as to how the print system will be configured. For example, which system(s) will be servers, which will be clients, will the LPD Gateways be required, how will the name space be managed, and so forth. You can find more details on these decisions in the Advanced Printing Software Installation Guide.

When you are ready to perform the installation, locate the Associated Products CD, Volume 2, and mount it:

```
# mount -r /dev/disk/cdrom0c /mnt
```

```
Then use setld to install the Advanced Printing subsets:
setld -l /mnt/Advanced_Printing/kit
```

*Note:* You can also install the Advanced Printing subsets via RIS. Once the RIS server is configured to serve this layered product, install it with a similar setld command:

```
setld -l ris-server:
```

Follow the setld prompts and install the subsets needed for this system. For more details, again refer to the Advanced Printing Software Installation Guide.

### 8.7.2 Configuring

Although you can enter configuration commands manually, as will be shown later, the simplest way to initially configure the Advanced Printing subsystem is to run the pd_get_started script. This partial example shows setting up the initial environment, which includes the spooler, supervisor, LPD outbound gateway, and queues (both logical and physical). Several of the individual steps are removed, but the final menu shows what has been accomplished. It is just a matter of following the prompts and filling in the requested information.

```
# /usr/pd/scripts/pd_get_started

               Compaq Advanced Printing Software Setup

                         *** MAIN MENU ***

  1  Create/Delete Servers

  2  Startup/Shutdown Servers

  3  Create Printer/Queue Combination

  4  Display Servers and Printers

  5  Exit

Enter the number that corresponds to your choice:[5] 1

.
.
.
Do you want job-sheets printed at the start of every job?
([y]/n)

               Compaq Advanced Printing Software Setup

                     *** PRINTER DEFINITION ***

          1  Printer name:            laser01
          2  Printer attribute file:
Digital_LN17_Level2PS.paf
          3  Printer connection:      ip-socket
          4  Printer address:         192.168.24.139
          5  Two-sided printer:       Yes
```

```
              6  Job separator pages:      Yes
              7  Spooler name:             justice_spl
              8  Supervisor name:          justice_sup

              9  Create new printer as specified above.

              q  Return to Main Menu

Enter the number that corresponds to your choice:[9]
Creating queue laser01_q
Creating physical printer laser01_pp
Creating logical printer laser01
Creating initial-value-job object laser01_IVJ_DEFAULT
Creating initial-value-document object laser01_IVD_DEFAULT

Logical printer information:

printer-name  printer-realization  printer-state  enabled
------------  -------------------  -------------  -------
laser01       logical              idle           yes


Physical printer information:

printer-name  printer-realization  printer-state  enabled
------------  -------------------  -------------  -------
laser01_pp    physical             idle           yes

Users can submit print jobs on the new printer using the pdpr
command like this:

  $ pdpr -p laser01 -x "sides=2" /etc/motd

Would you like to print a test job? ([y]/n)

A test job has been successfully submitted.

Printer laser01 is set up.
```

### 8.7.3 Managing the Environment

Managing the Advanced Printer environment is slightly different from managing the regular BSD printing environment, although the general approach is similar. This section is not intended to provide a comprehensive guide to managing the Advanced Printing software environment; however, given the initial configuration produced by running /usr/pd/scripts/pd_get_started, this section will highlight some important elements of the environment.

Knowing some of the commands used to manage the printers is a good starting point. Table 8.2 contains a list of the more useful ones.

**Table 8.2** *Useful Advanced Printing Commands*

| Command | Function |
|---|---|
| pdpr | Submit print job |
| pdls | List jobs pending on a printer or printer attributes |
| pdcreate | Create a printer (logical or physical) |
| pdenable | Enable the printer for printing |
| pdclean | Clean/delete jobs from the printer |
| pdpause | Pause printing on the printer |
| pdresume | Resume printing on the printer |
| pdresubmit | Resubmit a job that isn't yet printing to another printer |
| pdpromote | Move a job to the front of the queue |

#### 8.7.3.1 The Name Space

In any distributed environment, it is a good management technique to have a central repository for names. The Advanced Printing Software supports existing distributed name databases such as the Network Information System (NIS) and Lightweight Directory Access Protocol (LDAP), as well as local file naming. For more details on how to set this up for Advanced Printing, see the Advanced Printing documentation.

#### 8.7.3.2 Printers and Queues

The pd_get_started program creates the Servers (Spooler and Supervisor) and an initial printer (physical and logical). To add another independent printer, simply re-run the program and follow the prompts. A more interesting operation, however, is adding another printer to the original logical printer. This method allows for two printers to be fed by a single logical queue. This is the fan-out method mentioned earlier.

To add a new physical printer, laser02_pp, to be fed by the logical printer, laser01_q, is fairly simple. When the new physical printer is created, it is associated with the existing logical printer:

```
# pdcreate -c printer -X \
/usr/opt/APX110/share/cap/Digital_LN17_Level2PS.paf \
-x printer-address=192.168.24.138  \
```

```
-x associated-queue=laser01_q justice_sup:laser02_pp
```

Now enable it for printing:

```
# pdenable laser02_pp
```

To verify that the logical printer laser01 will fan out to both physical printers, use the pdls command to check which physical printers are associated with the logical printer:

```
# pdls -c printer -r printer-associated-printers -s line \
laser01

laser01: printer-associated-printers = laser01_pp
                                       laser02_pp
```

#### 8.7.3.4 Security

There are three levels of operations that users of the Advanced Printing system can perform:

- End-user
- Operator
- Administrative

The operations that these groups of users are allowed to perform are determined by Access Control Lists (ACLs). Certain users are allowed to perform Operator or even Administrator functions on certain printers. Refer to the System Administration and Operation Guide for Advanced Printing for complete directions.

### 8.7.4 LPD Gateways

To maintain compatibility with existing printing, there is an LPD Inbound Gateway and LPD Outbound Gateway. By configuring these two gateways you can ensure that applications that can only print to the BSD-based printers continue to function and other printers in your environment that may only understand LPD remain accessible.

#### 8.7.4.1 LPD Inbound Gateway

The LPD Inbound Gateway can either replace or coexist with the BSD/lpd printing environment. If configured to replace the lpd print system, all printing is done through the Advanced Printing system. If configured to coexist, lpr and lp can still be used, and applications that know only about BSD printing will still operate.

To complete the loop so that lpd can use the Advanced Printing printers, add an entry to /etc/printcap that associates the BSD printer with an Advanced Printing printer. This printer is called a "gateway printer." To create a gateway printer, add an entry with "rm=@dpa" and "rp=printername," where printername is the logical printer name in Advanced Printing. For example:

```
lp20|laser_old:\
:lp=:\
:rm=@dpa:\
:rp=laser01:\
:sd=/var/spool/lp20:\
:mx#0:
```

Any BSD print jobs submitted to laser_old are sent to the Advanced Printing printer laser01.

To configure the LPD Inbound Gateway, run the script /usr/pd/scripts/inbound_gw_config.sh. In this example, the gateway and lpd are configured to coexist:

```
# /usr/pd/scripts/inbound_gw_config.sh


   Compaq Advanced Printing Software Inbound Gateway
Configuration Script


   The Inbound Gateway is a daemon that allows users to print
using
   ASU and lpr/lpd, and have those print jobs be transferred to
printers
   on the Compaq Advanced Printing Software system.  This
script
   will set up your system to run the Inbound Gateway.

Do you wish to use the Inbound Gateway? ([yes]|no) yes

   The Inbound Gateway can either take the place of lpd on
   this system (if all printers will be accessed through
   Compaq Advanced Printing Software) *or* it can
   run in conjunction with lpd so that both printers accessed
   through Compaq Advanced Printing Software and printers
   accessed using traditional lpd filters (defined in
   /etc/printcap) can be used simultaneously.  Unless you are
   running out of process slots on your system, Compaq
```

```
   recommends you answer yes to the following question.

Will both lpd printers *and* Compaq Advanced Printing Software
printers be used on this system?  ([yes]|no)

   You can choose to start the inbound gateway daemon now,
   or you can wait until the next time the system starts up.
   Note that if an inbound gateway daemon is already running
   on this system, it will be stopped and restarted after all
   configuration paramenters are entered.

Do you want to start the Inbound Gateway now? ([yes]|no)

   You have requested the following:

        Use Inbound Gateway:                     YES
        Use Gateway *and* lpd:                   YES
        Start Inbound Gateway now:               YES

   Is this correct?  ([yes]|no)

Updating /etc/rc.config ...

Starting Inbound Gateway daemon on justice.alf.dec.com
/usr/pd/sbin/in.bsd-gw -l

Inbound Gateway Setup Complete
```

Based on the application there may be some lpr-Advanced Printing Software mapping issues. Refer to the Advanced Printing Software System Administration and Operation Guide for the details.

#### *8.7.4.2 LPD Outbound Gateway*

The LPD Outbound Gateway provides a mechanism whereby jobs can be sent to a remote printer using the LPD protocol. This is accomplished by converting the print job to an RFC1179 request and sending it to the remote lpd daemon. Obviously, the remote system must support the LPD protocol.

To create a physical printer that will route print jobs to a remote lpd host, include the attribute printer-address with the following format:

```
printer-address=remotehost,printername,protocol_conformance
```

where protocol_conformance is one of:

- 1179
- Solaris

- DIGITAL UNIX
- Xerox

For example, to set up a printer called office01 on LPD host justice.abc.com (a Tru64 UNIX system), the printer-address attribute would look like this:

```
printer-address="justice.abc.com,office01,DigitalUNIX"
```

There are some limitations on the mappings of Advanced Printing to the LPD system, so refer to the Advanced Printing Software System Administration and Operation Guide for details.

# 9

# Processes and Resources

## 9.1 Process Management

Tru64 UNIX provides a rich computing environment due to its multiprocessing and multiuser nature. The ability for multiple users to run multiple jobs simultaneously provides great flexibility to end users. Of course, this ability is not limited to Tru64 UNIX, nor even just to UNIX itself, but exists in a variety of computing environments, such as large mainframe environments, vendor proprietary systems such as Compaq's OpenVMS, and Microsoft's Windows 2000. UNIX, however, and Tru64 UNIX in particular, has gained a reputation since the early 1970s as the operating system of choice for supporting software development efforts, especially large team projects, and multiuser database applications, such as those based on Oracle, Informix, or Sybase.

A Tru64 UNIX system administrator comes to this environment needing the skills to understand and manage this multiprocessing capability. In UNIX, a single job, whether it has a system function, such as authenticating user logins or receiving and handling print requests, or is a user activity, such as compiling a C++ program or querying a database, is called a *process*. Managing these processes, which can be as few as a couple of dozen processes on an individual workstation, or many thousands of processes on a large database or Web server, is an important part of a system administrator's responsibility.

In this chapter, we discuss the various attributes of a process, how these attributes interrelate, and which attributes can be adjusted to change the behavior of a process. In addition, the parent/child process relationship is covered. This relationship is important in understanding how processes start and finish. Controlling processes includes the various ways to start a process, changing the state of a process by sending signals to the process, and the concept of foreground and background processes. Tru64 UNIX also provides several methods of scheduling processes to be run at a future date. This capability is used extensively by system administrators to schedule periodic maintenance processes, such as system backups, to run without user intervention.

## 9.2 Process Overview

A process is composed of executing code and its address space. A program and a process are not necessarily one and the same; a single program can be made up of many processes. There are frequently performance benefits to breaking large or complex programs into multiple processes on a UNIX system. Each active process has an entry in the system process table, which is managed by the system scheduler. Processes are the mechanism by which all work, whether system task or user application, is performed on a Tru64 UNIX system.

The process table is a memory structure that contains information about each running process. This information includes the process identification number, or PID, the current state of the process (such as RUNNING or SLEEPING), accounting data such as the amount of CPU time used, and the actual command or program associated with the process. The process table is used by the system scheduler to assign CPU usage to individual processes based on their priority. The system scheduler is part of the first process created, which has a PID of zero (0). The second process, init, is always PID 1 and is the ultimate parent from which all subsequent processes are spawned.

The maximum number of processes that can run simultaneously is derived from the "maxusers" system parameter. The Tru64 UNIX documentation defines maxusers as the number of simultaneous users that a system can support without straining system resources. The formula for calculating the maximum number of processes changed in Tru64 UNIX version 5.0. Before V5.0, the formula was:

```
(maxusers*8) + 20
```

Beginning with V5.0, the formula is:

```
(maxusers*32) rounded up to a power of 2
```

For example, with maxusers set to 1000, a V4.0 system can run up to 8,020 simultaneous processes, while a V5.0 system can run up to 32768 processes.

The default value of maxusers is 32 in older versions of Tru64 UNIX. This is a very conservative value, perhaps suitable for an individual workstation, but definitely too low for most systems. Beginning in V5.0, the kernel sets the value of maxusers at boot time, based on the amount of physical memory in the system. The relationship between maxusers and physical memory is shown in Table 9.1.

The minimum possible value of maxusers is 8. The maximum is 16,384 (4,096 prior to V5.0.)

When the maximum number of processes is reached, the kernel writes a "pid table is full" message in the /var/adm/messages file and to the kernel event-logging system, similar to the following:

```
Apr 23 11:07:44 martin vmunix: pid table is full
```

You may also see a more informative message, such as the following:

```
The fork function failed.  Too many processes already exist.
```

To resolve this situation, increase maxusers to an appropriate value. Increasing maxusers has become progressively easier in successive versions of Tru64 UNIX. Prior to V4.0, it was necessary to modify the maxusers value in the kernel configuration file (/sys/conf/<HOSTNAME>), rebuild the kernel, and reboot the system with the new kernel. In version 4, maxusers could be specified in the proc subsystem stanza of /etc/sysconfigtab; this value was loaded at boot time and remained in effect while the system was up. In version 5, the initial value of maxusers is loaded from /etc/sysconfigtab, but it is now possible to raise (but not to lower) the value while the system is running. As such, it is now possible to resolve an "out of processes" problem without rebooting the system.

**Table 9.1** *Default Value of maxusers in Tru64 UNIX Version 5*

| Physical memory size | Value of maxusers |
|---|---|
| Up to 32 MB | 16 |
| More than 32 MB, less than 256 MB | 128 |
| At least 256 MB, less than 512 MB | 256 |
| At least 512 MB, less than 1 GB | 512 |
| At least 1 GB, less than 2 GB | 1024 |
| 2 GB or more | 2048 |

The following example illustrates increasing maxusers from 32 to 200 on a running system:

```
# sysconfig -q proc maxusers
proc:
maxusers = 32
```

This shows that the current value is 32.

```
# sysconfig -r proc maxusers=200
maxusers: reconfigured
```

The sysconfig –r command changes the value. To verify the change:

```
# sysconfig -q proc maxusers
proc:
maxusers = 200
```

This confirms that the value currently in use is now 200. But what happens on the next reboot? Check the contents of /etc/sysconfigtab:

```
# sysconfigdb -l proc
 proc:
        maxusers = 32
        max_proc_per_user = 10000
```

The sysconfig –r command did not change the value of maxusers in /etc/sysconfigtab, so on the next reboot, maxusers will revert to 32. To change the value in /etc/sysconfigtab, you can use either dxkerneltuner(8) (a graphical interface) or sysconfigdb(8) (a command line utility). To use the latter, it is necessary to create a stanza file containing the desired subsystem parameter values. Then use sysconfigdb to merge the changes into /etc/sysconfigtab:

```
# cat proc.stanza
proc:
maxusers = 200
# sysconfigdb -m -f proc.stanza
Warning: duplicate attribute in proc: was maxusers = 32, now
   maxusers = 200
```

To verify that the value was changed successfully:

```
# sysconfigdb -l proc
proc:
        maxusers = 200
        max_proc_per_user = 10000
```

## 9.3 Process Attributes

Tru64 UNIX stores a variety of attributes about each active process in a kernel memory data structure. This structure, proc, is defined in the /usr/include/sys/proc.h header file. The following sections describe some of the more interesting process attributes:

- Process Identifier (PID)
- Parent Process Identifier (PPID)
- Process Group Identifier (PGID)
- Process Owner's Real and Effective User Identifier (UID/EUID)
- Process Owner's Real and Effective Group Identifier (GID/EGID)
- Process Priority
- Resource Utilization
- Controlling Terminal (if any)
- Process State

### 9.3.1 Displaying Process Attributes

The attributes of active processes can be displayed using the ps(1) (process status) utility. Running ps with no comman-dline arguments prints information about processes associated with the controlling terminal:

```
$ ps
PID TTY    S       TIME COMMAND
21281 ttyp0  S   0:00.08 -ksh (ksh)
```

This default output format displays the process ID (PID), the controlling terminal (TTY), the state (S), the CPU time used by the process (TIME), and the command that is running (COMMAND). The Tru64 UNIX ps utility has a variety of command line switches that specify which attributes to display and how to display them. There are two distinct command line sets, based on the System V (SYSV) and BSD "flavors" of UNIX. The SYSV comman-dline set is used when the arguments are preceded with a dash "-"; otherwise, the arguments are considered to be BSD format. Some examples follow.

An example of SYSV process display output:

```
# ps -ef

UID  PID  PPID  C    STIME  TTY  TIME     CMD
```

```
root 0    0      0.0  Jun 03 ??    15:20.91 [kernel idle]
root 1    0      0.0  Jun 03 ??    0:35.07  /sbin/init -a
root 3    1      0.0  Jun 03 ??    1:30.53  /sbin/kloadsrv
root 22   1      0.0  Jun 03 ??    12:15.65 /sbin/update
root 95   1      0.0  Jun 03 ??    0:16.80  /usr/sbin/syslogd
root 97   1      0.0  Jun 03 ??    0:00.04  /usr/sbin/binlogd
root 349  1      0.0  Jun 03 ??    0:20.21  -accepting
  connections (sendmail)
root 401  1      0.0  Jun 03 ??    0:25.62  /usr/sbin/os_mibs
root 403  1      0.0  Jun 03 ??    3:47.75  /usr/sbin/snmpd
root 420  1      0.0  Jun 03 ??    0:00.58  /usr/sbin/inetd
root 453  1      0.0  Jun 03 ??    0:01.02  /usr/sbin/cron
root 469  1      0.0  Jun 03 ??    0:00.02  /usr/lbin/lpd
root 536  1      0.0  Jun 03 console 0:00.42 /usr/sbin/getty
 console console vt100
mcheek    28727 28801  0.3  17:13:51  ttyp0 0:00.90
 -ksh (ksh)
root 6959  28727  0.0  18:47:47  ttyp0  0:00.19  ps -ef
```

A look at the same system, with the BSD process display output:

```
# ps auxw

USER  PID  %CPU  %MEM  VSZ  RSS  TTY  S  STARTED  TIME
 COMMAND
root  0  0.0  7.5  76.0M  4.6M  ??  R <  Jun 03  15:20.91
 [kernel idle]
root  1  0.0  0.1  440K  40K  ??  I  Jun 03 0:35.07
 /sbin/init -a
root  3  0.0  0.0  904K  0K  ??  IW  Jun 03  1:30.53
 /sbin/kloadsrv
root  22  0.0  0.1  1.55M  56K  ??  S  Jun 03 12:15.65
 /sbin/update
root  95  0.0  0.2  1.61M  120K  ??  S  Jun 03  0:16.80
 /usr/sbin/syslogd
root  97  0.0  0.0  1.59M  0K  ??  IW  Jun 03  0:00.04
 /usr/sbin/binlogd
root  349  0.0  0.1  1.86M  72K  ??  I  Jun 03  0:20.21
 -accepting connections (sendmail)
root  401  0.0  0.2  2.84M  104K  ??  S  Jun 03  0:25.62
 /usr/sbin/os_mibs
root  403  0.0  0.1  1.68M  48K  ??  S  Jun 03  3:47.75
 /usr/sbin/snmpd
root  420  0.0  0.1  1.62M  64K  ??  I  Jun 03  0:00.58
 /usr/sbin/inetd
root  453  0.0  0.2  1.59M  120K  ??  I  Jun 03  0:01.02
 /usr/sbin/cron
root  469  0.0  0.0  1.70M  0K  ??  IW  Jun 03  0:00.02
 /usr/lbin/lpd
root  536  0.0  0.0  432K  0K  console  IW +  Jun 03  0:00.42
 /usr/sbin/getty console console vt100
root  7202  0.0  0.4  1.75M  264K  ttyp0  R +
 8:49:07  0:00.06  ps auxw
```

```
mcheek  28727  0.1  0.4  1.88M  264K  ttyp0  S  17:13:51
 0:00.88  -ksh (ksh)
```

### 9.3.2 Process Identifiers

Each active process is assigned a process identifier, or PID, which is a unique positive number. There is also a special process with a PID of zero; the ps command shows this as the "kernel idle" process. Despite the name, this process is far from idle. It contains numerous threads that perform all of the kernel's "housekeeping" functions. In some cases, this "idle" process may actually be the largest and busiest process on the system. PID 1 also represents a special process, the /sbin/init program, which initializes the system and changes the system run level as needed.

Beginning in Tru64 UNIX version 5, PIDs include information showing which cluster member a process is running on. The "local" PID is stored in the lowest 19 bits of the PID and therefore can range from 0 to 524,287 (2^19 – 1). The cluster member ID is stored in bits 19–24. Thus, a version 5 PID is equal to:

```
(member_id * 2^19) + local_pid
```

A standalone system (i.e., one that is not part of a TruCluster), has a member ID of zero. For example, since init is always process 1, we see the following on a standalone system:

```
% ps -ef | grep init
root 1 0 0.0 10:48:09 ?? 0:00.04 /sbin/init -a
```

The number 1 (immediately after "root") is the PID. Now let's try the same thing on a system that's part of a cluster:

```
% ps -ef | grep init
root 524289 524288 0.0 Jan 21 ?? 0:01.05 /sbin/init -a
```

In this case, init's PID is 524289. If we break this into the local PID and cluster member fields, we see that the PID value is (1 * 2^19) + 1. This represents a local PID of 1, as expected, and a cluster member ID of 1. We can verify the member ID as follows:

```
% /sbin/sysconfig -q generic memberid
generic:
memberid = 1
```

Let's try another cluster member:

```
% ps -ef | grep init
root 1048577 1048576 0.0 Jan 21 ?? 0:06.05 /sbin/init -a
```

On this system, init has a PID of 1048577, or (2 * 2^19) + 1, which breaks down to a local PID of 1 and a cluster member ID of 2. Checking the member ID:

```
% /sbin/sysconfig -q generic memberid
generic:
memberid = 2
```

The PID is simply a value used by the kernel to report status changes to the user, and by which a user can identify individual processes when, for example, sending a signal to a process. A PID is assigned to each new process in a somewhat random manner, and there is no correlation between a process and a PID. In addition, a PID is unique only among active processes; PIDs are reused as needed by the system. Never make any assumptions about which PID will be assigned to an active process. Instead, use the ps utility and search for the command name of the desired process in order to obtain the PID of that process. For example:

```
# ps -ef | grep syslogd
root    95   1    0.0  Jun 03 ??   0:16.80
/usr/sbin/syslogd
```

### 9.3.3 PPID and PGID

In addition to the PID, two other process identifiers are assigned to a process when the process is created: the parent process identifier (PPID) and process group identifier (PGID). These two IDs are inherited from the process's parent process rather than being generated and, consequently, do not have the uniqueness requirement of the PID.

The parent process identifier (PPID) of a particular process is simply the PID of the parent process that started this particular process. All processes are children of some other process and, except for the "kernel idle" process (PID 0), can ultimately trace their lineage back to init (PID 1), the ancestor of all other processes.

The PPID is a default output field in the SYSV version of ps. The PPID is useful to the system administrator in tracing process ownership, especially when it becomes necessary to terminate processes. Whenever possible, send processes the termination signal (via the kill(1) command) in the reverse order of creating. This avoids zombie processes and other unpleasant situations where processes can hang. (See Section 9.5 for more information on zombie processes.)

The process group identifier (PGID) is a number similar to the PID, except that instead of identifying a single process, the PGID is used to identify a set of processes or a process group. An example of a process group would be a set of commands in a pipeline issued from a shell prompt. For example, the following command,

```
# cat /etc/passwd | grep ksh | cut -d: -f1 | sort
```

which displays a sorted list of user IDs whose default shell is /bin/ksh, consists of four distinct processes (the cat, grep, cut, and sort commands) in a pipeline, each with their own PID. All four processes, however, will have the same PGID. This is especially useful if, for instance, such a pipeline were a long-running job and you wished to terminate the job. Instead of having to search for and then specify each process's PID in a kill command, you could specify just the PGID, and the termination signal would be broadcast to each member of the process group. Process groups are the foundation for the job-control facility in the C shell and Korn shell.

### 9.3.4 Real and Effective User/Group Identifiers

A process inherits its user identifier (UID) and group identifier (GID) from its parent. The UID and GID of a process are used by the kernel's access control facilities to determine file and directory access privileges for the process. This is what prevents a nonprivileged user process from, for example, writing to /etc/passwd and changing the root password. In addition, UIDs are used to define which signals a process may receive. This protects the system by preventing a regular user from killing important system processes such as init or cron.

The UID and GID are maintained by the system administrator in the /etc/passwd and /etc/group files. When listing processes with the ps(1) command using the SYSV -f switch, the UID is translated by ps to the corresponding user name. Without this switch, ps displays UIDs as numeric values.

It is often necessary to allow a regular user process to temporarily assume greater privileges. For example, a user must be able to edit the normally read-only /etc/passwd file in order to change the user's password. To solve this problem, UNIX allows programs to be configured such that the program assumes additional privileges when run by a nonprivileged user. A program that runs with an additional group privilege is called a set-group-identifier (SGID) program. Similarly, programs that run with an additional user privilege are called set-user-identifier (SUID) programs. When a SUID program is run—for example, the passwd(1) program that allows users to change their password—that process has an additional identifier, the effective user identifier (EUID), which specifies the additional user privilege that the process possesses. Continuing the example of the passwd(1) program, the EUID of the password-changing process is zero (root), since the passwd program is set to be SUID to root. The passwd program assumes the access privileges of the root user in order to modify the password of the executing user in the password file. Similarly, the effective group identifier (EGID) of a process is set when running a SGID program.

Tru64 UNIX also uses a third user identifier, the login UID (LUID). The LUID is determined when a user logs in, and remains unchanged until the user logs out. For example, if user "ajones" with a UID of 123 logs in and then uses the su(1) command to become the superuser, the user process will have a UID of 0 (root), but its LUID will remain 123 (ajones).

### 9.3.5 Process Priority

Tru64 UNIX processes are scheduled for execution based on an attribute called the *process priority*. This parameter is a number between 0 and 63, with a lower number indicating a higher scheduling priority. The highest numbers (44 to 63), which represent the lowest scheduling priority, are assigned to user jobs. Priority numbers 32 to 43 are used by system jobs, while 0 to 31 are reserved for real-time jobs. The process priority is maintained internally by the kernel, and process priorities are dynamically updated based on a number of variables, such as the "nice value" of a process.

The concept of nice value is the primary way for a system administrator to either start a process with a higher or lower scheduling priority, or change an already running process's priority. A process's nice value is a number between -19 and 19 that is added to the process's priority number. Since a lower priority number indicates higher priority, a lower (negative) nice value further reduces the priority number, thereby increasing the process's scheduling priority. A process with a positive nice value increases the process's priority number, thereby reducing the process's scheduling priority. This causes the process to be "nicer" to the system, hence the name.

By default, a process starts with a nice value of zero, which neither increases nor decreases the process priority. The nice(1) command is used to start a process with a nonzero nice value:

```
$ nice -n 15 sort bigfile.txt -o sorted.txt
```

This syntax starts and runs the sort command with a nice value of 15, which lowers the process's scheduling priority, thereby increasing its execution time. The nice value (-n) is an optional parameter, for example:

```
$ nice cc *.c &
```

This command compiles a group of C programs in the background with the default nice value of +10.

Only the superuser can specify nice values less than zero. For example, the following command runs with a nice value of -10, which increases the scheduling priority and prevents regular user processes from delaying its execution:

```
# nice -n -10 du -ks /home/*
```

The nice(1) command is used only to start processes with modified nice values. Once a process is already running, its nice value also can be modified via the renice(8) command. The renice command is very flexible for the system administrator; either a single process or groups of similar processes can be reniced. To change the nice value of a single process, simply specify the process identifier to be reniced:

```
# renice -n -12 -p 783
```

This changes the nice value of process ID 783 to negative 12. Multiple PIDs may be specified on the command line.

The renice command can also be used to change groups of similar processes, either by specifying process group identifiers (PGIDs) to change all processes in a process group, or by specifying usernames or user identifiers (UIDs) to change all processes owned by a particular user. Renice is flexible enough to allow all three types of changes on a single command line. For example, the following command changes the nice value of process IDs 2001 and 2005, processes in process group 771, and processes owned by jsmith:

```
# renice -n -2 -p 2001 2005 -g 771 -u jsmith
```

One final restriction of renice is that while the superuser may both increase and decrease the nice value of processes, a nonprivileged user may only increase the nice value of processes owned by that user. A user may never decrease the nice value, even if the nice value was previously increased by that user. For instance, if user jsmith increases the nice value of a job from zero to +10, jsmith may not return the nice value to zero; only the system administrator can reduce a nice value.

In addition to the nice value, there are a variety of other factors that influence the value of process priorities. These include the amount of CPU time that a process has used recently, the amount of memory the process is using, and the number of jobs already in the run queue waiting for CPU time.

Both the process priority value and the nice value can be displayed with the ps command by specifying the -l switch. The process priority is displayed in the PRI column, while the nice value is displayed in the NI column of the ps output.

### 9.3.6 Resource Utilization

As a process executes, the kernel keeps track of the process's utilization of a variety of system resources. These resources include:

- CPU usage
- Memory utilization
- Elapsed time
- Disk I/O and paging
- Number of context switches
- Number of signals received

These resource utilization statistics are stored in the proc kernel structure for each process, are updated dynamically by the kernel for all processes, and are available to the system administrator (and regular users as well) via the ps command. This information is useful, for example, in identifying runaway processes by examining CPU utilization, or in determining the memory usage, both physical and virtual, of a particular process.

The most frequently useful process utilization information is the CPU and memory statistics. The CPU utilization of a process is monitored by examining two fields, %CPU and TIME, in the ps output. Memory utilization is tracked in the %MEM, RSS, and VSZ columns. These columns are displayed by using either the SYSV "ps -eo VFMT" option, or the BSD "ps u" option.

%CPU is a dynamically computed value that represents the percentage of a single CPU's resources that a process is consuming. Thus, the maximum amount of CPU time for all processes totaled together is equal to the number of CPUs multiplied by 100%; for example, a system with four CPUs could total up to 400%. It is possible that a single multithreaded process could show a CPU time greater than 100%; although this may look a little strange, it is a normal consequence of a multiprocessor system. A process that is consistently at or near the maximum possible utilization may possibly be a runaway process. It may also, however, be perfectly normal for a process's %CPU to be high, depending on what the process is and what it is doing.

TIME is the total time that a process has actually been executing on a CPU. This value is cumulative since the process was started, and can be hours or days on a long-running process. This value is not the total elapsed ("wall clock") time, just the total time that the process has actually been running on a processor.

%MEM is the percentage of real (physical) memory used by a process. RSS is the current resident set size (i.e., the amount of physical memory the process is actually occupying), while VSZ is the total virtual memory size of a process. Both are displayed in kilobytes. A process's VSZ will always have a value, while the RSS column can vary between the VSZ value and zero. The RSS value can be zero if a process is swapped out to disk and no longer resident in real memory, either due to the process being idle and moved to swap space by the system, or due to a memory shortage when lower priority processes are swapped out. When confronted with a low-memory or out-of-memory situation, these three memory utilization fields from the ps output should be examined to determine which processes are consuming both real and virtual memory.

#### 9.3.6.1 Process Resource Limits

Several process resources are restricted by limits imposed by the command shell or the Tru64 UNIX kernel. The current process limits can be displayed by using the built-in shell commands "limit" (in the C shell) and "ulimit" (in the Korn shell.) For example, in the C shell:

```
% limit
cputime        unlimited
filesize       unlimited
datasize       131072 kbytes
```

```
stacksize     2048 kbytes
coredumpsize  unlimited
memoryuse     505816 kbytes
descriptors   4096 files
addressspace  1048576 kbytes
```

The Korn shell command shows the same information in a slightly different format:

```
$ ulimit -Sa
time(seconds)  unlimited
file(blocks)  unlimited
data(kbytes)  131072
stack(kbytes)  2048
memory(kbytes)  505816
coredump(blocks)  unlimited
nofiles(descriptors)  4096
vmemory(kbytes)  1048576
```

The –S flag instructs the ulimit command to display the "soft" process limits. The –H flag displays the "hard" limits, as in this example:

```
$ ulimit -Ha
time(seconds)  unlimited
file(blocks)  unlimited
data(kbytes)  1048576
stack(kbytes)  32768
memory(kbytes)  505816
coredump(blocks)  unlimited
nofiles(descriptors)  4096
vmemory(kbytes)  1048576
```

Soft limits can be raised by the limit or ulimit command, up to the corresponding hard limit. A hard limit, once set, cannot be increased. The hard and soft limits for some resources are derived from kernel parameters found in the "proc" (process) subsystem. The values of interest are as follows:

```
% sysconfig -q proc
proc:
per_proc_stack_size = 2097152
max_per_proc_stack_size = 33554432
per_proc_data_size = 134217728
max_per_proc_data_size = 1073741824
max_per_proc_address_space = 1073741824
per_proc_address_space = 1073741824
```

These parameter values look suspiciously like some of the shell limits shown above. For example, the limit command returned a stack size of

2048 kbytes, and the value of per_proc_stack_size is 2097152, which is exactly the number of bytes in 2048 kbytes. You might conclude from this that the shell limit is derived from the kernel parameter, and this conclusion is correct. Other process limits—though not all of them—are similarly derived from kernel parameters. Table 9.2 contains information about each limit.

Every process includes a text segment, which contains executable code and other constants; a data segment, which contains defined data storage; and a stack segment, which contains the program stack. The data and stack segment sizes are limited, as shown in Table 9.2, while the text segment is not specifically constrained. However, the *total* size of the text, data, and stack segments is limited by the virtual memory size limit. There is one further constraint in older versions of Tru64 UNIX: the total size of the text, data, and stack segments, plus all shared memory segments attached to the process, is limited by kernel parameter "vm_maxvas" in the "vm" (virtual memory) subsystem. This limit was removed in V5.0.

**Table 9.2** *Process Resource Limits*

| Resource | "limit" field name | "ulimit" field name | "ulimit" switch | Derived from |
|---|---|---|---|---|
| CPU time | cputime | time | -t | (none) |
| File size | filesize | file | -f | filesystem type and quotas |
| Data segment size | datasize | data | -d | (soft) per_proc_data_size<br>(hard) max_per_proc_data_size |
| Stack segment size | stacksize | stack | -s | (soft) per_proc_stack_size<br>(hard) max_per_proc_stack_size |
| Core dump size | coredumpsize | coredump | -c | (none) |
| Resident set size (physical memory in use) | memoryuse | memory | -m | Physical memory in system |
| Number of open files | descriptors | nofiles | -n | (soft) open_max_soft<br>(hard) open_max_hard |
| Virtual memory size | addressspace | vmemory | -v | (soft) per_proc_address_space<br>(hard)<br>max_per_proc_address_space |

An additional limit (imposed by the kernel, not the shell) is the "max_proc_per_user" parameter in the proc subsystem. This parameter, which defaults to 64, defines the maximum number of processes that a nonprivileged user can execute at any one time. This limit prevents a non-privileged user from accidentally or maliciously creating a huge number of processes, which could consume all of the system's available process slots. The default value of 64, however, is not enough for certain applications; to raise it, change the value of max_proc_per_user using dxkerneltuner or sysconfigdb, and reboot the system.

One "hidden" limit to be aware of is that, because a single user surely can't run more processes than the entire system is allowed to run, max_proc_per_user can be no larger than the system maximum number of processes (minus 10, to reserve a few slots for system processes). If you attempt to set max_proc_per_user higher, the system will silently reset it to the maximum possible value. For example, if maxusers is set to 32 on a V5.0 system, the system can run a maximum of 1024 (32*32) processes. If you try to set max_proc_per_user to a higher number, say 10,000, the system will lower the value to 1014 (1024 minus 10)—without giving you any warning or error message.

### 9.3.7 Controlling Terminal

Most processes, with the exception of system processes started at boot time, are associated with a particular terminal. This controlling terminal is normally the terminal where the user who started or owns the process is logged in. If, however, a user runs a job in the background and then logs out, that process is no longer associated with a terminal. This is indicated by "??" in the TTY field of the ps output. System processes, or daemons, not associated with a terminal also have a "??" in the TTY field of the ps output.

Knowing the controlling terminal is useful when it becomes necessary to identify all processes associated with a particular logged-in user. Simply run the who(1) command to determine which terminal to query, then specify the terminal of interest to the ps command to display all processes associated with that terminal. For example:

```
# who
mcheek  ttyp1  Jun 4  11:35 <- What are the processes
  associated with the tty?
styler  ttyp2  Jun 4  13:11
jsmith  ttyp4  Jun 4  15:51
tlee    ttyp5  Jun 4  09:14
```

```
# ps -ft ttyp1
mcheek  28727  28801  0.3  11:37:51  ttyp1  0:00.90  -ksh (ksh)
mcheek  29178  28727  0.0  11:52:33  ttyp1  0:01.02  -vi main.c
```

### 9.3.8 Process State

The kernel maintains the current state of all active processes in the proc structure. Even though Tru64 UNIX is a multitasking operating system, the perception that multiple processes are actually running at the same time is somewhat of an illusion. Only one process can run at any one time on a particular processor; on multiprocessor systems, the number of processors dictates the maximum number of concurrent processes. When a process is not actually running, it can be in several other states, including sleeping, waiting for its next turn to run, idle, stopped, or halted.

The process state is displayed in the S column of the ps output as a sequence of one or more characters. The first character indicates the status of the process. Additional characters after the first indicate additional state information, including whether the process has been swapped out or if the process's scheduling priority (or nice value) has been altered. See Table 9.3 for the definition of the process state indicator characters.

The ps command shows the state of processes as accurately as possible. However, process states can change quickly, and there may be discrepancies between the ps command's snapshot and the actual process state. This does not usually cause problems, but it is something to be aware of.

The BSD format of ps displays process state information by default. To display the process state when specifying SYSV ps switches, simply add the "–l" parameter to generate a "long" listing. The process state is displayed in the S column. For example:

```
# ps -efl

F  S  UID  PID  PPID  %CPU  PRI  NI  RSS  WCHAN  STARTED
 TIME  COMMAND
3  R <  0  0  0  0.0  32  -12  4.6M  *  Jun 03  19:28.34
 [kernel idle]
80048001  I  0  1  0  0.0  44  0  40K  pause  Jun 03  0:35.36
 /sbin/init -a
8001  IW  0  3  1  0.0  44  0  0K  sv_msg_  Jun 03  1:30.53
 /sbin/kloadsrv
8001  I  0  22  1  0.0  44  0  56K  pause  Jun 03  14:51.74
 /sbin/update
8001  S  0  95  1  0.0  42  0  120K  event  Jun 03  0:21.45
 /usr/sbin/syslogd
```

Table 9.3 *Process State Indicator Characters*

| Character | Process State |
|---|---|
| R | Runnable (waiting for its turn on a CPU) |
| U | Uninterruptible (waiting for a kernel event) |
| S | Sleeping (less than 20 seconds) |
| I | Idle (sleeping longer than 20 seconds) |
| T | Stopped |
| H | Halted |
| W | Swapped out |
| > | Exceeding memory soft limit |
| N | Niced (process priority reduced) |
| < | Process priority raised |
| + | Process group leader |

## 9.4 The ps Command

The ps(1) command is the system administrator's window into the state of all processes running on a Tru64 UNIX system. Every process statistic collected by the kernel is available for display via the ps command's many options. By default, each version of ps (SYSV or BSD) only displays a few common fields, such as the PID, the process owner, the process start time and CPU time, and the command being executed. To display any of the less common process statistics, such as a process's nice value or the process group identifier (PGID), additional format options must be specified on the ps command line. In addition, the ps -o switch provides the ability to customize the ps output to display any combination of fields that you wish to see. This can be very useful in generating custom reports of system process activity. For instance, to display the PID, the total elapsed time, the current CPU time, the time processes have spent executing in system and user spaces, and the running command—in that order and for all processes on the system—run the following ps command:

```
# ps -A -o pid -o etime -o cputime -o systime -o usertime -o
  command
  PID  ELAPSED   TIME  SYSTEM  USER  COMMAND
  0     36-09:52:31  22:59.78  22:59.78  0:00.00  [kernel idle]
  1     36-09:52:31  0:35.83   0:34.72   0:01.11  /sbin/init -a
  3     36-09:52:30  1:30.59   0:58.19   0:32.40  /sbin/kloadsrv
  22    36-09:52:20  17:06.41  17:00.09  0:06.32  /sbin/update
  95    36-09:52:14  0:23.17   0:19.73   0:03.44
    /usr/sbin/syslogd
  97   36-09:52:14  0:00.13  0:00.11  0:00.02  /usr/sbin/binlogd
  277 36-09:52:07  1:46.42  1:17.01  0:29.41  /usr/sbin/portmap
  349 36-09:52:02  0:39.12  0:38.13  0:01.00  -accepting
    connections (sendmail)
  401 36-09:52:00  0:36.32  0:24.92  0:11.40  /usr/sbin/os_mibs
  403 36-09:52:00  4:13.62  3:43.14  0:30.49  /usr/sbin/snmpd
  420 36-09:51:53  0:01.22  0:01.16  0:00.06  /usr/sbin/inetd
  453 36-09:51:52  0:01.95  0:01.81  0:00.14  /usr/sbin/cron
  469 36-09:51:49  0:00.04  0:00.04  0:00.01  /usr/lbin/lpd
  536 36-09:51:38  0:00.42  0:00.40  0:00.03  /usr/sbin/getty
    console console vt100
  18804  01:42:42  0:00.32  0:00.19  0:00.12  -ksh (ksh)
  19570  0:00  0:00.07  0:00.05  0:00.02 ps -A -o pid
    -o etime -o cputime -o systime -o usertime -o command
```

Consult the ps(1) reference page on your system for a list of available output specifiers that can be used with the -o option.

## 9.5 Process Parent/Child Relationships

Every process on a UNIX system is created by another process calling the fork() system call, and is termed a child process of the creating parent process. A child process inherits the privileges of its parent in addition to the parent's priority, signal state, environment, and all other parameters stored in the "proc" structure of the parent process. In fact, except for the PID and PPID, a child process is initially a clone of its parent until either the child, the parent, or a privileged user modifies the process parameters.

The parent/child relationship is important to keep in mind when managing processes, especially in a problem situation. For instance, if a process begins forking new child processes uncontrollably, you must find and kill the runaway parent process to fix the problem. Killing the child processes in this case would address only the symptom, not the true cause of the problem.

The parent/child relationship also comes into play when discussing "zombie" processes. A zombie process is a process that has exited, but whose parent process has not acknowledged the child's exit. Zombie processes are identified in a ps listing by the string "<defunct>" in place of the process command. Zombies themselves are usually not a problem for system administrators, since the only impact is that the zombie continues to occupy a process table slot. The various conditions that can cause zombie processes, though, may be of concern. These causes can include a hung or blocked parent process, which is unable to catch the exit signal of its child processes, poor programming practices, or system problems.

Zombie processes are so named because, like the zombies of horror movies, they appear alive (in the ps output), but actually are not. This explains why trying to kill a zombie process is futile; the process is already dead. The only way to rid yourself of zombie processes, other than rebooting the system, is to cause the parent to acknowledge that its children have exited. If the parent process is a user shell, such as the Korn shell or C shell, sometimes just having the user press Return at the shell prompt is sufficient to clean up its defunct child processes. If that fails, or the parent process is not a shell or is hung, a more drastic measure is to kill the parent process itself. When a process exits, its remaining children are "adopted" by the init process, which will immediately acknowledge the exited children and remove the zombies from the process table.

## 9.6 Controlling Running Processes

Tru64 UNIX processes are controlled by a mechanism known as signals. A signal is simply that: a message sent by one process to another process. A signal can also be thought of as the software equivalent of a hardware interrupt. A signal can originate from a user application program or from an interactive session via the kill(1) command. There is a defined set of signals for a variety of software and hardware conditions that may arise during the execution of a process; see Table 9.4 for a list of these signals.

**Table 9.4** *Tru64 UNIX Signal Definitions*

| Signal Number | Signal Name | Meaning |
|---|---|---|
| 1 | SIGHUP | Hangup |
| 2 | SIGINT | Interrupt |

**Table 9.4** *(continued)*

| Signal Number | Signal Name | Meaning |
|---|---|---|
| 3 | SIGQUIT | Quit |
| 4 | SIGILL | Illegal Instruction |
| 5 | SIGTRAP | Trace trap |
| 6 | SIGABRT | Abort program |
| 7 | SIGEMT | EMT instruction |
| 8 | SIGFPE | Floating-point exception (or other arithmetic exception) |
| 9 | SIGKILL | Kill |
| 10 | SIGBUS | Specification exception |
| 11 | SIGSEGV | Segmentation violation (memory access violation) |
| 12 | SIGSYS | Invalid argument to system call |
| 13 | SIGPIPE | Broken pipe |
| 14 | SIGALRM | Alarm clock |
| 15 | SIGTERM | Termination |
| 16 | SIGURG | Urgent condition on I/O channel |
| 17 | SIGSTOP | Stop |
| 18 | SIGTSTP | Interactive stop |
| 19 | SIGCONT | Continue after stop |
| 20 | SIGCHLD | Child process exited |
| 21 | SIGTTIN | Background read |
| 22 | SIGTTOU | Background write |
| 23 | SIGIO | I/O possible (or completed) |
| 24 | SIGXCPU | Exceeded CPU limit |
| 25 | SIGXFSZ | Exceeded file size limit |
| 26 | SIGVTALRM | Virtual time alarm |
| 27 | SIGPROF | Profiling time alarm |
| 28 | SIGWINCH | Window size change |
| 29 | SIGINFO | Information request |
| 30 | SIGUSR1 | User-defined |
| 31 | SIGUSR2 | User-defined |

A Tru64 UNIX system administrator's primary method of controlling processes is by sending them signals with the kill command. The kill command is a misnomer, since issuing a kill command,

```
# kill <PID>
```

does not necessarily kill the process. What actually happens is that the kill command sends a signal to the process (or processes) specified on the command line, which may or may not cause the process to die. In fact, some signals, including SIGUSR1, do not terminate processes. By default, unless a particular signal is specified, kill sends the SIGTERM signal (signal number 15), which politely asks the process to terminate.

Several other common signals are SIGHUP (signal number 1), SIGKILL (signal number 9), and SIGSTOP (signal number 17). A SIGHUP signal tells the process to hang up, and is the signal sent to all processes assigned to a terminal when a user logs out. SIGKILL is the familiar signal for killing a process; it should be used as a last resort for ending a process, since it will terminate the process immediately without giving it a chance to perform any final "cleanup" actions. SIGSTOP is a signal that tells a process to temporarily stop execution; it is commonly sent to a process in response to the shell "stop" character, usually Control-Z. The SIGKILL and SIGSTOP signals are unique in that they cannot be caught or ignored by the receiving process. This ensures that there exists a method for stopping or killing unruly or runaway processes.

Signals may be specified on the kill command line either by signal number or by signal name (minus the "SIG" prefix.) When specifying the signal name, case is ignored. For example, the following three commands are equivalent:

```
# kill -9 4321
# kill -KILL 4321
# kill -kill 4321
```

In addition, multiple processes may be signaled by specifying their PIDs:

```
# kill -HUP 4456 4458
```

The hang-up (HUP) signal is a commonly used signal for the system administrator. Several system daemons, such as inetd(8), syslogd(8), and bootpd(8), will reread their configuration files upon receiving a HUP signal. This allows you to modify a daemon's configuration file and cause the change to take effect without stopping and restarting the daemon. For example, the following command,

```
# kill -HUP 'cat /var/run/inetd.pid'
```

will cause inetd(8) to reread /etc/inetd.conf, since /var/run/inetd.pid contains the PID of the currently running inetd daemon.

Two PIDs have special significance when signaled with the kill command. Specifying zero (0) as a PID sends the signal to all processes having a process group ID (PGID) equal to the PGID of the sender, except PIDs 0 and 1. Specifying -1 as a PID behaves differently depending on the effective user ID (EUID) of the sender. If the EUID is not 0, or root, the signal is sent to all processes with a UID equal to the EUID of the sender, except PIDs 0 and 1. However, if the EUID of the sender is 0, or root, the signal is sent to *all* processes on the system, again excluding PIDs 0 and 1.

## 9.7 Allocating CPU Resources

Tru64 UNIX systems, particularly large servers, frequently support a mix of different user and application types. A single server might support a production database, a development group creating new software, and users accessing their e-mail. In such cases, it's important to ensure that the various applications receive enough resources to accomplish their tasks—without interfering with all the other applications trying to accomplish their own tasks. Tru64 UNIX provides several methods for allocating CPU resources to specific users, groups, processes, or applications. These include:

- Partitioning the system (dependent on system hardware)
- Defining processor sets
- Binding processes to CPUs or processor sets
- Using the class scheduler

### 9.7.1 System Partitions

System partitioning is the ability to organize a system's physical resources (processors, memory, and I/O devices) into several smaller "virtual machines," or partitions. Although this capability is a function of the underlying hardware, rather than the operating system, it is an important tool for Tru64 UNIX administrators. The larger members of the AlphaServer family provide this ability, allowing one large server to operate as several, completely independent partitions, each running its own copy of Tru64 UNIX—or even another operating system, such as Compaq's OpenVMS.

Partitioning is useful in cases where complete system-level independence is desirable. For example, you might wish to run a production version of your application or database in one partition, and a test version in another partition. Or you might wish to run one partition at a newer version of Tru64 UNIX, in preparation for upgrading your entire system. The disadvantage to partitioning a system is that the allocation of resources is not dynamic; you can't, for example, move processors from one partition to another while the systems are running. To reconfigure the partitions, you must shut down each partition, perform the reconfiguration, and then restart the partitions. There are also hardware-dependent restrictions on how partitions can be configured.

The details of creating and using partitions vary depending on the specific model of AlphaServer being used. For this reason, you should consult the hardware documentation for your system for more information.

### 9.7.2 Processor Sets

Tru64 UNIX gives you the capability to divide your system's CPUs into "processor sets" (or "psets" for short). Processor sets are groups of one or more processors that are treated as "virtual" processors for scheduling purposes. By default, the system creates a default processor set that includes all processors. The pset_info(1) command lists the current processor sets on the system:

```
# pset_info

number of processor sets on system = 1

pset_id  # cpus   # pids   # threads  load_av    created
  0         3       62        240       3.40     05/10/2001
11:41:14

total number of processors on system = 3

cpu #     running  primary_cpu  pset_id  assigned_to_pset
 0          1          1           0     05/10/2001 11:41:14
 1          1          0           0     05/10/2001 11:41:14
 2          1          0           0     05/10/2001 11:41:14
```

This system has one processor set (the default processor set, which always has a pset_id of 0), containing three processors. We can get more information on the individual processors with the psrinfo(1) command:

```
# psrinfo -v
Status of processor 0 as of: 05/15/01 18:55:03
  Processor has been on-line since 05/10/2001 11:41:14
  The alpha EV6.7 (21264A) processor operates at 667 MHz,
        and has an alpha internal floating point processor.
Status of processor 1 as of: 05/15/01 18:55:03
  Processor has been on-line since 05/10/2001 11:41:14
  The alpha EV6.7 (21264A) processor operates at 667 MHz,
        and has an alpha internal floating point processor.
Status of processor 2 as of: 05/15/01 18:55:03
  Processor has been on-line since 05/10/2001 11:41:14
  The alpha EV6.7 (21264A) processor operates at 667 MHz,
        and has an alpha internal floating point processor.
```

To create a new processor set, use the pset_create(1) command:

```
# pset_create
pset_id = 2
```

This creates a new processor set with a pset_id of 2, but at this point it's an empty processor set. That is, it contains no processors yet.

```
# pset_info

number of processor sets on system = 2

pset_id  # cpus   # pids   # threads  load_av    created
  0        3        61        239        3.57     05/10/2001
11:41:14
  2        0         0          0        0.00     05/15/2001
18:55:36

total number of processors on system = 3

cpu #     running  primary_cpu  pset_id  assigned_to_pset
 0          1          1           0     05/10/2001 11:41:14
 1          1          0           0     05/10/2001 11:41:14
 2          1          0           0     05/10/2001 11:41:14
```

Now we can add a processor to the new processor set:

```
# pset_assign_cpu 2 1
# pset_info

number of processor sets on system = 2

pset_id  # cpus   # pids   # threads  load_av    created
  0        2        56        233        0.01     05/10/2001
11:41:14
  2        1         0          0        0.00     05/15/2001
18:55:36
```

```
total number of processors on system = 3

cpu #     running  primary_cpu  pset_id  assigned_to_pset
 0           1          1          0     05/10/2001 11:41:14
 1           1          0          2     05/16/2001 09:17:45
 2           1          0          0     05/10/2001 11:41:14
```

To remove a processor set, use the pset_destroy command:

```
# pset_destroy 2
processor set 2 has active processors/tasks/threads assigned to
it.
destroy anyway? (y/n): y
# pset_info

number of processor sets on system = 1

pset_id  # cpus   # pids   # threads  load_av    created
  0         3        56        233       0.00     05/10/2001
11:41:14

total number of processors on system = 3

cpu #     running  primary_cpu  pset_id  assigned_to_pset
 0           1          1          0     05/10/2001 11:41:14
 1           1          0          0     05/16/2001 09:19:56
 2           1          0          0     05/10/2001 11:41:14
```

The usefulness of processor sets will become apparent in the next section.

### 9.7.3 Binding Processes

The ability to define processor sets is an interesting feature, but is not, by itself, particularly useful. However, in conjunction with the ability to bind processes to a particular CPU or processor set, it becomes a powerful tool for allocating your CPU resources. Binding a process simply means that the process can run only on the CPU or processor set to which it is bound. This allows you to divide up your CPU resources so that different jobs all receive a fair share of the available resources but do not interfere with each other.

Fair allocation of resources is becoming increasingly important due to the trend of consolidating multiple functions into a single large server. For example, you might have a large database application, a software development group, and hundreds or thousands of e-mail users, all sharing the same server. Assuming this server has a reasonable number of CPUs, you could divide it into three processor sets, dedicating one processor set to the database application, one to the developers, and one to the e-mail users.

Processes can be bound using either system calls within an application or command-line utilities; the latter method is of the most interest to system administrators. There are two command-line utilities for binding processes: runon(1) and pset_assign_pid(1). The runon command runs a new process on either a particular CPU or a processor set, while pset_assign_pid assigns an already running process to a specified processor set. Both utilties have an option to bind a process exclusively; that is, *only* the specified process is allowed to use that CPU or processor set.

For example, consider the configuration created in Section 9.7.2:

```
# pset_info

number of processor sets on system = 2

pset_id  # cpus   # pids   # threads  load_av    created
  0         2       56       233        0.01     05/10/2001
11:41:14
  2         1       0        0          0.00     05/15/2001
18:55:36

total number of processors on system = 3

cpu #     running  primary_cpu  pset_id  assigned_to_pset
 0          1          1           0     05/10/2001 11:41:14
 1          1          0           2     05/16/2001 09:17:45
 2          1          0           0     05/10/2001 11:41:14
```

There are two processor sets: pset 0 contains CPUs 0 and 2, while pset 2 contains CPU 1. Now the runon command, in conjunction with the "-o psr" (show processor) option of the ps command, illustrates binding a process to a CPU:

```
# runon 2 ps -o cmd,psr | grep ps
grep ps               2
ps -o cmd,psr        ~2
```

The output shows processes whose names contain the string "ps", listing only the command name and the processor that is running the process. Both processes are running on CPU 2, but the tilde before the 2 on the last line indicates that the ps command is bound (by the "runon 2" command) to CPU 2. The grep command is also running on CPU 2, but it is not bound to do so; it could just as easily execute on a different CPU.

The –p option to runon specifies a processor set rather than a particular CPU. Modifying the above example slightly:

```
# runon -p 2 ps -o cmd,psr | grep ps
grep ps              0
ps -o cmd,psr        1
```

In this example, runon is binding the ps command to processor set 2, which contains CPU 1. The output shows that ps does in fact execute on CPU 1, while the grep command is running on CPU 0. At first glance, it seems strange that there is no tilde before the 1 to indicate that the ps command is bound to CPU 1; after all, CPU 1 is the only processor in pset 2, so binding a process to pset 2 effectively binds it to CPU 1. The reason the tilde is absent is that the membership of a processor set is dynamic. If the process were running for an extended period of time, other processors could have been added to or removed from pset 2 while the process was running. In such a case, the process could have executed on any processor that was a current member of pset 2.

### 9.7.4 Class Scheduling

Class scheduling is another method of allocating CPU resources to specific users or applications. You can create any number of classes and define the maximum percentage of available CPU time that each class is allowed to consume. Users and groups may be assigned to these classes; any jobs started by these users are subject to the CPU time constraint for their class. In addition, you may run any job in a particular class by using the runclass(1) command.

The class_admin(8) command is used to set up and manage class scheduling. The first time that you run class_admin, it will ask several questions to define its default behavior:

```
# class_admin

        Class Scheduler Administration

 configure:

Shall processes that have not been explicitly assigned to a
defined class be assigned to a 'default' class?  Enter (yes/no)
[no]:

Enforce class scheduling when the CPU is otherwise idle?
(yes/no) [yes]:
```

```
How often do you want the system to reset class usage?
Enter number of seconds (1):
```

The class_admin utility can run either in interactive mode (if you just enter "class_admin"), or it can accept class scheduling commands as arguments on its command line. For example, to create a new class called "low_priority" that is limited to 20% of CPU time, you could enter the following at the command line:

```
# class_admin create low_priority 20
low_priority created at 20% cpu usage.
```

or in interactive mode, at the "class>" prompt:

```
class> create low_priority 20
```

Class scheduling must be explicitly enabled to take effect:

```
# class_admin enable
Class scheduling enabled and daemon /usr/sbin/class_daemon
started.
```

To display the current class scheduling configuration, use the "show" command:

```
# class_admin show
Configuration:
 -Processes not explicitly defined in the database are
  class scheduled.
 -If the processor has some idle time, class scheduled
processes are not
  allowed to exceed their cpu percentage.
 -The class scheduler will check class CPU usage every 1
seconds.

current database: /etc/class/part.default
Class scheduler status: enabled

Classes:

 default targeted at 80%:
    class members:
    Every one not listed below
 low_priority targeted at 20%:
    class members:
    none.
```

Once a class is defined, you can add users to the class:

```
class> add low_priority uid 115
uid 115 added to low_priority.
```

Alternatively, you can run a specific job in the class by using the runclass command:

```
# runclass low_priority backup
```

Now looking at the class scheduling configuration after performing the above commands:

```
# class_admin show
Configuration:
 -Processes not explicitly defined in the database are
  class scheduled.
 -If the processor has some idle time, class scheduled
processes are not
  allowed to exceed their cpu percentage.
 -The class scheduler will check class CPU usage every 1
seconds.

current database: /etc/class/part.default
Class scheduler status: enabled

Classes:

 default targeted at 80%:
    class members:
    Every one not listed below
 low_priority targeted at 20%:
    class members:
    uid 115        pgrp 43006
```

Process group 43006 is the one that created the backup job, and the output shows that it is a member of the low_priority class. All processes in this process group inherit the class membership.

The above simple example illustrates the basic idea of class scheduling. Much more complex setups are possible; for more details, see the class_scheduling(4) and class_admin(8) reference pages.

## 9.8 Foreground and Background

UNIX is a multiprocessing operating system, and as such, supports the simultaneous execution of many processes. Many of the processes necessary for the proper operation of a UNIX system are always running. These system processes, or daemons, are typically started as part of the system boot sequence and are not associated with a terminal or user. These processes are running in the "background" in a noninteractive fashion. In contrast, when a user is logged onto the system, interactively editing a file or listing the contents of a directory, such tasks are running in the "foreground." Foreground processes are processes for which a command interpreter, or shell, is currently waiting.

A process is put into the background by running it with the "&" operator, either from the shell command line or from within a script. Putting a process into the background returns the shell prompt immediately and allows the execution of additional commands. Long-running commands are good candidates for background processing. For example, the following find(1) command lists information on every file on the system and places the output into a file for later review:

```
# find / -ls > /tmp/find.out &
5051
#
```

On a large system with many thousands of files, this command clearly could take a considerable amount of time to finish. By appending the "&" character to the end of the command, the shell places the command into the background for processing by the system. The process ID of the find command (5051 in this case) is returned by the shell, and the shell prompt returns immediately for additional interactive commands.

A background process inherits its controlling terminal, in addition to all other process parameters, from its parent process. If the process table entry for the background process is examined, the controlling terminal field (TTY) displays a value:

```
# ps -ef -p 5051
UID   PID   PPID  C     STIME     TTY    TIME     CMD
root  5051  4988  35.0  14:33:12  ttyp1  0:02.04  find / -ls
```

However, as discussed earlier, if a controlling terminal's primary process terminates, such as when a user logs off the system, all children of that primary process (typically a shell) are sent a SIGHUP signal which, by default, causes the remaining child processes to terminate as well. In the find example above, if the user who issued the command logs off before the find command completes, the find command is terminated. To avoid this and allow for processes to continue running after the initiating user logs off, UNIX provides the nohup(1) command, which executes a process so it will ignore any hang-up

(SIGHUP) or quit (SIGQUIT) signals. To run the find command again, this time making it immune to the hang-up signal, insert "nohup" at the beginning of the command line:

```
# nohup find / -ls > /tmp/find.out &
5077
#
```

If a process is started using nohup, it will continue running even if the creator logs off intentionally or is inadvertently disconnected.

The controlling terminal of processes started with nohup remains the same as the parent process until such time as the parent process terminates (for example, when the user who placed the process in the background logs off the system). When this occurs, the controlling terminal field in the ps output is displayed as "??" and, since the parent process has terminated, the init process (PID 1) adopts the background process. When this happens, the ps command shows the parent process ID (PPID) as 1:

```
# ps -ef -p 5077
UID  PID  PPID  C  STIME  TTY  TIME  CMD
root  5077  1 7.9  14:26:52  ??  0:10.97  find / -ls
```

If nohup is used and the output of the command is not redirected to another file, nohup automatically appends all output from the process into a file named "nohup.out" in the current directory (at the time the command is issued), and reminds the user of this with a brief message:

```
# nohup find / -ls &
5194
Sending output to nohup.out
#
```

If the nohup command creates a nohup.out file, the permissions are set to owner read and write only (600). If the nohup.out file in the current directory cannot be created or appended to, due to permission problems (e.g., if the file is not writable by the user running the nohup command), nohup attempts to create/append to $HOME/nohup.out. If nohup is also unable to write to $HOME/nohup.out, execution of the command is aborted with an error message:

```
$ nohup find / -ls &
5211
nohup: cannot open/create nohup.out
```

```
$ whoami
mcheek
$ ls -l ./nohup.out $HOME/nohup.out
-rw---  1 root  system   0 Jun 10 11:17 ./nohup.out
-rw---  1 root  system   0 Jun 12 14:40 /home/mcheek/nohup.out
$
```

If this occurs, simply remove the nohup.out file(s), change the permissions to allow appending to the file, or change to a different directory when issuing the nohup command. Note that subsequent execution of commands with nohup will not overwrite existing nohup.out files, but will append output to nohup.out. This can result in a nohup.out file containing the output of more than one process. To capture only the output of a single process when using nohup, either explicitly redirect a process's output into a unique file, or remove any existing nohup.out files prior to running the command.

## 9.9 Scheduling Processes for Future Execution

UNIX systems are intended to run continuously so as to be available at all times for user activity. This activity can either be of an interactive nature, where users are actually logged in doing work, or processes running in the background without any user interaction. There are a variety of reasons to run jobs in an unattended fashion; perhaps the job needs a large amount of system resources, and the system is relatively idle during the middle of the night or over a weekend. Another reason is simply to increase the utilization of the system by performing some processing during otherwise idle periods. A system administrator also needs the ability to run processes unattended. These include regularly scheduled jobs such as backing up the system, rotating error logs, and scanning file systems. In addition, a system administrator occasionally needs to schedule an ad hoc job for a future one-time execution. An example of this is scheduling an automatic system shutdown and reboot during the wee hours of the morning.

Tru64 UNIX provides three tools for scheduling jobs:

- cron
- at
- batch

Each tool has a similar, but distinctly different purpose. cron(8) is used to schedule jobs to execute repeatedly, on a regular schedule. at(1) is used to schedule an ad-hoc job for execution once, at a user-specified date/time.

batch(1) is also used to schedule the single execution of a job; however, batch runs jobs only when the system load level permits.

### 9.9.1 cron and crontabs

The cron facility is the most common method of scheduling processes for future execution. The cron facility is composed of two main parts: the cron daemon itself, which is always running while the system is in multiuser mode, and the cron tables (crontabs), which contain the commands to be run and their execution schedules. In addition, there is a mechanism to restrict the ability to submit jobs for execution via cron; by default, all users can submit jobs to cron.

The cron daemon is the primary component of the cron facility and is normally started when the system is booted. There should only be one instance of cron running, since cron exits only when explicitly killed or when the system shuts down. The cron daemon logs its startups in /var/adm/cron/log. When cron starts, or when it is signaled that a crontab has been modified, cron reads all existing crontab files, which are located in the /var/spool/cron/crontabs directory. This avoids the overhead of checking the crontab files for changes on a periodic basis.

Each crontab file contains a list of commands for cron to execute on behalf of a particular user, along with the scheduling information that defines when to run the commands. Each line of a crontab contains the following six fields:

1. The minute of the hour (0 to 59)
2. The hour of the day (0 to 23)
3. The day of the month (1 to 31)
4. The month of the year (1 to 12)
5. The day of the week (0 to 6 for Sunday to Saturday)
6. The command to be executed

The first five date fields may be a single integer to indicate a single value, a comma-separated list of integers for multiple values, two integers separated by a dash to indicate an inclusive range of values, or an asterisk (*) to indicate all possible values for a date field. For example, to redirect the output of a ps command into a file every 15 minutes on Monday through Friday, the following crontab entry will do the trick:

```
0,15,30,45 * * * 1-5 /usr/bin/ps -ef >> /tmp/ps.out
```

These fields schedule the ps command to run at 0, 15, 30, and 45 minutes past the hour; every hour of the day; every day of the month; every month of the year; on days of the week 1 through 5 (Monday through Friday). Note that the full pathnames of the ps command and the output file are used. Specifying full pathnames in a crontab is strongly recommended to avoid "command not found" errors or output files in odd places. If the cron-executed command generates errors or output that is not redirected, cron e-mails this output to the crontab owner. To avoid these emails, always redirect output or errors to a log file or to the bit bucket (/dev/null).

A crontab is named for its owning user. The default Tru64 UNIX root crontab is /var/spool/cron/crontab/root, and contains the following entries:

```
#
#     root crontab file
#
15 4 * * * find /var/preserve -mtime +7 -type f -exec rm -f {}
\;
20 4 * * * find /tmp -type f -atime +2 -exec rm -f {} \;
30 4 * * * find /var/tmp -type f -atime +7 -exec rm -f {} \;
40 4 * * * find /var/adm/syslog.dated -depth -type d -ctime +5
-exec rm -rf {} \
;
#0 3 * * 4 /usr/sbin/acct/dodisk > /var/adm/diskdiag &
```

A line beginning with a pound sign (#) is considered to be a comment and is ignored by cron. Take advantage of this and insert liberal comments into your crontabs for future reference. In addition, a crontab entry can be "commented out" to temporary disable execution of that job by inserting a pound sign at the beginning of the line.

The cron daemon executes the specified command from the owner's $HOME directory with a default environment, defining HOME, LOGNAME, SHELL (/usr/bin/sh), and PATH (/usr/bin). If additional environment variables are necessary, or if a different shell is desired, such as /usr/bin/ksh or /usr/bin/csh, you must explicitly specify them. Except for simple one-line commands, it is recommended that shell scripts be created that contain all necessary environment variables and the resulting script be specified in the crontab file.

The proper way to create or edit a crontab is with the crontab(1) command. The crontab command does two important things: it places the new or edited crontab file into the protected /var/spool/cron/crontabs directory, and it signals the cron daemon to re-read all the crontabs because there has been a change to their contents. There are two methods to submit changes to cron using crontab: manually, and with the crontab -e command. The manual method is suitable for situations where crontab changes may be scripted, while the crontab -e command is usually appropriate for interactive edits to a crontab file

The manual method:

1. Become the user that corresponds to the appropriate file in the crontabs directory. For example, if you want to submit commands that will run as user adm, use the su(1) command to become user adm.
2. Use the crontab command with the -l flag to copy the appropriate file from the crontabs directory to a temporary file. For example, if you are user adm, you could use the following command:

```
$ crontab -l > /tmp/temp_adm
```

3. Edit the temporary file and add the commands you want to run at a specified time.
4. Use the crontab command and specify the temporary file to submit the commands to the cron daemon:

```
$ crontab /tmp/temp_adm
```

Using the crontab –e command:

1. Become the user that corresponds to the appropriate file in the crontabs directory.
2. Run crontab specifying the edit (-e) command line switch, and you will be placed in the editor specified by the EDITOR environment variable, or /usr/bin/vi by default. Simply make the desired changes to the crontab entries, and crontab will submit the changes to cron when the edit session is completed:

```
$ crontab -e
```

The system administrator can restrict access to cron services in one of two ways. If there are a small group of users permitted to use cron, simply list their account names, one per line, in /var/adm/cron/cron.allow. If cron.allow does not exist, the crontab command checks for the existence of /var/adm/cron/cron.deny to determine which users are denied access to cron services. If neither file exists, only the root account is permitted to submit a job to cron. Normally, cron.allow is absent and cron.deny is an empty file, meaning that all users have access to cron.

### 9.9.2 at

While the cron facility and its crontab scheduling files are for regularly scheduled jobs, the at(1) command submits a job to be executed only once at a user-specified future time. Jobs submitted via the at command are packaged into a script and placed in the /var/spool/cron/atjobs directory for future execution by the cron daemon. The at command provides a more complete job environment by including all active environment variables in the resulting script file. The at command also allows specifying which shell is used to run the job, via the [-c | -s | -k] switches for C shell, Bourne shell, and Korn shell, respectively. The default shell is the Bourne shell, /usr/bin/sh.

The at command's job submission syntax is very flexible, allowing an English-like date/time argument in addition to a more conventional CCYYMMDDhhmm.SS format. For example, either of these commands will schedule a system reboot for the following Saturday at 2:00 A.M.:

```
# at 2 am Saturday /sbin/reboot
# at -t 200104280200.00 /sbin/reboot
```

The at command writes the job number and the scheduled time to standard error upon job submission, for example:

```
job root.869299200.a at Sat Apr 28 02:00:00 2001
```

The format of the job name is user.xxxxxxxxx.y, where the "user" argument identifies the user who submitted the job; xxxxxxxxx is a 9-digit number based on the scheduled date; and y indicates the job type, as shown in Table 9.5.

**Table 9.5** *Job Type Indicators for at(1) Command*

| Character | Job Type |
|---|---|
| a | at job |
| b | batch job |
| e | ksh job |
| f | csh job |

The job name is also the name of the packaged script located in /var/spool/cron/atjobs. The following is the atjob script from the previous reboot example:

```
# ls -l /var/spool/cron/atjobs
total 1
-r—r-Sr—  1 root   daemon    648 Apr 24 18:10 root.869299200.a
# cat /var/spool/cron/atjobs/root.869299200.a
: at job
export EDITOR; EDITOR='/usr/bin/vi'
export HOME; HOME='/'
export LOGNAME; LOGNAME='root'
export MANPATH; MANPATH='/usr/man:/usr/local/man'
export PATH; PATH='/usr/bin:/sbin:/usr/bin/X11:/usr/tcb/bin'
export PWD; PWD='/usr/bin'
export SHELL; SHELL='/bin/sh'
export TERM; TERM='vt220'
export USER; USER='root'
export VISUAL; VISUAL='/usr/bin/vi'

cd $HOME  # cd to user's home directory
cd /usr/var/spool/cron/atjobs  # working directory
#ulimit 18014398509481983  # commented out till Sys V shell
umask 22  # file creation mask
/usr/bin/sh << 'QAZWSXEDCRFVTGBYHNUJMIKOLP'
/sbin/reboot
  # shell and jobname
```

The at command also provides options to manage at jobs:

```
# at -l  (List all scheduled at jobs)
root.869299200.a  Sat Apr 28 02:00:00 2001
root.869530564.a  Mon Apr 30 18:16:04 2001
root.869098583.a  Wed Apr 25 18:16:23 2001
mcheek.868997800.a  Tue May 1 14:16:40 2001

# at -r -u mcheek  (Remove all scheduled jobs owned by
  mcheek)
at file: mcheek.868997800.a deleted
# at -n root  (List the number of jobs in the queue for the
  specified user)
3 files in the queue
```

Similarly to cron, the system administrator can enforce access to at services by placing user names in /var/adm/cron/at.allow or /var/adm/cron/at.deny. The at command checks these files when a user attempts to submit an at job. By default, all users are permitted to use the at command.

### 9.9.3 batch

The batch(1) command is simply an interface to the at command that submits a job for execution when the system load level permits; batch is intended to be run interactively, with the commands to be scheduled to be read from standard input. Depending on how busy the system is at the time of submission, batch jobs may be executed immediately or queued in the /var/spool/cron/atjobs directory for execution at a later date. The following is an example of batch submission of a sort job:

```
# batch
/usr/bin/sort /tmp/bigfile.txt -o /tmp/sorted.txt
<Ctrl-D>
job root.868928098.b at Mon Jul 14 18:54:58 1997
#
```

Since jobs submitted with the batch command are actually at jobs, the at command is also used to list and delete batch jobs.

# 10

# *Performance Monitoring and Tuning*

## 10.1 Overview

The performance of a UNIX system is best defined as the ability of the system to accomplish a given task or set of tasks. Good performance is a moving target that depends on a great many variables, including user perception, performance indexes, and available system resources. A system administrator is frequently called upon to evaluate and improve the performance of a system; the ability to do so to the satisfaction of the user community can be a challenging task. In this chapter, we discuss the performance indexes available to you in quantifying system performance, define the four primary system resource categories that affect UNIX system performance and the tools to measure them, and provide strategies for translating user complaints into objective information useful for evaluating performance problems.

Once the performance of a system has been quantified and performance problems have been identified, the next step is tuning. Tuning is the process of adjusting the system configuration to compensate for an identified performance bottleneck. Following the discussion of performance indexes and system monitoring, we outline a tuning methodology that aims for the best overall performance over time.

## 10.2 Performance Management

Performance management is an ongoing process of continued system monitoring and configuration adjustments to maintain an acceptable level of performance. In order to successfully manage performance, a system administrator must understand:

- Performance indexes
- System resources and their performance characteristics
- Performance management strategies

## 10.3 Performance Indexes

There are a variety of factors that affect the performance of a Tru64 UNIX system, and frequently these factors are non-technical and beyond a system administrator's control to change. Understanding the nature of these factors is the first step in being able to effectively manage the performance of a UNIX system.

Perhaps the most important factor is understanding your system environment and workload. Simply put, it is difficult to identify abnormalities without first knowing what is normal. This understanding is gained over time by monitoring a system to determine its average throughput and behavior. Knowing a system's typical workload also allows an administrator to see trends in system activity over time and to predict the effects of changes to the system, applications, or usage patterns.

Regardless of whether a system administrator has been involved with a particular system from its inception (and therefore was part of a system's design, installation, and configuration) and early use, or simply inherited an existing system that has been running for months or years, an administrator should spend some time with the system in order to answer system characterization questions such as:

- What are the types of applications running on the system?

  Database

  Development

  Graphics
- World Wide Web or other network service
- What is the average number of users on the system at each time of day?
- What are the busiest times of operation?
- Which jobs run at which times of the day?
- What are the known resource-intensive jobs?
- What is the average response time at various times of the day?

(Note: response time is defined as the time interval between entering an interactive command and the appearance of a response.)

The answers to some of these questions are learned by being logging into the system and monitoring its behavior. Tru64 UNIX provides tools and utilities that allow the system administrator to view the usage of various system resources. The next section (10.4.), "System Resources," covers the usage of these tools and the interpretation of their output. Over time, a system administrator will come to understand what is "normal" for a given system. Normal, of course, is a relative term and assumes that the workload does not change. For example, a system that supports an organization's financial activity may seem quite speedy during the first part of the month, but may become nearly unusable around the end of the month as the system is under stress to complete the month-end close-out. In this case, both situations are normal as long as it is understood what the system is being asked to do and when. If, however, the system's response time were to increase dramatically in the middle of a month, this behavior would most likely be considered abnormal and worthy of investigation.

Some of the other characterization questions listed above are best answered by working closely with the user community and understanding their needs and perceptions. Users tend to accept an average response time as normal, and jobs are expected to complete in the same amount of time every time they are run. These expectations are not always valid, but exist nevertheless. In a time-sharing system, such as Tru64 UNIX, an individual user's response time can vary greatly depending on the other work going on at the same time. Users who come from a PC-only background, for example, may not understand this, and it is up the system administrator to educate them rather than effect a change to the system's behavior.

In addition, you may discover that a user's perception of reduced response times or increased execution times may be due to factors outside your control. For example, a user may be connected to the system via a slower connection than usual, resulting in a slower response just to that user's terminal. The system may be running well within the range of acceptability but may seem slower to that user. Keep in mind that the purpose of the system is for the completion of productive work for everyone, regardless of system irregularities, when you are called upon to evaluate the inevitable user complaints.

A Tru64 UNIX system administrator needs to develop the skills to interpret user complaints. One of the most important of such skills is patience. You will occasionally receive feedback that "the system seems slow." When this happens, work with the user(s) to quantify their perceptions by enlisting their help in collecting the basic information you will need:

- What is the user's measured response/execution time versus normal?
- Are reported "hung" processes truly hung?
- Did the problem occur suddenly, or did it degrade over time?
- Is this the first time this behavior has been experienced?
- Can the problem be duplicated?
- How many (and which) users were on the system at the time of the problem?
- Is the problem on the local system or a remote system?

Going through this process with users will help educate them and hopefully impress upon them the importance of collecting useful data rather then just yelling that the system is slow. Thus, you will also be making them part of the process of identifying the problem and finding the solution.

## 10.4 System Resources

A Tru64 UNIX system can be a complex environment with many variables that impact performance. A system administrator may initially feel overwhelmed when first presented with a performance problem. In reality, though, there are only four categories of system resources, and all performance issues are related to the availability—or lack—of these resources:

- CPU
- Memory
- Input/output (I/O)
- Network

Once an administrator understands these four resources and how to view their usage, it becomes easier to identify which resource is a bottleneck to the timely completion of work. After describing the particulars of each resource, we discuss the utilities available for characterizing the usage of the resource, and strategies for translating this usage information into conclusions on any performance issues.

### 10.4.1 The CPU Resource

The CPU capacity of a UNIX system is defined by the quantity, type, and speed of its processor. All Tru64 UNIX systems contain one or more Alpha processors. In the following discussion, "the CPU" refers to the total CPU capacity of a system, whether that consists of one or more actual processors. The CPU is the resource that actually executes instructions, and is frequently perceived by users to be the primary factor in specifying overall system speed. The speed of a given machine is a function of that system's CPU cycle time; the greater the clock speed of the process, the faster the CPU. However, doubling the clock speed of the Alpha chip in a system may not automatically double the overall speed of a system. The same notion holds true for the number of CPUs in the system. A system containing two CPUs is not likely to be exactly twice as fast as a system with only one CPU of the same type. There are a number of other factors that influence the speed with which individual instructions are executed on a given system, such as:

- Number of CPUs in the system
- Complexity of the instructions being executed
- Effectiveness of memory caches (See Section 10.4.2, "The Memory Resource")

In addition, there is the issue of process scheduling and priority. A process with a higher priority will typically negatively impact a process with a lower priority. By default, Tru64 UNIX favors interactive processes over compute-intensive processes by maintaining or raising the priorities of the interactive processes. A system administrator must be able to monitor CPU utilization and process scheduling status in order to understand and identify performance problems.

The CPU is always running in one of two modes, kernel mode or user mode, at any one time. Kernel mode (sometimes referred to as system mode) is a privileged processor access mode that handles most operating system functions. For example, handling hardware and software interrupts and processing system calls are done in kernel mode. User application processes, on the other hand, run in user mode, which is less privileged than kernel mode. If a user process makes a system call, however, the CPU switches to kernel mode to process it.

There is no rule of thumb regarding an acceptable ratio of CPU time spent in kernel mode versus user mode. The distribution depends on a variety of factors including the type of applications running (database, graphics, development, networking, etc.), the number of system calls the applications make, and the state of the system (system health, number of users, etc.). It is therefore crucial that a system administrator have the experience to know what is "normal" for a given system.

#### 10.4.1.1 Tuning CPU

CPU performance issues usually fall into one of the following three categories, each of which prevents user processes from being executed and completed in an acceptable time frame:

- The CPU is at capacity.
- The CPU is busy doing things other than the desired task(s).
- The CPU is idle, waiting for other resources.

##### 10.4.1.1.1 CPU at Capacity

If the amount of work being demanded of the CPU in a given system exceeds the capacity of that CPU, the system's response time will increase as jobs queue up waiting for the CPU, which is working at 100% trying to keep up. In this instance, there are only two things to be done: purchase more CPU capacity, or demand less of the existing CPU resource. Assuming that buying more hardware is usually not feasible, a system administrator must look at either reducing the priority of jobs or shifting the execution of compute-intensive jobs to times when the CPU is not in such demand, such as the middle of the night or during the weekend.

A CPU at capacity is usually considered a bad situation. However, for certain classes of systems, it simply means that the system resources are being very effectively utilized. The way to tell if your system falls into this category is almost entirely based on user perception. If the CPU utilization is at or very close to 100%, users are getting work done, and response time is reasonable, then the system has reached a special point known as "CPU nirvana." Once you reach this point, if the system workload is well known and not expected to grow, then there is nothing for you to do. This is admittedly a rare event in computing. In practice, your system will usually not fit these criteria, and if you ever have a system that reaches this point, you should be planning to add more CPU capacity immediately. CPU utilization on most working systems will never remain constant, and a slight increase in workload could make the system unusable for everyone. Although unspent CPU cycles are wasted and will never be returned, it is almost always a good idea have some extra CPU capacity to meet temporary or long-term increases in demand.

##### 10.4.1.1.2 CPU Busy

The CPU may have high utilization but users may still see unacceptable response times. In this case, the CPU may be busy doing something other than the work the users are asking of it. Remember that the CP.U's kernel mode is a higher priority mode than user mode, and certain events will preempt the execution of user processes, forcing the CPU to stop executing user code in favor of other work. One such event of particular interest to a system administrator is a hardware interrupt. If there exists a hardware problem on the system, the CPU will be notified via such an interrupt and be required to deal with the error. If repeated errors, such as disk or memory errors, are present, the CPU may be constantly interrupted and user work will suffer. If you suspect such a situation, examine the system error logs; a perceived performance problem may actually be a hardware problem. It is almost always the case that a busy CPU will be a problem with another resource, rather than CPU. The vmstat(1) and ps(1) tools that come with Tru64 UNIX, as well as some freeware tools like vmubc, top, and monitor, can help you determine the processes or kernel subsystems using up the CPU cycles. It's a good idea to familiarize yourself with these tools and how they work before you actually need them.

#### 10.4.1.1.3 CPU Idle

Today's high-speed processors, such as the Alpha processors in Tru64 UNIX systems, are faster than ever and continue to get faster still. Memory and disk performance, though also always improving, continue to lag behind. If the jobs being run on a system require large amounts of memory or disk I/O, you may find the CPU sitting around doing nothing waiting for the I/O subsystem to catch up. Since the CPU is so much faster than the I/O on any UNIX system, there will always be some amount of CPU wait time. If, however, the CPU is idle most of the time during busy periods, there may be a severe I/O bottleneck that needs to be examined. When investigating a high CPU idle percentage, always examine the disk load before assuming that the entire system is simply idle.The vmstat(1) command has a little-known switch, -w, which displays the percentage of time the CPU is in an I/O wait condition.

### 10.4.2 The Memory Resource

There are several types of memory on a Tru64 UNIX system that differ in purpose, speed, capacity, and cost. A system administrator must understand the characteristics of each to identify and fix memory resource problems. The three types are:

- Real memory (RAM)
- Virtual memory
- Cache memory

#### 10.4.2.1 Real Memory

The primary and most familiar type of memory in a Tru64 UNIX system is composed of Random Access Memory chips, or RAM. This memory is typically what is meant when referring to the memory size of an individual system. For example, an Alphastation with 64 MB of memory has 67,108,864 bytes of memory storage. The total, or physical, memory on a running Tru64 UNIX system includes the Compaq console code, the Tru64 UNIX kernel, and the kernel's associated data structures. The memory remaining after system initialization loads these system resources is termed "available" memory and is the amount of memory available to user processes. Since Tru64 UNIX uses a shared memory model, the user processes will usually have part of their address space resident in real memory and part in swap space. The process's pages must be loaded into RAM in order for the Alpha CPU to execute its instructions. Therefore, the amount of real memory on the system is important. We will discuss the difference between real and virtual memory shortly, but for now be aware of this distinction.

To determine the physical memory configuration of a Tru64 UNIX system, use vmstat -P. See Figure 10.1 for a representative output from the vmstat command.

Note that a fairly significant amount of real memory is occupied by the Tru64 UNIX kernel and associated data structures. The size of the kernel and its data structures is determined by which kernel options are selected when the kernel is built. To minimize the size of the kernel (and thus the amount of physical memory occupies), select only the kernel options that are necessary or appropriate for your system. See Chapter 4, "System Configuration," for guidelines in building a Tru64 UNIX kernel. Note that more recent versions of Tru64 UNIX allow many subsystems to be installed and removed dynamically from the system at run time. Thus, there are fewer "opportunities" to rebuild the kernel than there used to be.

#### 10.4.2.2 Virtual Memory

Tru64 UNIX, similar to many other modern operating systems, supports a facility whereby the total addressable memory size is independent of the physical memory installed in the system. This ability, called virtual memory, allows a system to apparently have a much larger addressable range than the amount of real memory installed in the system. The basic unit of memory, virtual and physical, is the page, which is a fixed 8 KB in size in current versions of Tru64 UNIX. The virtual memory facility, which is managed by the Tru64 UNIX kernel, works by transparently moving pages between physical memory,

**Figure 10.1** *Determining the Memory Configuration.*

```
# vmstat -P

Total Physical Memory =    512.00 M  ❶
                      =     65536 pages

Physical Memory Clusters:

 start_pfn       end_pfn      .     type  size_pages / size_bytes
         0           256             pal        256 /    2.00M
       256         65534              os      65278 /  509.98M
     65534         65536             pal          2 /   16.00k

Physical Memory Use:

 start_pfn       end_pfn            type  size_pages / size_bytes
       256           278       unixtable         22 /  176.00k
       278           288        scavenge         10 /   80.00k
       288          1123            text        835 /    6.52M
      1123          1337            data        214 /    1.67M
      1337          1716             bss        379 /    2.96M
      1717          1954          kdebug        237 /    1.85M
      1954          1960         cfgmgmt          6 /   48.00k
      1960          1962           locks          2 /   16.00k
      1962          2282       unixtable        320 /    2.50M
      2282          2296            pmap         14 /  112.00k
      2296          2302            logs          6 /   48.00k
      2302          3308        vmtables       1006 /    7.86M
      3308         65534         managed      62226 /  486.14M  ❷
                                  ============================
         Total Physical Memory Use:           65277 /  509.98M  ❸

Managed Pages Break Down:
       free pages = 34152
     active pages = 7201
   inactive pages = 3838
      wired pages = 17045
        ubc pages = 6878
     ==================
            Total = 69114

WIRED Pages Break Down:

   vm wired pages = 2854
  ubc wired pages = 3381
  meta data pages = 1958
     malloc pages = 7463
     contig pages = 549
   user ptepages = 510
  kernel ptepages = 68
    free ptepages = 8
     ==================
            Total = 16791

❶ Physical memory installed in the system
❷ Number of managed pages used by processes (excluding UBC)
❸ Total memory utilisation
```

where instructions can be run, and temporary holding areas on disks, known as swap areas. The kernel basically plays a "shell game" with processes and data, moving idle objects to disk and recalling objects from disk back into physical memory when needed. There are two types of virtual memory operations that the operating system performs: paging and swapping.

#### 10.4.2.2.1 Paging

The paging operation consists of moving a single page or a small group of pages between disk and physical memory. It is conceivable (in fact common) that a process's memory image would be too large to fit into available physical memory, and only part of the process can be resident at any one time. UNIX has the ability to execute such a process through the mechanism of paging. If the process references a location in virtual memory that is not currently resident, the kernel generates a page fault on behalf of the process to bring the required page into physical memory. A page fault is a hardware interrupt that instructs the Tru64 UNIX memory manager to move the required page from disk to physical memory. In doing so, the memory manager may be required to move another page from physical memory to disk to make room. Some amount of paging results from normal activity on a UNIX system, and the amount of pageins and pageouts is monitored via the vmstat(1) command. If pageins or pageouts are constant or excessive, this could indicate a physical memory shortage.

There are several different types of page faults. Some page faults, known as hard page faults, require a disk I/O to complete and are expensive in system resource terms. An "expensive" system operation is one that will take a long time to execute and will likely force the process to wait for its completion. Other types of page faults, known collectively as soft faults, are not expensive and can be handled by the system without a disk I/O. There are four types of soft page faults monitored by vmstat(1): fault, cow, zero, and react.

- fault—An address translation fault has occurred.
- cow—A copy on write fault (usually resulting from a fork() operation).
- zero— A zero-filled page was requested.
- react—A page is reactivated from the system-wide inactive page list.

#### 10.4.2.2.2 Swapping

The process of swapping is similar to paging in that virtual memory pages are moved between disk and physical memory. The primary difference is that instead of moving a single page or small groups of pages, swapping moves all pages associated with a particular process between disk and memory. This operation on a process is known as a swapout and is initiated by the Tru64 UNIX memory manager for one of the following reasons:

- A memory shortage so severe that the paging process cannot free memory fast enough

- Processes have been inactive for more than 20 seconds

Swapping is usually the result of insufficient physical memory on the system. Swapping is a very expensive system operation and should be avoided at all costs. On more recent versions of Tru64 UNIX, the occurrence of swapping has been all but eliminated. Paging is the preferred method for the system to reclaim memory due to the fact that it is a far less expensive operation than swapping.

In extreme cases of memory shortages, a condition known as thrashing can occur. Thrashing occurs on a system when the requested memory resources far exceed the available physical memory, and the system spends more time performing memory-related tasks such as paging and swapping than executing user application code. The name thrashing is derived from how the disks behave in this situation.

#### *10.4.2.3 Cache Memory*

Cache memory is a type of high-speed memory that typically acts as a buffer between a slow resource, such as disks or network, and a fast resource, such as our speedy Alpha processor. There are several types of caches that, though important and desirable, are not directly under the system administrator's control; that is, the sizing of these caches is not configurable. Examples of these caches are the CPU's on-chip cache and disk controller hardware caches, such as those provided by the Compaq StorageWorks family of controllers (HSZ70, HSG80, etc). The two cache memories that are configurable in Tru64 UNIX are:

- Traditional buffer cache (file system metadata cache)
- Unified buffer cache (UBC)

Each of these caches is defined as a percentage of physical memory; the percentages can be configured by the system administrator.

##### 10.4.2.3.1 Traditional Buffer Cache

As users and processes access a Tru64 UNIX system's UNIX File Systems (UFS), the file system metadata (directories, symbolic links, inodes, and blocks) is cached in the traditional buffer cache. If every implied disk transfer really had to occur, a UNIX system would spend a great deal of time waiting for the completion of I/O. However, through the use of this traditional buffer cache, which contains recently used disk blocks, typically over 80% of all disk transfers will be satisfied from the contents of this cache, dramatically reducing disk I/O.

By default, the size of the traditional buffer cache is 3% of physical memory. This is a reasonably sane default, except in special situations where such a value may incur unacceptably high physical memory usage. For example, an Alphastation workstation with 64 megabytes of memory will have a traditional buffer cache size of approximately 1.9 MB. However, on a system whose physical memory is 4 GB, the cache size would be almost 123 MB, which is possibly excessive. Reducing the size of the cache on such a system to 2% (82 MB), or even 1% (41 MB) of physical memory is probably sufficient. This has the pleasant side effect of increasing the total available memory for user processes. As an example, if your system is using the Advanced File System (AdvFS) for all of its local file systems and does not use UFS, then the traditional buffer cache can be safely reduced to 1%. Ideally, if this were the case, you'd want to simply turn this cache off in order to avoid wasting any memory on it. However, this cache cannot be completely eliminated; 1% of physical memory is the smallest cache size that can be configured.

Another variable to keep in mind when sizing the traditional buffer cache is that its purpose is caching file system metadata. If there are a small number of file systems on a system (for example, on a database server where the bulk of the disk space is accessed by the database management system in character (raw) mode), a smaller traditional buffer cache may be warranted, since the raw mode access bypasses all Tru64 UNIX I/O buffering.

The traditional buffer cache size is specified in the kernel configuration file or in /etc/sysconfigtab by the "bufcache" keyword. For example, placing the following entry in the kernel configuration file, rebuilding the kernel, and booting from that new kernel would set the traditional buffer cache size to 2%:

```
bufcache 2
```

See Chapter 4, "System Configuration," for instructions on building a new kernel. If you alter this value using sysconfigtab, you can avoid a kernel rebuild; you would add the following entry and simply reboot the system:

```
vfs:
  bufcache = 2
```

To determine if the traditional buffer cache is sized appropriately, examine the hit rate. The hit rate is the percentage of time that requested data is in the cache, preventing a physical disk I/O. Use the dbx(8) debugger to examine the cache statistics (see Figure 10.2). A good hit rate is 97% or better. If the hit rate is below 97%, you may want to consider increasing the bufcache attribute to increase the size of the traditional buffer cache, thereby increasing its effectiveness.

#### 10.4.2.3.2 Unified Buffer Cache

Tru64 UNIX uses a second type of cache called the Unified Buffer Cache (UBC), which is different in two ways from the Traditional Buffer Cache. Whereas the Traditional Buffer Cache caches file system metadata (directories, symbolic links, inodes, and blocks), the UBC buffers file contents. In

**Figure 10.2** *Calculating the traditional buffer cache hit rate.*

```
# dbx -k /vmunix
dbx version 5.1
Type 'help' for help.

thread 0xfffffc007fe20a80 stopped at  [thread_block:3102
,0xfffffc00002d2130]     Source not available

warning: Files compiled -g3: parameter values probably wrong
(dbx) pd bio_stats
struct {
    getblk_hits = 43848279  ❶
    getblk_misses = 104437  ❷
    getblk_research = 0
    getblk_dupbuf = 122
    getnewbuf_calls = 105800
    getnewbuf_buflocked = 0
    vflushbuf_lockskips = 7
    mntflushbuf_misses = 0
    mntinvalbuf_misses = 0
    vinvalbuf_misses = 0
    allocbuf_buflocked = 0
    ufssync_misses = 0
}
(dbx) quit
#bc
scale = 5
(1 - ( 104437 / (104437 + 43848279) ) ) * 100  ❸
99.76300  ❹
#

❶ Total number of block misses
❷ Total number of block hits
❸ Calculate the hit percentage
❹ The Traditional Buffer Cache hit rate percentage
```

addition, the size of the UBC is dynamic, whereas the traditional buffer cache is fixed at a certain percentage of physical memory. The UBC grows and shrinks in response to changing system demands and can potentially grow to utilize all of physical memory. Heavy file system activity will increase the number of physical memory pages reserved for the UBC, and heavy virtual memory demands, such as requirements to run large executable files, will reduce the number of pages reserved for the UBC, thereby reclaiming those pages back into user memory space.

The upper and lower bounds of the UBC can be specified by setting two kernel attributes in the vm subsystem. These attributes are set in the kernel subsystem database (/etc/sysconfigtab). By default, the maximum percentage of physical memory that the UBC can grow to is 100%. The ubc_maxpercent attribute can be set to specify a different maximum value. Similarly, the ubc_minpercent attribute, which defaults to 10%, specifies the minimum percentage of physical memory that the UBC will shrink to when page reclamation occurs. Note that the ubc_minpercent value is not the minimum value that the UBC can be. Often, the UBC starts below the ubc_minpercent value, and it is possible for the UBC to never grow above this minimum value.

To determine the effectiveness of the unified buffer cache, monitor the cache hit rate. This is the percentage of times that requested data was found in the UBC, requiring a physical I/O to retrieve the data. This value can be calculated with the dbx(8) debugger (see Figure 10.3). A good hit rate is 95% or better. If the hit rate is below 90%, you may want to consider increasing the ubc_minpercent attribute to increase the minimum size of the UBC, thereby increasing its effectiveness.

#### *10.4.2.4 Tuning Memory*

Memory performance issues are typically caused by either an insufficiency in one or more of the three types of memory resources, or an inefficient use of existing memory resources. The former situation is addressed by either adding more of the required resource (RAM, cache, or swap space), or demanding less of the existing memory resource, e.g., by shifting usage to off-peak hours. The latter situation is where a system administrator can make adjustments. Several suggestions to focus on are:

- Kernel configuration
- Traditional/unified buffer cache sizing
- Swap space configuration

**Figure 10.3** *Calculating the unified buffer cache hit rate.*

```
# dbx -k /vmunix
dbx version 5.1
Type 'help' for help.

thread 0xfffffc007fe20a80 stopped at  [thread_block:3102
,0xfffffc00002d2130]    Source not available

warning: Files compiled -g3: parameter values probably wrong
(dbx) pd ufs_getapage_stats
struct {
    read_looks = 49678827  ❶
    read_hits = 48551227  ❷
    read_miss = 1128369
    alloc_error = 0
    alloc_in_cache = 0
}
(dbx) quit
# bc
scale = 5
( 48551227 / 49678827 ) * 100  ❸
97.73000  ❹
#


❶ Total number of read attempts
❷ Total number of read hits
❸ The UBC cache hit rate percentage calculation
❹ The UBC cache hit rate percentage.
```

#### 10.4.2.4.1 Kernel Configuration

When a Tru64 UNIX kernel is built with the doconfig(8) command, the size of the resulting vmunix file is determined by the selected kernel options (see Chapter 4), or by specifying values for certain kernel parameters in the kernel configuration file. If the kernel contains unneeded options, the resulting vmunix file could be unnecessarily large, consuming valuable physical memory. To conserve RAM, select only the kernel options appropriate for a particular system. Additionally, specifying unused or nonexistent devices or pseudo-devices such as network or disk interfaces, disks, or tapes, also increases the size of the kernel by linking additional code into the kernel. Remove any such extraneous devices from the kernel configuration file, and then rebuild the kernel.

In addition, certain kernel configuration file parameters, such as "maxusers," which is used to size a variety of kernel tables and structures, should be set appropriately for a given system. The maxusers parameter is, by definition, the number of simultaneous users that your system can support without straining system resources. Setting maxusers higher than necessary wastes physical memory. Determining an optimal value for maxusers can sometimes be difficult, but making an assessment of the projected use of the system can point you in the right direction. For instance, on a large server that will have several hundred interactive users, each running a large number of processes, it may make sense to set maxusers to 512 or higher. On the other hand, a small desktop workstation that will have only a single user running a handful of windows will probably be fine with a maxusers value of 32. Unless your system is very memory constrained, the best approach is to double maxusers when it becomes necessary to increase it; otherwise, just leave it alone.

#### 10.4.2.4.2 Traditional/Unified Buffer Cache Sizing

Proper sizing of both the traditional buffer cache and the unified buffer cache is important in order to maximize the available memory for user processes, while retaining adequate buffer space to prevent I/O performance degradation. The traditional buffer cache's default size of 3% of physical memory is sufficient unless the physical memory in the system is greater than two gigabytes, in which case we recommend reducing the size to 2% of physical memory.

The unified buffer cache (UBC), on the other hand, is dynamically sized and is controlled by specifying a high-water value (ubc_maxpercent) of 100% (of physical memory) by default, and a low-water value (ubc_minpercent) of 10% by default. If more real memory is needed to execute a system's processes, and the system is not doing a great deal of I/O, you can reduce the amount of memory made available to the UBC by setting the ubc_maxpercent parameter to 50%. This prevents the UBC from growing beyond half of physical memory rather than taking the entire 100% if necessary. On systems doing a great deal of I/O, such as an NFS server or a development system, you may wish to increase the initial size of the UBC (presumably reducing actual I/O) by raising the ubc_minpercent parameter above the default of 10% of physical memory. To determine if the ubc_minpercent value is set too high, causing a real memory shortage and resulting in higher paging activity, monitor the pageout rate using the vmstat(1) command.

#### 10.4.2.4.3 Swap Space Configuration

There are several swap space configuration issues that impact virtual memory performance on a Tru64 UNIX system. The first of these is swap space size and layout. The amount of storage space set aside for the swap area should be at least one times the size of a system's physical memory and two or more times physical memory if the system is running many large jobs simultaneously. Though there is no performance penalty for having more swap space than necessary, there will definitely be problems if there is not enough swap space. Large programs will either be prevented from running or killed midstream if insufficient swap space is available, depending on the swap allocation method selected.

For best performance, spread your swap space across multiple disk devices and, if possible, multiple disk controllers as well. Use the fastest disks available in a system when configuring swap space. By having multiple smaller swap partitions, each on its own disk, rather than one large swap partition on a single disk, the system is able to stripe swap activity across multiple disks, thereby increasing performance. In order to provide the best swap space interleaving, as this striping is termed, activate all swap partitions at system bootup by placing them in the /etc/sysconfigtab file, as detailed in Chapter 4, "System Configuration." The swapon –s command displays the current swap space configuration and status. See Section 10.7.4 for a usage example of the swapon(8) command.

The second swap space consideration is the swap space allocation mode. The swap space on a Tru64 UNIX system usage is determined by two allocated modes: immediate mode or deferred mode. These two modes differ in when swap space is allocated and result in different swap space requirements.

- Immediate mode, which is also called eager mode, causes a chunk of swap space to be allocated as soon as a process starts and is reserved for the life of that process.
- Deferred mode, which is also referred to as lazy mode, delays the allocation of swap space until the system needs to write a memory page to swap space.

Tru64 UNIX's default swap allocation mode is immediate mode. This causes the operating system to reserve swap space for every process when the process starts, and again whenever it allocates memory. Immediate mode typically forces the system administrator to configure more swap space than is probably required.

Deferred mode, or overcommitment mode, on the other hand, causes the reservation of swap space to be postponed until the swap space is actually required for a pageout. Deferred mode requires less configured swap space and may cause the system to perform better, since less swap space overhead is required. However, since the swap space is not reserved until needed, the swap space may be unavailable when it is required, and the operating system may terminate the process. Unfortunately, in deferred mode, the system will occasionally kill processes other than the one needing the swap space, and the system does not discriminate between system processes and user processes. You should ensure that you have configured sufficient swap space if you are going to run in deferred mode. If the system decides to kill processes for lack of available swap, it will log this information in the current user.log file.

Immediate swap mode will be configured if the vm_swap_eager parameter in /etc/sysconfigtab is set to the value "1" when the system boots up. On the other hand, if the value of this parameter is set to "0" on system boot, then deferred mode is used. For example, put the following entry into the /etc/sysconfigtab file and reboot to convert from immediate swap mode to deferred mode:

```
vm:
  vm_swap_eager = 0
```

After running this system in deferred mode, change the following entry to go back to immediate mode:

```
vm:
  vm_swap_eager = 1
```

Generally, adding real memory to a system is the best way to increase performance of that system. However, a system administrator frequently does not have that luxury and has to work with what is available to increase memory performance.

### 10.4.3 I/O Resource

The I/O resource on a Tru64 UNIX system is typically related to the disk subsystem. Disk performance on a system is usually the greatest determining factor in that system's perceived overall performance. Modern CPUs, memory, and networks all have greater throughput than disks and, therefore, understanding disk I/O problems is key to configuring and tuning disk subsystems.

Systems with disk performance problems usually fall into one of two categories:

- Disk-bound systems
- Swap-bound systems

#### 10.4.3.1 Disk-Bound System

A system is disk-bound if there is a large amount of disk traffic on one or more disk drives and the CPU is spending a great deal of time idle, waiting for disk I/Os to complete. If a system is disk-bound, there are two things to focus your attention on: the physical disk layout, and the file system type and configuration on those disks. Both are important and go hand in hand; but, depending on a particular system, one may weigh more heavily than the other.

Since most disk performance problems are related to the physical disk configuration, it makes sense to start with the disk subsystem. There are a variety of strategies to investigate in order to increase disk throughput, and most attempt to avoid saturation of an individual disk, which should be avoided if at all possible. These strategies include:

- Use the fastest disks possible.
- Spread disks across as many buses as possible.
- Where possible, use many small disks rather than a few large disks.
- Use disk controllers with hardware cache, such as Compaq's HSx family of controllers.
- Use disk mirroring, either software such as the Logical Storage Manager (LSM), or hardware such as an HSZ controller.
- Balance disk load by distributing file systems across multiple disks or controllers.

The iostat(1) command is invaluable in determining if one or more disks on a system are saturated, or "hot." At a typical time during the workday, if one disk's transfer rate is significantly higher than that of the other disks, or worse, if one disk is supporting all I/O while the remaining disks are idle, this is indicative of an unbalanced disk subsystem. In this situation, the only remedy is to distribute the disk usage more evenly among all the disks or controllers. This may involve physically relocating disks between disk controllers, or moving file systems between disks to balance the usage.

This type of physical layout is especially crucial for a database system that uses raw space, rather then file systems, for data storage. A database server using raw devices bypasses the entire operating system buffering and caching system and, thus, depends more heavily on the efficient distribution of I/O across disks. The same principle holds true if the AdvFS Direct I/O feature is being used to bypass the buffer caches.

Once the disk subsystem has been examined, the next area of focus is the file system configuration and layout. The two primary local, general-purpose types of file systems supported by Tru64 UNIX are UFS and AdvFS, and each has its own unique tuning issues and strategies.

#### *10.4.3.2 UFS*

The UNIX File System (UFS) is the first of two local file system types supported on a Tru64 UNIX system, and this file system type is very common. There are a number of options and techniques available to a system administrator to tune a UFS file system. One or more of the following tips may suit your environment:

- Mirror file systems with Compaq's Logical Storage Manager (LSM). Mirroring a file system can be used to improve disk reads and also increase availability. On the other hand, mirroring typically slows down write operations.
- Defragment file systems if necessary. Using the dbx(8) debugger, examine the ufs_clusterstats, ufs_clusterstats_read, and ufs_clusterstats_write structure, to determine whether a disk is fragmented. See Figure 10.3 for an example of examining a kernel data structure. If the values in these UFS clustering structures show that clustering is not effective, the disk may be fragmented.

  Tru64 UNIX does not currently provide an automated mechanism for defragmenting a UFS file system. However, it is possible to defragment a file system with this procedure:

  1. Back up the file system data to tape or another disk partition.
  2. Unmount the fragmented file system.
  3. Recreate the file system, using newfs(8).
  4. Mount the file system.
  5. Restore the file system data to the newly recreated file system.

- Adjust the number of inodes to match the file system usage. If the file system has fewer, larger files, reduce the density of inodes with the newfs –i command when creating the file system.
- Adjust the fragment size to match the file system usage. By default, the fragment size on UFS is 1KB. This is appropriate on a file system containing many small files of 1KB or less. However, a larger fragment size (8 KB) is less wasteful of disk space and provides better performance for a file system that contains larger (greater than 16 KB) files. The frag-

ment size is specified with the newfs command when the file system is created.

- Adjust the maximum number of blocks per cylinder group. This value, the maxbpg parameter, is set when a UFS file system is created or an existing file system is modified by the tunefs(8) command. The default value for maxbpg is approximately one-fourth of the total blocks in a cylinder group, and this default is designed to benefit file systems containing average file size. Access performance on large files is degraded by the restriction of this parameter. The maxbpg parameter should be set higher than the default only on a file system that contains only large files (1 MB or larger). If maxbpg is changed for an existing file system, the files must be laid out on the disk again, similar to a defragmentation procedure, to gain the benefit.

#### 10.4.3.3 AdvFS

The Advanced File System (AdvFS) is another local file system on Tru64 UNIX systems. AdvFS provides significant performance and tuning advantages over UFS. Whereas certain tuning operations, such as defragmentation, on a UFS file system can only be done manually, AdvFS allows online defragmentation. Also, with an additional license, you can utilize Compaq's AdvFS Advanced Utilities to provides even more features such as multiple volume capacity, online reconfiguration, performance tuning, and online backups.

Some strategies for improving AdvFS performance include:

- Dedicate an entire disk to a single AdvFS file domain, rather than multiple file domains on a single disk, to avoid disk contention.
- Defragment AdvFS filesets frequently. Use the defragment and defragcron utilities, which allow online defragmenting without reducing file system availability. Without using these tools, you can, similarly to UFS, back up, recreate, and restore filesets to defragment them. This, however, forces filesets to be unavailable during the operation. The defragment utility can also be used to monitor the fragmentation of your AdvFS domains, without actually doing anything.
- Use AdvFS fileset quotas to limit the amount of space an individual fileset may consume of the file domain. It frequently makes sense for an AdvFS file domain to contain multiple filesets, and quotas prevent a single fileset from using all available space.

- Stripe individual files across multiple physical disks (or volumes) to increase performance. The optional AdvFS Advanced Utilities contain a utility to allow distributing individual files across specific disks within a file domain. This can provide better file access throughput and some degree of load balancing across disks and/or controllers.
- Consider using the AdvFS Direct I/O feature with commercial database products, such as Oracle, to get the performance advantages of raw disk I/O with the manageability of a file system.
- If you have older domains that have were created in a pre-Tru64 version 5.0 environment, consider converting these domains from the older AdvFS V3 on-disk structure to the newer AdvFS V4. There are significant changes and improvements in the AdvFS V4 structure that warrant converting to its use. Unfortunately, there is no online procedure for performing this conversion, and the only way to do this is by backing up, recreating, and restoring the file system.
- Very large file systems (over 200 gigabytes) require the features available from the optional AdvFS Advanced Utilities, such as, on-line backups, multiple volumes, file migration, and usage balancing.

### 10.4.4 Network Resource

The network resource is technically an I/O-type resource, but since so many modern Tru64 UNIX applications depend on multiple networked systems (e.g., Web servers), it is worthwhile to discuss network performance issues separately. In any case, good network performance is, by its nature, a hard thing to pin down. The state of a network is dependent on a variety of factors, many of which may be out of a system administrator's control. For example, network performance is affected by:

- Applications, both local and remote
- Network controllers, both type and capacity (Ethernet, SLIP/PPP, Token Ring, FDDI, ATM, etc.)—again, both local and remote
- The communications gear inconnecting the affected systems
- The capabilities of the local and remote hosts

Just like the other three performance resources (CPU, memory, and I/O), network performance is impacted when the demand for resources exceeds the supply of resources. This is usually manifested in network congestion caused by one of two issues:

- A physical problem with either network hardware or software somewhere in the network
- Network traffic that simply outstrips the capacity of the existing network resource

Neither of these problems is fixable by tuning. In the first case, something is broken and needs to be fixed, and in the second case, the solution is to either reduce the demand on the resource or add more resources.

Identifying network throughput bottlenecks is the first step in investigating perceived network issues. By finding such bottlenecks, you can quickly rule out problems with systems under local control. As an example, if the performance of a link between two systems suddenly degrades, the strategy might be to first measure the throughput rate by transferring several large files via ftp(1) and recording the transfer rate. There is a simple freeware program called ttcp (test TCP), available for download from multiple Internet locations, that is very helpful in characterizing network throughput. (Here is where knowing the performance characteristics of a "normal" network connection becomes invaluable. If you know what a typical transfer rate is, it becomes an easy step to compare the two transfer times and quickly ascertain if there is, in fact, a problem.) Once it is determined that the transfer rate has degraded, the next step is to trace the network path, capturing the hops and times and looking for abnormal values. Use the ping(1) and traceroute(1) utilities for this data collection. Hopefully, this will point you in the right direction to a solution. Obviously, this is just an example, but it shows how a step-by-step troubleshooting process is essential in troubleshooting network performance problems.

There is, however, one Tru64 UNIX–specific network parameter to be aware of and possibly adjust. This parameter, netisrthreads, specifies the number of network threads configured on a Tru64 UNIX system. The only issue with this parameter is to avoid having it set needlessly high. You can check the status of netisrthreads by examining the output of the netstat –m command. If the number of network threads configured exceeds the peak number of currently active threads, your system may be configured with too many threads. If this is the case, reducing the value for netisrthreads will free up memory for use by user processes. To change this value, specify the following lines in /etc/sysconfigtab:

```
net:
        netisrthreads = n
```

where n equals the number of network threads to configure. After making this change in /etc/sysconfigtab, reboot the system.

## 10.5 Finding Performance Bottlenecks

Finding a performance problem is the first step in fixing such a problem. The following is a simple four-step approach to identifying Tru64 UNIX bottlenecks:

1. Examine the system load average using the uptime(1) command.
   - Load average higher than normal: There may be a performance bottleneck. Continue to Step 2.
2. Determine how the CPU is spending the majority of its time. Use the vmstat(1) and iostat(1) commands.
   - User mode abnormally high: CPU resource may be at capacity.
   - System mode abnormally high: If system interrupts are exceptionally high, there may be hardware problems. Examine the binary error log for issues. (See Chapter 12 for details on troubleshooting hardware issues.)
   - Idle mode higher than normal: Memory resource may be reaching capacity, causing increased paging/swapping. Continue to Step 3.
   - Idle mode abnormally high: Disk (I/O) resource may be at capacity. Continue to Step 4.
3. Monitor the available memory and the paging rate. Use the vmstat(1) command.
   - If the total number of available pages (vmstat(1) "free" field) is less than the value of the sysconfig parameter vm_page_free_target, the system may be paging. Investigate possible causes of paging and swapping.
4. Determine if the disk usage is balanced evenly across the disks/controllers. Use the iostat(1) command.
   - If one or more disks have significantly higher activity (tps and/or bps) than the other disks, balance the disk load across all disks/controllers.

## 10.6 Resolving Performance Bottlenecks

Performance bottlenecks, once identified, are nearly always due to a lack of one or more of the four performance resources (CPU, memory, I/O, or network). A system administrator has three strategies for compensating for such resource bottlenecks:

- Increase the capacity of the limiting resource:

  By adjusting the system configuration (kernel parameters, etc.)

  By purchasing additional hardware
- Reduce the demand on the limiting resource:

  By running fewer simultaneous jobs or moving some jobs to off-peak times

  By redesigning the application(s) on the system
- Shift the demand from the limiting resource to another resource:

  By running application(s) remotely on other, less busy systems

  By distributing files and file systems across multiple disks/controllers

  By increasing system buffer cache size to reduce disk I/O, thereby reducing memory available to users

## 10.7 Performance Monitoring Utilities

Tru64 UNIX provides several native tools to monitor resource utilization. These include:

- uptime(1)
- iostat(1)
- vmstat(1)
- swapon(8)
- netstat(1)
- collect(8)

### 10.7.1 uptime

The uptime(1) command's primary purpose is to report how long a system has been running. In addition, uptime indicates how many users are logged in and displays three load average values. The load average numbers give the number of jobs in the run queue for the last 5 seconds, the last 30 seconds, and the last 60 seconds, and can be a rough indicator of how "busy" a system is. For example:

```
$ uptime
16:59 up 26 days, 21:12, 10 users, load average: 2.81, 2.80,
   2.65
```

These three load average numbers tell us that, on average, there were fewer than three jobs waiting for CPU time over the last 60 seconds. This particular system is a large database server with eight CPUs and a modest load. Load average numbers of zero usually indicate an idle system:

```
15:40 up 6 days, 17 mins, 9 users, load average: 0.00, 0.00,
   0.00
```

Extremely high load averages ( > 10 ), on the other hand, may indicate a CPU bottleneck as jobs are queued waiting for CPU resources. Since the load average numbers are only one parameter, however, you must perform additional investigations to determine the performance issue, if any.

One way to understand a system's activity is to periodically run the uptime command over several days and review the output. For example, to run uptime every 15 minutes and place the output into a log file, put the following line in your crontab:

```
0,15,30,45 * * * * /usr/bin/uptime >> /tmp/uptime.log
```

Be sure to monitor the size of the uptime.log and truncate or remove as necessary, for the log will grow by approximately 70 bytes every 15 minutes. After running uptime in this manner for several days, review the log file and determine what the busiest times of the day are, both in login activity and load averages.

### 10.7.2 iostat

The iostat(1) command is primarily a tool for displaying terminal and disk I/O statistics. However, iostat also displays useful information about CPU utilization. The iostat command's syntax is:

iostat [drive ...] [interval [count]]

Table 10.1 describes the arguments of the iostat command.

**Table 10.1** *iostat(1) Arguments*

| Argument | Meaning |
|---|---|
| drive... | Forces iostat to display information on specific drives. If drive is not specified iostat displays the first four drives (even if more than four disk drives are configured in the system). |
| interval | Causes iostat to report once each interval second. The first report is for all time since a reboot, and each subsequent report is for the last interval only. |
| count | Specifies the number of reports. |

For example, iostat 1 10 would produce 10 reports at 1-second intervals. You cannot specify count without interval, because the first numeric argument to iostat is assumed to be interval.

**Example:**

```
$ iostat
tty  dsk1  dsk2  dsk3  dsk4  cpu
tin  tout  bps   tps   bps   tps   bps   tps   bps   tps   us   ni   sy   id
0    39    5     0     5     0     2     0     6     0     5    0    23   72
$ iostat 5 5
tty  dsk1  dsk2  dsk3  dsk4  cpu
tin  tout  bps   tps   bps   tps   bps   tps   bps   tps   us   ni   sy   id
0    39    5     0     5     0     2     0     6     0     5    0    23   72
0    59    0     0     0     0     0     0     0     0     7    12   43   38
0    59    0     0     0     0     0     0     0     0     7    12   45   36
0    58    0     0     0     0     0     0     0     0     7    12   41   40
0    58    0     0     0     0     0     0     0     0     7    12   48   33
$
```

See Table 10.2 for a description of the output fields from the iostat command. The first invocation of iostat displays a summary of activity since the system was last started. This summary line is always displayed as the first output line when running iostat. The CPU fields (us, ni, sy, and id) indicate that, on average, the CPU has been idle 72% of the time and busy running system and user instructions the remaining 28% of the time. The second iostat session also displays the summary line first, followed by four "snapshots" of current system activity at five-second intervals. At this time, the CPU is busier than average, and each time the CPU utilization is approximately 63% (the average sum of the us, ni, and sy field.s) Note that the CPU fields, in addition to the other fields, are displayed as rounded integers, so it is possible for the sum of the four CPU values to equal less than 100%.

The iostat output is useful in identifying CPU resource limitations. While the system is running a typical or representative workload, run iostat

**Table 10.2** *iostat(1) Output*

| Field | Meaning |
|---|---|
| tin | The number of characters read per second from terminals (collectively) |
| tout | The number of characters written per second to terminals (collectively) |
| bps | For the specified disk, the amount of data (in kilobytes) transferred per second |
| tps | For the specified disk, the number of disk transfers per second |
| us* | The percentage of time the CPU has spent in user mode |
| ni* | The percentage of time the CPU has spent in user mode running low priority (niced) processes |
| sy* | The percentage of time the CPU has spent in system mode |
| id* | The percentage of time the CPU has spend idling |

**Note:* If the system has multiple CPUs, these values are calculated across all CPUs.

with an interval of five seconds and no count and monitor how the CPU is spending its time.

### 10.7.3 vmstat

The vmstat(1) command is used to display virtual memory statistics such as free memory, pageins and pageouts, and page faults. Additionally, vmstat shows the number of running processes categorized into running or runnable, waiting interruptibly, or waiting uninterruptibly. The type and quantity of interrupts, systems calls, and context switches per second is also displayed, along with CPU usage statistics. The CPU information is displayed by vmstat similarly to the iostat command. The vmstat command's syntax is:

```
vmstat [interval [count]]
```

Table 10.3 describes the arguments of the vmstat command.

**Example:**

```
$ vmstat 5 5
Virtual Memory Statistics: (pagesize = 8192)
  procs       memory         pages
intr       cpu
```

**Table 10.3** *vmstat(1) Arguments*

| Argument | Meaning |
|---|---|
| interval | Causes vmstat to report once each interval seconds. The first report is a summary since the last reboot, and each subsequent report is for the last interval only. |
| count | Specifies the number of reports. |

*Note:* For example, vmstat 2 5 would produce 5 reports at two-second intervals. You cannot specify count without interval, because the first numeric argument to vmstat is assumed to be interval.

```
    r   w   u  act free wire fault  cow zero react  pin pout  in
      sy  cs us sy id
    4 563 128  69K  19K  36K  912M 199M 314M  187K 133M  22K  2K
     76K  7K 14 37 49
    4 563 128  69K  19K  36K     4   16   17     0   27    0  4K
     48K  9K  5 75 20
    5 563 127  69K  19K  36K   165   15   26     0   25    0  5K
     50K 10K  6 76 18
    6 563 126  69K  19K  36K   115   24   32     0   37    0  5K
     49K 10K  6 77 18
    4 563 128  69K  19K  36K    13    0    0     0    0    0  2K
     49K  6K  5 60 35
$
```

See Table 10.4 for a description of the output fields from the vmstat command. Each invocation of vmstat displays a summary of activity since the system was last booted as the first line of output. The example vmstat session displays the summary line first, followed by four "snapshots" of current system activity at five-second intervals. At this time, for instance, the pageins (pin) and pageouts (pout) are effectively zero, indicating minimal paging. Also, the number of free memory pages is 19K, indicating approximately 159 MB available.

The vmstat output is helpful in identifying memory resource limitations. While the system is running a typical or representative workload, run vmstat with an interval of five seconds and no count, and monitor the memory free value, plus the number of pageins (pin) and pageouts (pout) and page faults.

### 10.7.4 swapon

The swapon(8) command is primarily used to activate swap areas, and is called for this purpose at system startup, and optionally after the system is up to add

**Table 10.4** *vmstat(1) Output*

| Field | Meaning |
|---|---|
| r | Number of threads that are running or are runable |
| w | Number of threads waiting interruptably |
| u | Number of threads waiting uninterruptably |
| act | Total number of pages on the active list, the inactive list, and the unified buffer cache (UBC) least-recently-used (LRU) list |
| free | Total number of pages that are clean and available for use |
| wire | Total number of pages that are currently in use and cannot be used for paging |
| fault | Number of address translation faults that have occurred. |
| cow | Number of copy-on-write page faults |
| zero | Number of zero-filled-on-demand page faults |
| react | Number of pages that have been faulted while on the inactive list |
| pin | Number of requests for pages from a pager |
| pout | Number of pages that have been paged out |
| in | Number of nonclock-device interrupts per second |
| sy | Number of system calls called per second |
| cs | Number of task and thread context switches per second |
| us* | Percentage of user time for normal and priority processes |
| sy* | Percentage of system time |
| id* | Percentage of idle time |

*Note:* If the system has multiple CPUs, these values are calculated across all CPUs.

additional swap space without rebooting the system. In addition, the swapon command's "-s" command line argument displays the status of the swap space on a Tru64 UNIX system. For example:

```
# swapon -s
Swap partition /dev/disk/dsk48b (default swap):
    Allocated space:        507114 pages (3.87GB)
    In-use space:            26157 pages (  5%)
    Free space:             480957 pages ( 94%)
```

Total swap allocation:

```
Allocated space:        507114 pages (3.87GB)
Reserved space:         163593 pages ( 32%)
In-use space:            26157 pages (  5%)
Available space:        343521 pages ( 67%)
```

This status display lists information for each individual swap area and summarizes the total swap space for the system. The important value to monitor is total available space. If the amount of available space is constantly around—or worse, below—10%, more swap space is urgently needed. In this event, allocate additional swap space immediately, using the swapon command. Your system will normally send out a warning to the console and the messages file when the swap space falls below 10%. When you see this message, it is a signal to begin to monitor, and possibly increase, the swap space on the system. Once again, understanding what is "normal" swap usage on the system will assist you with discovering anomalous behavior.

### 10.7.5 netstat

The netstat(1) command is a multipurpose tool that provides a variety of information about the state of the network and network interfaces. From a performance monitoring standpoint, the netstat –m command is very useful. Specifying the "-m" switch causes netstat to display information about memory allocated to data structures associated with network operations. This information is useful when trying to determine where and how memory is configured on a Tru64 UNIX system. For example:

```
# netstat -m
    874 Kbytes for small data mbufs (peak usage 1148 Kbytes)
   1494 Kbytes for mbuf clusters (peak usage 7240 Kbytes)
   2039 Kbytes for sockets (peak usage 2274 Kbytes)
    538 Kbytes for protocol control blocks (peak usage 865
Kbytes)
    174 Kbytes for routing table (peak usage 185 Kbytes)
      6 Kbytes for interface addresses (peak usage 14 Kbytes)
    < 1 Kbyte for socket options (peak usage < 1 Kbyte)
    370 Kbytes for socket names (peak usage 509 Kbytes)
    < 1 Kbyte for ip multicast options (peak usage < 1 Kbyte)
    < 1 Kbyte for ip multicast addresses (peak usage < 1 Kbyte)
      3 Kbytes for interface multicast addresses (peak usage 4
Kbytes)
      0 requests for mbufs denied
      0 calls to protocol drain routines
5497 Kbytes allocated to network
```

```
Network threads:   3 netisrthreads configured (peak active   3)
```

This gives you an idea of one way to use netstat(8). Chapter 7 contains more information about Tru64 UNIX networking in general.

### 10.7.6 Collect

It has been stressed before that it is important to understand what is considered "normal" activity on the system, so that "abnormal" behavior can be compared with it. In these types of cases, a "baseline" of previous performance levels is invaluable in putting this new performance problem in perspective. The collect utility, if configured to run automatically, is a performance monitoring tool that collects system performance information. This information forms the baseline of normal activity.

Furthermore, there is a graphical user interface (GUI), called collgui, that you can run against the collection of data to get a quick picture of historical system performance. The collect utility itself is available on patched V4.x systems and is standard on V5.0A systems and later. The collgui tool is in a separate kit and is officially not supported by Compaq; however, it is very useful in visually tracking performance trends. The collgui kit can be found at:

```
ftp://ftp.digital.com/pub/DEC/collect
```

To turn on the "autorun" feature of collect so that it survives reboots and keeps a historical record of the system's performance, execute this command as root:

```
# rcmgr set COLLECT_AUTORUN 1
```

You might be concerned that this tool itself will impact the system's performance. Since collect is a very lightweight tool and tunable as far as its collecting interval and the specific statistics that it monitors, it typically takes less than 1% of the system CPU. It can also be configured to suspend and resume operation based on the amount of free disk space, so you do not have to be overly concerned about storage space for the compressed data files.

**Example:**

The collect utility is not just a tool that produces historical data. You can also use collect on the live system with a command such as the one shown below. This command will run with an interval of two seconds and will only report on the selected subsystem "disk".

```
# collect -i 2 -s d
Initializing (2.0 seconds) ... done.

#### RECORD    1 (990531569:0) (Tue May 22 06:39:29 2001) ####

# DISK Statistics
#DSK      NAME  B/T/L    R/S RKB/S  W/S WKB/S   AVS    AVW  ACTQ
WTQ  %BSY
   0      dsk0  0/0/0      0     0    0     0  0.00   0.00  0.00
0.00  0.00
   1    cdrom0  1/0/0      0     0    0     0  0.00   0.00  0.00
0.00  0.00
   2      dsk1  5/1/0      0     0    0     0  0.00   0.00  0.00
0.00  0.00
   3      dsk2  5/2/0      0     0    0     0  0.00   0.00  0.00
0.00  0.00
   4      dsk3  5/3/0      0     0    0     0  0.00   0.00  0.00
0.00  0.00
   5      dsk4  5/4/0      0     0    0     0  0.00   0.00  0.00
0.00  0.00
   6      dsk5  5/5/0      0     0    0     0  0.00   0.00  0.00
0.00  0.00

#### RECORD    2 (990531571:0) (Tue May 22 06:39:31 2001) ####

# DISK Statistics
#DSK      NAME  B/T/L    R/S RKB/S  W/S WKB/S   AVS    AVW  ACTQ
WTQ  %BSY
   0      dsk0  0/0/0      0     0    0     0  0.00   0.00  0.00
0.00  0.00
   1    cdrom0  1/0/0      0     0    0     0  0.00   0.00  0.00
0.00  0.00
   2      dsk1  5/1/0      0     0    0     0  0.00   0.00  0.00
0.00  0.00
   3      dsk2  5/2/0      0     0    0     0  0.00   0.00  0.00
0.00  0.00
   4      dsk3  5/3/0      0     0    0     0  0.00   0.00  0.00
0.00  0.00
   5      dsk4  5/4/0      0     0    0     0  0.00   0.00  0.00
0.00  0.00
   6      dsk5  5/5/0      0     0    0     0  0.00   0.00  0.00
0.00  0.00
Ouch!
```

## 10.8 Summary

We have barely scratched the surface of monitoring and managing performance on a Tru64 UNIX system. However, it is our hope that we have impressed upon you the importance of being familiar with a system and understanding what is "normal" before attempting to make adjustments. Performance problems are usually resource deficiencies, and the first step is identifying which resource is constrained. Once the resource limitation is isolated, the system administrator's next step is to adjust either the workload or the resource, if possible, or collect justification for increasing the resource, such as purchasing more hardware.

# 11

# *Backups*

## 11.1 System Backups

System backups are often a neglected or completely overlooked function on all too many UNIX systems. The reasons for this are many and varied. Many novice system administrators are simply unfamiliar with the variety of backup utilities available, while more experienced administrators may consider backups to be "grunt" work. In other cases, backups are not a priority with management or users . . . until, of course, the inevitable occurs and data or files are lost. Statistics have shown that most companies that are unable to recover quickly from a data loss often never recover. The key to preventing this situation is developing and implementing a backup strategy. Given the information presented in this chapter one should be able to easily develop one's own backup strategy. Following that, the various backup tools and utilities provided on Tru64 UNIX systems will be discussed. The focus will be on those utilities that are part of the base Tru64 UNIX product, but several alternative backup solutions will be briefly mentioned.

## 11.2 Backup Strategy

Backups on a Tru64 UNIX system must be more than an occasional file system dump to a tape. Developing an effective backup strategy is an important responsibility for a Tru64 UNIX system administrator. Such a backup plan must take into account the type of data to be backed up, how frequently the data should be saved, or more importantly, how much data can afford to be lost, the amount of time available for the backup operation itself, and the tools available. Finally, backing up the system is only half of a complete backup strategy. Being able to restore from the system backups, whether the entire system or just a file or two, is equally important. A complete backup strategy must backup the entire system. This may not mean, of course, copying every file to tape every night. It may mean backing up key file systems nightly, or even more frequently if necessary, while only backing up some of the more static system areas, such as the root and /usr file systems, on a weekly basis. The key is having an understanding of your system's data and use.

An effective backup strategy should address at least the following issues:

- What will be backed up?
- When will the backups occur?
- How will the backups be done?
- Selection of backup device and media
- Backup and restore documentation
- Restore dress rehearsal

Additionally, planning for the following items will make a good backup strategy a great one:

- Offsite storage
- Disaster recovery plan

### 11.2.1 What Will Be Backed Up?

Determining what to back up is the first step in developing a backup strategy. Of course the answer is "everything," right? Given unlimited resources and time, backing up everything would be ideal. However, the requirement for systems to be available around the clock, and the ever-increasing amount of disk space on today's modern UNIX systems, probably precludes backing up every file each night. Of course, if time and resources permit, doing a daily complete backup is certainly an option. If this is the case, by all means do so and avoid the added complexity of managing incremental backups. If this is not a feasible option, however, the system administrator must decide the frequency with which to copy the system's data to the backup media. The answer to this question requires some thought the nature of the system users' data, the amount of data the users can afford to lose, and the restore strategy.

The two categories of data on a Tru64 UNIX system are system data, which is primarily located in the root, /usr, and /var file systems, and user data, which can be anywhere, including in the previously listed system file systems. Obviously, to be able to restore the entire system, it is necessary to have a backup copy of the entire system. This usually means copying all files to a backup media such as tape. However, if resources such as time or tape capacity are limited, an option to consider is to identify parts of the system that exist on the vendor's distribution media. This can include third-party applications, static sections of the operating system such as the man pages, or even the entire base operating system itself. In the event of a system problem requiring a full system restoration, it would be necessary to reload these subsystems from the manufacturer's media. Obviously, this is a drastic measure requiring careful consideration. Perhaps a better strategy would be to make separate backups of these static subsystems outside of the normal backup schedule and archive these backups. This certainly is a more sound strategy for the base operating system as it avoids having to reload the base system from scratch.

### 11.2.2 When Will the Backups Occur?

There are three factors to consider when deciding the scheduling of system backups: how frequently to run the backups, what time of the day to start the backups, and will the system be in single- or multiuser mode during the backup window. Each of these questions must be answered before an appropriate backup strategy can be defined. Also, all three of these questions are usually best answered by the end users themselves. The actual owners of the data should have an idea of how often to run backups and at what time during the day they would cause the least impact.

How often to run regularly scheduled backups is directly related to how dynamic the user's data is. If the data to be backed up is fairly static (unchanging over time), it may make sense to back up only once a week. However, if a system is actively updated around the clock, perhaps a single nightly backup is insufficient and several backups a day are necessary. The basic question to pose is "What is the minimum amount of data that can be lost?" If the answer to this question were 24 hours worth of updates, then a single daily backup would suffice. If, however, no more than four hours of updates can be lost, for example, then the backup strategy must take into account this requirement and ensure that changes are safeguarded. This may seem like a drastic example, but as systems become more mission critical, the requirement for no data loss whatsoever is becoming normal.

If, or more likely when, you are faced with such a requirement of no data loss, your backup strategy must be more than simply copying files off to tape. Modern database systems, such as Oracle, provide a facility where database transactions are logged, thus providing the ability to restore the database to any point in time. Normal tape backups still must be done, of course, but the database itself effectively continues to back itself up between tape backups.

The database facility does not protect your data from accidental or intentional deletions, of course, and this is the reason that regularly scheduled backups are still vital. In the event a critical table is dropped in error, the database will happily log the table as dropped. The tape backups from the previous evening will be required to restore data lost in this manner.

Another type of system backup is to use clusters, thereby having completely redundant systems. Compaq's TruCluster product is such a configuration. TruCluster supports a redundant environment that prevents system or component failures from taking an application or service down. Similarly, using either mirroring or RAID can protect your data from individual disk failures. Just like databases, though, neither TruCluster nor disk mirroring will protect your data from human error, such as the accidental deletion or modification of an important file. This point cannot be stressed enough: The use of redundant hardware, whether duplicating entire systems using TruCluster, or redundant disks/controllers and mirroring, or RAID, does not preclude regularly scheduled backups. Do not rely on such system configurations as a backup method. When a user mistypes a command and deletes an important file, the fact that the file system is mirrored does not in any way prevent that file from being deleted. Clusters and disk mirroring are primarily used to increase system availability, and as such, are important tools.

The second aspect of when a backup will occur is deciding what time of the day the backup process itself should be executed. The answer to this question may at first glance be easy: the middle of the night; and, depending on your environment, it's likely this may be the case. However, there are situations in which the middle of the night may be the worst time to do backups. If your organization is global and international users use a system, perhaps the best time would be early morning, U.S. time; 4:00 A.M., for instance. Another possibility is that the system's busiest time may be the middle of the night, and a backup starting at 1:00 A.M. would further load the system. One such system supported interactive users from 7:00 A.M. to 4:00 P.M. and processed nightly downloads from 8:00 P.M. to 7:00 A.M., leaving only four hours between 4:00 P.M. and 8:00 P.M. in which to do backups. Therefore, the backup process was started each day at 4:00 P.M. in the afternoon. This example points out the necessity of knowing a particular system's workload when scheduling system backups.

Finally, the question of whether the backup will be done while the system is running in multiuser mode or single-user mode must be considered. Given the opportunity, having the system in single-user mode would ensure the most reliable or consistent backups, since no users will be actively using the system and all files will be closed. However, it is unlikely that many systems can afford to be unavailable to users to do regular off-line backups. Additionally, the risk of inconsistency in online, or hot backups, is fairly low. If AdvFS or LSM are being used, it may also be possible to perform online and consistent backups with very little or no downtime at all. The AdvFS clone fileset and the LSM snapshot are examples of facilities available with the operating system to make online backups not only possible, but easy. One recommendation is to do offline backups only when it makes sense and the system is unavailable to users anyway, for instance, after an initial system install or major upgrade, and to do online backups the rest of the time to minimize system downtime.

The primary exception to this may involve systems that run database systems such as Oracle and Informix, since the database files themselves are typically large and are not static while the database engine itself is running and there are no interactive users. For this reason, the database vendors provide methods and utilities for either doing hot backups directly or check-pointing the database to allow traditional backup tools to safely back up the data files. In these cases, the additional requirements of such applications must be taken into consideration when planning a backup strategy. Perhaps it may be that in order to accomplish backups on a system running a large database, it may be necessary to use both the database vendor's backup tool and a traditional UNIX backup utility. In such a situation, it will be necessary for the system administrator to work closely with the database administrator (DBA) to coordinate system backups.

### 11.2.3 How Will the Backups Be Done?

The method of actually copying system files to backup media can be thought of as the meat of the backup process. Actually, the process of copying data off to tape is fairly straightforward. There are several utilities provided with the Tru64 UNIX operating system that provide sufficient functionality for most systems. These tools are all command line programs that are each suited for a different type of backup and generate backups that are fairly portable, thus allowing them to be read by equivalent tools on other vendors' UNIX implementations. The four utilities are:

- tar
- vdump/vrestore
- dd
- cpio

In addition, Compaq has bundled a single-user version of Legato's Networker backup program with Tru64 UNIX. This program, renamed Networker Save and Restore (NSR) by Compaq, provides both a command line and a graphical user interface to system backups. The bundled version of NSR supports backups of a single system to a local tape drive and may not be suited for larger site requirements. Compaq also offers an upgrade to this basic product that allows backing up of multiple clients across a network and supports multiple, complex tapes devices, including jukeboxes and changers. NSR is a richer backup tool than any of the four native Tru64 UNIX backup utilities, supporting multiple backup sets and schedules, e-mail notification of backup success and failure, indexing of backed up files allowing quick restoration, and flexible user interfaces for both backup and restore.

#### 11.2.3.1 tar(1)

The tar utility is a simple tool that can be used to save multiple files and directories quickly and easily. The tar(1) tool, which stands for Tape ARchiver, can write either directly to tape, floppy disk, or other magnetic media, or can create a single archive file on disk. A tar archive file, sometimes referred to as a "tar ball," is usually identified by a filename with a .tar suffix. The tar utility has become a de facto standard on the Internet for packaging and distribution of files. Understanding the use of tar, both for creating and unpacking archives, is a must-have skill for a UNIX system administrator.

The syntax of the Tru64 UNIX tar utility may at first glance appear complex, but there are actually only five main command line switches that specify tar's function (see Table 11.1).

The remaining switches are modifiers that define how tar behaves. See Table 11.2 for a list of the most common modifiers.

Typically, only a handful of switches are used with tar in normal operation. For instance, to copy a directory to the default tape device, the following minimal tar command will do the job:

```
# tar -c /data
```

Since a specific tape drive or archive file is not specified (via the "-f" switch), this command copies the contents of the /data directory to /dev/tape/tape0_d0. If /dev/tape/tape0_d0 does not correspond to a tape drive on the system, tar will dutifully create a archive file named tape0_d0 in the /dev/tape directory. Since the /dev directory is a subdirectory of the root

**Table 11.1** *tar(1) Required Arguments*

| Argument | Meaning |
|---|---|
| c | Create a new archive; if the destination is a tape, the archive is written to the beginning of the tape instead of after the last file. Directories are recursively copied to the archive. |
| t | List the contents of the specified archive. |
| x | Extract the named files from the archive. If no file argument is given, the entire archive is extracted. Directories are recursively extracted. |
| r | Write the named files to the tape after the last file. |
| u | Add the named files to the tape archive if the files are not already in the archive or if the files have been modified since they were last copied to the tape. |

Note: These five flags are all mutually exclusive. Only one of these flags may be specified at a time.

**Table 11.2** *Common tar(1) Argument Modifiers*

| Argument | Meaning |
|---|---|
| v | Verbose mode. Normally tar is silent as it performs its work. If the v switch is specified with the t argument, additional information about each file in an archive is displayed. |
| f | The next argument is the name of the archive instead of the default value of /dev/tape/tapen. If the name of the file is a - (dash), tar writes to standard output or reads from standard input, whichever is appropriate. |
| b | The next argument is the blocking factor for tape records. The default is 20 (larger values can be specified at the risk of creating a tape archive that some systems' tape drives might not be able to restore). Use this flag only with raw magnetic tape archives. This flag is appropriate only when writing archives to tape, as the block size is determined automatically when reading tapes. |
| p | This switch tells tar to restores files to their original modes, ignoring the present umask. Set-user-ID and sticky information will also be restored if the user is root. |
| P | The next argument specifies the prefix that is to be stripped off of the file names copied to or extracted from archives. |
| s | This switch tells tar to strip off any leading slashes from pathnames during extraction. This is useful when restoring an archive that was created on a system with a different file system structure, or when the archive was created with absolute pathnames. |

*Note:* These flags are modifiers to the required flag (Table 11.1). This is not an exhaustive list of modifiers. See the man page for tar(1) for the entire set of modifiers.

file system, it is easy to fill up the root file system with an error of this type. For this reason, it is recommended to always use the "-f" switch and explicitly specify the archive destination. For example:

```
# tar -c -f /dev/tape/tape0_d0 /data
```

One confusing aspect of the tar command is whether or not to specify a hyphen (-) at the beginning of a flag set. In some UNIX vendors' implementations of tar, including very old versions of Tru64 UNIX, the minus sign is optional. Modern versions of Tru64 UNIX, on the other hand, do not allow this option. If a hyphen is specified in front of a flag that requires an argument, the argument must follow immediately after the flag. If no hyphen is specified in front of a set of flags, the arguments, if any, must follow the entire flag set in the order of the specifying flags. For example, the following two tar commands are equivalent:

```
# tar -c -f /dev/tape/tape0_d0 -b 20 /data
# tar cfb /dev/tape/tape0_d0 20 /data
```

Both these commands create an archive on /dev/tape/tape0_d0 with a blocking factor of 20, which contains the contents of the /data directory.

The opposite of creating archives is, of course, extracting files from a tar archive. An example of this operation is:

```
# tar xf /dev/tape/tape0_d0
```

This will extract the entire contents of the archive residing on a tape. Similarly, an archive can be a single tar(1) formatted file. For example:

```
# tar xf /tmp/data.tar
```

Where files extracted from an archive are restored is determined by the manner in which the files were copied to the archive in the first place. If, when creating an archive, the files are specified with an absolute pathname, for example:

```
# tar cf /dev/tape/tape0_d0 /etc
```

the files will be restored to their original location when the archive is extracted—in this case, the /etc directory. However, if a relative pathname is specified when creating an archive:

```
# cd /etc
# tar cf /dev/tape/tape0_d0 .
```

In this case, the files will be restored relative to the current directory from which the archive is extracted. In this example, extracting this archive from the root directory will also restore the files back into the /etc directory. However, if the archive is extracted from, say, the /tmp directory, the files will be restored into /tmp/etc, possibly a new directory.

If an archive has been created containing files with absolute pathnames, such as those beginning with a slash (/), it may be inappropriate to extract these files as they could overwrite existing files. In this situation, simply add the "-s" switch to the tar command line to strip the leading slash from the files in the archive and restore the files relative to a location other than the root file system. For example:

```
# tar tf /dev/tape/tape0_d0
/etc/passwd
/etc/passwd.dir
/etc/passwd.pag
# cd /tmp
# tar xfs /dev/tape/tape0_d0
# ls /tmp/etc
passwd     passwd.dir     passwd.pag
```

Another common tar(1) argument is "-t" which stands for "Table of Contents." The "-t" flag displays the contents of a tar archive. Specified without the "-v" modifier, only the file names are listed. The "-v" modifier tells tar to list the file names in a format similar to that produced by an "ls -l" command. For example:

```
# tar tf /dev/tape/tape0_d0
/etc/passwd
/etc/passwd.dir
/etc/passwd.pag
# tar tvf /dev/tape/tape0_d0
-rw-r—r—   0/0   1074 Jul 13 13:57:29 2001 /etc/passwd
-rw-r—r—   0/0   4096 Jul 11 10:46:41 2001 /etc/passwd.dir
-rw-r—r—   0/0   4096 Jul 13 13:57:29 2001 /etc/passwd.pag
```

One handy use of the tar command is to copy directory hierarchies between disks while maintaining file permissions and ownerships. It would be a simple matter to create an archive of a directory hierarchy, then extract that archive to another place on the system. Since tar provides the ability to write to standard output and to read from standard input, the following command pipeline copies a directory structure without having to create an intermediate archive:

```
# cd fromdir; tar cf - . | (cd todir; tar xfBp -)
```

By specifying a minus sign (-) as the argument to the "-f" switch, the tar on the left side of the pipe (|) writes the archive to standard output, which is then read by the tar(1) command on the right side of the pipe, which reads standard input. For example, to copy the contents of the /usr/data hierarchy to the /home/data subdirectory, use the following command:

```
# cd /usr/data; tar cf - . | (cd /home/data; tar xfBp -)
```

Remember that this operation is only a copy; the original hierarchy is not removed. If a move-type operation is desired, simply follow this pipeline with an "rm –r /usr/data" command.

The tar utility is most useful for ad hoc backups and for packaging files for transport. The tar format is considered to be an industry standard; thus archives are fairly portable among the different vendor implementations of UNIX. In addition, there are tar-like utilities for non-UNIX systems, such as Windows 2000. However, since the tar utility lacks robust error checking and correction and the ability to do incremental backups, it is not an ideal choice for regular system backups. It is handy, though, for quickly backing up a file or directory or two, either to magnetic media, such as tape or floppy, or to a tar archive on disk.

#### 11.2.3.2 vdump/vrestore

The vdump(8) utility (and corresponding vrestore(8) utility) is the most flexible and robust backup utility in the base Tru64 UNIX operating system. The vdump/vrestore utility pair support backing up and restoring AdvFS filesets, UFS file systems, NFS file systems, and MFS or memory file systems. The similar dump/restore utility pair support only backing up and restoring UFS file systems. For this reason, using vdump/vrestore is recommended for all dump/restore operations. Additionally, there is a third derivative of this command pair: rdump/rrestore, for Remote dump and Remote restore. The rdump/rrestore are for backing up UFS file systems to and restoring from remote backup devices, such as a tape drive on another system. Beginning in version 5.0, the rvdump/rvrestore utilities were introduced for remote backup and restores. Unfortunately, in versions prior to 5.0, vdump/vrestore did not directly support this remote facility. In Section 11.2.3.4, "Incremental vdumps," we will detail a method of accomplishing remote vdump/vrestore for Tru64 version prior to 5.0. In this section, references to vdump and vrestore will apply to vdump/vrestore, dump/restore, and rdump/rrestore, except where noted. The vdump and vrestore utilities are designed to back up and restore entire filesets (or UFS file systems, in the case of dump/restore). However, the vdump utility provides the ability to backup individual directories, though not individual files, and the vrestore utility allows recovery of individual directories or files. Incremental backups are supported, which makes rdump an acceptable method of doing regular system backups.

#### 11.2.3.3 vdump(8)

Since the vdump utility only does backups, as opposed to the tar command that is used for both backup and restore operations, its syntax is fairly straightforward. The command-line switches of the vdump command are listed in Table 11.3.

**Table 11.3** *vdump(8) Arguments*

| Argument | Meaning |
|---|---|
| -0-9 | Specifies the dump level. A level 0 dump backs up the entire fileset to the backup device. The default dump level is 9. |
| -C | Causes vdump to compress the data as it is backed up. This minimizes the size of the resulting dump file at the expense of the time needed to do the compression. |
| -D | Dumps only the specified subdirectory of a fileset to the backup device. When the flag is used, the dump level specification is ignored, and a level-0 backup is run regardless of the dump level that is specified. Without the -D flag, the vdump command backs up the entire fileset that contains the subdirectory. Only a single subdirectory may be backed up. |
| -F #_of_buffers | Specifies the number of in-memory buffers to use. The valid range is 1 through 64 buffers; the default is 8 buffers. Specifying more buffers may increase the performance of the vdump. |
| -N | Disables the rewinding of the tape and placing the tape offline after completing the vdump session. By default, when the dump command finishes backing up a file system, it rewinds the tape and takes it offline. The -N flag is the default when the -f parameter is a no-rewind tape device; e.g., /dev/nrmt*. |
| -V | Displays the version of vdump. |
| -b #_of_blocks | Specifies the number of blocks (1024-bytes each) for writes. The valid range is 1 to 64 blocks; the default is 60 blocks. |

**Table 11.3** *(continued)*

| Argument | Meaning |
|---|---|
| -f device | The next argument is the destination of the saveset, which can be a device, file, or a - (dash). If the name of the file is - , vdump writes the saveset to standard output. |
| -h | Displays usage instructions for vdump. |
| -q | Quiet mode. Only error messages are displayed. |
| -u | Updates the /etc/vdumpdates file with a time-stamp entry from the beginning of the backup. |
| -v | Verbose mode. Displays the names of files as they are backed up. |
| -w | Displays the filesets that have not been backed up within one week. |

To back up a single file system, the following vdump command is sufficient:

```
# vdump -0 -f /dev/tape/tape0_d0
path    : /
dev/fset : root_domain#root
type    : advfs
advfs id : 0x342ab78e.000c3270.1
vdump: Dumping directories
vdump: Dumping 63516207 bytes, 131 directories, 1151 files
vdump: Dumping regular files
vdump: Status at Fri Jul 25 21:32:05 2001
vdump: Dumped 63516295 of 63516207 bytes; 100.0% completed
vdump: Dumped 131 of 131 directories; 100.0% completed
vdump: Dumped 1151 of 1151 files; 100.0% completed
vdump: Dump completed at Fri Jul 25 21:32:05 2001
#
```

In this example, vdump performs a level-0 dump, or all files/directories, of the root file system to the primary tape drive. Since the "-q" switch was not specified on the command line, vdump prints out informational messages as the vdump progresses.

A recommended switch to use with vdump is "-u," which updates the /etc/vdumpdates file. The /etc/vdumpdates file is a text file that vdump uses to keep track of when file systems were last backed up and at which dump level. If incremental backups are instituted with vdump, it is imperative that the "-u" switch be used. An example /etc/vdumpdates file includes entries like the following, defining the fileset name, dump level, and date:

```
usr_domain#home 0 Mon Jul 21 02:00:22 2001
/dev/disk/dsk1c 0 Thu Jul 24 02:00:13 2001
usr_domain#home 5 Thu Jul 24 06:30:07 2001

usr_domain#home 9 Fri Jul 25 06:45:51 2001
```

In this example, usr_domain#home represents an AdvFS fileset mounted on /home, and /dev/disk/dsk1c represents a UNIX file system mounted elsewhere. If you perform a level-8 backup of the usr_domain#home, for example,

```
# vdump -8 -u -f /dev/tape0_d0 /home
```

using this /etc/vdumpdates file, the following occurs:

- The vdump command ignores the /dev/disk/dsk1c entry, since it does not match the specified fileset, usr_domain#home.
- The vdump command ignores the level-9 entry, since this entry is equal to or higher than the level-8 backup you requested. This leaves only the level-0 and level-5 entries.
- Of the two remaining entries, the vdump command chooses the entry with the most recent dump date, which is the level-5 entry.
- The vdump command backs up all files that were created or modified after the dump date of the level-5 entry.

When a vdump operation is started, if a file system entry with that specific dump level does not already exist in the /etc/vdumpdates file, the vdump command appends a new record to the file for the dump level; otherwise, the vdump command overwrites the existing record for that dump level, changing the backup date to reflect the most current backup session. This occurs after all files in the named file system are successfully backed up.

#### 11.2.3.4 Incremental vdumps

Incremental backups are a way of reducing the amount of time and backup media a backup consumes by backing up only the files that have changed since the last backup. By consulting the /etc/vdumpdates file, the vdump utility is able to manage incremental backups and determine which files have changed. The main drawback to incremental backup strategies is that the system administrator must manage the multiple tapes between level-0 dumps in order to completely restore a system. Consider the following 28-day incremental backup schedule:

```
SM T W T F S
05 4 7 6 9 8
05 4 7 6 9 8
05 4 7 6 9 8
05 4 7 6 9 8
```

A full (level-0) dump is performed once a week, with incrementals the remaining days of the week. The number of dump files to perform a full restore can vary from 1 to 4, depending when during the week a restore becomes necessary. Following this schedule would mean a minimum of 7 tapes in the backup rotation; a better idea would be to have the full 28 tapes in a rotation, especially since tapes are relatively inexpensive compared to lost data. In any case, if this type of schedule is adopted, it is important to safeguard all tapes between level-0 dumps to complete a full restore. For instance, if the system required a full recovery on a Wednesday morning before that day's backup, it would be necessary to first apply the level-0 dump from Sunday, then apply the level-5 dump from Monday, followed by the level-4 dump from Tuesday, to restore the system to the state it was immediately after Tuesday's dump. In this example, any changes after the Tuesday backup would be lost.

This 28-day incremental vdump(8) schedule can be run by inserting the following entries in root's crontab. This example only backs up the /home file system:

```
0 2 * * 0 /sbin/vdump -0 -u -f /dev/tape/tape0_d0 /home
0 2 * * 1 /sbin/vdump -5 -u -f /dev/ tape/tape0_d0 /home
0 2 * * 2 /sbin/vdump -4 -u -f /dev/ tape/tape0_d0 /home
0 2 * * 3 /sbin/vdump -7 -u -f /dev/ tape/tape0_d0 /home
0 2 * * 4 /sbin/vdump -6 -u -f /dev/ tape/tape0_d0 /home
0 2 * * 5 /sbin/vdump -9 -u -f /dev/ tape/tape0_d0 /home
0 2 * * 6 /sbin/vdump -8 -u -f /dev/ tape/tape0_d0 /home
```

Obviously, if a system has many file systems, this method of individual crontab entries would be very unmanageable. A better solution is a single script that is run each night, which backs up all desired file systems at the appropriate dump level that is determined by the current day of the week.

One capability the vdump utility does not directly provide is the ability to send the backup across the network to a tape drive on a remote system. The rdump utility does support this functionality by requiring the specification of a remote system name and a tape device on that system via the "-f" command line parameter. The format of the rdump's "-f" option is "machine:device" as in the following example:

```
# rdump -0 -u -f saturn:/dev/tape/tape0_d0 /
```

This command does a level-0 dump of the root file system to the /dev/tape/tape0_d0 tape drive on the remote system saturn. This command also updates the /etc/dumpdates, which is functionally identical to the /etc/vdumpdates file for the vdump command. Additionally, the remote system's /.rhosts file must contain the name of the local, or client, machine. This requirement is necessary to provide a trusted host relationship between the two systems (remote and local).

The main drawback to the rdump command is rdump's inability to back up AdvFS filesets. This remote backup functionality is achievable using rvdump or the vdump command by the use of a workaround. The workaround is to run the vdump command on the local system with the output of the vdump sent to standard output by specifying a hyphen (-) to the "-f" parameter. The standard output is then piped to a remote shell on the remote system running a dd(1) command to its local tape drive. (See Section 11.2.3.6. for information on the dd command.) The following example backs up the root file system to the /dev/tape/tape0_d0 tape drive on the remote system saturn:

```
# vdump -0 -u -b 64 -f - / | rsh saturn dd
of=/dev/tape/tape0_d0 bs=64k
```

This example command is equivalent to the previous rdump. Note that the block size must be specified to both the rdump command (-b 64) and the dd command (bs = 64k). This workaround has the same requirement as the remote system's /.rhosts file, which must contain the name of the local, or client, machine. The rvrestore utility can be used to perform a remote restoration from a backup created using vdump or rvdump. See the vrestore section for information on the reverse of this workaround—restoring from a remote system's tape drive with the vrestore command.

#### 11.2.3.5 vrestore(8)

The vrestore(8) utility restores files from archives written by the vdump or rvdump utilities. Similarly to vdump, the vrestore/rvrestore utilities are like its restore/rrestore counterparts. The vrestore command line parameters are listed in Table 11.4.

Restoring a single file or an entire system is easily accomplished with the vrestore command. For example, to restore the password file from a vdump(8) of the root file system, use the following vrestore command:

**Table 11.4** *vrestore(8) Arguments*

| Argument | Meaning |
|---|---|
| -D | Restores the file(s) to the directory specified by this parameter. By default, files are restored to the directory where the vrestore command was invoked. |
| -V | Displays the version of vrestore. |
| -f device | The next argument is the destination of the saveset, which can be a device, file, or a - (dash). If the name of the file is - , vrestore reads the saveset from standard input. |
| -h | Displays usage instructions for vrestore. |
| -i | Invokes vrestore in interactive mode. After reading directory information from the archive, a shell-like interface is displayed that allows files to be selected interactively. See Table 11.5 for a listing of the interactive vrestore commands. |
| -l | Displays the vdump archive structure. |
| -m | Do not preserve the ownership or permissions of restored files. |
| -o opt | Specifies the action to take when a file being restored already exists. Note that only the file name is checked for collision. The following options are recognized: |
| yes | Overwrite existing files without asking. The default option is yes. |
| no | Do not overwrite existing files. Conflicting files are not restored. |
| ask | Query where to overwrite an existing file. |
| -q | Quiet mode. Only error messages are displayed. |
| -t | Displays the names and sizes of all files contained in the vdump archive. |
| -v | Verbose mode. Displays the names of files as they are restored. |
| -x | Extract files from a vdump archive. If the last command line option is a file specification vrestore extracts only the file(s) that match, or no file list is pecified, all files in the archive are restored. |

```
# vrestore -x -f /dev/tape/tape0_d0 ./etc/passwd
```

Note that the backed-up files in a vdump are stored using a relative pathname. In a vrestore, this means that by default, the files are restored in the directory where the vrestore command was invoked. In this example, if the vrestore was run from the root file system, the password file would have been restored to /etc/passwd, overwriting any existing /etc/passwd file. The final parameter in this command specifies the file(s) to be restored. This parameter can be a single file or a directory, which restores the directory and its contents, including any subdirectories. Multiple files and/or directories separated by spaces can be specified to be restored. This parameter, however, cannot be a wildcard. For instance, the following vrestore commands are all legal:

```
# vrestore -x -f /dev/tape/tape0_d0 ./etc
# vrestore -x -f /dev/tape/tape0_d0 ./.profile ./.rhosts
# vrestore -x -f /dev/tape/tape0_d0 ./etc/passwd ./etc/group
./sbin
```

This vrestore example, on the other hand, is not legal:

```
# vrestore -x -f /dev/tape/tape0_d0 ./etc/pass*
```

A useful vrestore flag is "-t", or Table of Contents. This flag displays the date the save-set was created, the filenames of the save-set, and the size in bytes. For example:

```
# vrestore -t -f /dev/tape/tape0_d0 | head
vrestore: Date of the vdump save-set: Wed Oct 1 01:00:05 2000
./etc/
./etc/sia/
./etc/sia/matrix.conf @-> /etc/sia/bsd_matrix.conf
./etc/sia/OSFC2_matrix.conf, 2387
./etc/sia/bsd_matrix.conf, 2191
./etc/disktab, 30278
./etc/group, 480
./etc/passwd, 1074
./etc/profile, 402
./etc/rc.config, 4835
```

The vrestore command supports an interactive mode that allows quick selection and recovery of files and directories, especially when the files to be recovered are spread around a directory hierarchy. This interactive mode is specified by the "-i" command line switch. Once the interactive mode is entered, the save-set is accessed from a shell-like interface that allows selection of files to be restored. This interface has a set of interactive commands for navigating within the save-set directory structure and selecting and extracting files. See Table 11.5 for a list of these commands.

**Table 11.5** *vrestore(8) interactive mode commands*

| | |
|---|---|
| add arg | Adds the files in the saveset specified by arg to the list of files to be restored from the device. Files on the list of files to be restored are prepended with the * (asterisk) character when they are listed with the ls interactive command. |
| cd [arg] | Changes the current saveset directory to the directory specified with the arg parameter. |
| delete arg | Deletes all files and their subdirectories specified by the arg parameter from the list of files to be restored from the device. An expedient way to select wanted files from any directory whose files are stored on the device is to add the directory to the list of files to be restored and then delete the ones that are not wanted. |
| extract or restore | Restores all files added to the list of files to be restored to the previously specified destination. |
| help or ? | Displays help information for the interactive commands. |
| ls [arg] | Lists files in the current saveset directory or the directory specified with the arg parameter. Directory entries are appended with a / (slash) character. Entries that have been marked to be restored are prepended with an * (asterisk) character. |
| pwd | Prints the pathname of the current saveset directory to the standard output device. |
| quit or exit | Exits immediately, even when the files on the list of files to restored have not been read. |
| verbose | Toggles the -v modifier (see the -v flag of the vrestore command). The name of each file restored from the device is written to the standard output device. |

The following is an example of an interactive vrestore session in a save-set of a root file system:

```
# vrestore -i -f /dev/tape/tape0_d0
vrestore: Date of the vdump save-set: Wed Oct 1 01:00:05 2000
(/) ls
.:
  #.mrg..DXsession        .cshrc        .login     .new...cshrc
   .new...login    .new..DXsession        .profile
.proto...cshrc
   .proto...login  .proto..DXsession        .rhosts         .tags

     bin          dev/          etc/         genvmunix
     ome/           lib          mdec/           mnt/
     opt/        osf_boot          proc/      real.profile
     sbin/          subsys/          sys           tcb/
     tmp/           usr/          var/         vmunix
```

```
(/) add .profile
(/) add .rhosts
(/) ls
.:
  #.mrg..DXsession        .cshrc        .login    .new...cshrc
   .new...login   .new..DXsession     *.profile
.proto...cshrc
   .proto...login  .proto..DXsession       *.rhosts         .tags

     bin         dev/         etc/       genvmunix
     home/          lib         mdec/         mnt/
     opt/       osf_boot          proc/     real.profile
     sbin/        subsys/           sys          tcb/
     tmp/        usr/         var/        vmunix
(/) cd /etc
(/etc/) ls
.:
       acucap          atm.conf           atmhosts
       auth/       autopush.conf          binlog.conf
     csh.login          disktab              dt/
        eca/          exports            fdmns/
       fstab          ftpusers          gettydefs
       group           hosts         hosts.equiv
      ifconfig        inetd.conf       inetd.conf.sav1
       inittab      latautopush.conf         lprsetup.dat
        magic           motd             namedb/
       networks            nls/           ntp.conf
      ntp.drift           passwd          passwd.dir
      passwd.pag           phones              ppp/
       profile          protocols          rc.config
        remote             rmt            routes
         rpc             sec/          securettys
       services        services.sav1          setup.conf
        shells             sia/             sm/
        sm.bak/          snmpd.conf           srconf/
        state         strsetup.conf           sudoers
       svc.conf          svid2_login          svid2_path
    svid2_profile          svid3_login          svid3_path
    svid3_profile           svid3_tz         sysconfigtab
 sysconfigtab.PreUPD       sysconfigtab.lite          syslog.conf
     termcap           ttysrch         ultrix_logi
     ultrix_path        ultrix_profile             uucp/
     uugettydefs          vdumpdates             visudo
         vol/             yp          zoneinfo/
(/etc/) add passwd
(/etc/) extract
#
```

This example adds /.profile, /.rhosts, and /etc/passwd to the list of files to be restored, then recovers those files from the save-set with the extract command.

Finally, since the vrestore command lacks the remote restore capability of the rrestore command, the workaround to accomplish a restore from a remote system's tape drive is presented. This workaround only supports noninteractive vrestores via the "-x" flag as remote interactive vrestores are not possible, since the shell-like interface that the interactive option of vrestore invokes will not work with an rsh. For instance, the following command restores the /etc/passwd file from a vdump save-set that resides on the remote system saturn's tape drive:

```
# rsh saturn dd if=/dev/tape/tape0_d0 bs=64k | vrestore -x -f -
./etc/passwd
```

This workaround has the same requirement as the remote vdump workaround; that is, that the remote system's /.rhosts file contain the name of the local, or client, machine.

#### 11.2.3.6 dd(1)

The dd(1) command is a specialized utility for copying data from one place to another. See the dd reference page for details of the command's options. The three most common options are if, of, and conv, which refer to Input File, Output File, and CONVersion, respectively. As part of a dd copy operation, dd can also perform certain conversions to the data. For instance, dd can be used to convert an ASCII file to EBCDIC, or all alphabetic characters in a file can be converted to uppercase:

```
# dd if=text.ascii of=text.ebcdic conv=ebcdic
# dd if=text.lower of=text.upper conv=ucase
```

As such, the dd command is not really a general-purpose backup utility. However, dd is a useful tool when applied in special situations. Since dd's input and output is specified to be a file, dd can read from and write to special device files just as handily as to normal operating system files. For example, suppose it became necessary to duplicate a disk drive—one possible motivation for doing this could be to clone a system for deployment. The dd command is perfect for this type of task. The following commands will copy the contents of disk dsk0 to disk dsk1:

```
# disklabel -z dsk1
# dd if=/dev/rdisk/dsk0c of=/dev/rdisk/dsk1c conv=noerror,sync
```

For this operation to succeed, the two disk drives should be identical in size and ideally should be the same model. The initial disklabel command removes any existing disk label from disk dsk1. This is necessary, as the dd command will not proceed if the target disk has a disk label. Note that both the input file (if) and the output file (of) are specified as the raw or character device. Finally, the two conversion options (noerror and sync) are specified to ensure that dd stays synchronized in the event that either disk has bad sectors. Upon completion of this dd command, the contents of disk dsk0 and dsk1 will be identical. This type of disk-to-disk copy operation can take a tremendous amount of time (hours or days) to complete, depending on the size of the disks and the type and number of I/O channels.

Another situation where the dd command is useful is as a method for copying a data stream off to tape. You have already seen the dd command used in the following workaround:

```
# vdump -0 -u -b 64 -f - / | rsh remotesystem dd
of=/dev/tape/tape0 bs=64k
```

The vdump command writes the save-set to standard output, which is piped to a dd process on a remote system via the rsh command. This dd command reads from the standard input (since an "if" parameter is not specified to dd) and writes the data directly to the raw tape drive. In this example, the dd command is simply a method used to redirect the output to the tape drive properly.

#### *11.2.3.7 cpio(1)*

The cpio(1) utility is a tool for copying files to and from cpio archives. The cpio utility, which stands for CoPy Input Output, can write archives either directly to tape or other magnetic media, or can create a single archive file on disk. As a general purpose backup tool, cpio is of limited use for two primary reasons: cpio does not support backing up special files, such as device files located in the /dev directory, and cpio cannot back up files with pathnames that exceed 128 bytes. However, some sites continue to use cpio despite its limitations; therefore, a system administrator may occasionally be called upon to restore a cpio archive. This most often occurs when a software package is delivered in a cpio archive, which is sometimes seen as a "least common denominator" format. The cpio utility is a "legacy" UNIX command compared to relative newcomer utilities such as vdump. In addition, cpio, along with tar, is a standard UNIX file format that can be read from any vendor's UNIX. For this reason, an understanding of cpio's somewhat arcane syntax can be quite useful in certain situations.

The cpio command is used both to create archives and to restore files from archives; not surprisingly, there are two main cpio command-line switches to accomplish these two functions:

- cpio –o This command reads filenames from standard input and copies these files to a specified archive (either tape or a operating system file).
- cpio –i This command reads a cpio archive from standard input and copies from it the specified files.

These descriptions identify one unique characteristic of cpio: cpio expects to get its input, whether this is a list of files to back up or an existing archive to restore, from standard input. For example, to back up all the files in the /home subdirectory to a tape drive with cpio, use the following command:

```
# find /home -print | cpio -o -O/dev/tape/tape0
```

The find(1) command is used to generate a list of all the files and directories under /home. This list is then piped to cpio, which copies the files specified in the list to the tape device specified by the –O flag.

The restoration of files from a cpio(1) archive is somewhat more straightforward:

```
# cpio -idm -I/dev/tape/tape0
```

This command restores the files previously saved onto /dev/tape/tape0 by cpio. The "d" flag specifies that any directories saved in the archive should be recreated by cpio if necessary, and the "m" flag tells cpio to maintain the last modification time when the files were archived.

Finally, it is often useful to be able to display the contents of a cpio archive. A variation of the "cpio –i" command displays the filenames contained in an archive. This command is:

```
# cpio -it -I/dev/tape/tape0
```

The cpio command is not quite obsolete, for it continues to be used by some people to generate "portable" archives that can be read by many different flavors of UNIX. Therefore, knowing how to list and extract the contents of a cpio archive continues to be a useful and necessary skill. This section gives just a small taste of this tool's capabilities. It is suggested that anyone looking for more information see the cpio reference page for the other flags that further modify cpio's functionality.

### 11.2.4 Selection of Backup Device and Media

This section endeavors to assist the Tru64 UNIX administrator with choosing the type of backup device and media that suit his or her environment best. At many sites, there simply is no choice given to the system administrator, and if that's the case, this section can be skipped. For others, it is important to understand the advantages and disadvantages of each in order to make an informed backup decision. In general, there are two ways to go with selecting a backup device: disk or tape. We discuss each option in the following two sections.

#### *11.2.4.1 Disk Backups*

Traditionally, choosing a backup device and media has meant choosing some sort of tape device, however more sites are choosing to perform on-line backups to disk. This sort of disk-to-disk backup is supported by many intelligent disk controllers and software-based mechanisms today and their primary advantage is they can be performed very quickly. This section is devoted to providing a framework for the administrator to either select or rule-out this option. There are many choices that could be made with disk backups so it is important to understand your requirements before you begin. The kinds of questions you need to answer are the following:

- What level of data inconsistency can be tolerated?
- Are you using file systems or raw?
- Are your file systems AdvFS or UFS?
- What hardware or software do you have available or can be purchased?
- Can you do your backups while the data are off-line or do you need data to be on-line all the time?
- Is speed more important than money?

So, what do we mean when we say the word "consistency?" Well, as with other things, this term may have different meanings depending on whom you talk to. We define three types of "consistency" we will be referring to throughout our discussion in this section and it is important for you to be aware of these when you are deciding which type of disk-to-disk backup is best for your site.

- Data consistency—This type of consistency involves the complete "snapshot" of a file system at a specific moment in time. Since UNIX file systems maintain some of their metadata and buffers in memory, it is necessary to flush all of this back out to storage before making the backup. This type of consistency maintains that the data and metadata are always completely in sync with one another for the entire time the backup progresses. The easiest way to do this would be to unmount the file system beforehand. However, this may not be desirable since the data and applications cannot be available while the file system in not mounted. This is the kind of backup you can get using on-line methods available such as AdvFS cloning.
- Metadata consistency—This type of consistency, also known as crash consistency, means the metadata for the file system can be recovered back to a state where the file system can be mounted and data can be accessed. This would be the same thing as if the system went down unexpectedly due to a system crash or power off while it was doing active work. With file systems in Tru64 UNIX, metadata consistency can be maintained so that the file system can be mounted again. If you are using UFS, the fsck(8) tool can be used for file system recovery. This has the advantage of simplicity, but it may also take a long period of time to recover. With AdvFS, on the other hand, recovery is much faster because of its transaction log-based nature. Be aware, however, that once the metadata is made consistent in either case, there is no assurance that the application files will also be data consistent. In addition, if file systems are not being used, then the metadata recovery is the responsibility of the application.
- Application consistency—This is type is similar to data consistent, but in this case the application must also force its buffers to flush and be consistent while making the backup. With application consistency, the guarantee is that the application will see the data from the backup exactly the same as the point at which the backup was taken. The application must have the ability to flush its own buffers and place itself into a standby mode for the time that the backup will be in-progress. If this feature is not available in the application you intend to use, shutting it down gracefully may be the only alternative. Either way, there is no mechanism built into Tru64 UNIX to insure this level of application consistency. If your application is smart enough to deal with this level of inconsistency, then you do not need to shut it down or place it into standby mode.

One site may have a different understanding and requirement for data consistency than another one. For a growing number of critical systems, a backup option is really only relevant if it allows the administrator to perform the backups in a completely consistent manner. On the other hand, another person might be able to get by with a metadata consistent backup. Which one you choose depends on whether your application can recover from data inconsistency in the same way that UFS or AdvFS deal with the system-level equivalent. We suspect that most people will want complete consistency, but will probably settle for metadata consistency if they cannot take their application off-line. Therefore, for our purposes, a completely consistent backup is one that maintains all three types of consistency discussed above. An inconsistent backup is one that fails an application consistency test and therefore is not usable because the application cannot continue once the data has been restored from it.

Another choice you must make when deciding upon the disk-to-disk option is what technology you wish to use and is available to you for making the data consistent prior to making the backup itself. One of the following is a necessary technology in Tru64 UNIX to make the disk-to-disk backup in at least a metadata consistent manner:

- LSM snapshot—This is a feature of the LSM subsystem and of course requires that LSM be in use before you can take advantage of it. The LSM snapshot makes another mirrored copy of the data on an LSM plex and then allows the mirrored copy to "snap off" and make its own logical volume. The new logical volume is an exact copy of the original volume at the time of the "snap off." This type of copying technology will create a metadata consistent backup if used while the file system is on-line, or data consistent if taken while the file system is off-line. Also, the LSM utilities that allow this operation are an added-cost option to the base Tru64 UNIX license.
- AdvFS clone fileset—This is a feature of the Advanced File System Advanced Utilities and will make at least a data consistent backup. A clone fileset of an existing fileset will be made at some moment in time. The advantage is of having a data consistent backup, however there is no "snap off" capability like in the LSM snapshot case. Therefore, the disk-to-disk backup must be made manually by the system administrator using vdump/vrestore or similar tools. This could easily be automated using scripts. As with the LSM utilities, the AdvFS Utilities that allow this operation are also an added-cost option to the base Tru64 UNIX license.

- Hardware-based snapshot. This is the most expensive, but fastest method of making a metadata consistent backup. A hardware-based, intelligent controller (such as an HSG80) can "snap-off" another unit very quickly similar to the LSM snapshot capability. The difference is the hardware solution can do the job much more quickly and with less overhead on the Tru64 UNIX operating system. So, the advantage of this approach is high speed, but it also costs money to invest in the controllers. If you already have this type of controller, then it is possible you can get this functionality with no additional costs. However, check with the hardware vendor to find out if there are no additional licensing involved in using the snapshot tools.

Even if someone had one or more of these technologies available, it would only make sense to use this option under a certain set of circumstances. For example, if the cost of a completely duplicated disk array were a factor, this would not be a viable option and the lower cost of tape backups would be more appropriate. The following lists some of the necessary prerequisites to consider performing disk backups:

- Intelligent controller, LSM snapshots or AdvFS clone filesets.
- Double the available disk space.
- Continuous availability of data.

The disk backup has the following advantages over traditional tape-based backups:

- Very fast—The disk-to-disk copy operations of this option tends to be much faster than a traditional disk-to-tape backup strategy.
- Little or no loss of data availability—Generally a disk-to-disk backup can be performed while the data is on-line and active. Whether the file system can remain consistent during the snapshot operation depends on the type of on-line backup used and the configuration of the file systems (today). Clone fileset backups can be performed consistently in all cases whereas LSM snapshot and hardware-based backups will only remain consistent if a single AdvFS volume is used. As of this writing, a data consistent on-line, multi-volume AdvFS domain backup is not supported other than with clone filesets. If a single AdvFS volume were used and either LSM or hardware-based snapshotting were employed, then a metadata consistency could be obtained.
- Simple recovery—The recovery in the case of a disk failure would be to simply make the system use the backup disks in place of the failed disks. No recovery from backup step is needed like in the tape restore strategy.

The primary disadvantage of the disk-to-disk backup option is the very high cost associated with having duplicated storage. However, from a pure performance perspective, it is best to use an intelligent controller (such as an HSZ, HSG or HSV) and make your copies at the hardware level. In addition, this off-loads the disk-to-disk copies from the operating system to the controller, thus freeing up system resources for other tasks. Performing the snapshots in hardware will greatly improve overall performance and avoid wasting resources of the computer systems but it will put a limit on the configuration of AdvFS file systems.

More information on how to safely perform hardware-assisted disk-to-disk backups is available at the Compaq best practices web page:

```
http://www.tru64unix.compaq.com/docs/best_practices/
  BP_SNAPSHOT/TITLE.HTM
```

Also, there are references in Appendix B that discuss the AdvFS cloning and LSM snapshotting features and how best to apply those at your site.

#### 11.2.4.2 Tape Backups

Selecting backup media to which to trust your regular system backups is often a decision already made for you. Whichever model tape drive ships with your system is often your only choice. If, however, you are lucky enough to be able to be involved in the selection of a backup device, there are several issues to consider:

- The capacity of a tape drive
- The speed of a tape drive
- Media availability, cost, and size

The first and foremost issue is the capacity of the tape drive as compared with the amount of data to be regularly backed up. It makes no sense to purchase a single, small 4-gigabyte tape drive when the system has hundreds of gigabytes of disk storage. Conversely, a 280-gigabyte multitape jukebox is probably overkill for a desktop workstation with just two gigabytes of disk space. There is no quick and easy formula for determining what is a good ratio of tape capacity to disk capacity, but a rule of thumb we recommend is to have enough tape capacity to be able to back up the entire system unattended. This requirement for an unattended backup can be accomplished either by a single tape with sufficient capacity or by a multitape changer with the backup spanning multiple tapes. Note that this does not mean having equal amounts of tape space and disk space, only being able to copy all the data to tape.

Another consideration in selecting a tape is tape speed. You must be able to complete the backup procedure in the amount of time allotted. This is not as important an issue as it has been in the past, now that backup technology has progressed beyond paper tape and 9-track tapes. Most modern tape technology is fairly quick, supporting high-speed interfaces and cache buffers to increase tape throughput. If a system is constrained by either tape drive capacity or speed, an option to consider is multiple tape drives. If tape drive speed is the concern, connecting multiple tape drives to the system on individual interfaces (e.g., SCSI channels) is recommended.

The final issue in selecting a backup device concerns the media. Choose a tape drive whose media is convenient. The convenience factors include cost, availability, and ease of storage. If all the existing systems in an organization are using 4mm DAT media, it may be wise to consider a 4-mm DAT drive for a new system, rather then selecting an 8mm tape drive. Choosing a common format could considerably reduce the administrative hassles presented by a "foreign" media format. This media factor is likely to have the least weight in your decision, but it should still be considered.

The most common tape drive on a Compaq system is the 4mm DAT drive (TLZ10), which has a capacity of 12 GB uncompressed (up to 24 GB compressed). This tape drive is usually shipped as the default drive on most Compaq systems. The advantages of this drive are a good size capacity, fair backup speed, and widely available and inexpensive media. The next step up in Compaq's tape lineup is DLT, or Digital Linear Tape. Compaq's SDLT 110/220 tape drive provides 110 GB uncompressed (up to 220-gigabytes compressed). DLT's biggest advantages are high capacity and very high data transfer rate. Both the media cost and physical size for DLT are greater than for 4mm DAT. Though DLT and 4mm DAT are currently Compaq's main backup architectures, Compaq's backup technology includes other tape formats such as quarter-inch cartridge (QIC) and optical drives.

### 11.2.5 Backup and Restore Documentation

The final requirement of a sound backup strategy is sufficient documentation of the backup and restore process. Ideally this should include written procedures and examples of how the backups were done, where the backup media is stored, and how to recover from these backups in the event of a file or system loss. This documentation should be printed out and located in a place where any staff member who would be called upon to perform a restore has access to it. These procedures can certainly be online, but having hard copies of the instructions to restore a file or system may prove invaluable in a crisis. This might even be helpful to the plan's author, because in a crisis situation anyone could miss a crucial step or two and waste time or inadvertently damage the file system or backup tapes. In a crisis, one simply cannot afford to leave anything to chance.

At a minimum, this documentation should clearly state the schedule of the backups, the level of the backups if incremental dumps are being done, the location of the backup media (both the backup rotation tapes and blank media for any ad hoc backups) the exact commands that generated the backups, and the restoration procedures and commands. The restore instructions should provide procedures for restoring individual files or directories and for recovering the entire system, both the operating system and the user applications and data. It is in the system administrator's best interest to create this backup and restore documentation so that even a user with limited system administration skills can at least restore files.

Another requirement of backup and restore documentation is that the information must be updated if and when the backup or restore process changes. For instance, if new disks are installed on a system and the backup process is amended to back up newly created file systems, it is imperative that the backup and restore documentation be updated to reflect this change. Other changes that should be incorporated into this documentation could include new backup hardware or software, changes in the backup strategy, and staffing reorganizations.

### 11.2.6 Restore Dress Rehearsal

Developing and implementing a backup strategy is well and good. However, if there is a flaw in the backup procedure or the recovery documentation is incorrect or there is a hardware issue preventing valid backups, the wrong time to find out is in a recovery situation. For this reason, it is imperative that the backup and restore procedure be tested as often as is feasible. This rehearsal is simply to validate the backups themselves and to ensure that the restore instructions in the backup and restore documentation are accurate.

The least that should be done is to restore several files or directories from a recent regular system backup using the documented recovery procedures. For instance, assuming a recent vdump of the root file system were inserted into the primary tape drive, the following commands would recover a fairly large file (/vmunix) and compare the restored file with the original file:

```
# vrestore -x -v -f /dev/tape/tape0_d0 -D /tmp ./vmunix

vrestore: Date of the vdump save-set: Wed Oct 1 02:45:44 2000
r /tmp/./vmunix, 11323768
# cksum /vmunix /tmp/vmunix
1731969811 11323768 /vmunix
1731969811 11323768 /tmp/vmunix
```

The cksum(1) command displays the checksum and byte count for the files specified on the command line. If the checksum value and the byte count are the same for the two files, you can assume that the file was successfully backed up.

The second phase of a restore rehearsal is to shut down a system and recover it from a regular system backup. Ideally, a second test system would be the best place to test a full system recovery. However, it may not be practical to simulate a system failure and completely restore a system from tape. One possible reason for this restriction may be that there is only one system and you cannot afford the system to be down. If this is the case, an alternative strategy could be to test restoring key user file systems to a spare disk partition. If this is successful, the restore strategy may have to be:

1. Rebuild the system from the Tru64 UNIX Installation Media.
2. Recreate the necessary user file systems.
3. Restore the user applications and data from backups.

Obviously such a strategy would be more time consuming as the system would have to be reinstalled from scratch, and some amount of system configuration would be necessary before the system could be considered successfully restored. This configuration activity would include recreating user accounts, reconfiguring the network, and possibly loading optional Compaq layered products. The best recovery solution would be to restore the entire system from the last full backup.

## 11.3 Optional Backup Strategy Components

Once a backup strategy is developed and the necessary components detailed in the previous section are in place, several other items may be considered that will further enhance such a backup strategy. These optional components are typically not necessary for most organizations, but completing some or all will greatly enhance your ability to withstand even the most severe data or system loss.

### 11.3.1 Off-site Storage of Backups

The purpose of regular system backups is to be able to recover from a system or user error that causes a file loss. At a minimum, such a loss could be the accidental deletion of a file or directory by a user, or the failure of a single hardware component that causes the loss of many files, or even the entire operating system, such as a disk crash. Given adequate backups, these losses can quickly be recovered from tape. The next severe system problem is a catastrophic hardware failure that causes the loss of some or all of the computer system itself. Such a failure could entail replacing some or all of the computer system in its entirety and being forced to restore the system from backups. A system failure of this scope would require a full system recovery; but if the backup strategy is sound, such a recovery is straightforward in approach.

One aspect of a backup strategy that has not been covered is the storage of the media from regular system backups. All too frequently, the entire rotation of nightly backup tapes are simply stored in the same room the computer resides in, often stacked on or near the system cabinet itself. Even if the tapes are not kept in the computer room, they are still stored in the same building as the computer, which is somewhat safer, but still not ideal. Both of the previously described types of data loss are recoverable from backup tapes that are stored on-site. However, there is a final failure, a loss of a facility or building, that would destroy the computer and the backup tapes. Such a loss would include a fire, flood, or other natural disaster, not to mention man-made catastrophes. An important piece of a good backup strategy is the storage of backups at an off-site location. A common practice is not to send every backup off-site, only a representative snapshot that would allow recovery to a known state, perhaps a monthly full backup. Ideally, an acceptable off-site location would be secure, geographically distant enough not to be vulnerable to natural disasters common to the location of the computer, and close enough to facilitate a relatively quick (within 24 hours) recovery of the tapes. There are companies that provide such vaulting services, including pickup and delivery, secure and climate-controlled vaults, and even tape-labeling services. Of course, such services cost money and may or may not be feasible. If, however, a computer system supports mission-critical applications and the organization must ensure that the computer and data can be recovered from any failure, no matter how catastrophic, off-site storage of backups is a must.

### 11.3.2 Disaster Recovery Plan

In addition to off-site storage of backups, the development of a disaster recovery plan (DRP) can reduce the risk that a catastrophic failure could prevent the restoration of a system. A DRP complements the backup and recovery document discussed earlier in this chapter. Where the backup and recovery document details how a backup was done and how to recover from that backup, a DRP has a larger scope. A DRP should outline the process to follow in the event of the total loss of the computer system, the computer room, or the entire facility. Some of the issues to explore when developing a DRP are what system functionality is critical to the continued operation of the organization, where can replacement systems and facilities be obtained, even on a temporary basis, and which personnel will need to be involved in carrying out a DRP in the unlikely event of a disaster.

Developing a DRP should be a joint effort between the operations staff such as the system administrator, the user community, and possibly facilities staff. In addition, a DRP, once created, must be revisited periodically to ensure that the information contained within is still accurate. Certain data tends to be volatil—efor example, contact information for company personnel, such as telephone numbers, pager numbers, and responsibilities. Other fundamentals that may change over time are the assumptions made during development of the DRS, such as the minimum time to recovery, the order of system recovery, and the strategy for system or facility restoration.

## 11.4 Summary

System backups are a critical responsibility for a UNIX system administrator. Developing and implementing a robust backup strategy is a requirement for being able to quickly and accurately restore data that will eventually be lost. The ability to restore an accidentally deleted file will demonstrate to your users that the system is in good hands.

Compaq provides several different utilities for backing up a Tru64 UNIX system. Of these, the vdump/vrestore pair is the most versatile. Whichever backup tool you select, whether one provided with the base Tru64 UNIX product, the Networker Save and Restore tool, or a third-party backup application, spend sufficient time with it to understand its ability and options. Do not wait until a crisis to discover that the backups you have been dutifully making every night are invalid. Test your backup procedure frequently by doing test restores. Finally, the backups process should not require massive amounts of resources to manage if sufficient system administration time and energy have been devoted to developing the process up front.

# 12

# *System Logging and Troubleshooting*

## 12.1 Introduction

When something goes wrong and a Tru64 UNIX system crashes, the first person to be called is the system administrator. Unfortunately, these events seem to happen at the most inopportune time. Whether it is in the middle of an important demonstration, crunch time at month's end, or simply in the middle of the night, it is up to you to quickly diagnose the problem, identify a solution, and get the system back up. This skill is probably best defined as problem management. Problem management is a broad topic that includes dealing with hardware and software errors, handling system crashes, and administering the system logging facility. Tru64 UNIX is a complex system, and often a system administrator's only recourse when confronted with a system problem is to provide as much diagnostic information as possible to your support organization, whether that be Compaq's Customer Support Center or another organization. This information can include system crash dumps and hardware, software, and system error log entries. This chapter will provide some insight into how to interpret the output of these problem-reporting facilities as well as how to correlate system problems with their resulting crash dump output or error-log events. Then, as your knowledge and experience increase, these same Tru64 UNIX problem management facilities can allow for a more proactive problem resolution.

At your disposal in this effort are several Tru64 UNIX facilities to assist you in this problem management effort. These are:

- The system logging facility
- The binary error logging facility
- The event management logging facility

- The crash dump process

These facilities are simply mechanisms used by the system to capture information. Sometimes these are errors, sometimes warnings, and sometimes just informational. The following sections will cover the issues of administering these tools. This includes determining what information is to be collected by these facilities, ensuring that there are adequate system resources to capture the desired information, configuring the tools appropriately, and naming strategies to follow when examining the collected information either before or after a system problem arises. In addition, the utilities provided by Compaq for examining this information will be detailed. Understanding the information these facilities can provide is an important factor in being able to quickly diagnose and recover from system problems.

## 12.2 The System Log

Modern UNIX implementations such as Tru64 UNIX provide a centralized facility for collecting and recording messages. This facility, commonly referred to as the "syslog," is the primary logging mechanism used by many system processes and utilities. In addition, due to syslog's architecture, non-system applications, including user and administrative scripts, are able to send messages to syslog for disposition. Because syslog is typically the destination for error messages from system processes, understanding how syslog works and how to interpret and manage the entries in syslog's configuration file is important to effective system administration. The syslog facility has two components: the syslog daemon, /usr/sbin/syslogd, and the syslog configuration files. The primary configuration file is /etc/syslog.conf, and the file that identifies which remote hosts are allowed to forward syslog messages to this one is, /etc/syslog.auth. In Tru64 UNIX V5 and later, the /etc/syslog_evm.conf file is also read by syslogd and identifies what to forward to the Event Manager.

### 12.2.1 syslogd

The syslog daemon is an executable system utility normally started at run level 3 during system startup and is always running while the system is in multiuser mode. The syslogd daemon reads messages sent to it from system processes, the kernel itself, and user applications. These messages can be informational only, warnings, or errors that need attention. The messages themselves are single lines, optionally containing a priority value indicating the severity of the message. These priorities are defined in the /usr/include/sys/syslog_pri.h header file. Messages are received by syslogd from three sources:

- The device special file /dev/log, the domain socket
- The device special file /dev/klog, which reads kernel messages
- Other systems across the network, via a socket specified in /etc/services

Most system processes and utilities, and optionally user applications, submit messages to syslog using the syslog(3) function call or the logger(1) command. These messages are relayed to syslog via the device special file /dev/log. Kernel messages are similarly sent to syslog through the device special file /dev/klog. Finally, syslog may receive messages from other systems via the network using a network socket specified in the /etc/services file, provided that the /etc/syslog.auth file allows it—see Section 12.2.4.3 for more information about /etc/syslog.auth. The point in mentioning these syslog message sources is to identify these files when troubleshooting syslog problems. For instance, if kernel messages are not being received and logged by syslog, ensure that the /dev/klog file exists:

```
# ls -l /dev/klog
crw- - - - -    1 root   system    3,   0 Apr 24 22:00 /dev/klog
```

If the file is missing or not correct (e.g., is it a character special file?), simply re-create the klog file:

```
# cd /dev
# ./MAKEDEV klog
```

Similarly, if syslog messages are not being received from other systems via the network, as part of your troubleshooting effort, ensure that the /etc/services file exists and contains the following entry:

```
syslog  514/udp
```

Note that the /dev/log file is a socket that is created and maintained by the syslogd itself and exists only while syslogd is running. If the /dev/log file is absent, it is likely that the syslog daemon is not running. Simply restart syslogd and the /dev/log socket will be created:

```
# /usr/sbin/syslogd
```

### 12.2.2 Starting and Stopping syslogd

The syslog daemon, syslogd, is usually started when the system starts from the syslog startup script, /sbin/rc3.d/S09syslog, which is actually a symbolic link to the /sbin/init.d/syslog script. Due to its importance in the error-logging process syslogd is started fairly early in the run level 3 boot process; however, any kernel messages logged before syslogd gets started are stored in the kernel's preserved message buffer. The syslog daemon reads its configuration file when it starts up and rereads the configuration file when it receives a hang-up signal (e.g., kill –HUP <pid>). The configuration file is simply a set of rules that instruct the syslog daemon what messages to log and where to log those messages.

When syslogd starts, it creates the file /var/run/syslog.pid if possible. This file contains a single line with the process ID (PID) of the syslogd process. This file can then be consulted to obtain syslogd's PID when it is necessary to stop or restart syslogd. For example, to terminate syslogd, use either of these commands:

```
# kill 'cat /var/run/syslog.pid'
```

or

```
# /sbin/init.d/syslog stop
```

Running the syslog script with a "stop" will kill syslogd by using the "kill" command above.

### 12.2.3 Disabling and Enabling syslogd Console Messages

A common destination for syslog messages is the system console. Depending on the amount of activity or the health of the system, the volume of messages printed on the console may be very low. Occasionally, however, the system administrator needs to diagnose one or more ongoing system problems from the console. If the syslog daemon is sending frequent messages to the console in this situation, it may be difficult to troubleshoot problems. Beginning with Tru64 UNIX version 4.0, there is a new command, /usr/sbin/syslog, that allows enabling and disabling syslog-generated console messages. If you are working from the console and find syslog informational messages hampering your effectiveness, simply issue this command:

```
# /usr/sbin/syslog console_off
```

This will disable syslog messages. Remember to re-enable syslog messages when the console work is completed so that the messages will once again be sent to the console:

```
# /usr/sbin/syslog console_on
```

If console messages are disabled and the system is rebooted, the default behavior of enabled syslog console messages is restored.

### 12.2.4 The Syslog Configuration Files

The Tru64 UNIX V5 syslog facility has three configuration files, /etc/syslog.conf, /etc/syslog_evm.log, and /etc/syslog.auth. These files are simply text files that the syslogd daemon reads at startup or after receiving a hang-up signal.

#### 12.2.4.1 /etc/syslog.conf

This configuration file contains entries that specify the facility (see Table 12.1), which is the part of the system that produced the message; the message severity level (see Table 12.2), and the destination to which the syslogd daemon should send the message.

**Table 12.1** *Available syslog Facilities*

| Name(s) | Description |
|---|---|
| kern | Kernel messages |
| user | User-level messages |
| mail | Mail system messages |
| daemon | System daemon messages |
| auth | Security/authorization messages |
| syslog | Messages generated by syslogd itself |
| lpr | Printer subsystem messages |
| news | Network news subsystem messages |
| uucp | UUCP subsystem messages |
| cron | Clock daemon messages |
| megasafe | Polycenter AdvFS |
| local0 | Reserved for local use |
| local1 | Reserved for local use |
| local2 | Reserved for local use |

**Table 12.1** *(continued)*

| Name(s) | Description |
|---|---|
| local3 | Reserved for local use |
| local4 | Reserved for local use |
| local5 | Reserved for local use |
| local6 | Reserved for local use |
| local7 | Reserved for local use |

**Table 12.2** *Available syslog Priorities*

| Name(s) | Number | Description |
|---|---|---|
| emerg | 0 | System is unusable |
| alert | 1 | Action must be taken immediately |
| crit | 2 | Critical conditions |
| err | 3 | Error conditions |
| warning | 4 | Warning conditions |
| notice | 5 | Normal but significant condition |
| info | 6 | Informational |
| debug | 7 | Debug messages |

Each line of the syslog configuration file contains a single entry. See Figure 12.1 for an example of an /etc/syslog.conf file.

The syntax and format of the /etc/syslog.conf file must be followed exactly, as the syslog daemon will stop reading the syslog.conf file if an error or format violation is encountered. This means that a simple typographical error in the middle of the syslog.conf file will prevent syslogd from seeing any entries after the error. The most common error is using spaces to delimit the facility and severity levels from the destination. The only permitted delimiter is one or more tab characters—spaces are not allowed in a syslog.conf entry.

**Figure 12.1**
*An example of /etc/syslog.conf.*

```
#
# syslogd config file
#
# facilities: kern user mail daemon auth syslog lpr binary
# priorities: emerg alert crit err warning notice info debug
kern.debug/var/adm/syslog.dated/kern.log
user.debug/var/adm/syslog.dated/user.log
mail.debug/var/adm/syslog.dated/mail.log
daemon.debug /var/adm/syslog.dated/daemon.log
auth.debug/var/adm/syslog.dated/auth.log
syslog.debug /var/adm/syslog.dated/syslog.log
lpr.debug /var/adm/syslog.dated/lpr.log

msgbuf.err/var/adm/crash/msgbuf.savecore

kern.debug/var/adm/messages
kern.debug/dev/console
*.emerg *
```

The first half of a syslog.conf entry specifies the source and severity of messages for which syslog should watch. The facility and its severity level must be separated by a period (.). For example:

```
kern.debug              /var/adm/syslog.dated/kern.log
```

More than one facility can be specified on a line by separating the multiple facilities with commas (,):

```
mail,lpr.info /var/adm/syslog.dated/misc_info.log
```

Additionally, more than one facility and severity level can be specified on a line by separating them with semicolons (;):

```
auth.info;syslog.debug /var/adm/syslog.dated/syslog.log
```

Finally, an asterisk (*) may be specified in place of a facility, indicating that messages generated by all parts of the system are to be logged. All messages of the specified severity and greater will be logged:

```
*.emerg    *
```

A Tru64 UNIX–unique facility.severity pair is "msgbuf.err." This facility.severity pair is crucial for recovering any messages that may be pending in the kernel syslog buffer in the event of a system crash. When a Tru64 UNIX system recovers from a system crash, any such messages recovered are placed in the file specified as the "msgbuf.err" destination in the syslog.conf file. When syslog starts, it looks for this file and, if it exists, processes any messages contained within and deletes the file. The default syslog.conf entry to provide this functionality is:

```
msgbuf.err              /var/adm/crash/msgbuf.savecore
```

The second half of a syslog.conf entry specifies the destination where syslog will log the messages that match the "facility.severity" criteria defined by the first half of the syslog.conf entry. There are four possible destinations for messages:

- A file name that begins with a leading slash (/)—The syslog daemon will append messages to this file. Note that this can be an ordinary file or a device special file such as /dev/console, which will cause all messages sent to this destination to appear on the system console.
- A host name preceded by an "at" sign (@)—Appropriate messages are forwarded to the syslog daemon on the named host (if the named host's /etc/syslog.auth permits it). The named host must have a record in its /etc/syslog.auth if it is to receive these messages.
- A comma-separated list of users—Appropriate messages are written to those users if they are logged in.
- An asterisk (*)—Appropriate messages are written to all users who are logged in.

Tru64 UNIX has the ability to create daily syslog log files. If you specify a path such as /var/adm/syslog.dated/mail.log for the "destination," a new directory and associated log files will be created each day of the form /var/adm/syslog.dated/date/file where "date" is the day, month, and time; and "file" is the log file, such as mail.log. For example:

```
mail.debug              /var/adm/syslog.dated/mail.log
```

This is a nice feature because it produces a day-by-day account of the messages received. For example, an entry such as the mail.debug entry above will cause syslogd to log mail debug messages in the following file if the syslog were to be started or restarted on June 2nd at 6:54 P.M.:

```
/var/adm/syslog.dated/02-Jun-18:54/kern.log
```

Furthermore there is a symbolic link, "current" in the /var/adm/syslog.dated directory that always points to the current date, which makes it easy to find the current set of syslog log files. Simply specify /var/adm/syslog.dated/current.

Be aware that if a syslog destination is a normal file (e.g., begins with a leading slash in /etc/syslog.conf), syslog always appends to that file and the file will grow indefinitely. Monitor such log files and trim them when necessary to avoid filling your file system(s). The following is an example of trimming /var/adm/messages:

```
# cp /var/adm/messages /var/adm/messages.1
# cp /dev/null /var/adm/messages
```

Note that the existing messages file is copied to a backup; then the original messages file is emptied by copying the /dev/null file to it. This technique is used here rather than simply deleting the original messages file because if a syslog log file is removed, the log file will not be re-created until the next time syslogd is restarted.

As mentioned before, the facility.severity level pair(s) must be separated from the destination by one or more tabs. Blank lines and lines beginning with a pound sign (#) are considered comments and are ignored. Finally, the /etc/syslog.conf file should not be world-writable. The appropriate permissions on this file are 644, or readable by everyone and writable only by the owner, which is bin.

As an example of some of syslog's configuration rules, consider the following sample syslog.conf entries:

```
kern.*	/dev/console
*.notice;mail.info	/var/adm/syslog/mail.log
kern.err	@saturn
*	/var/adm/messages
*.emerg	*
*.alert;auth.warning root
```

These example configuration file entries log messages as follows:

- Log all kernel messages onto the system console.
- Log all notice (or higher) level messages and all mail system messages except debug messages into the file /var/adm/syslog/mail.log.
- Forward kernel messages of error severity or higher to the syslogd on saturn.
- Log all messages into the /var/adm/messages file.

- Inform all logged-in users of any emergency messages and inform the root user, if logged-in, of any alert message or any warning message (or higher) from the authorization system.

#### 12.2.4.2 /etc/syslog_evm.conf

The /etc/syslog_evm.conf file specifies which syslog messages to forward to the Event Manager (EVM). The entry format is facility.priority[+]. These facilities and priorities are roughly the same as for syslog.conf. The optional plus sign (+) indicates that if the priority is higher than listed, it is also forwarded; otherwise, only the priority specified is forwarded.

Consider this fragment of an /etc/syslog_evm.conf file:

```
*.emerg
kern.info+
user.notice
```

All emergency messages are forwarded, kernel messages of informational priority and higher are forwarded, and only messages generated by users with the priority of notice are forwarded.

#### 12.2.4.3 /etc/syslog.auth

Finally the local syslogd does not accept syslog messages from just any remote host. If the remote host is not listed in the /etc/syslog.auth configuration file, but the file exists, syslog messages from that host are not processed to the log. If the file does not exist, then syslogd will accept messages from any host. It should be noted that the /etc/syslog.auth file is not created at installation time, so the default behavior is to allow all remote hosts to forward syslog messages. The format of this file is simply the list of fully qualified remote host names, one per line:

```
justice.abc.com
liberty.xyz.com
```

A local host with these entries would accept syslog messages from both justice.abc.com and liberty.xyz.com.

### 12.2.5 Default syslog.conf

When the syslog daemon starts, it looks for /etc/syslog.conf by default. An alternate configuration file may be specified on the syslogd command line when starting syslog. For example, to start syslog and use /var/adm/syslog.txt, use the following syntax:

```
# /usr/sbin/syslogd -f /var/adm/syslog.txt
```

If the syslog configuration file is absent, syslog defaults to these message rules:

```
*.err   /dev/console
*.panic   *
```

These defaults instruct syslog to send all error messages to the console and all kernel panic messages to all logged-in users. No files are written.

### 12.2.6 Sending Messages to Syslog from Scripts

Since syslog is the primary logging mechanism for the operating system, it occasionally may make sense to use syslog for logging in custom system administration or user scripts. The way to send messages to syslog from a scrip—tor the command line, for that matter—is the logger(1) command. The logger command provides an interface to the syslog() routine. The syntax of the logger command allows specification of the facility and severity, and provides the ability to either specify the text of the message to be logged on the command line or indicate a file whose contents will be the text of the message. For example:

```
# logger -p user.debug "Program error"
```

will cause syslog to log the following message:

```
Apr 24 22:12:01 justice bly: Program error
```

in the destination specified in /etc/syslog.conf for the "user.debug" facility.severity pair.

## 12.3 The Binary Error Log

While syslog exists on all modern implementations of UNIX, the Binary Error Log facility is unique to Tru64 UNIX. This facility—normally referred to as the binlog, from the name of the system daemon responsible, binlogd—generates the binary error log. The binlog is a mechanism, similar in functionality to syslog, which collects and logs messages from the kernel. The types of messages that the binlog daemon logs are hardware and software errors and operational events, such as system startups and shutdowns. Obviously, these messages are of great interest to a system administrator, and understanding how to examine and interpret the binary error log is the key to successfully troubleshooting system problems. The binlog facility has two components—the binlog daemon, /usr/sbin/binlogd, and the binlog configuration files /etc/binlog.conf and /etc/binlog.auth. In addition, since the resulting binary error log is, as its name implies, in a binary format, there are three utilities provided by Compaq to view and manipulate this log. In order of their appearance on the scene they are uerf(8), DECevent, and Compaq Analyze.

### 12.3.1 binlogd

The binlog daemon is an executable system utility normally started at system startup and always running while the system is in multiuser mode. The binlogd utility reads messages sent to it from the system kernel. These messages can be informational only, warnings, or errors that need attention. The messages contain a priority value indicating the severity of the message. Messages are received by binlogd from two sources:

- The device special file /dev/kbinlog
- Other systems across the network, via a socket specified in /etc/services (if /etc/binlog.auth allows it)

The system kernel itself submits messages to binlog via the device special file /dev/kbinlog. Additionally, binlog may receive messages from other systems via the network using a network socket specified in the /etc/services file. The only reason for mentioning these two sources for messages is to identify places to check when troubleshooting binlog problems. For instance, if kernel messages are not being received into the binary error log, ensure that the /dev/kbinlog file exists:

```
# ls -l /dev/kbinlog
crw- - - - -  1 root  system  31,  0 Apr 24 22:11 /dev/kbinlog
```

If the file is missing or not correct (for example, is it a character special file?), simply re-create the kbinlog file:

```
# cd /dev
# ./MAKEDEV kbinlog
```

Similarly, if other Tru64 UNIX systems are sending binary error log messages to a particular system but the messages are not being logged, ensure that the /etc/services file exists and contains the following entry:

```
binlogd  706/udp
```

Further, ensure that the /etc/binlog.auth file is properly configured (Section 12.3.3.2).

### 12.3.2 Starting and Stopping binlogd

The binary error log daemon, binlogd, is usually started when the system starts from the binlog startup script, /sbin/rc3.d/S10binlog, which is actually a symbolic link to the /sbin/init.d/binlog script. The binlog daemon is started fairly early in the boot process due to its importance in the error-logging process.

When binlogd starts, it creates the file /var/run/binlogd.pid, if possible. This file contains a single line with the process ID (PID) of the binlogd process. This file can then be consulted to obtain binlogd's PID when it is necessary to stop or restart binlogd. For example, to terminate binlogd use either of these commands:

```
# kill 'cat /var/run/binlogd.pid'
```

or

```
# /sbin/init.d/binlog stop
```

Running the binlog script with a "stop" will kill binlogd by using the "kill" command above.

### 12.3.3 The Binlog Configuration Files

The binlog facility has two configuration files, /etc/binlog.conf and /etc/binlog.auth, that are read when binlogd starts up, and reread when it receives a hang-up signal. Like the syslog configuration files, these are also text files.

#### *12.3.3.1 /etc/binlog.conf*

The binlog.conf file contains entries that specify the event code (Table 12.3), which is the source of the message; the message priority level, which can be

**Table 12.3** *Available binlog Events*

| Number | Description | Category |
|---|---|---|
| 100 | CPU machine checks and exceptions | Hardware |
| 101 | Memory | Hardware |
| 102 | Disks | Hardware |
| 103 | Tapes | Hardware |
| 104 | Device controllers | Hardware |
| 105 | Adapters | Hardware |
| 106 | Buses | Hardware |
| 107 | Stray interrupts | Hardware |
| 108 | Console events | Hardware |
| 109 | Stack dumps | Hardware |
| 199 | SCSI CAM events | Hardware |
| 201 | CI port-to-port driver events | Software |
| 202 | System communications services events | Software |
| 250 | Generic ASCII informational messages | Informational |
| 300 | ASCII startup messages | Operational |
| 301 | ASCII shutdown messages | Operational |
| 302 | Panic messages | Operational |
| 310 | Timestamp | Operational |
| 350 | Diagnostic status messages | Operational |
| 351 | Repair and maintenance messages | Operational |

severe, high, or low; and the destination to which the binlogd daemon should send the message.

Each line of the binlog.conf configuration file contains a single entry. See Figure 12.2 for an example of the default /etc/binlog.conf file.

The syntax and format of the /etc/binlog.conf file must be followed exactly, as the binlog daemon is as unforgiving of configuration file errors as the syslog daemon.

**Figure 12.2**
*An example of /etc/binlog.conf.*

```
#
# binlogd configuration file
#
#format of a line:   event_code.priority        destination
#
# where: event_code  - see codes in binlog.h and man page,
# * = all events
#        priority    - severe, high, low, * = all priorities
#        destination - local file pathname or remote system
#  hostname
#
*.*                          /usr/adm/binary.errlog
dumpfile                     /usr/adm/crash/binlogdumpfile
crdlog                       /usr/adm/binary.crdlog
```

The first half of a binlog.conf entry specifies the event code and priority of messages for which the binlog daemon should watch. The event code and priority level must be separated by a period (.). In addition, an asterisk (*) may be specified in place of both an event code and a priority, indicating that all event codes and all priorities, respectively, are to be logged.

The second half of a binlog.conf entry specifies the destination where the binlog daemon will log the messages that match the "event_code.priority" criteria defined by the first half of the binlog.conf entry. There are two possible destinations for binlog messages:

- A file name that begins with a leading slash (/)—The binlog daemon will append messages to this file. Note that this file should be an ordinary file, since the resulting messages are logged in a binary format.
- A host name preceded by an at sign (@)—Appropriate messages are forwarded to the binlog daemon on the named host (if the named host's /etc/binlog.auth permits it). Since the binlog is a Tru64 UNIX facility, it is only reasonable to forward binlog messages to other Tru64 UNIX systems.

A special binlog.conf entry is necessary for recovering any error messages that may be pending in the kernel binary event-log buffer in the event of a system crash. When a Tru64 UNIX system recovers from a system crash, the savecore(8) command recovers any such pending messages from a system dump and places them in /usr/adm/crash/binlogdumpfile. When binlog starts, it looks for this file and, if it exists, processes any messages contained within and deletes the file. The default binlog.conf entry to provide this functionality is:

```
dumpfile /usr/adm/crash/binlogdumpfile
```

The primary binary error-log destination specified by the "*.*" event-code.priority pair is always appended to by binlogd. This binary.errlog file should be monitored and trimmed when necessary to avoid running out of disk space. Another reason to trim the binary.errlog is to keep the log to a manageable size to reduce the timetaken by queries against the file. To trim the binary.errlog and save current entries do the following:

```
# kill -USR1 'cat /var/run/binlogd.pid'
```

This renames the current binary.errlog to /usr/var/adm/binlog.saved/binary.errlog.saved then creates a new version of the binary.errlog file. There is a pre-written crontab(1) entry to routinely do this. If you choose to use it, log in as "root," run "crontab –e," and remove the comment character "#" from the entry:

```
#0 2 1 * * kill -USR1 'cat /var/run/binlogd.pid'
```

Note that the binary.errlog is a context dependent symbolic link (CDSC) and must not be deleted. For more information about CDSLs see the hier(5) man page.

Within the binlog.conf file, event code and priority pair(s) must be separated from the destination by spaces or tabs. Blank lines and lines beginning with a pound sign (#) are considered comments and are ignored. Finally, the /etc/binlog.conf file should not be world-writable. The appropriate permissions on this file are 755, or readable and executable by everyone and writable only by the owner, which is bin.

#### 12.3.3.2 /etc/binlog.auth

The local binlogd does not accept binlog messages from just any remote host. If the /etc/binlog.auth file does not exist or exists but is empty or contains no valid remote host names, the binlogd will not accept forwarded messages from any remote host. If the file does exist, then binlogd will accept messages only from the listed hosts. The format of this file is simply the list of fully qualified remote host names, one per line:

```
justice.abc.com
liberty.xyz.com
```

A local host with these entries would accept binlog messages from both justice.abc.com and liberty.xyz.com.

### 12.3.4 Default binlog.conf

When the binlog daemon is started, it looks for the /etc/binlog.conf by default. An alternate configuration file may be specified on the command line when starting binlog. The default /etc/binlog.conf file delivered by Compaq (Figure 12.2) is usually sufficient for most systems—all event classes and severity levels are logged to /usr/adm/binary.errlog.

### 12.3.5 Examining the Binary Error Log

As mentioned previously, the log file generated by the binlog daemon is a binary file not directly human-readable. The format of the binary error log (binary.error) is such that the binlog daemon can quickly process and append events it receives. An advantage of the binary error log not being ASCII is that events can be extracted and sorted quickly by the Compaq-supplied tools. Three utilities are available for examining and manipulating the messages contained in the binary error log:

- uerf(8), the UNIX event report formatter
- dia(8), the DECevent management utility
- ca(8), the Compaq analyze fault analysis utility

#### *12.3.5.1 uerf*

The uerf utility is a legacy part of the base Tru64 UNIX operating system and is a tool to translate the binary error log produced by the binlog daemon into human-readable output[1]. Run with no options, the uerf command simply reads the file specified as the destination for the "*.*" entry in the /etc/binlog.conf file, typically /var/adm/binary.errlog, and prints on standard output each entry in chronological order, oldest events first. This default ordering is not tremendously useful, for the most recent events are usually the ones of immediate interest, especially when investigating a problem. A commonly specified command line option, -R, outputs the records in reverse chronological order, showing the most recent events first.

1. Although uerf is no longer supported, discussing it first is useful to get a perspective of the tools and to understand the progress that has been made.

Note that the binary.error log file is owned by root and belongs to the adm group, and that the default permissions are 640. If you want to use the uerf command to translate the default binary.errlog, you must belong to the adm group or be root. Optionally, you can change the ownership or permissions to allow others to access this file via the uerf command. For instance, to allow all users to read the file:

```
# ls -lL /var/adm/binary.errlog
-rw-r—    1 root      adm       323016 Apr 24 22:41
/var/adm/binary.errlog
# chmod 644 /var/adm/binary.errlog
# ls -lL /var/adm/binary.errlog
-rw-r-r-    1 root      adm       323016 Apr 24 22:41
/var/adm/binary.errlog
```

*Note:* the "L" switch was used above since the file is a CDSL or Context Dependent Symbolic Link. These symbolic links are used in Tru64 UNIX V5 and later to keep the member-specific files, like log files and configuration files, separate across members in a cluster where the file system is shared. Using the "L" tells "ls" to follow the link instead of reporting on the link itself.

This change will persist across reboots as long as the file is not removed or renamed, in which case the binlogd will re-create the file with the original default permissions. There is probably not a good reason to allow world access to the binary.errlog, but it can be done.

Obviously, since the binary.errlog contains all binlog events since the binary.errlog was started, one after another, sorting out useful information would seem at first glance difficult. However, by using several of uerf's command line parameters, you can request to see only certain types of events, events related just to particular disks, events in a specified time range, or summaries of the events categorized by quantity. Additionally, as uerf's output can be many pages, piping this output to a favorite pager, such as more(1) or pg(1), is recommended. Some commonly used uerf commands are:

- Display the most recent system startup events, including the system configuration information:

```
# uerf -R -r 300 | more
```

- Show a summary report of all events in the binary.errlog:

```
# uerf -S
```

- Show all events between 8:00 A.M. on February 18, 2001 and 6:00 P.M. on February 20, 2001:

```
# uerf -t s:18-feb-2001,8:00 e:20-feb-2001,18:00
```

- Show all events from a backup binary.errlog with most recent events first:

```
# uerf -R -f /var/adm/binary.errlog.old
```

- Show all memory-related events, such as single-bit corrected read data and double-bit uncorrectable errors, in reverse chronological order with the most detailed output:

```
# uerf -R -M mem -o full
```

These and the many other uerf command line parameters detailed in the uerf reference page can be combined, as in the last example above, to further narrow the search query. All specified parameters are combined together using a logical AND by uerf when determining matching events. Basically, the uerf command allows the system administrator to query the binary.errlog for the records of interest. For example, if you suspect a particular disk is beginning to fail, keep a watch on the binary error log for events from that disk. Perhaps run the following uerf command each night before midnight via cron(8) to e-mail you the disk-related events since the last midnight:

```
uerf -R -D -t s:00:00
```

Useful though it may be, the uerf command does not provide absolutely every useful piece of information that exists in the binary error log, though specifying the "-o full" command line switch does provide more detailed output. The uerf command's main advantage is that, to this point, it will exist on all Tru64 UNIX systems. To address uerf's translation shortcomings, Compaq created a more advanced tool to replace uerf: DECevent.

#### *12.3.5.2 DECevent*

DECevent is an optional product available directly from Compaq's customer support organizations, on the Associated Products CD or downloadable from the Compaq DECevent Web page:

```
http://www.support.compaq.com/svctools/decevent/
```

Per the Web page, "DECevent is a rules-based hardware fault management diagnostic tool that provides error event translation. During translation, the binary portion of an event log is transformed into human-readable text. These events can then be displayed on the screen or printed." DECevent is simply a better uerf. DECevent, or dia as the DECevent executable is called, mostly has the same syntax as uerf and reads the same binary.errlog as uerf. See the man page for dia for the differences.

It is immediately apparent that the DECevent output is more detailed than the equivalent uerf output, and although much of the DECevent output is unintelligible to the average person, this is exactly the level of detail that the Compaq field engineers and Customer Support Center specialists need to quickly identify and resolve problems.

The DECevent product is actually two components, the Translation module and the Analysis/Notification module. The Translation piece of DECevent is the uerf-like functionality and is available to all Tru64 UNIX users[2]. Compaq strongly recommends getting DECevent, if only for this Translation piece, for platforms that are not supported by Compaq Analyze (for example, CA is not supported on the AlphaServer 4100). The Analysis/Notification module is only available to those Tru64 UNIX users having a support contract with Compaq and requires a Product Authorization Key (PAK) license to activate. Basically, the DECevent Analysis/Notification functionality provides automatic proactive monitoring of a system's binary error log for identified error conditions and notification when such errors are detected. This notification can take several forms, including E-mail notification either directly to Compaq field engineers or to the system administrator. If you do have a support agreement with Compaq, contact your support representative for information on getting and configuring DECevent's Analysis/Notification module.

To diagnose problems on the EV6 platforms and later, you must use Compaq Analyze. The exception to this rule is that DECevent will work on the AlphaServer GS60 and GS140 systems.

#### 12.3.5.3 Compaq Analyze

Compaq Analyze (CA) is a product on the Associated Products CD and is available from Compaq to customers who are under hardware warranty, or

2. In fact many of the uerf switches work the same way with dia.

have a hardware service contract or a service obligation[3]. You can find out more about Compaq Analyze by visiting the CA Web page:

```
http://www.support.compaq.com/svctools/webes/ca/ca.html
```

To quote the Web page, Compaq Analyze is "a rules-based hardware fault management diagnostic tool that provides error event analysis and translation." Compaq Analyze is a replacement for both uerf and DECevent that does both bit-to-text (BTT) translation as well as multievent correlation analysis. Used with DSNlink (http://www.support.compaq.com/dsnlink/), CA can perform remote notification to the Compaq Service Center.

CA reads the same binary.errlog that uerf and DECevent read but uses different syntax and has a different translation and analysis engine. The idea behind this new syntax is that once familiar with CA, it does not matter whether the platform is UNIX, OVMS, Windows NT, or some newly added operating system the command is the same. Currently there are three syntax flavors of CA on Tru64 UNIX: the old common syntax, a DECevent-like syntax and the new common syntax. The default syntax is configurable and this setting is system-wide. To set the default CA syntax for your system use the command

```
ca syntax n|u|x
```

where "n" is for the new common syntax, "x" is the old common syntax and "u" is for the UNIX-like DECevent syntax.

Whether you use uerf, dia, or ca, the concept is the same. The tool translates the binary error log into something that can be understood by a system administrator or support specialist. You should use the more recent tool based on the compatibility of the tool and your system type (i.e., use ca on all new systems, dia on most pre-EV6 Alphas). Also ca and dia have the added functionality of analysis. Table 12.4 lists some of the more useful ca commands and the dia equivalent and describes what they do.

In addition to the CA command line interface, there is a GUI-based interface that you can access by Web browser. See the documentation for instructions on setting up your browser. Point your browser to port 7902 for the system that you want to analyze:

3. A V5.x Tru64 UNIX system administrator should become familiar with ca as it will be the one tool to use with many existing and future hardware platforms.

**Table 12.4** *Useful ca and dia Commands*

| Desired output | CA command | DIA command |
|---|---|---|
| Bit-to-text output in reverse order | ca tra rev* | dia –R |
| Summary of events | ca sum | dia –o summary |
| Provide analysis of events | ca ana | dia ana |
| Specify alternate binary.errlog for bit-to-text formatting | ca tra input <filename> | dia –f <filename> |

* Assumes "ca syntax n"

```
http://justice.alf.dec.com:7902
```

From this view you can see both an analysis of the events from the binary.errlog as well as the full view of the BTT translation. See Figure 12.3 for an example of the full binary.errlog view from the CA GUI.

To see the detailed BTT view, click on an event. See Figure 12.4.

Compaq Analyze is part of a suite of service tools from the Web-Based Enterprise Services (WEBES) kit. This kit also includes the Compaq Crash Analysis Tool (CCAT); and the Revision and Control Management Tool (RCM). CCAT is discussed briefly in Section 12.5.2.

Some of the WEBES tools communicate with a new daemon, desta (Distributed Enterprise Service Tools Architecture), or the Director daemon. If CA is installed, desta monitors the system log files for new events to translate or analyze. It also responds to manual analysis. If CCAT is installed, desta processes any crash files during the boot process. It also responds to manual crash dump analysis commands.

## 12.4 Event Management (EVM)

New as of Tru64 UNIX V5.0 is the Event Manager or (EVM). EVM serves to unify events from a variety of channels into a single source. EVM works in cooperation with syslogd and binlogd (and any other configured channel). This section will give a brief overview of what EVM is and how to use it.

Consider the participants of the EVM system:

- Events—indications that something interesting happened

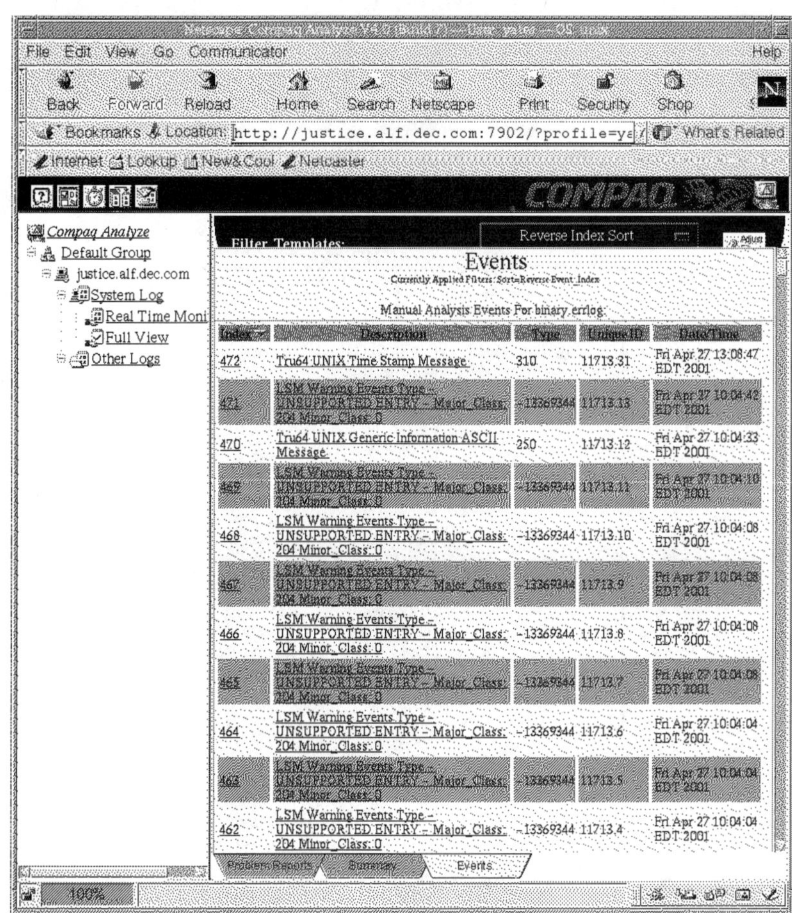


**Figure 12.3** *Compaq Analyze view of the binary.errlog.*

- Event channel—facility used to post or retrieve event information
- Event poster—component that posts an event to the EVM daemon
- Event subscriber—an entity interested in particular indications

The way EVM works is that something interesting happens (an event), a component creates an EVM event package that describes what happened, the component posts the event to the EVM daemon, the daemon receives the event and enhances it based on its template event database, the daemon then sends the event, to any subscribing clients that have registered an interest in this type of event and the subscribing client receives the event and may perform some action because of it. Additionally the system administrator may use the evmget(1) command to look at the event.

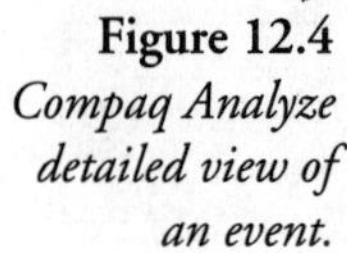

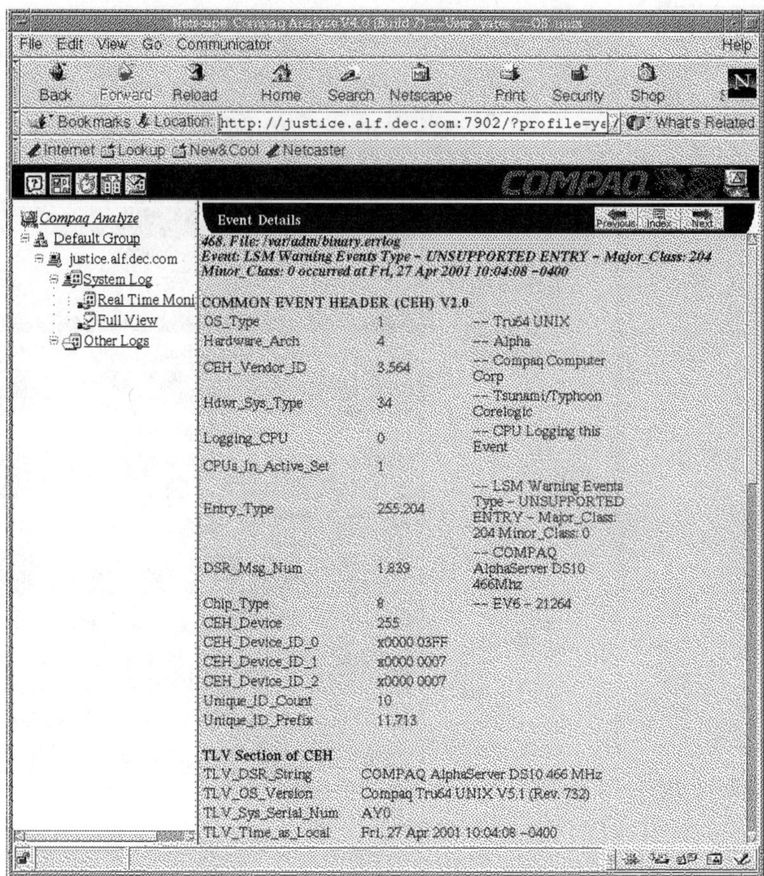


**Figure 12.4** *Compaq Analyze detailed view of an event.*

## 12.4.1 EVM Commands

The EVM command-line utilities can be used to show, retrieve, sort, and post events. There is also a SysMan EVM interface, but it is not covered here. The five EVM command-line utilities are:

- evmshow—converts binary events into human-readable format
- evmget—retrieves events
- evmsort—sorts a stream of events
- evmwatch—subscribes to a set of events
- evmpost—posts events

#### 12.4.1.1 evmshow

Perhaps the most used EVM command line utility is the evmshow command. You must use this command to view the stored events because they are in binary format. To display the contents of an old log file use a command such as:

```
# evmshow /var/evm/evmlog/evmlog.20010606
```

To insert a timestamp re-run the command specifying that the timestamp be included:

```
# evmshow -t "@timestamp @@" /var/evm/evmlog/evmlog.20010606
```

For details about the EVM command-line utilities, see the man page or the EVM documentation.

#### 12.4.1.2 evmget

The evmget command is used to retrieve a stream of binary EVM events. The evmget command makes a connection to a child process of the EVM daemon, the get-server, and based on the authorization checks by the get-server, processes events for which the user is authorized. Normally this is passed to the evmshow command:

```
# evmget -f "[priority > 300]" |evmshow -t "@timestamp @@"
```

This command will retrieve all events for which the user is authorized that have a priority greater than 300 and displays them with a timestamp through the evmshow command. Notice the use of the –f switch (filter) to select only certain events.

#### 12.4.1.3 evmsort

Since the events are likely to be in no particular order when evmget retrieves them, there needs to be some sorting done along the way. That is precisely what evmsort does. The evmsort command reads the binary events and can be used in a pipeline with evmget. Building on the previous example but adding a sort:

```
# evmget -f "[priority > 300]" |evmsort \
  |evmshow -t "@timestamp @@"
```

View the evmsort man page to see how you may "fine tune" your sort based on different fields.

#### 12.4.1.4 evmwatch

The evmwatch utility is for viewing events in real-time. Again the output will be processed through evmshow and again you may use a filter to select only certain events—for example, those with a priority greater than 300:

```
# evmwatch -f "[priority > 300]" |evmshow -t "@timestamp @@"
```

There is no need for an evmsort in the pipeline since these events will be displayed as they occur. The timestamp will be displayed with any events.

#### 12.4.1.5 evmpost

Finally the evmpost utility, as its name implies, posts events to the EVM daemon. It takes input as a file or stream of event sources, converts it into the binary EVM format, and posts it to the EVM daemon for distribution. One simple example of this is posting a system administrator event that a particular operation completed successfully:

```
# evmpost -a "Disk dsk23 was successfully replaced"
```

## 12.5 The Crash Dump Process

When a Tru64 UNIX system encounters a problem so severe, whether a software issue in the kernel or an unexpected hardware fault, that further operation is impossible or just unwise, the operating system will halt operation. This immediate halt typically results in a panic and, if the auto_action console prompt is set to boot, a system reboot. When a system crashes in this manner, the operating system copies an image of the contents of all or part of the physical memory to swap. The partial_dump attribute from the "generic" subsystem of /etc/sysconfigtab tells the operating system whether to write a partial or full dump; partial dumps are the default and are normally sufficient to diagnose the problem. Furthermore, the default value of compressed_dump (also in "generic") is "1," which saves considerable disk space but might be a problem if you use tools that require an uncompressed dump file—you can always use expand_dump(8) to uncompress a vmzcore file. As part of the reboot process, savecore(8) checks if a memory image from a system crash exists, and if so, moves that image from disk to an operating system file and along with another program creates several other ancillary files that, together, are called the Crash Dump Files. The system administrator and/or an experienced Compaq support engineer can then use these Crash Dump Files to determine the cause of the crash.

In order to ensure that these Crash Dump Files are created, it is important to understand the sequence of events in a crash dump recovery so that sufficient system resources, primarily disk space, are preallocated. The following topics will be covered:

- The Crash Dump sequence
- Guidelines for deciding how much disk space to allocate
- Forcing a hung system to generate a crash dump

### 12.5.1 The Crash Dump Sequence

When a Tru64 UNIX system crashes, an image of the memory is copied to disk, specifically to the swap area(s). Which swap areas are copied to is determined by the size of the memory image to be saved, and the number and size of the available swap areas:

- If the memory image fits in the primary swap area (identified as the first entry in the comma-separated list of swap devices in the swapdevice attribute—this attribute is found in the "vm" subsystem of the /etc/sysconfigtab file), the memory image is written into this primary swap area, starting at the end of the partition. The image is placed far from the front of the primary swap partition to avoid being overwritten when the system is next rebooted.
- If the memory image does not fit into the primary swap area, the memory image is written into the secondary swap areas (also identified as by swapdevice in the /etc/sysconfigtab file).
- If the memory image is too large to fit into the secondary swap areas, the memory image is written to the secondary swap partitions until those partitions are full. The remaining part is then written to the end of the primary swap partition.
- If the memory image is too large to fit into all swap areas combined, no crash dump is created.

After the memory image is copied to the swap area(s), the system reboots. During the reboot process at run level 2, the /sbin/init.d/savecore startup script runs the savecore program and determines if a crash dump has been created and if sufficient file system space exists in which to save the crash dump. If a crash has occurred and a crash dump was successfully saved and there is enough file system space, savecore begins to copy the memory image from the swap area(s) into a file system, /var/adm/crash, by default.

After savecore has successfully saved a crash dump, two files are produced:

- vmzcore.N—The compressed physical memory image at the time of the crash
- vmunix.N—The running kernel at the time of the crash

As the system continues to boot, crashdc(8) runs at run level 3 to produce:

- crash-data.N—A human-readable crash summary file

The value of N is maintained by savecore in the "bounds" file in the crash directory. This value is simply a sequence number that is incremented after each crash, with the first crash being number 0. As crash dump files can be quite large, especially the vmzcore.N files, ensure that crash dump files that are no longer needed are removed to avoid running out of disk space.

When diagnosing a system crash, an experienced crash dump analyst will need all three files in order to troubleshoot what caused the crash and how to prevent future instances. You may be required to transfer the crash dump files for a particular crash to a Compaq customer service center for analysis. While such crash dump troubleshooting is beyond the scope of this text (for more information on this topic, see the Tru64 UNIX Kernel Debugging Guide), it is at least interesting to examine the crash-data.N file, for this file contains a summary of the system at the time of the crash. It is sometimes possible to determine from the contents of the crash-data.N file alone if a particular process, or possibly a hardware problem, may have caused the crash.

### 12.5.2 Compaq Crash Analysis Tool

The Compaq Crash Analysis Tool (CCAT) is a diagnostic tool for Compaq Services customers. It allows customers to automatically or manually diagnose system crashes. The CCAT analysis may include a solution, workaround, or troubleshooting technique for the crash. As mentioned earlier, CCAT is part of the Web-Based Enterprise Service (WEBES) suite of diagnosis tools:

```
http://www.support.compaq.com/svctools/webes/
```

During the reboot after a system crash, in fact at run level 3, CCAT runs to see if the crash matches the footprint of a fixed problem or not. In either case, it generates a call (if DSNlink is also installed) to Compaq's Customer

Support Center for either the delivery of the solution (if it found a match) or to have a new crash analyzed. The key is that as the system boots, some diagnosis is already being performed and may, in fact, provide a solution to the crash completely behind the scenes.

You can find more information about DSNlink at the DSNlink Web page:

```
http://www.support.compaq.com/dsnlink/
```

### 12.5.3 Crash Dump Disk Space Guidelines

There are two types of disk space to consider when planning for Crash Dump disk space: swap space and the crash file system. Both types must be sufficient to hold at least one crash dump. The crash dump is an image of physical memory, but since partial dump is usually all that is required plus the fact that the dump file is compressed (by default), the space requirement is cut down significantly and is, as a rule, about 50% of the size of physical memory. This figure will vary widely based on how much memory is currently in use and how it is configured. For example, a lightly loaded system with 256 MB of physical memory with partial_dump and compressed_dump enabled may require a mere 4 MB for the vmzcore.N file.

The first place a crash dump is saved is the swap partition(s), and a very large swap space is not needed to capture a partial dump. But even though a large swap space is not a requirement for the crash dump process, Compaq recommends swap space of three times the size of physical memory. An exception to this rule of thumb is that Very Large Memory (VLM) systems with physical memory sizes over two gigabytes are normally tuned so they do not page or swap. On these types of systems, it may simply be unnecessary to allocate even one times physical memory for swap. In this case Compaq recommends having the ability to temporarily add additional swap space to capture a crash dump if such a system were to begin crashing. Once a crash dump is captured and the reason for the crashes is identified, reassign the extra swap space.

The second place a crash dump is saved is to the crash file system, which is /var/adm/crash by default. Again, the file system where the crash dump files will be saved must be sufficiently sized to hold at least one crash dump—that is, approximately 50% the size of physical memory. If /var/adm/crash is not appropriate, set the run-time configuration variable SAVECORE_DIR to another location. For example, to set /usr/crash as the crash directory, issue this command:

```
# rcmgr set SAVECORE_DIR /usr/crash
```

Again, if it is unreasonable on a VLM system to keep a large amount of disk space available in a file system on a permanent basis, simply be prepared to point the SAVECORE_DIR to a temporary location in the event of system crash problems, at least until a crash dump is captured.

### 12.5.4 Forcing a Crash Dump

It is possible for a Tru64 UNIX system to stop responding in any way as the result of a software or hardware problem. When this occurs, a crash dump is not generated, due to the system's being in a hung state. In order to force a crash when a system is hung and generate a crash dump that may indicate the cause of the system hang, do the following:

- If the system has a HALT button on the operator control panel:
  1. Press the HALT button to bring the system to the "triple chevron" console prompt (>>>).

     (*Note:* If the system has a switch for enabling and disabling the HALT button, set that switch to the ENABLE position.)
  2. At the console prompt, type "crash" and press <Return>.
- If the system does not have a HALT button:
  1. Press the Ctrl-P key sequence at the system console.
  2. At the console prompt, type "crash" and press <Return>.

These steps will halt the system and initiate the generation of a crash dump, saving a memory image at the time of the halt, and, one hopes, containing information about the original system hang. After the crash dump save is complete, boot the system to complete the generation of the crash dump files. If you were to look at the crash-data.N file, you would see a panic string of "hardware restart," indicating a forced crash.

There are times when a crash dump would be useful to troubleshoot a problem that is not considered a "hang" and it may be desired not to force a crash since that will result in system downtime. In this case, dumpsys(8) can be used to take a snapshot of memory and produce crash files much the same way that a forced crash would. Keep in mind, however, that using dumpsys is not quite the same as a forced crash since memory will continue to change while dumpsys runs.

## 12.6 Summary

As this chapter outlined, Tru64 UNIX provides several tools and facilities to assist in identifying, diagnosing, and preventing system problems. Between syslog, binlog and EVM, Tru64 UNIX's logging is very complete, giving you, the system administrator, a great deal of useful information about software and hardware errors. Finally, once a problem is so severe that the system cannot continue, the crash dump facility is available to provide a dump of core memory for faster analysis.

# Electronic Resources

## A.1 Mailing Lists

There are a couple of mailing lists that are of direct interest to Tru64 UNIX system administrators. These mailing lists contain a great deal of useful information and can be an invaluable resource. Be aware, though, that mailing lists can easily overwhelm you with their volume. An active mailing list can and will generate hundreds of e-mails a day. One useful strategy when subscribing to mailing lists is to use an e-mail client with filtering capabilities and to transfer incoming mailing list traffic into another folder for later perusal. In addition, many mailing lists provide the ability to receive "digests" where you are periodically sent a summary of list activity. Such digests typically are sent weekly or monthly, depending on the list volume. Some mailing lists are also archived, allowing easy keyword searching through months or years of list activity.

*Note:* Always regard information read in a mailing list with caution, especially if the list is unmoderated. Although there will always be experts who happily share their experience and knowledge, there are also less experienced folks who, either through error or malice, provide incorrect information. Never blindly believe a single person's contribution. Always substantiate any piece of information if you are unsure of its source or validity. Remember as well that even the experts can make mistakes. Mailing lists are frequently valuable sources of useful and pertinent information, but you should tread carefully.

### A.1.1 Tru64-UNIX-Managers List

The Tru64-UNIX-Managers list is a quick-turnaround troubleshooting aid for people who administer and manage Alpha systems running Tru64 UNIX. Its primary purpose is to provide a Tru64 UNIX system administrator with a quick source of information for system management problems that are of a time-critical nature. This list allows any subscriber to pose a question to the entire list or contribute to another individual's question.

To subscribe to the list, send an e-mail to majordomo@ornl.gov containing the command "subscribe tru64-unix-managers".

The Tru64-UNIX-managers list is archived at:

```
http://www.ornl.gov/its/archives/mailing-lists/
```

Additionally, the following URL provides the ability to keyword search the entire Tru64-UNIX-managers list archive:

```
http://www-archive.ornl.gov:8000/
```

And a couple more archive search engines:

```
http://www.geocrawler.com/lists/3/Miscellaneous/530/0/
```

```
http://www.xray.mpe.mpg.de/mailing-lists/tru64-unix-managers/
```

### A.1.2 Tru64 UNIX Patch List

The Tru64 UNIX Patch list is a nondiscussion list provided by Compaq Computer Corporation that announces the latest patches on the Tru64 UNIX operating system and layered software products. These notices cover both Public and Entitled patches. While the Entitled patches are available only to contract customers, the Public patches are readily available via anonymous FTP from:

```
http://ftp.support.compaq.com/public/unix/
```

also view:

```
http://www.support.compaq.com/patches/
```

To subscribe to the mailing list and receive individual patch notices, click on the "join mailing list" link on this page.

## A.2 USENET Newsgroups

There are several USENET newsgroups that may be of interest toTru64 UNIX system administrators. These newsgroups typically have an even higher "noise ratio" than mailing lists, and the recommendation is again to be cautious with information presented in a newsgroup.

- comp.unix.tru64—The primary Tru64 UNIX discussion group
- comp.unix.osf.misc—Miscellaneous Tru64 UNIX discussions
- comp.unix.admin—General UNIX system administration topics
- comp.admin.policy—General UNIX system administration policy issues
- comp.security.unix—UNIX security
- comp.security.misc—Miscellaneous system and network security
- comp.unix.questions—A forum for general UNIX user questions
- comp.unix.wizards—Advanced UNIX topics

## A.3 Web Resources

The World Wide Web has grown tremendously since its inception and is now a valuable resource. Some Web pages are extremely broad in content, while others are narrowly focused or address single topics. The pages listed below are a good starting point for Tru64 UNIX system administrators. Many of these pages provide links to other associated pages. Over time, you will build a personal set of favorite pages.

Note that online resources do change, and these addresses may not apply in the future. Readers may always use a Web search engine to identify the new location if an address is not found.

### A.3.1 The Tru64 UNIX Homepage

Compaq Computer Corporation has created a comprehensive Tru64 UNIX Web site with many useful and informative links to other Web pages related to Tru64 UNIX at:

```
http://www.tru64unix.compaq.com/
```

### A.3.2 Tru64 UNIX Technical Documentation

Compaq Computer Corporation has created a Web resource containing the entire documentation set for Tru64 UNIX. This includes online versions of the Release Notes, Installation Guide, and System Administration Guide. This online library is an invaluable reference and may be found at:

```
http://www.tru64unix.compaq.com/faqs/publications/pub_page/
  doc_list.html
```

### A.3.3 The Compaq Services Online

The Compaq Services Division homepage provides a variety of online services, including access directly to the Compaq Business Critical Services call-logging systems and problem-diagnosis systems, the Tru64 UNIX patch repositories, and miscellaneous product support information.

```
http://www.compaq.com/support/
```

### A.3.4 Tru64 UNIX Patch Services

The Patch Services page provides easy access to Tru64 UNIX patch kits, including publicly available and contract-only patches. Users are permitted to search for individual patches either through a Search and Download utility or via traditional FTP access:

```
http://www.support.compaq.com/patches/
```

### A.3.5 The Alpha Systems Firmware Update Page

The firmware update page provides online access to current and past versions of the Alpha system firmware images. In addition, this Web page is also the place to check for interim firmware versions released between regular firmware CD-ROM distributions:

```
http://gatekeeper.research.compaq.com/pub/DEC/Alpha/firmware/
```

### A.3.6 Tru64 UNIX Freely Available Software

This page contains a list of free and demo software:

```
http://tru64unix.compaq.com/demos/
```

```
ftp://gatekeeper.research.compaq.com/gatekeeper.home.html
```

### A.3.7 Compaq DECevent Homepage

The DECevent utility, an optional product that can be used in place of the uerf(8) program, is a highly recommended addition to a Tru64 UNIX system. The latest version may be downloaded from:

```
http://www.support.compaq.com/svctools/decevent/
```

### A.3.8 WEBES Homepage

The Web-Based Enterprise Services (WEBES), kit, which includes Compaq Analyze and the Compaq Crash Analysis Tool:

```
http://www.support.compaq.com/svctools/webes/index.html
```

### A.3.9 Compaq Best Practices

This site has recommendations that will help a system administrator in areas such as:

- Performance
- Networking
- Patches
- Cluster
- Security
- Programming

```
http://www.tru64unix.compaq.com/faqs/publications/best_practices/
```

Check back often since this is a "living" Web page.

### A.3.10 Tru64.org

This site has lots of resources including mailing lists, articles, and FAQs. It should be noted that it is not affiliated with Compaq Computer Corporation.

```
http://www.tru64.org/
```

### A.3.11 Compaq Authorized Training Vendors

Bruden Corporation and The Institute for Software Advancement are two Compaq Authorized Training Vendors:

```
http://bruden.com/
```

```
http://www.softadv.com/
```

### A.3.12 User Group

The Encompass Compaq User Group (formerly DECUS, US Chapter) Website contains lots of useful links:

```
http://www.decus.org/encompass/index.shtml
```

### A.3.13 Test Drive

At this Web site you can "test drive" Tru64 UNIX (and other operating systems for that matter):

```
http://www.testdrive.compaq.com/os/
```

B

# Recommended Supplemental Reading

Many of the Tru64 UNIX topics mentioned in this book are so broad that they would require an entire book to cover them completely. Happily, excellent texts on both Tru64 UNIX-specific and standard UNIX subsystems already exist. Rather than attempting to adequately address these topics, the reader is encouraged to refer to one or more of the following titles when working with these topics, some of which are considered the "bibles" of their subjects.

## B.1 AdvFS, LSM, TruCluster


Hancock, Steven M. *Tru64 UNIX File System Administration Handbook.* Digital Press, 2000.

Fafrak, Scott, and Lola, Jim. *TruCluster Server Handbook.* Digital Press, 2001.


## B.2 TCP/IP Networking, DNS, NFS, and NIS


Albitz, Paul, and Liu, Cricket. *DNS and BIND,* Fourth Edition. O'Reilly & Associates, 2001.

Hunt, Craig. *TCP/IP Network Administration,* Second Edition. O'Reilly & Associates, 1997.

Stern, Hal, Eisler, Mike, and Labiaga, Ricardo. *Managing NFS and NIS,* Second Edition. O'Reilly & Associates, 2001.

Tanenbaum, Andrew S. *Computer Networks,* Third Edition, Prentice Hall, 1996

## B.3 Sendmail

Costales, Bryan, and Allman, Eric. *sendmail*, Second Edition. O'Reilly & Associates, 1997.

## B.4 Backup

Preston, W. Curtis. *UNIX Backup & Recovery.* O'Reilly & Associates, 1999.

## B.5 UNIX Internals

McKusick, Marshall Kirk; Bostic, Keith; and Karels, Michael J. *The Design and Implementation of the 4.4BSD Operating System.* Addison-Wesley, 1996.

# *Index*

**B**

## C

E

## K



## L

N



O



P

T